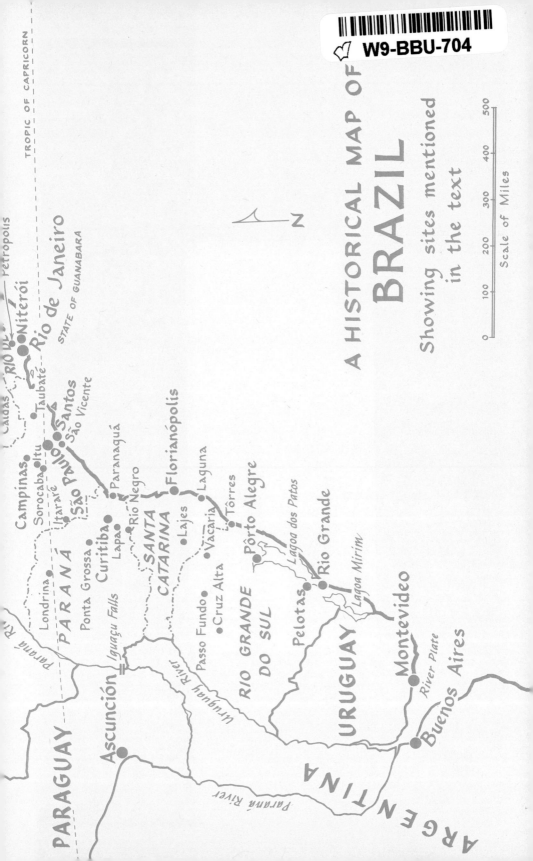

A HISTORICAL MAP OF
BRAZIL

Showing sites mentioned
in the text

N

Scale of Miles

0 100 200 300 400 500

TROPIC OF CAPRICORN

Petrópolis

Niterói

Rio de Janeiro

STATE OF GUANABARA

RIO DE ...

Caldas

Taubaté

Santos

São Vicente

São Paulo

Itu

Sorocaba

Campinas

Itararé

Paranaguá

Rio Negro

Florianópolis

Laguna

Curitiba

Lapa

Lajes

Vacaria

Tôrres

Pôrto Alegre

Ponta Grossa

SANTA
CATARINA

Londrina

PARANÁ

Iguaçu Falls

Passo Fundo

Cruz Alta

RIO GRANDE
DO SUL

Lagoa dos Patos

Rio Grande

Pelotas

Lagoa Mirim

PARAGUAY

Ascunción

Paraná River

Uruguay River

URUGUAY

Montevideo

River Plate

Buenos Aires

ARGENTINA

Paraná River

A History of Modern Brazil
1889–1964

José Maria Bello

A History of Modern Brazil
1889-1964

Translated from the Portuguese by
James L. Taylor

With a New Concluding Chapter by
Rollie E. Poppino

1966
Stanford University Press
Stanford, California

A History of Modern Brazil, 1889–1964 was originally published in Portuguese in 1940 under the title *História da República (1889–1902)*. Subsequent editions extended the coverage of the book to 1930, to 1945, and to 1954. The present volume is based on the 4th edition (1959), the last to appear in the author's lifetime.

Stanford University Press
Stanford, California
© 1966 by the Board of Trustees of the
Leland Stanford Junior University
Printed in the United States of America
L.C. 65-21494

Publication of this book was assisted by a grant from the
Rockefeller Foundation and the Latin American Translation Program
of the Association of American University Presses.

Publisher's Note

This volume is a translation of Bello's *História da República,* 4th edition (1959), with alterations in organization and detail to make the work more useful to non-Brazilian readers. Much of the author's general background material on American and European history, especially the history of World War II, has been removed. On the other hand, events familiar to a Brazilian audience have seemed to us to require more elaboration, as well as a more strictly chronological treatment, for non-Brazilians. In making the necessary changes, we have been careful to retain not only the author's facts but also his interpretations and emphases; in short, our changes have been confined to matters of organization and sequence. Chapters 1–10 and 22–24, in particular, have been radically reorganized.

We wish to express our profound gratitude to James L. Taylor for scholarly aid and advice far beyond the responsibilities normally assumed by a translator; to Professor Rollie E. Poppino for an exceptionally deft job of expanding chapter 24 and for writing chapter 25; and to Aidan A. Kelly for devising and carrying out the complex editorial strategies that have made this book what it is. We are grateful also to the Rockefeller Foundation and to the Latin American Translation Committee of the Association of American University Presses for their indispensable support. The Index and the Chronology were prepared by Mr. Taylor. The maps were prepared especially for this edition by David J. Pauly.

Contents

Translator's Note

The excellence of Mr. Bello's book is attested by the reception its several editions have had among his countrymen. The excellence of this English-language version, if it has any, is of a different kind. As the Publisher's Note on page v suggests, corrections, additions, annotations, eliminations of redundancy, and transpositions have been made throughout the text, and Professor Poppino's superlative review of events since 1946 in chapters 24 and 25 has been added. Our effort has been to make the book as useful as possible for readers of English with little or no knowledge of Brazilian history.

The general procedure by which the text was arrived at may be of interest. I first did a relatively literal translation, straightening out syntactical snarls, converting to the past from the historical present, eliminating various digressions, and supplying a minimum of annotation. This version was then edited by Mr. Aidan Kelly of Stanford University Press and referred to me for checking, accompanied by editorial queries of every conceivable sort, some of them unanswerable from the sources available to me. The unedited manuscript was read by Professor Poppino, the first proofs by Mr. Kelly and myself, the second proofs by me and Mr. J. G. Bell of the Press; errors and infelicities were routed at all stages, though many no doubt remain.

A word about the Index. Owing to the well-known Brazilian custom of referring to others by anything but their full names, some difficult choices face the indexer of a book on Brazil. In this book, for instance, the leader of the naval revolt in 1893 is usually called Custódio de Melo, but Mr. Bello also refers to him as Custódio José de Melo, as Admiral Melo, and simply as Custódio. With a few exceptions (which are cross-indexed), I have arbitrarily listed all names under the last part of the name as most often used by the author, sometimes adding missing parts in brackets: Melo, Custódio José de. I have retained the author's spelling of all proper names.

JLT

A Brief Chronology of Brazilian History

by James L. Taylor

THE COLONIAL ERA

1500   Brazil discovered by Pedro Alvares Cabral, Portuguese navigator.

1532   First permanent Portuguese settlement.

1565   Founding of Rio de Janeiro.

1580–1640   Portugal and Brazil under the dominion of Spain.

1624–54   Dutch in control of northeastern Brazil.

1788–92   Period of the Inconfidência (or Conjuração) Mineira, an unsuccessful attempt to establish a republic of Brazil. It was headed by an army officer who had been a dentist and is best remembered by his nickname, Tiradentes (the Tooth-puller). He was executed April 21, 1792, and is now honored as Brazil's greatest martyr.

1808–21   The Portuguese royal family in Brazil.

THE BRAZILIAN EMPIRE

1822   Declaration of independence, September 7. Coronation of Pedro I.

1825–27   War with Argentina over the southernmost Brazilian territory (Banda Oriental), which resulted in the birth of Uruguay as an independent nation.

1831   Abdication of Pedro I. Beginning of the regency.

1835–45   War of the Farrapos in Rio Grande do Sul.

1840   Coronation of Pedro II (reigned 1840–89).

1850–52   War with Uruguay and Argentina.

1864–70   War with Uruguay (1864–65) and Paraguay.

1871   Promulgation of the law of the "ventre livre" (free birth).

1888   Abolition of slavery, May 13.

THE REPUBLIC

1889   Overthrow of the monarchy and proclamation of the Republic. The Provisional Government to 1891.

1891   Promulgation of the first republican constitution and election of the first President.

1893–95   Civil war in Rio Grande do Sul. Naval revolt.

1896–97   The Canudos rebellion in Bahia.

1917   Brazil declares war on Germany.

1924–27   Rebellion in São Paulo and other states.

1930   Revolution and ousting of Washington Luís. Vargas heads a provisional government.

1932   "Constitutionalist" counterrevolution in São Paulo.

1934   The second republican constitution. Vargas elected President by Congress.

1937   Coup d'etat and proclamation of the Estado Novo. Vargas becomes dictator. The third republican constitution.

1942   Brazil declares war on Germany and Italy.

1945   The Estado Novo overthrown and Vargas ousted by the military.

1946   The fourth republican constitution.

1950   Vargas reelected President by popular vote.

1954   Military demands Vargas's resignation. Vargas commits suicide. Interim presidency with military consent.

1956   Juscelino Kubitschek inaugurated as President.

1960   Brasília becomes the new Federal District and capital of Brazil.

1961   Inauguration and resignation of President Jânio Quadros. After a constitutional amendment introducing parliamentary government, João Goulart inaugurated as President.

1963   National plebiscite abolishes the parliamentary system.

1964   Goulart deposed by military revolt, and Marshal Castello Branco elected President by Congress.

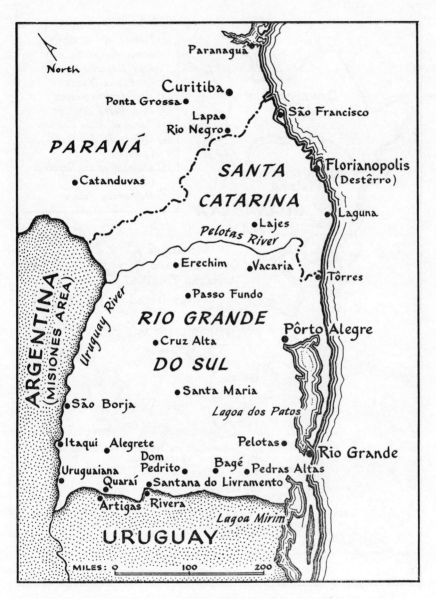

MAP 1: Area of Rio Grande do Sul, showing sites mentioned in the text.

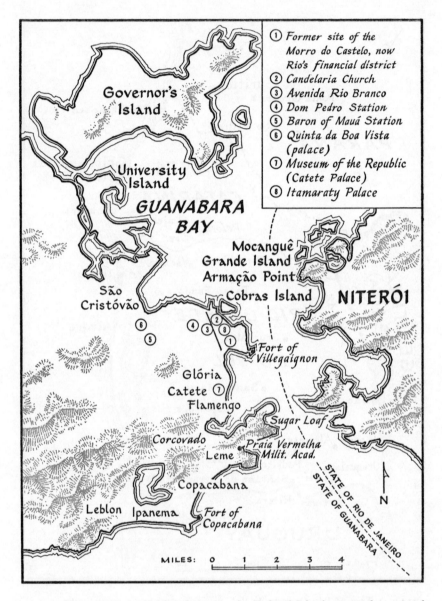

Governor's
Island

University
Island

GUANABARA
BAY

Mocanguê
Grande Island
Armação Point
Cobras Island

São
Cristóvão

NITERÓI

⑥ ④ ③ ⑧
⑤ ①

Fort of
Villegaignon

Glória
Catete ⑦
Flamengo

Sugar Loaf

Corcovado

Praia Vermelha
Leme   Milit. Acad.

Copacabana

STATE OF RIO DE JANEIRO
STATE OF GUANABARA

N

Leblon   Ipanema   Fort of
Copacabana

MILES: 0   1   2   3   4

MAP 2: City of Rio de Janeiro, formerly the Federal District, now the state of
Guanabara.

Author's Preface

From the Preface to the First Edition, 1940

It is somewhat rash to write the history of a regime that has existed for barely half a century. There is a lack of perspective. The patina of time has not yet given things that vague poetic touch that renders events and persons of the distant past, even trifling events and mediocre persons, both sad and beautiful. The landscape of Brazilian history strikes one as monotonous. Rarely do the decent and orderly figures in it rise above the common level. Because of this, in the early days of the Republic the psychologically extraordinary personality of the two-faced, dissembling Floriano Peixoto places him in bold relief.

This study of the history of Brazil's republican period is part of my self-imposed attempt to understand my country. From this viewpoint, this book complements other books of mine. Here, as in my earlier work, I have tried to be sincere and objective, forgetting my passions, aversions, and sympathies, and tending always toward benevolence in judging men.

From the Preface to the Second Edition, 1952

History, if such a definite literary classification exists, presupposes minute, objective analyses, at least to the extent that objectivity is possible. What I have written is more a synthesis of forty years of the nation's life, a synthesis that interprets, in an attempt to tie together on a higher level, the most varied manifestations of our collective activities. It is also therefore a judgment, subject to mistakes, but always in good faith. I know of no other attempt to systematize and condense the Republic's history. Thus, I have been obliged to turn for information not only to the sparse official documents but also to monographs and pamphlets, nearly all tainted by the political passions of the time. Various foreign books, although not serving me in any way as models, have

---

As the sideheads indicate, this is a composite preface derived from the prefaces to the four editions of the book published during the author's lifetime. In preparing it, I have omitted those sections of the original prefaces that seemed likely to be of little interest to readers of the present edition. JLT

helped me to become well-informed about the most recent happenings in my country, to better understand her, and in consequence to love her more strongly and to have faith in her future. Among others I might mention *America in Our Times (1896–1946)* by Dwight Lowell Dumond, *La Troisième République (1870–1935)* by Jacques Bainville, and *L'Italie Contemporaine (1871–1915)* by Benedetto Croce.

American and European writers on the contemporary history of their countries have, besides any intrinsic advantages over a modest Brazilian writer who might venture into the same field, many extrinsic ones, such as profuse documentation, readers who are habitually polite and tolerant, and above all an atmosphere of ideas in ferment, an atmosphere in which subterranean currents of thought influence political, social, and economic movements. By contrast, we in Brazil are quite deficient, as are other peoples in our situation, in great ideological aspirations. Our biggest achievements always smack of empiricism, of improvisation imposed by the circumstances of the occasion. . . . It is thus unrewarding to search our history for any great lines of matured thought and great clashes of interests such as are present, for example, in the United States. Perhaps because of this I have especially stressed the economic changes that mark the Republic's history. Though I am no agnostic and am averse to a materialistic concept of history, it seems to me that when one studies countries like Brazil, the economic facts, and their immediate impact on the government's successive financial experiments and general policy, are of capital importance.

From the Preface to the Third Edition, 1956

I have had to overcome many research difficulties to arrive at the facts, some of them confusing, some dramatic, some simply picturesque, about the epoch of transition and uncertainty Brazil has lived through. I wrote a friend about this book that I felt like a rubber collector in the wild Amazon jungle searching among a thousand different kinds of trees in the tangled growth for the rubber trees that would repay his efforts. Which were the main facts, which the secondary? Does not an apparently minor event often have, because of its unforeseen consequences, marked historical significance?

I am quite aware of the risks run by writers of contemporary history. Among these are always the sketchiness of the documentation and the immediate reflexes of one's own sympathies and passions. The pitfalls are no fewer, however, along the path of those who propose to reconstruct the distant past. . . . No one succeeds in getting entirely outside himself. After all, in history as in the other sciences described by Dilthey as "of the spirit," the dialogue between Me and the Other Me is permanent. The objective judgment of the historian of any epoch is therefore relative. Gibbon, Mommsen, and Ferrero, for example, were equally proficient in Roman history, but their conclusions were very different.

I was quite young when I read Taine's *Origins of Contemporary France*. Imbued with a rigid determinism, as were most of the young men of my generation, I accepted his judgment of the French Revolution and of Napoleon as final. Later, when I returned to French history through other authors, from the romantic to the most modern, my faith in the old master was irreparably shaken. Other ideas and other reflections revealed to me the schematic, mechanical, and precarious element in what he called the "backbone" of his thought, which was inspired by Hegel. The moral: do not write history, contemporary, modern, or ancient. To carry the argument to its logical conclusion, do not write about anything.

As against the alleged disadvantages of contemporary history there are, naturally, uncontested advantages. The writer does not have to make the difficult psychological switch to the environment of the dead past. He calls up a world that is his own, that he has experienced directly, figures with whom he has rubbed elbows or of whose passage traces still remain, currents of ideas and sentiments that have merged with his own; in short, the climate in which he has lived. This does not mean, however, that he should confine himself to dull and colorless daily news items. He reaches conclusions, makes inductions and deductions, interprets and judges; he intervenes, therefore, with his own imagination, intuition, and susceptibility. In a recent book H. I. Marrou quotes a certain English historian as saying that "history is no more than autobiography writ large." There is truth in the sally.

In his excellent *Minha Formação no Recife,* Gilberto Amado relates that on arriving in the old city as an adolescent to study law, he was eager to learn what he could of the "human side" of his illustrious fellow citizen from Sergipe, Tobias Barreto. He plied an erudite Pernambucano, a former friend and disciple of Tobias, with questions. Barreto's look, his voice, his gestures, his walk, his clothes—what were they like? The *érudit* remembered nothing. Theoretical and bookish, he was incapable of observing the reality of life around him. Gilberto tried again with another former disciple and friend of the Sergipano philosopher; but this man, though an imaginative and sensitive writer, could answer nothing either, because he talked only about himself. Another lesson to retain: an arid imagination and an excess of egotism are negative assets for any kind of literature, including history. . . .

If I may be permitted to speak of myself, I was actually a "militant politician" in the so-called Old Republic. At a little over forty years of age, I was a Federal Senator with a nine-year mandate, and recognized governor-elect of my native state, Pernambuco. The 1930 revolution put a sudden stop—and I soon accepted the fact that it was a permanent one—to my political career. I suffered, like nearly all of my companions of that period, honest and poor as they were, the hardships that subversions of constitutional order, so frequent in vast and turbulent Latin America, often have in store for men in politics. Nevertheless, I never found it hard to admit the poor judgment, lack of foresight, and mistakes of the men formerly in power. I felt no bitterness, and perhaps not even any longing for what I had lost, although the experience was harsher than others I had had. Still less do I hold rancor against the winners. I can only lament, as a Brazilian, that the victorious revolutionaries, owing to their leaders' want of ideas and other deficiencies, did not seize their extraordinary opportunity to bring the nation the benefits they had promised, but instead reduced it to the state of total crisis that today cripples and degrades it.

In writing about this book, my keenly intelligent friend Barbosa Lima Sobrinho has remarked that it takes little note of mass movements. According to him, I am a historian of the elite, thanks to my roots in the "rural patriarchy" of Pernambuco. I cannot, of course, analyze myself to judge how much I have retained of the Pernambucan cane fields. But I am persuaded that the masses have played only a small part in the historical evolution of a hierarchical society of masters, dependents, and slaves, restricted to a primitve type of agrarian economy. . . . The incipient class consciousness of the urban working classes is a new phenomenon in Brazil. It began with the rapid growth of manufacturing industries, and the resulting dominant influence of the cities, and was heightened by the Vargas labor laws, whose execution was so perverted by the interference of demagogues and exploiters.

On looking back over the typewritten pages of this book, I asked myself if I had not been unjust in my judgment of a personality so apparently complex and so contradictory as that of ex-President Vargas. I had regular contacts with him when he was a deputy and Finance Minister, but far fewer contacts after he became President. His undeniable human virtues overcame whatever prejudice I might otherwise have felt against him. I am indebted to him for some personal courtesies. However, it is not the man Vargas who is important to a biographer, but the head of state, the guide, the manager. . . .

From the Preface to the Fourth Edition, 1959

Certain critics have thought it strange that I have not expanded this book into a vast treatise of the Republic's history in all its aspects. Actually, the task would have required only a little more patience or leisure time. But it did not attract me, nor would it ever. . . . What I have attempted is a synthetic interpretation of the life of my country in all its manifestations. . . . This is therefore in some ways more the modest effort of a sociologist than the work of an objective historian concerned only with a succession of events.

Some critics have objected to my dividing up the history of the Republic into four-year presidential terms, as if these were meaningful units in themselves. No one knows better than I that they are not. Republican politics, like monarchic politics, has never had a profusion of exceptional figures, men of the kind that seem to make history instead of being passively led by it. Most of the Republic's administrations did not even try to vary the routine of office, but were content merely to serve out their terms. . . . The authoritarian regimes tried in Brazil have been no more outstanding in this respect than the ordinary constitutional ones. In dividing up this history according to presidential terms, I merely sought to establish a sensible framework that would make the task of analysis easier.

Some of my amiable critics have noted in this work (as in everything I write, according to them) a certain tendency to disenchantment, if not at times to vague pessimism. I do not think they are right. I am as far from pessimism as from optimism. Brazil, as I say in another book, is my constant torment. I see her great, rich, strong, decent, and happy, but the reality frequently and harshly shatters my illusions. The land—using the term in its broadest meaning—is not of the most fertile, contrary to what its boosters, old and young, believe or want to believe. To build an advanced political and technological civilization in Brazil has never been, is not now, and never will be an easy task. The obstacles are growing greater on all sides. . . . However, the vastness and complexity of the job to be done should stimulate those who are called upon to tackle it, both in government and in private enterprise. And those, too, whose work lies outside of material things can contribute to intellectual and artistic growth, to a civilization of the spirit that adds meaning, strength, and stability to the conquests of technological civilization. This study of my country's contemporary history may perchance be the small share of one who cannot render her greater aid, but who believes that in the crises here portrayed her future greatness has surely been in the making.

José Maria Bello

A History of Modern Brazil
1889–1964

1. A Survey of the Empire

Brazilian society — Literary and artistic influences — The clergy and the church-state dispute — Brazil's economic geography — Economic cycles — Abolition and the slave economy — Economic and political crises — Imperial fiscal and monetary policy — Excesses of centralization.

Brazilian society at the close of the Empire naturally reflected the general economic conditions of the country, which in turn were determined by the system of extensive cultivation of large rural landholdings made possible by slave labor. Its structure, therefore, was simple. There were essentially only two classes: at the top, the elite, composed of the plantation owners, the intelligentsia, and the titled nobility, all living directly or indirectly on the bounty of the immense land; at the bottom, the humble masses of slaves and tenant farmers held in bondage by the powerful agricultural clans.

The burgeoning urban class of business and professional men still had negligible influence. There was little industry other than the home type. The system of self-sufficient sugar-mill complexes in the North and large *fazendas* in the South hampered the development of a petty bourgeoisie in the country districts, and discouraged any wide exchange of goods and services. The need for currency was thus kept to a minimum.

Brazil was then, even more than today, a land without small towns and villages. But the rural civilization with its classic virtues and numerous faults (among them, clannishness, extreme traditionalism, and deadening routine) dominated the civilization of the cities, even though the cities were more exposed to the machine technology that was revolutionizing the West. Hundreds of thousands of immigrants settled on the fazendas in São Paulo during the closing years of the Empire, but without altering the traditional atmosphere of Brazilian life: generous, warm, and friendly. The unsanitary cities, lacking in conveniences and often swept by epidemics, were merely immense, ugly villages. The large rural families preferred to live on their vast estates, where they could have greater abundance at less cost and where their authority and social prestige remained intact. The old and large cities in the North—Belém, Recife, and Bahia [Salvador]—were almost autonomous centers of civilization. Rio de Janeiro, with four or five hundred thousand inhabitants scattered over the wide area of the future Federal District, was not the social center of the country, even though it was the capital. The less dense urban centers of São Paulo, Minas Gerais, and Rio Grande do Sul were of still less importance.

The reserved and frugal habits of Pedro II expressed themselves in a renunciation of material comforts. The modesty of the Second Reign was symbolized by the second-rate way of life in the imperial palaces in Rio, São Cristóvão, and Petrópolis, whose lack of comfort and conveniences was proverbial. It was a common thing for rich Brazilians in the North to go to Europe without ever visiting Rio. For an era in which the private reception was the form for high society, the number of drawing rooms to be found in Rio was small indeed. In an intimate letter to Eduardo Prado (published some years ago in a magazine in São Paulo), Ramalho Ortigão lamented, after a visit to Brazil toward the close of the Empire, that in the nation's capital there were no salons where ladies could show off their gowns. He added roguishly that one of his women friends had told him that in Rio there were only two ladies who could "lead a movement to promote elegance"; one had died and the other had moved to Europe.

The Emperor kept a close moral watch over public customs and habits. He felt an instinctive repugnance for men of doubtful integrity, and he would not forgive improper or indecent behavior. His famous "fateful pencil," with which he underlined the names of suspect persons, could inspire panic. The noble virtues of his private life were an example and even a stimulus to his political and administrative staffs. Money had not then become the universal measure of worth. The great majority of public men were models of honesty. And so strong was the tradition of uprightness that it carried over into the republican era, where it withstood even the tremendous temptation to speculate in the stock exchange during the *Encilhamento* [a period of inflationary boom and bust widely blamed on the financial policies decreed in 1890 by the Republic's first Minister of Finance, Rui Barbosa].

The intellectual climate of Brazil was necessarily one of conformity. The prevailing formalism, extending even to everyday clothes, was not conducive to intellectual boldness. Pedro II's bookish tastes, his preoccupation with humanism and exotic learning (such as Sanskrit and Arabic, of no interest to the country's intellectuals), naturally had some influence on the key men of his kingdom.

Until the early part of the nineteenth century, the intellectual life of Brazil had reflected that of Portugal, itself already barren, and was rarely stirred by outside influences. The start of Romanticism in Brazil (foreshadowed by Gonçalves de Magalhães's mediocre poetry) marks the beginning of an independent Brazilian literature. Shortly afterward, inspired by the somewhat dated writings of Chateaubriand and Fenimore Cooper, Brazil's national Romanticism merged with the Indianism of José de Alencar and Gonçalves Dias. This rather artificial form (especially as Alencar practiced it), which patriotically exalted the land's primitive inhabitants or unconsciously reacted against the long enthrallment to Portuguese culture, changed again under the influences of Byron and Victor Hugo and of social poetry. Brazil's two great poets, Castro Alves and Alvares de Azevedo,* are the highest exponents of these currents. When these had run their course, realism and Parnassianism came to the fore.

With the approach of the Republic, Brazilian literature entered one of its most brilliant phases. The men of letters, though confessedly anti-Romantics, proudly cultivated the old Paris Bohemian traditions of 1830. But in the end, in their realistic novels concerned with "human documents" and their cold and objective Parnassian poems, they were as far removed from the life of the nation as their predecessors.

Machado de Assis, who managed to free himself from such ephemeral French influences, was in a class quite by himself because of his British-style humor, his extraordinary psychological insight, and his stylistic artistry. In his younger days, when Romanticism was still in vogue, he delighted in writing short social novels (in which it would be hard to discover any hint of the future master) about the aristocratic life of the court, of which he, modest and shy as he was, could have had little personal knowledge. In the novels and humorous stories of his maturity, when his genius was at its height and his need for psychological flight from his chronic resentments became extreme, his characters became

---

* Antônio de Castro Alves, Brazilian poet and playwright, 1847–1871. Although he was only 24 years old when he died in a hunting accident, his works exerted a deep and lasting influence on Brazilian poetry. Manuel Antônio Alvares de Azevedo, Brazilian poet and short-story writer, 1831–1852. He was only recognized as one of Brazil's greatest poets when his poems and stories were published after his death from tuberculosis at age 20. JLT

symbols of human frailties, absurdities, and small miseries, universal in their essence but rooted all the same in Brazilian, especially Carioca, soil.

The French influenced Brazil's art as much as its literature. After going through an early "primitive" phase that confined itself to imitating the Italians and Portuguese, and that was more or less Gongoristic and rococo, the Brazilian painters and sculptors took their feelings and techniques almost exclusively from the French. In the twilight of the Empire, a nationalistic reaction set in that favored freer interpretation in painting Brazilian life. In music the French and Italian influences were about equal, and in religious and civil architecture the old Portuguese colonial tradition was among the best.

The spreading philosophic doctrines that since midcentury had been renovating European thought were beginning to give Brazil's culture an identity of its own. The philosophies of Comte and Spencer had had a great effect, even when poorly assimilated, on her academic, civil, and military circles. In the closing years of the Empire, the political essay attracted such brilliant minds as those of Joaquim Nabuco and Rui Barbosa. Both men were enthusiastic admirers of British institutions, although Nabuco's cultural background was almost entirely French.

The older representatives of the political and intellectual elite also followed with pleasure, or at least with ingenuous vanity, the debates in the British Parliament. Their mental background was essentially classical, though it derived also from the old climate of Coimbra, from the law faculties of Recife and São Paulo, from the Corpus Juris, and from the realm's jurisconsults. The Civil Code was merely something promised for the future—a promise, incidentally, that was not carried out until twenty-seven years after the republican victory.

The press had lost the passion of the regency period, preferring to adapt itself, more or less, to the pacific atmosphere of the Empire. Sensationalism was then unknown, and even the most popular and liveliest newspapers would by today's standards seem dull and poorly gotten-up. The regime of complete freedom under which they functioned encouraged doctrinaire journalists like Evaristo da Veiga and Justiniano José da Rocha. In a country so devoid of intellectual activities, unstimulated by books or cultural periodicals, the press became the best medium for the spread of ideas. Under its aegis, men of letters sought their own directions. The vicious and unpunished murder of Apulcro de Castro had perhaps intimidated the lampooners. Old political pamphleteers, such as Sales Tôrres-Homem of the distinguished *Libelo do Povo,* ultimately occupied positions in the councils of government.

In paid articles in the *Jornal do Comércio,** in its famous "by request" columns, the great political debates of the period were conducted, cheek by jowl with personal polemics, diatribes of every kind, petty libels, small complaints, and the affected salutations and greeting cards of a city profoundly provincial in its habits. The leading papers boasted of their political neutrality, and those that bound themselves to one of the parties that alternated in power were successful only when they fought one another. Toward the end of the Empire, the voice of the oppositionist press became louder. The burning abolitionist campaign of José do Patrocínio and the powerful articles of Rui Barbosa in the *Diário de Notícias* and *O País* clearly indicated the new spirit of combat.

The church had not become a highly effective social force in the Empire, partly because of the moral and intellectual mediocrity of its servants, mainly because of its subordination to the state, a situation quite in keeping with Pedro II's rigid regalism. The Brazilian church had not had the long and brilliant tradition of struggle that informed the French clergy, whose spiritual virtues and character had been strengthened during the period of revolution and the Napoleonic tyranny. Instead, the Brazilian church copied a Portuguese model. Blending in with the imperial bureaucracy, the clergy had no outside stimulus to fulfill its mission.

The Catholicism of the greater part of the ruling classes was like that of the Emperor: a sincere deism, a listless and formal observance, a permanent dread of being taken to be Papal supremacists or upholders of the Syllabus of Pius IX. In private family life, religious worship had a poetic and traditional form that was in many ways like the Roman worship of household gods. Among the masses, largely slaves and descendants of slaves, religious worship was naturally tinged with vivid reminiscences of African fetishism.

In such social surroundings, discipline and customs readily became lax. Cohabitation by priests, especially in the country districts, was readily condoned. Some members of the clergy, among them those who led great political battles or were feared as political bosses, unconcernedly flaunted their illegitimate offspring. Not only statesmen but Catholic priests as well were Freemasons in a state with an official religion that proscribed Freemasonry. The Brazilian prohibition of novitiates was rapidly extinguishing the monastic orders, whose rich patrimonies thereupon fell into the public domain.

Dom Vital de Oliveira, who had attained the Bishopric of Olinda

---

* Still one of Rio's most influential newspapers and perhaps the most valuable to historians. JLT

[onetime capital of Pernambuco] before he was thirty years old, decided [in 1872] to initiate a moralizing and disciplinary counteraction. Energetic and combative, somewhat like a young Lamennais, he forbade the clergy of his diocese to participate in ceremonies conducted by Masons. Following his own logic, and with the support of the Bishop of Pará, Dom Antônio de Macedo Costa, he went even further: he obliged members of the Catholic brotherhoods to abjure their Masonic oaths. When he was disobeyed, he interdicted both brotherhoods and churches. Thus was born a conflict between the church and the state, without whose express approval it was not possible to change the civil law under which the brotherhoods were constituted.

The cabinet, presided over by the Viscount of Rio Branco, a Masonic grand master, was not disposed to temporize with the two bishops. On their refusal to lift the interdicts, the government, supported by the Council of State, had them tried in court. They were condemned to four years at hard labor, but the penalty was changed to one of simple detention.

A year and a half later, when the Duke of Caxias was prime minister, they were granted amnesty by the government. But the grave dissension between the monarchy and the church, though it was readily forgotten by the Holy See, which had had centuries of diplomatic dealings with civil powers, left the Brazilian clergy feeling a resentment that time did not extinguish. If the clergy did not go so far as to adhere outright to the republican movement, at least it lost interest in the fate of the Empire.

However, it is mainly the economic life of the Empire that needs analysis, for here, certainly, the principal causes of its fall are to be found.

The indigenous peoples of Brazil at the time of its discovery were still living in the Stone Age, with an extremely rudimentary social structure. The Portuguese, therefore, did not encounter any such native cultural resistance in their new and enormous colony as they had confronted in the East Indies, or even such as the Spaniards had encountered from the Aztecs in Mexico and the Incas in Peru. In Brazil they implanted their typically Portuguese civilization in the midst of what they found. Of course the Negro, soon brought over from Africa, and the native Indian strongly influenced the common or, to use an old term, less noble aspects of the life of the Brazilian mass, born of the miscegenation arising from the intimate domestic contact of the three races. They broke down the strong virtues, already in decline, of the Portuguese colonizer, but they gave him others; they affected his language; they influenced his religious practices. But the prime bases of moral and political organization brought in by the superior element remained intact, as was true, incidentally, of all colonies during the era of discoveries.

Brazil's first economic frontier was, naturally enough, her Atlantic coast. Lacking people to populate and capital to develop the new and enormous colony, the Portuguese were obliged to confine themselves to scattered footholds along the seaboard, precarious trading posts in the poor and desert land of brazilwood. Little by little, by traveling the streams in the North, or by climbing the mountains along the southern edge of the plateau and then following the western flow of its rivers, the cattle herders at one extreme and the Paulista *bandeirantes** at the other effected the first great mobilization of Brazil's economic frontiers. The process of opening up the land did not, as it did in the United States, precede its control by the government. Pushing to the west, in search of adventure and easy wealth by capturing and enslaving Indians and by profiteering in mines, the Brazilian pioneers trudged over a tremendous area of land, nearly all of which was already politically defined. The discovery of gold and diamonds in the colony's third century caused a new displacement of internal frontiers. The bandeirante was succeeded by the traveling merchant, the gold prospector, the peddler, the mule driver, and the cattle herder, who made possible communication and trade between the coast and the distant backlands.

This occupation of the backlands, begun early and not yet complete, did not affect the primitive economic center of Brazil, the hot, humid sugarcane lands of the Northeast. Unable to depend on the lazy and intractable Indians to do the necessary rude and continuous farm labor, the Portuguese colonist had introduced the African slave during the colony's first century. The sugar plantations multiplied, principally in Pernambuco and Bahia, and soon became the focal points of the country's wealth and civilization. The sugar industry gave rise to a large class of proud and powerful feudal masters, who were virtually independent of the metropolitan state. This industry thus set the pattern of Brazilian society, which is only now being threatened by that of urban industrial civilization.

Even when the economic center of Brazil shifted from the sugar plantations of the North to the coffee fazendas of the South, the use of the same production methods left intact the old patriarchal society, whose psychology was in so many ways reminiscent of the primitive collective

* Predatory pioneers and adventurers who roamed the unknown interior of Brazil in the 17th and 18th centuries in armed bands called *bandeiras*. JLT

psychology of clans. The Fluminense* or Paulista coffeegrower, like the sugar baron in Pernambuco or Bahia, was profoundly attached to the soil. Moreover, he exhibited the same faults and virtues as the Northerner, with the difference, perhaps, that the man in the North had greater aristocratic pretensions, and was more prodigal, more improvident, more stay-at-home, more fearful of economic experiments, and politically more radical than his counterpart in the South.

The division of Brazil into airtight, hereditary *capitanias* [huge land grants] seemed to the Portuguese government the best way to protect the country against foreign greed. The form of colonization adopted by the British in North America and tried by the Portuguese in the Azores was being repeated in Brazil. The *capitães-mores* [grantees or donataries of the capitanias], proving ineffectual except in Pernambuco and São Vicente, had their powers curtailed by the Crown and themselves placed under an overall government in Bahia. With the appointment of an auditor-general and the granting of the right to appeal to Lisbon, Brazil took her first steps in judicial organization. The setting-up of the first appellate court in Bahia (suppressed during the period of Spanish dominion and restored when Portugal regained her independence) was a milestone in this field. The system of *municípios*† and the rudimentary legislative assembly that Maurice of Nassau had instituted during his fruitful rule of Pernambuco [under the Dutch, 1630–54] did not spread to the rest of Brazil. The Portuguese restoration, giving the heir to the throne the title of Prince of Brazil, and later raising the colony to the honorary status of a viceroyalty, slowly widened Brazil's sphere of local autonomy. The Crown's laws were as applicable in Brazil as in Portugal. Its absolutist regime freed the capitanias from the arbitrary rule of their grantee-governors and imposed the "King's justice" everywhere.

Though the *côrtes* [national assemblies], where an evolution toward representative democracy might have been peacefully fostered, had disappeared from Portugal (as, in fact, from nearly all of western Europe), there still survived certain types of municipal self-government that were reminiscent of the old forms. Certain communities in Brazil were granted privileges identical to those enjoyed in Portugal. Of popular origin were the justices of the peace, who, as João Ribeiro notes, were always to be found in the forefront of rebellions against authority.

---

* A Fluminense is a native or inhabitant of the state of Rio de Janeiro, but a Carioca is a native or inhabitant of the city of Rio de Janeiro. JLT

† County-like units of local government into which the states are divided. For a thorough discussion of the nature of the município, see *Brazil: People and Institutions* by T. Lynn Smith, 3d ed. (Louisiana State University Press, 1963). JLT

A decline in large-scale agriculture, brought on by the migrations of labor to the gold and diamond fields, caused a corresponding decline in the life of the munícipios, hitherto dominated by the sugar barons and *fazendeiros*. The Brazilians no longer struggled for local privileges but for "constitutionalism" and soon for political independence itself. During the colonial period, the land baron was scornful of the metropolis, or was a silent or outspoken adversary of its political and administrative machinery. He continued to grow more insubordinate, especially in Pernambuco, during the reign of Pedro I and the ensuing regency. He was essentially very much a regionalist, and for that reason was a federalist with strong republican tendencies. He accepted Pedro II's ascension without enthusiasm. Nevertheless, he soon succumbed to the government's strong political and bureaucratic centralism, feeling that, after all, the nation's political control would fall to him by reason of his economic ascendancy. Slavery and a centralized Empire harmonized splendidly with his interests as a land baron. The secret of Pedro II's long and peaceful reign is probably that what was to the advantage of the owners of latifundia was also to the advantage of the monarchy. The slow pace of Brazil's progress and the secondary position to which the cities were relegated might also be explained by the hegemony of the plantations' patriarchal civilization.

Sure of the support of the nation's leading class, the Emperor overlooked or slighted the other elements that could have reinforced his position—notably and foremost, the armed forces. Unique among kings, Pedro II did not wish or know how to identify the fortunes of the Crown with those of the military classes, which even after the victorious war with Paraguay were never able to attain the higher ranks in the hierarchy of imperial society.

After the close of the campaign against Paraguay in 1870, and with the example of the United States to ponder, the idea of abolition forced itself upon the conscience of the ruling classes and of the Emperor himself. In order to prevent a possible repetition of the North American tragedy, the Empire's cautious statesmen turned to slow or progressive solutions. The law of the *ventre livre** and the law that freed sixty-year-old slaves, which complemented the earlier law forbidding the slave trade, smoothed the way for the final liberation of the captives. In fact, Rio Branco's law of the ventre livre, so arduously won, only continued to postpone abolition, which could have taken place when the slave

---

* Literally, the law of the "free womb," that is, that all children born of slave mothers should be free. J L T

trade was abolished, for the duration of the Second Reign. But in the last decade of the monarchy, when the abolitionist campaign was revived, it captured the popular imagination and forced open the floodgates that had held it back. The old economic edifice of Brazil, built on slave labor, began to crumble everywhere.

After the social structure had been poisoned for many years by slavery, the question was resolved finally in a grand, sentimental gesture that damaged the pecuniary interests of those who supported the Empire, and disrupted the economy of large sections of the country. Headed by an impulsive ruler like Pedro I, or under the firm hand of a José Bonifácio* or a Bernardo de Vasconcelos, Brazil might have cleansed herself of the great stain of slavery before the Civil War in the United States and before the Paraguayan war. The heavy currents of European immigrants (disliked, incidentally, by Pedro II) that were pouring into the United States could have been partially diverted to Brazil's vast empty spaces to begin developing them economically and bettering them ethnically, as those immigrants had begun to do for Argentina.

If the displacement of Brazil's economic center to the South did not at once affect the dominant social class, it did open up new prospects for employing rural labor. In Rio de Janeiro province and in the valley of the Paraíba in São Paulo, the land and the slave continued to exist as one, as in Pernambuco and Bahia. However, between 1883 and 1889 about 300,000 immigrant farm workers, mainly Italian, arrived in São Paulo, and when coffeegrowing moved from northern to western São Paulo, the free labor of these settlers was found to be the answer to the problem of enforced slave labor. A fast-rising coffee industry could no longer afford the scanty production of the Negro field hand, disciplined by the overseer's whip and paid in kind by the kitchen of the big house, which was the traditional way in the North and in Rio de Janeiro. To the Paulista fazendeiro, the free labor of the immigrant, judging by the prosperity of the industry, seemed much more profitable. If the Republican Manifesto of 1870 had been written fifteen years later, its composers would not have needed to worry about treading on the toes of the Paulista slavocrats.

Furthermore, the growth of factories and urban business, though slow, had noticeably breached the long hegemony of the rural masters. The provinces, restricted to an economy of forced labor, were not strong enough to oppose the rapidly rising dominance of the free-labor regions

---

* José Bonifácio de Andrada e Silva (1763–1838), geologist, minister under Pedro I, tutor to Pedro II. Called the "Patriarch" of Brazilian independence. JLT

and of the newborn industries, which fact helped preserve Brazil from the tragic antagonisms that brought on the American Civil War.

The divergence of economic interests between the Brazilian provinces in the North and those in the South never reached the dangerous imbalance it did in the United States before the Civil War. Slavery, for example, had spread all over Brazil, though with greater or lesser intensity here and there, but had not divided the country into two great rival zones separated by a conventional line. The Negro had profoundly affected not only the racial composition of Brazil (to the point of creating the world's largest area of miscegenation) but Brazilian culture as well. To it he had contributed his kindheartedness, his improvidence, his passive, fatalistic resignation, and most of all his lack of initiative, self-confidence, and self-management, despite the fact that these three qualities were outstanding in the early Portuguese colonizers and in the first pioneers who ventured into the hinterland. After abolition the former slaves, wholly unprepared for autonomous living, abandoned their work on the farms and flocked to the towns and villages, swelling the idle masses living from hand to mouth. Their only conception of their newly granted freedom was that they were no longer subject to the overseer's discipline or, what to their childish minds amounted to the same thing, that they now had the right to indulge in idleness, lazy habits, and degrading behavior.

Thus the date May 13, 1888, marks both the emancipation of the slaves and the death agony of the Empire. Losing its forced labor, the economic lifeblood of its agriculture, the monarchy of Dom Pedro had no further chance of survival. It had neither the support of the army nor the backing of the middle classes. The ancient and often benign historic artifice was about to disappear forever.

The nature and extent of the country's economic activities and their immediate impact on public finances are worth a little study. Next to the constant displacements of its center of gravity, the outstanding feature of the Brazilian economy was its extremely irregular distribution over the country's immense geographical area. Before the ascendancy of coffee in the provinces of Rio de Janeiro, São Paulo, and Minas Gerais, the economic potentials of the North and South maintained a certain equilibrium. Brazil's economic frontiers did not extend very far beyond its coastal areas, where some three-fourths of its productive activities were concentrated. The prevailing economy of consumption was slowly moving toward one of export. The rapid rise of coffeegrowing had profoundly upset the old balance. The northern populations grew little, if at all. From 1870 (the end of the Paraguayan war) to the advent of the

Republic in 1889, the population indices rose from 100 to 120 in the northeastern provinces, while in Espírito Santo, Rio de Janeiro, Minas Gerais, and São Paulo, the increase was to around 148, and in the area from Paraná to Rio Grande do Sul, to 195.

The appearance of rubber in Amazonia attracted extraordinarily large numbers of outsiders to Pará and Amazonas, the two provinces in the far North. But except for the northeastern coast and the regions of the Southeast, Brazil was practically a desert. The central provinces of Amazonas, Goiás, and Mato Grosso, with only about 470,000 inhabitants, covered an area of 3,920,000 square kilometers [1,500,000 square miles]. Of the more than fourteen million total population, six million were located in the coffeegrowing provinces. The northeastern sugar area contained some four-and-a-half million inhabitants, and the provinces in the far South nearly one-and-a-half million. Of these inhabitants, one million were slaves, and the great majority of the rest were mestizos. There was almost universal illiteracy.

Even more accentuated than the demographic differences between the several regions of Brazil was the economic imbalance. A map of productive activities at the close of the Empire would not differ materially from a similar map of Brazil's last century as a colony. The area of effective economic exploitation would be shown by a faintly colored strip along the northern coast, which would become darker in the sugar zone of Pernambuco and Bahia, fade in Espírito Santo, and become darker once more in Rio de Janeiro. Then the strip would widen to take in the coffee regions and old mines of Minas Gerais and the valley of the Paraíba as far as São Paulo. The western part of São Paulo province was virtually an extension of the Mato Grosso desert. There would be spots of color along the coasts of Paraná and Santa Catarina, and in the area of the old German colonies in the latter province, where there were thinly settled pockets of population. In Rio Grande do Sul, the two large regions of grain farming in the hills and cattle raising on the plains were beginning to enjoy a prosperity that would grow with the advent of the Republic.

There was little intercommunication between these various zones. There was not, properly speaking, as there is not even today, a national economy or even a national market in terms of balances between production and consumption peculiar to the various sectors. Each province constituted a small, autonomous market, just as each port controlled a distinct hinterland of its own, which is still true today, although it is less extreme. Only the nationwide fiscal and monetary system provided an image of national political unity.

The 9,700 kilometers [6,000 miles] of railroads built by the monarchy followed the same pattern; they provided transportation from certain backcountry regions to the nearest points on the seaboard, but had no overall articulation. The inland roads over which the oxcarts and burro trains crept were bad and deficient. The same was true of the postal and telegraph services. In 1880 about fifty million government and private letters were handled by the post office. Ten years later this figure had risen to more than two hundred million.

Still, despite its limited enthusiasm for material progress, the Second Reign had built some important railroads at a time when their advantages were a matter of dispute. The construction of the first sections of the Pedro II line was a noteworthy technical undertaking. Starting from Recife and Bahia, the two lines extended toward the São Francisco river. The rail network in Rio de Janeiro, São Paulo, and Minas Gerais did form the basis for a national rather than regional system. The 12,000 kilometers [7,500 miles] of telegraph lines extended inland little by little, and submarine cables connected Brazil with the rest of the world. The first large sugar mills were subsidized by the government.

The merchant marine, born in 1808, had made good progress under its exclusive right to coastwise shipping, but fell back when this privilege was canceled in 1862. The transport lines on the Amazon and Paraná rivers were created by the Baron of Mauá's initiative.* Of the several port concessions, based on special import taxes to guarantee their construction and operation, only that of Santos had begun to be executed.

Thus, in João Ribeiro's happy phrase, Brazil was an archipelago of human islands with almost no intercommunication. Political and administrative centralization under the monarchy did not create economic unity for the country. Although only some agricultural products and raw materials were exported, practically all the manufactured goods and a large part of the consumer goods needed for the very low standard of living were imported. The attempt made during the reign of John VI to establish a small steel industry had not been pushed ahead. In the routine atmosphere of the Empire, Mauá's projects were almost a cause for scandal. After the alluvial gold beds were exhausted at the beginning of the century, the Brazilian subsoil lost all economic significance. "An essentially agricultural country," the old and somewhat pejorative description, was nevertheless exact and true.

But the agricultural wealth had no stability. The main products that composed it changed from time to time and moved from one area to

* Irineu Evangelista de Sousa, Baron (later Viscount) of Mauá, 1813–1889. A native of Rio Grande do Sul. Merchant-banker, founder of river transport lines, and builder of Rio's Mangue canal, dry docks, gas-lighting system, and streetcar lines, and of the Rio–Petrópolis railroad. JLT

another. During colonial days and until the mid-eighteenth century, the sugar in the Northeast was dominant, with cotton ranking second. Even during the gold and diamond cycle, which began and ended in the eighteenth century, the northern sugar plantation, because of the strength and stability of its social and economic structure, continued to represent Brazil. But in the mid-nineteenth century, the sugar industry was ruined by foreign competition, and the extraordinary rise of coffeegrowing in Rio de Janeiro province and along the Paraíba river in São Paulo hastened the transference of the national economy from northeastern to southern Brazil. The Northeast lost its economic leadership and therefore its political dominance.

Near the close of the monarchy rubber began to skyrocket, and at the same time coffee invaded and monopolized the national economy. In 1889 Brazil produced 57 per cent of the world's coffee, from which she derived her foreign trade balances. Coffee built São Paulo and supported Brazil; when coffee no longer depended on slave labor, it conspired to bring about a republican federation and abandoned the monarchy to its fate. In both monarchical and republican Brazil, the cultivation of a single product caused periodic crises, as it does everywhere, that impoverished the country and forced the government into dangerous, life-saving measures. The decline of the Second Reign was marked by the sugar crisis that abolition had greatly aggravated, and the fall in 1930 of the Republic of 1889 coincided with the Paulista coffee crisis.

We can say, therefore, that for each economic crisis related to a major product, there is a corresponding violent upset in the political order. The victory of the revolutionary movement in 1930 is explained by the gaps in the coffee economy, just as the republican triumph of 1889 marked the final stage in the move of the economic center from the North to the South, precipitated by the introduction of free labor.

The weakness of imperial Brazil's economy kept the public treasury in a permanent state of penury. The state could find no new sources of wealth to tap. It limited itself, therefore, to the old colonial fiscal system, though with less red tape and hairsplitting. In spite of some protectionist attempts, its tariffs were nearly always designed to produce revenue, 50 per cent of which was derived from import duties. Budgetary deficits occurred nearly every year, averaging between 20,000 and 30,000 contos (against a yearly revenue that rose from 100,000 contos in 1871 to only 150,000 contos in 1889).* The total revenue for the 66 years during

---

* The value of a conto—one thousand milreis—was about $500 at the exchange rate in 1871. Around the turn of the century it was $333, in 1925 it was $100, and today (1965) it is less than fifty cents. J L T

which the monarchy kept more or less regular budgets was 874,298 contos, whereas the total favorable trade balances did not exceed 430,000 contos. The problems of organization following the nation's independence, the civil struggles that preceded the Second Reign, the war with Paraguay, and public calamities accounted for the chronic deficits.

Foreign debts contracted after independence amounted to about 632,000 contos (at an assumed rate of 27 pence per milreis), of which 175,000 contos were still outstanding in 1889. By adding to this figure the consolidated internal debt of 543,000 contos, and the 75,000 contos of floating indebtedness, we arrive at a total of 793,000 contos, which, together with the 200,000 contos of paper currency in circulation, made up the one million contos that Rui Barbosa, finance minister of the Provisional Government, reported as the Empire's total debt.

The Viscount of Ouro Prêto, replying to Marshal Deodoro da Fonseca, his immediate successor as head of government, stated that the extraordinary expenses incurred under the monarchy had been 1,230,218 contos, of which 63,779 went for the wars of independence, the settlement of accounts with the old metropolis, and the wars of the River Plate and with Paraguay, 425,000 for physical improvements, 87,000 in aid to victims of public calamities, etc.* Since several credit transactions, both foreign and domestic, had produced a total of 870,000 contos, the Empire had spent about 360,000 contos of its ordinary revenues for the extraordinary expenses referred to.

Foreign trade during the last year of the Empire amounted to 525,000 contos. Of the 260,000 contos in exports, coffee accounted for 150,000. The volume of traffic in the port of Santos was almost equal to that in Rio, and greatly exceeded that in Recife and Bahia.

During colonial days Brazil was in a constant battle against a shortage of currency. In the interior certain agricultural products served as a medium of exchange. In order to organize the administration of his new seat of government, John VI resorted to every expedient. He founded the new Banco do Brasil as a bank of issue, which lasted until 1829. (On his return to Portugal [in 1821] he took with him all the money and precious metals he could lay hands on. The poverty became extreme. Copper was the only coined metal, and the door was soon opened to scandalous frauds.)

Upon the failure of the Banco do Brasil in 1829, a system of Treasury issues was begun, and the rate of exchange of the milreis for the pound

---

* These figures do not add up to 1,230,218, but they are the ones that Bello gives. It may be that the war expense is in error, and should be 637,790. That would leave a difference of 80,428, which Bello might have intended to be covered by the "etc." JLT

sterling was reduced on two occasions: from 67½ pence to 43½ pence in 1833, and then to 27 pence in 1846. A second Banco do Brasil could not be organized. A third bank with the sole right of issue resulted from the merger of the bank of the Baron of Mauá (already tied in with the Rothschilds) with the Banco Comercial. After the big crash of 1864, brought about largely by the worldwide depression, the sole right to issue paper money passed back to the Treasury, a system that prevailed until 1888, and the government's finances experienced a long period of relative order, interrupted unfortunately by the immediate consequences of the war with Paraguay.

At the end of the nineteenth century, nearly all of Europe was in a state of economic equilibrium. In general there prevailed parity of exchange, stable currencies, free circulation, moderate tariffs, and a leaning toward free trade. Economically the world seemed divided into two large and counterbalancing regions: the industrial, capitalist countries, and the agricultural countries with no accumulated wealth. Brazil willingly included herself in the second class, as a supplier of raw materials and agricultural products that were exchanged for manufactured goods. When her own reserves fell short of her needs, she obtained loans from the Rothschilds, an incarnation or extension of British capitalism, which had held her in its orbit from the time of her independence. Her moderately favorable balance of trade assured the interest payments. But this financial tidiness was no more than an illusion, since it did not reflect any economic vitality.

In the closing years of the monarchy, North American prosperity began to make a strong impression on Brazil's statesmen, who, with little knowledge of either foreign or domestic economics, were inclined to attribute it more to the political system of the United States than to her exceptional environment, climate, and people. Why, they asked, should Brazil not follow the example of the powerful republic to the north? The greatness of the American Union dated from the abolition of slavery in Lincoln's time; the new phase in Brazil's economic history would likewise date from the freeing of her own slaves.

In November 1888 the João Alfredo cabinet abandoned the system of inconvertible Treasury issues, and launched a new system of redeemable bank emissions, of which a future Central Bank of Issue would be the final goal. The realization of a foreign loan of six million pounds sterling encouraged public belief in a healthy national prosperity, of which the increase in the currency and the growth of banking credit were promising signs. There was an increase of 402,000 contos in the capital of corporations formed in Rio between May 1888 and November 1889—another factor behind belief in Brazil's economic vitality—which Ouro Prêto lost no opportunity to point out. (Later Rui Barbosa also called attention, as evidence of success, to the 1,200,000 contos in new capital of the corporations of the Encilhamento.)

The Viscount of Ouro Prêto formed his cabinet in the climate of confidence and optimism created by abolition. He succeeded in converting a large part of the foreign indebtedness and in obtaining a favorable domestic loan, and he held out hopes of a convertible currency in the near future. The stability of the rate of exchange (kept at par much more by the gold received from the foreign loan of 1887 and by foreign investments in the country after abolition than by true economic prosperity) explains to some extent his confidence in his plan to consolidate the emission of bank notes on the classic basis of a one-third gold reserve.

Putting the Alfredo plan into operation before the creation of the Central Bank of Issue—today still an unrealized dream—Ouro Prêto contracted with the Banco Nacional do Brasil to gradually replace the Treasury bills with others redeemable in gold. This same arrangement was made available to a second bank in Rio that did not make use of it, and to one in São Paulo that issued only a small amount of the new currency. The government committed itself to make no further emissions and to deliver to the Banco Nacional five per cent bonds in exchange for the Treasury paper redeemed by it. In times of political or economic crisis, the Banco would have the right to suspend conversion of its bills.

At the same time, as a temporary solution to the agricultural problems that had been brought on mainly by abolition, Ouro Prêto instructed the Treasury to lend to various banks 84,000 contos, out of the 100,000 raised by the domestic loan, at no interest. The banks would in turn be able to make farm loans at six per cent interest for periods of one to fifteen years. This completed the grand scheme for financial reform that Ouro Prêto contemplated, but which the republican revolution kept from being carried out. In any case it was probably less brilliant than its author imagined.

Today, as we analyze the economic and financial conditions that prevailed toward the end of the Empire, we find it hard to understand how a man as intelligent and experienced as Ouro Prêto could have considered a definitive overhaul of the Treasury and the consequent mintage of metal to be even possible. The euphoria of the market stimulated by the government, possibly to placate the feudal masters whose slaves had been freed and to create a more propitious climate for a peaceful succession to Pedro II, was bound to result in the crisis of the Encilhamento that soon afterwards marked the financial policy of Rui Barbosa.

Insofar as one can summarize moot questions that even today cannot be discussed with complete calm, the economic and financial situation bequeathed by the Empire to the Republic was that described above. It was seemingly brilliant, if one looks only at exchange parity and national credit, but the true state of affairs in the immense, impoverished land so ill-equipped for productive work was quite otherwise. The euphoria immediately preceding the death agony of the reign of Dom Pedro at least largely explains, if it does not justify, the uncertainties, the contradictions, the mistakes of the Republic's first fiscal administration.

To conclude this rapid inventory of the Empire, the special circumstances of public administration must also be reviewed. Progress in the provinces was made difficult by the centralization of government. Accordingly, the ideal of federation flourished more in the richer regions. The provincial presidents, appointed by the central government, were generally out of touch with local problems. They pursued their public careers by stages, seeking only to please their parties and the cabinets under which they served.

Distinguished statesmen, among them Tavares Bastos, had long pointed out the evil consequences of excessive centralism. The impoverished provinces in the North complained that they contributed more to the central government than they received from it; the rich provinces in the South complained that their initiative was being frustrated. Intelligent monarchists, such as Rui Barbosa and Joaquim Nabuco, thought it possible to reconcile empire and federation. The municípios had no political significance. The scandalously fraudulent electoral machine, composed of some 150,000 or 200,000 questionable and insignificant voters who were devoid of autonomy and civic consciousness, controlled local administrations. Public servants were honest and often diligent, but their close dependence on the central government created bureaucratic red tape and delays that robbed them of what efficiency they had.

The few statesmen and politicians who had not been deceived by the regime's shoddy veneer of parliamentarism occasionally pointed to the realities of the situation: the successive business depressions; the fickle policies about the right to issue money, now restricted to the Treasury, now to the banks, now allowed simultaneously to both of them; the high interest rates; the mortgages that burdened eighty or ninety per cent of rural properties; the lack of a national trading area; the extremely precarious transportation and credit systems; and the irrevocable poisoning of the national life by slave labor. Blinded by their egoism, only the small class of politicians, the Emperor in his dress suit, the land barons, the gold-braided ministers, the members of Parliament, who wore their

Prince Alberts in a sweltering climate and were preoccupied with the *Revue des Deux Mondes* and with what was being thought and said in the Parliament of Victorian England—only these could not see the monstrosity that Brazil was.

The life of the court, the whispered intrigues in the corridors of the ministries and the Parliament, took up too much of the time and attention of the heads of government, those of incontestable ability as well as those of sincere patriotism. The Emperor had long since lost any liking for detailed work or close supervision of administrative affairs. The great services of his long reign were largely forgotten in the atmosphere of general discontent. In a way, however, this atmosphere may have rendered the work of reconstruction, to which the Provisional Government committed itself, less difficult.

2. The Nature of the Monarchy

*The weak and artificial foundations of the Empire — The
Republic forestalled — Three causes of the Empire's fall —
The renascence of republicanism — Unrealistic imperial politics — Pedro II: the man and the head of state — The war
with Paraguay — The Empire's general staff — The twilight
of the monarchy.*

The great ease with which the Brazilian monarchy was overthrown on
the morning of November 15, 1889, has given rise to prolonged controversy among chroniclers and historians of every caliber. The disagreements that at once arose among the men who were most responsible (or
thought they were) for the advent of the Republic naturally made it
difficult for them to form any clear judgments. Their disputes appear
somewhat irrelevant to those who more than fifty years later pore over
the contradictory documents. They were vying for the honors of a bloodless triumph over a political regime that died of its own accord, consumed
by the disease to which it had been predisposed from the beginning.

Today, as we study the immediate causes of the Republic, we have
two advantages over those who first dealt with them: our detachment
from the passions of the time, and the lessons of new political experiences. The quick revolution of 1930 [when Vargas came to power] singularly enlarged our psychological understanding of what occurred in 1889.
Analogous facts, given Brazil's still far-from-settled moral climate, her
precarious economic and social conditions, and her lack of leaders with
political discernment, bring analogous results.

From the time of her independence Brazil has sought to discover her
destiny, the meaning of her existence. Soon tiring of experiments begun
with clamorous enthusiasm and ingenuous messianic pretension, she has
easily given herself over to still others. Basically her great capacity for
endurance rests upon her fear of something worse.*

---

* What the author means, apparently, is that Brazil has survived as an independent
nation since 1822, in spite of her many and great economic, social, and political ills
and the often violent attempts to cure them, because of Brazilians' willingness to put
up with the bad for fear of the worse, i.e., their fear of jumping from the frying pan
into the fire. JLT

The greatest praise that can be given the reign of Pedro II is that it lasted so long. Having been thrust upon the country in an "attainment of age" conspiracy that was a solution of the moment [in 1840, when Pedro was fourteen years old], it endured for half a century. This was the miracle—wrought more by Pedro's own actions than by the exotic institution that he built up, the monarchy. The day on which he clearly revealed his discouragement, his disenchantment, and his premature physical and mental decay, the ancient structure inevitably collapsed, so weak were its foundations. One might have said that Brazil's second Emperor neither knew how nor wanted to prepare for his successor. The strange apathy he displayed during the last phase of the monarchy seemed to be the fatalism of one who walks with open eyes to his doom.

The Empire, it has been said a thousand times, had run out of vital juices. Its patriarchal atmosphere, a kind of warm bath that lulled the nation, could not hold the interest of the younger generation, who were eagerly making contact with the great world currents of new ideas. Even its old civil servants had long since become disillusioned and apathetic about its perilous situation. (The political leaders of 1930 who held the key executive and parliamentary positions had lapsed into a similar frame of mind.) If, in the beginning, feelings of sentiment for the Boy-Emperor, the "nation's orphan," contributed much to the survival of his reign, respect and compassion for the aged and ailing monarch only prolonged its agony.

The France of 1830, her First Republic vanished, accepted the bourgeois rule of Louis Philippe, the "citizen king," as a compromise between her monarchic tradition and a parliamentary liberalism along British lines. The memory, still very much alive, of the revolutionary excesses of 1789 caused her to fear a republic. But eighteen years later, wearied of a government without boldness or magnificence, she applauded Lamartine's "scornful revolution," only to succumb four years later in the throes of renewed panic to the imperialism of Napoleon III. There is a certain similarity between the situations of France and Brazil.

The declaration of young Pedro's majority had forestalled the republic that should logically have emerged from the regency. It too was a form of compromise between the monarchy, which had brought about independence, and liberal idealism. Not until 1822, with the reign of Pedro I, had a consolidation of Brazil's independence become a possibility. The great men of that day, the illustrious José Bonifácio more than any other, had a perfect vision of the historic reality. The tumults during the regency had evident federalist and republican aspirations, and aroused in the small Brazilian elite a terrified apprehension of a national split-up. The famous defection of Bernardo de Vasconcelos clearly reflects the dread of radical liberalism that gripped the most eminent statesman of that period.

Because Brazil easily survived the revolutionary ferment during the most agitated and interesting phase of her history [i.e., the First Reign and the ensuing regency], her historians and sociologists have concluded that only the precipitate advent of the Second Reign could have preserved national unity. But hypothetical reconstruction of the facts might lead us to a different conclusion.

Menaced by poor or nonexistent intercommunication, by some states' superficial longings for separation, by the fond recollection of self-contained colonial provinces, and by a rudimentary economic system, Brazilian unity was nevertheless cemented by the natural affinities of language, religion, and race, and would have survived under a republic. She would have prolonged the period of revolutions for a time, like the other South American republics, but the violent intellectual and moral clashes of such a period would have given greater strength and solidity to the young democratic institutions of the nation. Thus Brazil would have come through the period of internal trial and strife, with a toughened fiber to her character, seventy years sooner than she did. The inauguration of Pedro II's rule, to repeat an old saw, was a mere salve that did not get at the cause of the inflammation. For this very reason the early hopes and confidence it raised were short-lived.

But we are not interested in reviewing the past merely to speculate on what might have been. We only wish to discover the causes of the Empire's dissolution within its own organism. Why and how did the Republic emerge so unexpectedly? Why were there no defenders of the old regime?

Historians agree in attributing the fall of the monarchy to three major causes: the religious dispute, the abolition of slavery, and the military issue. If these questions (or at least the last two, which were the most important) had not arisen, Pedro II would have ended his days on the throne. Perhaps, as Quintino Bocaiúva declared in his praise of the military's part in the monarchy's overthrow, Brazil would have continued living under a third reign, and a fourth. There is no doubt that the abolition of slavery was a big step toward the Republic. It is also clear that the support of the republicans by the military was a decisive factor. But it is equally true that the roots of the Empire were already so weak that any grave event would have toppled it.

Despite uncertainty and confusion, a large fraction of the Brazilian upper classes were always basically republican. Yet the monarchy was

the framework of the established order, whose legalistic and bureaucratic tradition had been inherited from Portugal. Fear of disrupting
the familiar and traditional forms was natural enough. A republic, to
many who remembered the French experiments of 1789 and 1848 and
observed the Spanish-American nations around them, seemed but an
invitation to disorder and tyranny. On the day these fears could be overcome, the monarchy would disappear. The esteem and public respect
that surrounded the person of the Emperor were not enough to block
the emergence of the Republic.

Brazilian historians, even the rare ones who concern themselves with
philosophic interpretation, date the decay of the monarchic principle far
back in Brazil's history. To Euclides da Cunha, for example, the Marquis of Paraná's party of "conciliation," which survived until 1860,
marked the start of the decline, or, as Joaquim Nabuco would later say,
the beginning of the flood tide of democracy. To Oliveira Viana, the
republican ideal "as an organized force and not as an isolated idea is
clearly related to the liberal reaction that followed the fall of the Zacarias cabinet in 1868" and brought about the organization of the Republican party in 1870. The overt intervention by the Emperor, not only in
the sacrifice of the Zacarias cabinet but also in handing over power to
the Conservatives under Itaboraí against a unanimously Liberal Chamber, brought about a general change in the political concepts of that day.
It set off a "progressive disbelief in the virtues of the monarchical parliamentary system and a growing aspiration for a new regime, a new order
of things."

Nevertheless, it is just that period after the end of the war with Paraguay that marks the zenith of the Second Reign. The ministry headed by
the Viscount of Rio Branco was its longest-lived, most fruitful, and most
brilliant cabinet. Dom Pedro was enabled to make his first visit to Europe, where he traveled in pleasant tranquility for almost a year. The
law of the ventre livre quieted abolitionist aspirations for a decade. Despite the lively repercussions it produced in the small Brazilian political
elite, the "bloodless coup" of 1868 was not essentially different from the
many others that filled the artificial parliamentary life of the Empire,
and had almost no effect on the public's belief or disbelief in the advantages of a parliamentary system.

The Emperor always arbitrated the rotation of the parties in power.
In a country with only incipient civic consciousness, where elections were
openly fraudulent, and where there did not and could not exist any
shadow of organized public opinion, he always retained for himself the
prerogative— admittedly beneficial—of limiting the length of each party's

stay in power. Except for minor public jobholders, the nation—disjointed, sparsely populated, poverty-stricken, and uncultivated—had little interest in the routine rotation of the parties in power. The small and rootless elite in the Parliament who strove to ape the English, even to their clothes, could not delude themselves about the comedy in which, after all, they were actors. In his famous arraignment of the Dantas ministry, Ferreira Viana echoed the sentiments of many when he declared "I am tired of being an actor in this political comedy," which fact, however, did not keep him from taking part in the ministerial councils.

It seems dubious, therefore, to ascribe the decadence of the Second Reign to any purely political event. Rather, we must seek the cause in the general conditions of the nation's economic and social life. Internal political events and their effects abroad were conditioned by a process of dissolution intrinsic to the Empire. The monarchy was always so foreign to the Brazilian temperament that a study of it as a specific form of government applied to the country must necessarily be limited. The monarchy, having been transplanted under extraordinary circumstances from Europe, where it represented a stratification created by centuries of history, and requiring as it did a mystic respect for its origins, never quite became a genuine superstructure in America. An analysis of the regime that was extinguished in 1889 reduces itself almost to a study of the figures by which it was defined, beginning, naturally, with the one at the summit. Hence we will do well to review the personality of Pedro II himself.

There is no one to the present time who has received greater attention from Brazilian biographers and historians. After the short period of Jacobinic exultation, during which it was the vogue to depreciate him, Pedro II has become the object of lasting tributes and praise. One could almost say that in the nearly unconditional eulogy there is a kind of return to the past. It is as if the Empire were filling Brazilians with nostalgic longings, as if they regarded the old king, the "grandson of Marcus Aurelius," as an impeccable model for Brazilian rulers. If privately his many virtues blot out his small defects, as a public figure, the guide and leader of a young nation, his faults are not so readily overlooked.

Meditating upon his long reign, we often get the impression that Pedro strove harder to implement his personal desires than to build a living nation. Actually he was not a statesman; he was wanting in vision, in liking for politics, and in boldness. A man who fulfilled his duties honestly, a sincere patriot imbued even with certain nativist predilections, he personified the highest type of public servant. The respectability of his private life was unassailable; his disregard for money was both great and instinctive, as was his distaste for dishonesty and immoral behavior. A person of little more than average intelligence, he was not really moved by art or by the poetic aspects of life. "I recognize," he said later in his *fé de ofício* [a sort of valediction] written during his exile, "that I am very deficient in the talents of the imagination. . . . Such knowledge as I possess I owe above all to pertinacity." He was fond of exercises of the mind, although his constant concern about social intercourse with foreign writers and savants overlaid perhaps a bit of provincial exhibitionism. Though sincerely liberal and generous by nature, he did not always find it possible to forgive and forget. He was sometimes willful and tenacious, even obstinate, as in his almost solitary insistence on prolonging the war with Paraguay until López had been killed, or in his haughty insistence on his prerogatives in dealing with the bishops of Pernambuco and Pará, but he was as a rule timid, essentially temporizing, and perhaps even disillusioned and skeptical.

His intelligence and even his kindliness were not glowing. He did not know how to make friends, how to inspire dedication and enthusiasm. He was detached even from the small world of intellectual mediocrities in whose conversation he took most pleasure. He was not highly esteemed by the politicians who served him for almost half a century, and was even less so by the most brilliant and independent Brazilian minds of that day. Public respect, however, was readily inspired by his sobriety, moderation, and well-balanced morality, so different from his father's impulsiveness. Like most men, he was psychologically much closer to his mother. From his grandfather, John VI, he received, perhaps, his peaceful nature, his love of work, his capacity for dissembling, and his unmatched keenness of insight as an administrator. His lonely and unhappy childhood, the irreparable mistakes of his early training, account for much of his grave and withdrawn character. He was, although without confessing it, proud of his ancestry, but was also modest, sober, and austere without effort; he disdained the glittering superficialities of the world. His disregard of etiquette, for instance, led him on occasion into comic breaches of protocol in foreign courts. With no fondness for politics, athletics, or social activities, he inevitably took refuge in the inner world of thought. But his was not, after all, a very wide world; it was not one that would permit him deep philosophic or religious understanding, or a more than mediocre esthetic responsiveness; as a result, his life may have seemed to him devoid of meaning.*

* His recently published letters to the Countess of Barral reveal a secret intercourse of which one would hardly have suspected him: a long "amorous friendship" with a fine and intelligent lady. But even in the abandon of an intimate correspondence (he

The precise daily office routine, the pleasures of censorship, his genius for unimportant details, perhaps offset to some extent his inner boredom, but contributed at the same time to a limitation of his intellectual horizons. He tried to tutor the nation like a patient schoolmaster, who supervises the life of his charges with detailed, bureaucratic discipline. Liberal by temperament and jealous of his aura as "philosopher-king," he tried to keep these sentiments within the bounds of parliamentary constitutionalism. But he knew better than anyone else that everything proceeded from his will. Instead of becoming a ridiculous tyrant like those who disgraced the republics of Latin America, as he could have done with impunity, he nobly made believe that he ruled a free nation.

As we can for almost all men, we can distinguish two distinct phases in Pedro's psychological development. The first of these was probably over before he was fifty, at the end of the war with Paraguay. He had by then become the supreme arbiter of life in a nation that was somewhat insulated from the rest of the world. Pedro, when he was barely out of his teens, had freed himself of those who had tutored him during the early days of his reign, and, feeling himself to be at the height of his powers, had begun to exercise a personal sovereignty. His youthful will, cold and stubborn, often betrayed itself in spite of his attempts to disguise it. With considerable adroitness, he took advantage of the diffuse aspirations for political peace by inducing the Marquis of Paraná to put together the so-called party of conciliation in 1853. This conciliation was an opportunistic amalgamation of parties that wiped out their ideological differences and cleared the field for the sovereign rule of the young Emperor. By means of the parliamentary machinery that had been imposed upon the country under singular circumstances, he became the great arbiter of Brazilian life, itself an expression of an economic system based on latifundian slavery.

Little by little, the clash of competing interests was held within bounds by the formation of two large parties, the Conservative and the Liberal, which were alternated in power, and by the rotating presidency of the Council of State. Pedro II presided over the peaceful activities of the nation like a patriarch, often renouncing the use of his powers so as to hold up to his people (and to foreign intellectuals, whose judgments

---

would burn her letters to him), he confirms the fixed nature of his psychology. He rarely indulges in a carefree expression of affection, but writes always in the same sober tone, the same dry, humorless style, equally preoccupied with both big and little things about Brazil, revealing above all the constant desire to escape his artificial and monotonous surroundings. J M B

greatly preoccupied him) the image of a free government. A loveless marriage gave him a wife who was a model of domestic virtues. His children completed the happiness of his home and filled him with hope. He became less withdrawn.

In Europe, constitutional monarchy approached its zenith. In 1837, the Victorian era, a sort of model for the universe, began in England. The romantic French Republic of 1848 fell before a new 18 Brumaire on December 2, 1851. The revolutionary wave that had spread over the Old World was slowly receding. In the triumphant beginnings of the machine age and economic liberalism, the leading nations of Europe believed that a temperate monarchy would achieve a just balance between tradition and progress—the perfect form of government. Thus, because of the influence of European monarchy, the system of slave labor, and the elimination of partisan ideologies, Pedro II was able to establish his reactionary empire unhindered. Had he possessed the genius of a true statesman, had he been able to grasp the meaning of Brazilian life, he might have been able to reinforce the country's weak foundations.

Brazil was grateful to him for peace and internal order, which seemed all the more precious when compared with the endemic disorders in the rest of the continent, symbolized, for example, by the tyranny of Rosas [Argentine dictator]. Pedro's policy of intervention in the River Plate area, inherited partly from the reign of John VI, partly from the historic rivalries between Portugal and Spain, had the object not only of saving Rio Grande do Sul from civil commotion, but also of guaranteeing the independence of Uruguay and Paraguay. This policy and the campaign against the slave trade, aggravated by the Christie incident, diverted the possible patriotic unrest of the people. The republican dream, which had been very much alive during and after the regency, became lost in the clouds. The insolent behavior of Christie, the British minister,* hurt Pedro's patriotic pride, but the war with Paraguay absorbed most of his care and attention. When the war ended, he returned to his old dreams of the abolition of slavery, but always with his habitual caution.

The Paraguayan campaign, as Joaquim Nabuco justly remarks, was Brazil's first great contact with the world beyond her borders. For good or ill, it brought her diplomacy into focus. She was abandoning her old isolation. The great intellectual currents of the century were beginning

---

* In 1862, upon Brazil's refusal of certain demands, the British minister William Dougall Christie retaliated by ordering a British warship to capture Brazilian merchant vessels in the vicinity of Rio. The monarchy promptly broke off relations with Great Britain and did not resume them for several years. JLT

to make themselves felt. Although the example of the South American republics was not edifying, it began to dissolve the monarchical idea, which in a republican and equalitarian America was anomalous anyway. The nightmare of slavery weighed on the best consciences. The Empire probably would not have survived a military defeat, even as the empire of Napoleon III was destroyed by such a defeat in the same year as the end of the Paraguayan war. But victorious at last in having López hunted down and killed, Pedro succeeded in postponing the disappearance of his own monarchy.

But Pedro was changing. He began to age prematurely in body and soul. One might have said that the heavy demands of the military campaign had exhausted him and destroyed whatever illusions he might have had about his mission in Brazil. Little by little he gave up the prerogatives that he had always guarded most jealously. Although he was as attentive as always to his routine daily duties, the higher functions and responsibilities of government seemed to weigh too heavily on him. His voyages to Europe and North America were largely escapes from the tedium that assailed his spirit.

Journeying hurriedly through country and city, commenting with a tourist's clichés on the glories of the past or the artistic beauties he saw, often failing to appreciate the worth of the eminent men he sought out —though he redeemed himself here by his grasp of Wagner's musical revolution and by his regard for the genius of Pasteur and Edison—Pedro endeavored to forget the cares of kingship. Nowhere does his lengthy travel correspondence (or other analogous documents) reveal the preoccupations of a statesman. He seemed indifferent to economic problems and unmindful of the first great social changes the machine age was making in the capitalist civilizations of Europe and the United States. He was much more interested, or made himself believe he was, in the study of Arabic or Hebrew.

He looked upon himself, at times, as a literate bourgeois or a vaguely sentimental businessman from the city on a long holiday among the museums and historic ruins of the Continent. He devoured books and let his mental curiosity range in all directions. But in intellectual output he did not go beyond a few mediocre sonnets and a few pages of equally mediocre prose. His letters, written without literary taste, reveal no spontaneity of idea or feeling, no strong emotional reactions to the things he most admired. They confirmed, nevertheless, the habitual nobility of his sentiments.

The members of his immediate family—wife, daughters, sons-in-law, grandchildren—were incapable of making up for his deficiencies by creating on their own an atmosphere of cordial public relations or personal warmth. It was a typically bourgeois family, of the stripe of Louis Philippe, in which no single person stood out. Everything therefore indicated to Pedro that the Empire would end with him. The nation would not tolerate even a hint that the sovereign power might pass into the hands of the Princess. Pious and estimable though she was, she was married to a foreign prince whom the public regarded, though perhaps unjustly, with profound antipathy.

The general staff of politicians who worked with Pedro II for fifty years also occupied prominent positions. In the moral qualities essential to public men, they gave the best possible impression. Nearly all of them were honest and diligent. But in general they had the same faults that inhibited the Emperor's actions: a lack of constructive boldness, an excessive formalism and legalism. They were victims of their own artificial parliamentarism. They neither translated nor brought to life the genuine aspirations of the nation. They lived the hothouse life of the court, the Parliament, and the Council of State; they were constantly preoccupied with imitating the English and French. At heart, in both politics and literature, most of them were old Romantics. They were university graduates and "doctors," proud of their classical, Latinist education (which did not, however, keep them from writing without elegance or from butchering the grammar of their own tongue). Absorbed in petty political intrigues and indifferent to the great social, philosophic, and economic questions of the day, rural proprietors, slave owners nearly all —such were the members of Pedro's general staff. The gap between them and the humble masses of slaves was enormous. The middle classes, the active and self-conscious bourgeoisie that constitute the backbone of representative democracies, did not exist, or at least had no political awareness. The economic and social system built on slave labor was necessary to the life of the Empire's ruling class and thus to the monarchy also. Perhaps, professionally handicapped and chained as they were by the unhappy institution that degraded Brazil and held her back, they could not have done more for her than they did.

In intelligence and culture none of them, certainly, was superior to Pedro II. True, during his reign there no longer flourished the great figures, energetic and positive, of the era of Pedro I and of the regency; there were no leaders of the caliber of José Bonifácio, Feijó, or Bernardo de Vasconcelos. Nevertheless, during the reign of Pedro II there were a number of brilliant men who on many occasions displayed statesmanlike vision or, to put it more modestly and truthfully, who revealed themselves to be capable members of the government. There were men such as

Paraná, Olinda, Uruguai, Itaboraí, Rio Branco, and Ouro Prêto. At least two others, Tavares Bastos and Mauá, as Vicente Licínio Cardoso observes with his usual clarity, displayed the highest degree of realistic and constructive intelligence during the imperial period, but being looked upon without great esteem by Pedro, they could not fully exercise their boldness of thought and action. The Emperor's extreme cautiousness was reflected in the whole of Brazilian life. Tavares Bastos spoke in a semi-desert, and Mauá had his wings clipped.

The Baron of Rio Branco, who was hardly adverse to the monarchy, later wrote that the political life of the Empire could be summarized as an undistinguished struggle for power between the Conservative and Liberal parties. The deep ideological differences that clearly separated the political elite of the regency period into opposite camps were obliterated in the climate of the Second Reign. The party of conciliation put together by Paraná made the revival of those differences impossible. In many ways, therefore, the bitter criticism of Angelo Ferraz is just: the conciliation perverted the parliamentary system and lowered the level of political contests from the national to the local plane.

The platform of the Liberal party, even after the reform movement, was *less* bold than that of the radicals in 1831, and was even carried out in part and without bias by the Conservatives. It did not broaden itself or go beyond winning liberal political victories along European lines, especially of the Louis Philippe variety. Economic problems were almost foreign to it. Until the end of the Empire, the political history of Brazil can be easily condensed into the somewhat monotonous succession of cabinets and parliaments. In the final years of the old regime the confusion became worse. The repeated attempts to clean up the parties by means of less scandalous elections were frustrated. The state of neglect into which the Emperor let his prerogatives fall, both *de jure* and *de facto,* did not signify a democratic victory that would have perfected and strengthened the parliamentary system. It seems, on the contrary, to have foreshadowed the end of the monarchy, just as the state of neglect that followed the liberal transformation of Napoleon III's empire foreshadowed its end.

The reign of Pedro II rendered two incomparable services to Brazil: completing her judicial system and training the nation in common respect for the law. It consolidated national unity with fewer hardships than the Republic might have created if it had succeeded the regency. It was honest and upright, but it was doomed at birth to a transient life. The slow functioning of its administrative machinery, the ideas and susceptibilities of the ruling classes, reflected too much of the King's own image. For half a century it busied itself with the surface of the nation, incapable of getting down to the core of things. Pedro II would have been an excellent figurehead ruler of some nation whose political and economic development had matured, like, for example, any of the present-day Scandinavian countries. But he was deficient in the great constructive qualities needed to govern a people newly born to autonomy, unsure of themselves in a vast territory, in the process of generating the greatest fusion of races ever seen, and displaying even today, from the cities on the seaboard to the wild backlands, every stage of man's agelong evolution.

The Republic we propose to study from its dawn to the present is even now atoning not only for its own mistakes, but also for those of its imperial heritage, a heritage of slavery, of timidity, of artifice—and so, among other things, of exaggerated value placed on academic degrees!

3. The Ascendancy of the Republican Idea

History and hibernation of the republican idea — Brazil's isolation on the continent — Foreign influences — The Republican Manifesto of 1870 — The republican movement — Brazil and Portugal — Spread of modern philosophy — The military ferment — Ouro Prêto — Psychological types — Antecedents of the Republic.

The example of the United States had aroused enthusiasm in the plotters of Minas Gerais at the end of the eighteenth century; the democratic ideal had replaced the old utopian, aristocratic republic of the Pernambucan nativists of 1710. The small Brazilian elite, educated in Europe's intellectual climate, were stirred by the ideals of freedom that had characterized the end of the eighteenth century and culminated in the French Revolution. When the Napoleonic dream came to an end, the liberal reaction united with the ardent aspirations for a system of political charters and limited powers. The fiction of the divine right of kings was replaced by the fiction of the sovereignty of the people exercised through legislative parliaments.

The constitutionalist agitation, which had spread to Portugal, propagated itself all the more easily in Brazil, the true seat of the monarchy since the arrival of John VI [1808]. The hesitant and harassed King had been coerced into accepting the constitution offered by the revolutionary junta in Pôrto, and soon afterward the Spanish constitution. Finally he fled the obligations he had assumed, thereby lending himself to the reactionary machinations of the Portuguese côrtes against the autonomies won by the old colony.

Brazil moved rapidly toward complete sovereignty on John's return to Portugal [April 1821], when Prince Dom Pedro I assumed the regency. The Brazilian patriots were able to maneuver the impulsive prince into uttering the *grito do Ipiranga,** which officially declared Brazil's inde-

* This refers to the cry "Independence or death!" with which the 24-year-old Pedro I declared Brazil's independence from Portugal. The historic event took place on the banks of Ipiranga creek near São Paulo, to which Pedro was returning from a visit to

pendence from Portugal. Even before this, the Prince had convoked a national constitutional assembly, whose sessions he inaugurated on May 3, 1823. The dissensions by the impatient assembly, jealous of its powers and infected by the passions of the three Andradas,* irritated the young, authoritarian Emperor, and provoked his coup d'etat of dissolution. Nevertheless, he personally granted the constitution that the Brazilians expected so much from and that did in fact take their liberal tendencies into account. The Pernambucan revolution of 1824 was an armed protest against the King's supposed right to override the assembly, although at bottom it revealed once more the invincible local repugnance for extreme administrative centralization.

The imperial constitution of 1824 measured up to the best political ideas of the time, but it was also a victory of centralism over federalism, then a bitter struggle in Brazil as in all of Latin America. Putting aside the old republican and federalist dreams inspired by the North American model, Brazil fell in with European-type monarchic and parliamentary constitutionalism. Political and economic centralism growing triumphantly throughout the civilized world—here was the great motivating ideal of 1824.

The Brazilian constituents, authors of the charter granted by the Emperor, cherished the romantic freedoms the French Revolution had popularized. Disciples of Montesquieu and Rousseau, they were convinced of the absolute truth of "liberal principles" and of "man's inalienable rights." Nevertheless, it was the book *Constitutional Policy,* itself a product of eighteenth-century philosophy, by the French publicist Benjamin Constant that had been their immediate source of inspiration. From it they adopted the moderating power exercised directly by the King and the tight administrative centralism of the Napoleonic tradition.

Since the ministers could be freely appointed by the Emperor and were not dependent on the Parliament, parliamentarism was in fact being perverted. The Additional Act of 1834, enlarging the autonomy of the provinces, principally through local assemblies, marked a victory for the federalists. However, it was annulled six years later by the authoritarian reaction of the one-time Liberal, Bernardo de Vasconcelos.

The period of regency that followed the abdication of Pedro I was

---

Santos, where two messengers from Rio caught up with him. They were carrying letters from his wife and José Bonifácio, informing him of new, oppressive demands just received from the Court in Portugal. The date, September 7, 1822, is the most celebrated in Brazilian history. JLT

* Three brothers, all born in Santos, São Paulo state, who rose to positions of prominence as Brazilian statesmen. The best remembered is José Bonifácio de Andrada e Silva, called "The Patriarch" of Brazil's independence. JLT

one of intense ideological conflicts. Brazil had arrived at the doors of the Republic when, by electing a regent, she took her first step in elective government. The revolution in 1835 of the *Farrapos*,* begun in defense of local autonomies, was headed in the direction of secession and the Republic. But the ascension of Pedro II to the throne in 1840 ensured the continuation of the monarchy, and marked the beginning of a long period during which the republican idea lay dormant.

After the ferment of the regency, the earlier short-lived nativist republican movements of 1817 and 1824 in Pernambuco, and the long-drawn-out war of the Farrapos, the imperial peace that followed Pedro's ascension reflected the people's fatigue much more than their belief in or enthusiasm for the regime. The inglorious revolt of the *Praieiros* in 1848, a last flare-up of the old Pernambucan spirit of rebellion, was the last revolutionary outbreak.†

It was largely Brazil's isolation from the rest of the western hemisphere that allowed the comparatively long life of the second monarchy. Her long eastern boundary on the Atlantic robbed her of effective contact with neighboring countries, except for Uruguay and Argentina, which at the time were under the degrading dictatorship of the caudillos. Her very language cut her off from the Hispano-American continental community. Her enthusiasm for the United States, so pronounced during the period between her independence and the regency, had abated considerably. In all truth, the first phase of the American expansionist policy [more or less between 1840 and 1860] had converted the ardent esteem for Washington's republic and its moral sense into a generalized prejudice against it. The real external influence on Brazil came from Europe.

With the fall of the Marquis [always referred to now as the Duke] of Caxias's cabinet in 1862, the policy of conciliation inaugurated by the Marquis of Paraná came to an end. The Progressive party, short-lived because of its own lack of cohesion, was formed by a coalition of the left wings of the Conservative and Liberal parties. The effects of the war with Paraguay were reflected in the Empire's parliamentary politics and added to its confusion.

On more than one occasion after the start of the war with Paraguay, conflicts between the civilian government and the military men cropped up. In 1868, with the campaign in full sway, Caxias, the commander-in-chief, clashed with the Zacarias cabinet. (The Prime Minister said after-

---

* A republican separatist insurrection in Rio Grande do Sul that began in 1835 and lasted for ten years. The name Farrapos, meaning "rags," was an allusion to the insurgents' lack of uniforms. JLT

† "Praieiros" was the nickname of the liberal elements whose official organ was printed in a shop on Rua da Praia in Recife. Their revolt was in protest against the composition of the 1848 imperial cabinet. JLT

ward that his cabinet "had suffered some scratches on its dignity.") The Emperor was forced to ask the Council of State which of the two should be sacrificed. The situation was smoothed over for a while, although the days of the Zacarias cabinet were numbered. Soon afterward, and contrary to all the procedural norms of the parliamentary system, it was dismissed from power by direct intervention by the Emperor, who turned the government over to the Conservatives under the Viscount of Itboraí.

The Liberal leaders, angered by the Crown's stroke, tried to patch up their old differences in an alliance committed to a program of "Reform or Revolution." The old liberal ideas were resynthesized in the pledges of the Manifesto of 1869: electoral and judicial reforms, abolishment of the draft and of the national guard, emancipation of the slaves. Meanwhile, a group of more sincere and impetuous politicians, weary of repeated and precarious party reconciliations, separated themselves from the monarchic policy of rotation of power and founded the Radical party. The Liberals' program of "reform" instead of "revolution" did not satisfy these less compromising and more rational Radicals, who did not offer a new coalition to fight Itaboraí's Conservatives or the "tyranny of the Crown," but instead offered their own short-lived party as the logical road to the Republic, at whose doors they were already standing.

From radicalism to republicanism the distance was short. It was easily wiped out by the victory of the French Third Republic, which resounded among the Brazilian ruling classes, who were always attentive to anything French. The Brazilian Republican Manifesto of December 3, 1870, was published three months after the fall of Napoleon III. To the Liberals' slogan, "Reform or Revolution," the 1870 Republicans opposed their own: "Centralization equals dismemberment; decentralization equals unity." The inauguration of the French parliamentary republic reawakened Brazilian republicanism, which had lain fitfully asleep since the regency, but those who dreamt of the new regime were inspired, as during the regency, by republican federalism.

After the end of the Paraguayan war, the nation intimately examined her conscience and her powers. In spite of the military victory, the causes of disenchantment and disappointment grew stronger. Brazil began to be more keenly aware of the moral affinities that bound her to the whole of America. The United States, freed of slavery by the Civil War, regained her old prestige. Her extraordinary prosperity, believed to result from her political system, became once more an ever-present example. The Spanish Republic of 1873, though short-lived, may have been another indirect influence, as was, perhaps, the Mexican revolt against Maximilian.

In 1870 Saldanha Marinho, a one-time member of the Liberal party, and Quintino Bocaiúva, newly returned from the United States and greatly enamored of the Argentine Republic, became the founders of the first republican club and newspaper. The Manifesto of that year, which consolidated the objectives of the new party, attracted signers from various bourgeois groups, most of them intellectual in nature, and from various parts of the country. Some of its most distinguished signers shortly reverted to their former positions.

The Manifesto of 1870 has been analyzed many times, not always charitably. In truth, it lacked fire, originality, and emotional appeal. Its long-drawn-out, digressive paragraphs of cold strictures against the Empire merely repeated criticisms already made in the Parliament and the press. Political questions or, more exactly, the mistakes and faults of representative government as then practiced were its principal topics. It made no effort to get down to the roots of the country's greatest economic and social ills. It avoided any mention of the crucial problem of slavery, the very essence of the monarchy. Even after the painful experience of the United States, the republicans of 1870 deemed it unwise to touch upon the subject. Federation, the abiding national aspiration, was the document's main theme.

Perhaps the political climate would not have permitted bolder ideas. By confining themselves to the program of the Liberals, who were more timid than the men of the regency, the authors of the Manifesto were conforming to accustomed moderation. They sidestepped the "Negro question" to avoid compromising their cause with the wealthy land-owners in the South. But they failed to foresee that the more intelligent landowners would, on their own initiative, be the first to abolish slavery, by employing foreign immigrants as paid laborers.

Nevertheless, in the Manifesto of 1870 is something new and unique: the dawning of what today we can call, without exaggeration, the American consciousness. If the Brazilian republicans did not forget Napoleon III's downfall in their criticism of the Empire, what vexed them most was that the monarchy was so alien to the American republican community. To quote from the document: "We are in America, and we want to be Americans. Our form of government is in essence and in practice both antinomian and in opposition to the rights and interests of the American states. Besides causing oppression within our borders, if continued it must perforce be a perpetual source of hostility and wars with the nations around us."

Once the first flurry of activity caused by the Manifesto had passed, enthusiasm for the republican cause declined. Political doctrines could not resound for long in patriarchal Brazil, then a poor and uncultured semidesert, a land of masters and slaves, in which no true middle class had yet arisen. Yesterday, even as today, and in all matters, the people took a pragmatic and somewhat dismal view of those who symbolized authority, whether friendly or unfriendly, generous or repressive. An appeal to the emotions rather than to reason would more likely have won adherents to the republican cause. This is what occurred in the abolitionist campaign of the same period and made it more successful than the campaign to change the form of the government.

The ardent abolitionist campaign had aroused the nation, and only those blinded with power or those who refused to see doubted that the form of government that had incautiously harnessed its fate to slave labor would be wrecked by it. The abolitionist propaganda somewhat overlapped that of the republicans. The Catholic clergy, still resentful over the question of sovereignty, wanted the Republic; the slavocratic barons wanted it, at least out of spite; the young military men, strongly influenced by Comtian philosophy, wanted it.

On the other side, the traditional monarchists stood by and did nothing. Opposed to the orderly and cautious republicans, who had Quintino Bocaiúva at their head, Silva Jardim and his small band of young men preached the revolution at public meetings. Ouro Prêto's efforts to rebuild the foundations of the old regime and to prepare for a successor to Pedro II did not deceive the intelligent men of the period.

Thus, the republican campaign moved slowly forward, somewhat disguised, in the protecting shadow of abolition. In November 1889, in his book *The Setting of the Empire,* Oliveira Viana notes the existence of 77 republican newspapers and 273 republican clubs in the entire country, and remarks on the minute social significance of the greater portion of them. The southern provinces, principally São Paulo, were more infected by the republican propaganda than those in the North. Actually the peaceful and temporizing propaganda for change in the political system carried on by the leaders in Rio de Janeiro and São Paulo was more in keeping with the conditions prevailing in those areas than with those in the poorer North, where political and social changes, as João Ribeiro justly observed, always tended to extremism and violence. And much more than it had the South, the burning, romantic character of the fight for abolition aroused the North and became its sole concern.

The first tangible result of the Manifesto of 1870 had been the formal organization, with rules and regulations, of the Republican Party of São Paulo, which held conventions in 1873 in Itu and in the capital city of the province. There the Paulista Republicans, finding it no longer possible to evade the problem of abolition, deplored any suspicions that their attitudes were radical. Despite the lone protest of Luís Gomes, they declared themselves against immediate abolition, subordinating it to the special conditions of each province and to the possible development of free labor. By accepting the principle of indemnification, they admitted as legitimate the ownership of man by man.

Such moderation, solemnly reaffirmed in the Parliament in 1885 by Prudente de Morais and Campos Sales, both of whom would later become great national leaders and Presidents of the Republic, placed the anti-dynastic party in a position less advanced than that of a large number of Liberal monarchists and even some Conservatives, who had already accepted the essential basis of the abolitionist campaign: the immorality of slave ownership. The young liberal politicians, friends of the *Conselheiro* Sousa Dantas—the "Englishmen of Senhor Dantas," as they were called—who included Rui Barbosa, in reckoning the Chamber's disposition toward emancipatory laws listed the three Republican deputies among the slavocrats.

Thus the election of the first Republican delegates to the monarchy's Parliament [in 1885] was not an especially significant event. They were, after all, cautious conservatives. If speeches in the Parliament and articles in the newspapers contributed to the fall of the Empire, many of them were composed by partisans of the Empire, both Conservative and Liberal, on occasions when they sided with the opposition. No one, for instance, did more indirectly to promote the Republic than Rui Barbosa, a monarchist in principle, by his articles in the press opposing the Ouro Prêto cabinet and defending the idea of a federation (which is a very difficult system in any case, even if it is not altogether incompatible with a monarchy).

Campos Sales wrote later that "what most characterized the conduct of the party, whose purpose was to radically transform the system, was the prudent and moderate tone of its militancy, its manifestly conservative leanings, and the unrelaxing, extraordinary vigor and imperturbable firmness with which it confronted its adversaries while heading straight for its goal." Campos Sales, like the other São Paulo Republicans, did not want radical abolition; he inclined to a gradual solution that would not upset the bases of the national economy.

By the time the idea of emancipation was accepted by the old-time Republicans, it had already all but won over the imperial family, the politicians, the young men in the military academies, and even the large landowners. The provinces of Ceará and Amazonas were also on the side of freedom, and in Rio de Janeiro the positivists demanded that the Republican candidates for Parliament expressly commit themselves to support abolition.

Nevertheless, the Republicans were able to offset their weakness as proselytizers by their adherence to party discipline, which was always a rarity in Brazil. They survived the defection of some of their most eminent early members. For example, in 1878 the Liberal cabinet of the Viscount of Sinimbu succeeded in attracting Lafayette Rodrigues Pereira, who had signed the Manifesto of 1870, to fill one of its posts [the Ministry of Justice]. The Republicans, however, withstood Lafayette's defection, as well as those of other early adherents. In the *Gazeta de Campinas* Campos Sales exhorted all sincere members of the Republican party to close ranks in defense of their doctrine. They would support the Sinimbu cabinet, he later stated, to the extent that its promised reforms would contribute to the victory of a federative republic. And here and there the Republicans sowed the seeds of constructive programs, such as the "Constitution of São Paulo" in 1878, which was within the framework of a "Federation of the United States of Brazil." In Rio Grande do Sul the Republican movement gained headway and was soon under the influence of the positivists.

In the North, Pernambuco seemed to be the liveliest center of propaganda. But the great, decisive conquest of the republican ideology was winning over the young men in the military schools. The spread of Comtist doctrines, which were so easily and dangerously assimilated by minds that were unformed or not inclined to philosophic inquiry (and such must have been the minds of the youths in the military academies), can be traced as the main factor in the growth of the military disaffection that precipitated the fall of the Empire.

The Brazilian elite, authors of the nation's independence and first monarchy, had their intellectual origin in Europe's liberal climate, but it was tempered by attendance at the University of Coimbra, where harmony between Romanticism and traditionalism was sought. Their political ideologies reflected the atmosphere of the old metropolis. Their impressions of the political movements in France and the United States were vivid, if fleeting, and their desire to imitate British parliamentarism was sincere, but Brazil's closest and most effective model was the Portuguese constitutionalism of the charter granted by Pedro IV and the one granted [in 1824] by her own Pedro I. Brazilians and Portuguese, already closely bound by all kinds of normal ties and by the same background of thought and culture, reacted similarly to the currents of political and literary thought and feeling. The monarchy of Pedro II would find its exact counterpart, in many respects, in the reigns of Portugal's Pedro V and Luís I.

The criticisms of their regime's faults and vices made by the Portuguese monarchists did not differ much from those made by the Brazilian monarchists and republicans. In the same language, but with more "sugar" in the Brazilian prosody (as Eça de Queirós would later say), they debated, they harangued, they indulged in rhetoric, they made verses in São Bento in Lisbon and in the Cadeia Velha in Rio de Janeiro. They displayed a tendency toward sentimentality, an identical fondness for old juridical phrases and formulas, an analogous ease in flight from reality and facts, balanced, however, by frequent bursts of common sense, the same insincerity in their promises, and the same stubborn attachment to political attitudes that lead to public office and feed personal vanity.

The rural society of immense, semidesert Brazil, tied to slave labor, was very different from that of small, subdivided Portugal, but the cultures of their cities were identical. The large cities of imperial Brazil, such as Rio, Bahia, Recife, and Belém, lived by the same customs and habits as Lisbon and Oporto. The narrow, unattractive Rua do Ouvidor in Rio— a kind of gallery of daily exhibitions and marketplace for Carioca vanities—was practically a replica of the Chiado in Lisbon.

The intellectual climate of the colleges founded in Brazil, especially of the law schools in Recife and São Paulo, was not much different from that of Coimbra. Candidates for degrees received the same kind of rigid, formalistic training in Roman and canon law. The Corpus Juris and the Ordinances of the Realm were their principal spiritual fodder. The doctrines of natural law seemed to overthrow the old scholasticism just as Cousin's eclecticism seemed to be the height of philosophic audacity. Political writers were principally influenced by the great French liberals, such as Tocqueville and Benjamin Constant. The most distinguished fell in with such conservative English writers as Burke and Bagehot.

Coincident with the end of the war with Paraguay and the literary rebirth in Portugal begun by the Coimbra generation of Antero de Quental and Eça de Queirós, rationalism and agnosticism, then at their height in Europe, spread rapidly in Brazil. To Tobias Barreto belongs the credit for introducing the "new thought." The "Recife School," with its youthful enthusiasm for Darwin's transformism, Spencer's evolutionism, and Haeckel's materialism, marked a great turning point in the development of Brazilian culture. Literary Romanticism evolved out of its primitive Indianesque form into the pompously elegant social poetry of the followers of Victor Hugo. Its most perfect expression was found in the genius of Castro Alves. The juridical interpretations of Savigny and Ihering rejuvenated the law schools. Thus these later intellectuals brought a new *Weltanschauung* into public life.

Nevertheless, these philosophic and literary influences did not inevitably turn the intellectuals toward the republican ideal. The writers, first to come under their spell, regarded forms of government as secondary to political liberalism, which developed perhaps more easily in parliamentary monarchies. This explains why even university-trained intellectuals such as Joaquim Nabuco and Rui Barbosa showed so little enthusiasm for the Republic; Barbosa held out against it until almost the last minute. Among the young military men, especially at the army school in Rio where Benjamin Constant* was a teacher, the great indoctrinating influence was the philosophy of Comte, with its mathematical bases, rudimentary morality, agnosticism, antimysticism, and strong biases toward dogmatism and discipline. For the rationalists and evolutionists of the civil academies, the supreme ideals were liberty and equality, but for the positivists the ideal was disciplinary authority. To the first, liberty and equality were as much at home in the republics of Switzerland and the United States as in the monarchies of Britain and Scandinavia. The morality of Comtism, on the other hand, thought the perfect state to be a dictatorial republic.

Neither the Emperor nor most of the politicians who surrounded him seemed to understand the mental transformation taking place in the new Brazilian generations, above all in the young military. Pedro II and his general staff were always sincerely antimilitaristic; they considered civil order primary and vital for democratic government. The army was low in the hierarchy of imperial society. The navy, with its more aristocratic background, was given preference over it. Its rather turbulent tradition during the first Pedro's reign forgotten, the army had been resigned to its secondary position until the war with Paraguay reminded it of its strength.

The blood sacrifice was a patriotic duty performed almost exclusively by the military classes. The meager volunteer forces were supplemented by recruits from the lowest social orders or by impressed slaves. The bourgeoisie and the aristocracy of the Empire remained far from the battlefields, but freely discussed and criticized the military operations. Very often the politicians in the cabinet or Parliament did not hesitate to place their small, partisan interests above the welfare of their country at war. It is to the honor of Pedro II's name and office that during the war he was the most sincere, conscientious, and zealous of all the civilians in defending the interests of those who were fighting for the fatherland in the swamps of Paraguay. No other Brazilian suffered from

* A Brazilian military engineer and, later, Republican War Minister, not to be confused with the French author and political theorist of the same name mentioned two paragraphs above. JLT

patriotic worry over the outcome of the war as much as he. When it
ended, he was not yet forty-five, but he was already a soul-stricken old
man, with white hair and a white beard.

Soon, however, his tendencies toward humanism and philosophic pacifism, so typical of the political elite of the period, reasserted themselves.
An army returning victorious from a foreign war was something of a
bugaboo to the Brazilian politicians; it would not do, therefore, to en-
hance its position in the nation. But the Brazilian politicians did not
push on to the logical extremes of this attitude; they did not follow the
French Republic of 1870 and forbid army men the right to run for public
office. Instead, they tried to draw their military greats such as Caxias,
Osório, Pelotas, Deodoro, and Floriano into partisan contests. The high-
ranking officers' discipline, and their esteem for and gratitude to the
Emperor, assured their loyalty to the established order. But the more recent and younger military men had a different attitude. Their contact
with fellow soldiers of other South American countries during the long
campaign in Uruguay taught them a different concept of their historic
role, including its less laudable aspects. The transfer of military studies
from the central school to a specialized academy also contributed noticeably to the development of class pride and feeling. The philosophy of
Comte thus found among the young military men the best soil for the
germination of a spirit of independence, which is always so close to a
spirit of defiance. The military engineers soon acquired the right to be
included among the "doctors," the highest of the official elite. The tur-
quoise in their class rings earned them much more prestige than the ruby,
emerald, and sapphire earned for the lawyers, physicians, and civil engineers. Despite the rather paradoxically pacifist influence of positivism,
the army's social standing was improved by its victory in the war with
Paraguay and the raising of the level of university studies. The army's
precarious economic conditions, its subordination to civilian partisan
interests, received attention as never before.

The Emperor, and especially the men of his government, lacked the
political discernment needed to prevent what later came to be known
as the military question. Their apparent success in 1875 after the grave
clash with the bishops of Pernambuco and Pará may have given them too
much confidence in the strength of civil authority. In spite of their
clumsy handling of the affair, they were able to reap the results of their
victory with apparent tranquility. The Brazilian clergy meanwhile swal-
lowed their humiliation in bitter silence. The attitude of Pope Leo XIII,
cautious and temporizing as always in his dealings with political power,
was not one to arouse the clergy to a more positive reaction.

With the army the situation was much different. By the very nature of their functions, the military developed a sense of honor far more heightened than that of the civilians. Their pride hurt, they reacted strongly and gained the immediate support of their entire class. Living somewhat apart from the civilian society and absorbed in their professional duties, they were easily given to doubt and suspicion. They imagined themselves, somewhat justly, to be poorly understood by civilians, who in turn felt misunderstood by the military. Thus arose the frequent occasions for misunderstanding that only open and unselfish attitudes (the surest road to success in dealing with the military of all times and countries) could avoid.

Abolitionist propaganda, infiltrating the military circles, brought about new motives for conflict. In 1884 the Liberal Prime Minister, Lafayette Rodrigues Pereira, was rudely answered by a Lieutenant Colonel Madureira when he asked about the festive reception that an army training unit gave to an abolitionist *jangadeiro* from Ceará. The Conservative ministry of Cotegipe, which followed soon after, tried to counteract the abolitionist propaganda in which republicans and monarchists, civilians and military men, were already involved. But this attempt at reaction only provoked new insubordinate movements. The doctrine of the soldier-citizen extolled by the positivists stimulated the military and ended up infecting even the highest-ranking officers, notably Pelotas and Deodoro.

From that time on, a multiplicity of incidents rendered the military question ever more acute. Finally, the direct intervention of the most esteemed and respected military leader, Marshal Deodoro da Fonseca, drove the wedge that finally and irreconcilably split the monarchy and the army. The government confessed that its prestige had been damaged. Protesting against the reported use of troops to round up fugitive slaves, the officer corps dealt a death blow to the degrading institution and indirectly to the Empire itself.

The Conservative cabinet of João Alfredo [Correia de Oliveira] imagined that removing Deodoro from the nation's capital and from the presidency of the newly formed Military Club might heal the rift. This illusion was soon compounded by the Liberal government of Ouro Prêto. Deodoro returned from Mato Grosso province with more prestige than ever among his fellow officers, and certainly fewer illusions about the Empire. The reception given the Ouro Prêto cabinet in the Parliament (when the priest-deputy João Manuel shouted "Long live the Republic!") and Benjamin Constant's welcoming speech to the officers of the Chilean ship *Almirante Cochrane* showed that the final break was rapidly approaching.

It was at this point that the republican leaders made their last-minute alliance with the military to lay the groundwork for a conspiracy to overthrow the monarchy. A smoother, more flexible statesman, more temporizing and more sensitive to the imponderables of the situation than the Viscount of Ouro Prêto, would probably have been able to postpone the fall of the throne for a while. But the monarchy's last prime minister was also the one who could least be expected to save it. Neither intransigence nor spectacular energy is always a virtue for men in government. An aptitude for realistic appraisal of and adjustment to new conditions created by the rapidly shifting events of social crises often transcends those basic qualities. Politics, as Joaquim Nabuco correctly wrote, is never a straight line. A man at the head of government fulfills his prime duty by not letting the storm unmast his ship. If a typhoon develops afterward, it will unleash its fury on the new captain. Ouro Prêto took charge of imperial Brazil at the height of her biggest historical and social crisis, abolition. Altering the whole economic structure of the nation by propelling nearly a million slaves into a freedom for which they had not been prepared, the law of May 13, 1888, touched the deepest roots of Brazilian life. Everywhere the spirit of passive obedience to law was lessened and the temptation to try radical solutions grew.

The monarchy became a thing of the past from the day of abolition. It lived out its melancholy twilight simply on what was left of its earlier strength, just as colonial Brazil persisted for a time after John VI had set up his court in Rio de Janeiro [in 1808]. Pedro II's morbid indifference to the fate of his own throne was a symbol of the times—better, of an order of things that was ending. The patriarchal economy of the slavocratic latifundia was, to repeat an old cliché, its flesh and blood, and rigid bureaucratic centralization was its political skeleton. The Republic promised a life of freedom and progress. Brazilians dreamed of a less torpid medium—above all, of something less artificial, something braver and bolder, better suited to the realities of their condition.

Loyal to his monarchic faith and confident of his repressive powers, Ouro Prêto believed he could crush the incipient revolution. His fiscal policy of easy credit and increasing currency was intended not only to meet the new and pressing needs for cash brought on by free labor working for wages, but also to open up a new era of optimism, of euphoria, of ambitious business and financial schemes that would end both secret and confessed civilian and military uneasiness. If the Republic had not come to pass, he would probably have been forced to make an about-face to avoid financial disaster. Politically his strategy did not go beyond the old and illusory recourse to unanimous Chambers and courageous reaction, in which he would soon find himself alone and of which he would unfailingly be the victim. For the final victory of the Republic, there now remained only Deodoro's supreme decision of November 15, 1889. Deodoro da Fonseca's great merit, the noble service he was able to render to Brazil, was that he incarnated at the opportune historical moment the century-old republican aspirations. Whatever his hesitations at the last minute, they are unimportant and merely reveal the excessive conscientiousness of his generous and impulsive nature.

Thus, to sum up the immediate origins of the Republic, we could say that two great forces had coincided: there was the direct action of the republicans and the indirect action of the monarchists, men for whom the Empire had lost its charm and who, especially after May 13, were a vast and dangerous body of defeatists. Among these theoretical monarchists who labored consciously or subconsciously for the Republic, one might distinguish Liberals, reformers, abolitionists, and federalists, as well as the discontented and indifferent, such as the Conservatives hurt by abolition. Among the republicans, too, it is possible to distinguish four different currents: the historic figures of 1870, principally the Paulistas, under the leadership of Quintino Bocaiúva; the ardent young men led by Silva Jardim, adept at revolutionary action in the press and in the streets; the young military men, imbued with the doctrines of Comte and inspired by Benjamin Constant; and, finally, the older military officers, symbolized by Deodoro, who went all the way to the Republic without having clearly defined doctrinal leanings, because of their *esprit de corps* and their intuitive certainty that the Empire's page in Brazil's history had been turned over forever.

It is certainly to this last group that the Republic owes its proclamation. In Deodoro da Fonseca we behold the great central figure of the republican victory. His impulsive courage freed Brazil from a superannuated political regime that was incapable of stimulating her energies. Nevertheless, the triumphant deed of November 15 was possible only because the ground had been prepared for it by the republican ideal, which, dormant since the advent of Pedro II, had been reawakened by men who revealed Brazil's sentiments and aspirations to her again. The constructive work of the Provisional Government, noteworthy for its honesty, patriotism, and extraordinary ability to improvise, is an honor to the men with whom Deodoro surrounded himself. In large measure that work compensates for the mistakes and faults incidental to the times and to the environment in which these men operated.

4. The Founding of the Republic

*Ouro Prêto and the Empire's last cabinet — Deodoro and the
conspirators — Floriano Peixoto — The events of November
15, 1889 — Last meeting of the Council of State — Banishment of the imperial family — Formation of the Provisional
Government — The nation's reactions.*

The Conservative ministry of João Alfredo, which had decreed abolition,
did not survive its own work for long. Weakened by dissension among its
political friends and stubbornly resisted by its opponents, it had been
forced to temporize with the rebellious spirit that pervaded the army
and, threatening to explode, placed the monarchy in serious danger. On
the advice of the Council of State, the Emperor refused to dissolve the
Chamber, as proposed in keeping with the old parliamentary practice by
his Prime Minister, and turned to the Liberals. Saraiva, held to be the
ablest statesman of the period, refused the job of forming a new cabinet,
but suggested Ouro Prêto, who accepted it.

Barely fifty years old, Ouro Prêto had not yet achieved great authority
as a leader, but was rightly considered, nevertheless, to be one of the Empire's most eminent statesmen. He was proud, energetic, courageous, and
upright. These excellent moral qualities were combined with a mind
that was clear, if lacking in literary brilliance, with undoubted culture
from his background as a jurist, and with a special taste for financial
problems. From his handling of the Navy Ministry in the Zacarias cabinet during the war with Paraguay while he was still a very young man, he
became known as a hardworking administrator.

In 1879 Ouro Prêto replaced Silveira Martins in the Sinimbu cabinet
as Minister of the Treasury. His term of office was filled with new undertakings. He distinguished himself in parliamentary debate at a time
when orators such as Silveira Martins, José Bonifácio the younger, the
Viscount of Rio Branco, and Cotegipe were in their glory and Rui Barbosa and Joaquim Nabuco were getting started. His principal concerns
were agricultural credits and balancing the budget. For these purposes

new taxes were necessary. Among these, the tax on railroad tickets and streetcar rides, known as the "penny tax," gave rise to a mass protest movement. This brought Ouro Prêto into his first direct contact with unpopularity on the streets, and was perhaps the first positive sign of the decadence of the Empire.

In 1889 Ouro Prêto was one of the organizers of the congress of the Liberal party. Here the guidelines for future action were laid down, but they were no great advance over the old liberal aspirations for civil marriage, freedom of religion, broadening the base of the vote, reforming provincial administration and the Council of State, and limiting the senatorial mandate. Rui Barbosa headed the dissidents who stood for increasing the autonomy of the provinces up to the limits of federation.

A month after the Liberal party congress, Ouro Prêto began forming a cabinet to carry out his party's winning program. Rui Barbosa, however, refused to accept an appointment, since he had not been able to convert Ouro Prêto to the federative principle, which, it was being said, Pedro himself would have accepted. The composition of the cabinet was up to the average of those preceding it: jurists and politicians, more or less skilled in parliamentary debate and intrigue in the corridors. Nevertheless, Ouro Prêto, probably to soothe the military, entrusted the Army and Navy portfolios to two high-ranking officers, thus going against the rarely broken tradition of civilian ministers.

Ouro Prêto felt, as did all the more clear-thinking statesmen of the period, that he would have to be on guard against the rapid dissolution of the monarchy. His words and attitudes before taking charge of the government show that, although he had no great enthusiasm for it in principle, he believed that only the monarchic system could serve Brazil. The Republic struck him as premature; worse than this, he associated it with the endemic caudillism of the rest of the continent. It would be possible, he felt, to meet the nation's desires for greater freedom, order, and material progress within the framework of the monarchy. All that was necessary to accomplish this was a determined government sure of its mission.

The political program he presented to Parliament offered ideas that had matured in the "liberal conscience of the nation." On the economic and financial levels it sought to speed up the development of natural resources, to revitalize agriculture through bank loans, to consolidate the public debt, and ultimately to give the currency a metallic base. But above all, the Ouro Prêto cabinet's openly stated main objective was to counteract republican propaganda and the revolutionary ferment in the army.

Thus if the government was progressive, in terms of the liberal gains

allowed by the narrow political philosophy of the times, its methods of
operation were still primarily those of repressive force. From the very
first, Ouro Prêto must have felt that he would have to act in a vacuum,
for his efforts were foredoomed to failure. The Emperor, tired, sick, and
abulic, was a mere shadow of his former self. Neither by force nor by
persuasion was the growing military insubordination to be halted. To
oppose the national guard to the army—an old French trick—would have
been the most self-defeating of remedies.

Brazil, disenchanted with the monarchy and hostile to the possibility
of a Third Reign, would never go along with the government's reactionary policies. Even the militant monarchists were calmly resigned to the
early end of the Empire. Some of those much in evidence, like Paulino de
Sousa, Conservative leader and President of the Senate, were vaguely
suspect of being pro-Republic. Saraiva was inwardly preparing himself
for immediate adherence to the Republic, which so many others, following the example of Antônio Prado, would at once accept as a fait accompli.

Oppositionist passion against the last imperial cabinet mounted from
the time of its introduction to the Chamber on June 11. The speech of
Father João Manuel, stigmatizing the government and hailing the Republic, was vehement, sarcastic, and prophetic. Ouro Prêto courageously
faced his opponents, contrasting the uncertainties and dangers of a
republic to the meritoriousness of the monarchy that "kept Brazil
prosperous and free." The opposition's campaign in the press went all
out.

After the May 13th triumph of abolition, forced upon the government
and Parliament by popular demand, the nation seemed to discover the
force of public opinion. The republican methods of propaganda changed
from temporizing to immediate action. In spite of his constantly reiterated monarchic preferences, Rui Barbosa, aiming his shots in the *Diário
de Notícias* at the Ouro Prêto government, hit the monarchy itself broad-
side. No one knew better than he how to aggravate the army's discontent
and exploit it against the government.

It was among the military that the final triumph of the Republic was
being hatched. The chronicle of what was called the military conspiracy,
an extension of the seething, years-old "military question," has been
written many times. But its exact reconstitution, if it has ever been possible, is not after all of much significance to one who looks in history
for the intimate ties that bind the facts together and give them meaning.
In trying to get close to the military in order to incite them even more
against the monarchy, the republicans applied the traditional lesson of
the revolutionaries of Latin America.

There were daily clashes between the military and the government in the Ouro Prêto cabinet. New republican manifestations occurred, as when some municipal chambers brought up the need for a constitutional convention to decide on the nation's political system in case of the Emperor's death. In normal times, small irritations such as the dismissal for the public good of the commandant of the military school in Ceará, or the arrest of the captain of the Treasury's guard, would soon be forgotten. But in their prevailing inflamed state of mind, the military classes were easily swayed to participate in the persistent activities of the republican conspirators.

In the army Deodoro had gained great prestige, equivalent perhaps to that which Caxias or Osório had enjoyed. Besides being a member of a family of renowned soldiers, he was brave, generous, and impulsive, had a brilliant record of heroism in the war with Paraguay, and displayed all the surface virtues needed for the historic mission being planned for him. A passionate class-consciousness had long been at work in his spirit, destroying his dedication to the political regime.

In this context, the attitudes of the two military chiefs Deodoro da Fonseca and Floriano Peixoto on the eve of the proclamation of the Republic were quite characteristic. Deodoro held back because of his personal consideration for Pedro II, whose "coffin he wanted to accompany to the cemetery." But at the last hour, three factors—the clever maneuvering of the republicans, Deodoro's injured professional pride, and his inner consciousness of the hollowness of the Empire—overcame his remaining scruples. Though he had been more or less active as a member of the Conservative party, the fate of the regime seems to have been of secondary importance to him. Floriano, who had been a member of the Liberal party, was a cold, calculating, double-dealing person to whom esteem for Pedro II or possible commitments to the Prime Minister meant little. The republican concept was repugnant to his authoritarian temperament. Nevertheless, at the decisive moment when he perceived that it would be useless or unpatriotic to combat the situation by throwing his general headquarters forces against Deodoro's rebelling troops, he accepted it with his habitual icy calm.

In mid-October, Deodoro was first frontally approached by Captain Mena Barreto, newly come from Rio Grande do Sul to "avenge" the affronts suffered by the army. Deodoro resisted, but left the door open for new attempts to influence him. Soon afterward, the same officer, accompanied by others, returned to insist on his demands, arguing that various of Ouro Prêto's measures, such as the mobilization of the national guard and the increase in the number of military police, were repressive. Having become more involved in the republican officers' plot, the old chief gave in at last. On November 11 he entered into personal contact with the civilian and military conspirators, notably Quintino Bocaiúva, Rui Barbosa, Aristides Lôbo, Francisco Glicério (representing the Paulista republicans), Benjamin Constant, and Solon Ribeiro. On the following day they dealt with the organization of the first republican government under the leadership of Marshal Deodoro. There remained only the last step, the military coup that would topple the throne.

Benjamin Constant and the small, stubborn group of young republican officers had thus finally succeeded in overcoming Deodoro's last scruples and his instinctive repugnance for meeting with the civilian conspirators. After he agreed to let them meet in his own home to plot the uprising, his attitude became irrevocable. For military men conscious of their duty, a breach of discipline, of their oath to defend the laws and the established government, must always be, we imagine, a sacrifice almost as great and painful as that of priests who abjure their faith. Since Deodoro agreed with the subversive movement, it is secondary to inquire how far he originally intended to go, whether only as far as the simple overthrow of the Ouro Prêto cabinet or all the way to the destruction of the Empire itself.

For the half-century of Pedro II's reign Brazil had witnessed no challenge to the legal order. For good or ill, cabinets were rotated in the pretence of accession to the political opinions expressed in partisan organs, of which the sovereign was supposed to be a kind of supreme arbiter. The forced removal of the head of government by a military rebellion would be a mortal blow to the regime. No public man, whether as tactful as Saraiva or as extreme as Silveira Martins, could exert enough authority to run the country after the military pronunciamento. The Crown could be saved only by a strong and energetic King who seized direct control himself and established a life-or-death dictatorship. Clearly, such a mission did not accord with the pacific temperament of Pedro II, who was old and sick as well.

It would not be easy to bring together, with a single sentiment and a single plan, all the opponents of the Ouro Prêto government and all the malcontents in the Empire. If all the civilian plotters were openly in favor of a violent change of regime, there were a number of different tendencies among the military. The leanings of a large part of the army were not known exactly. A great majority of the navy was held to be loyal to the Empire. Moreover, Marshal Deodoro's precarious health threatened the entire movement with failure.

Because of all this, the coup planned for November 15, apparently so easy, had in common with all attempts to suddenly transform political institutions a certain element of risk, of moves in the dark. One cause of uneasiness was the somewhat enigmatic attitude of Floriano Peixoto, who, as Adjutant General of the army, was the supreme defender of legality. In a famous letter a few days previously, he had asserted his loyalty to the Ouro Prêto government. The solidarity of the provincial garrisons was doubtful. And the nation itself—how would it receive a republic born of a military uprising? What would become of the old and respected Emperor? How would the nation adjust to the new political structure? Could all the possibilities for civil war be avoided?

To conspire is probably not very difficult. To bring about a revolution requires, most of all, audacity. The major problem that racks revolutionaries of good faith in their hour of victory is organizing the new order of things. Except for the idea of federation, the republicans (composed as they were of men from the most diverse origins: old-time pure doctrinaries of the Manifesto of 1870, liberals who only recently had begun severing their ties with the Empire, and military men driven by the positivist ideology) had not organized a definite rebuilding program. The main source of power for the victors of November 15 was the personal prestige of Deodoro, which alone was sufficient to command the allegiance of the military classes.

At daybreak on November 15, a telegram from Ouro Prêto reached Petrópolis, where the Emperor was spending the summer. It said that the First and Ninth Cavalry Regiments and the Second Artillery Battalion had revolted, and that Ouro Prêto intended to crush them "to teach respect for law and order." This telegram either did not reach the Emperor in person (having been intercepted, perhaps, by his medical aide) or failed to rouse him out of his morbid apathy. At eleven o'clock he received a second telegram from Ouro Prêto reporting the victory of the military insurgents and the surrender without a struggle of the military headquarters, where the gathered ministers had spent an anxious night. Only after receiving this second telegram did Dom Pedro decide to go down to Rio in a special train, accompanied by the Empress, his physician, and some other palace attendants.

On the historical level, the adventure begun on that day was the logical outcome of Brazil's political evolution, during which the monarchy was a phase in parentheses. But even so it was an enormous surprise, perhaps even for the republican leaders themselves. They could scarcely believe in their own rapid victory. After the parade-like march on the morning of November 15, they were left as stunned as the peaceful Rio townspeople. Their bewilderment is revealed by their attitudes during

the day. Nothing prevented the Emperor from coming down from Petrópolis to meet in the Rio palace with counselors and political leaders,
the formation of a new Liberal cabinet still being supposed possible.
Perhaps not one of the men whom the events of the morning had pushed
to the forefront knew all the facts exactly or perceived their immediate
consequences.

In this connection, one recalls the unjust (though nevertheless famous
and picturesque) statement attributed to Aristides Lôbo, "The nation
received the Republic with stupefaction." The people, even in the nation's capital, heard the proclamation with surprise or indifference: no
strong emotions over the disappearance of the Empire, no radiant enthusiasm for the new regime. This extraordinary indifference could of
course be attributed largely to the habitual apathy of the Brazilian
masses, so lacking in civic training. However, it could also be explained
by the nature of the conspiracy, developed as it was in the secrecy of
military gatherings and of "blood pacts" known to only a few civilians.

What had occurred in the military headquarters between the insurgent military chief and Ouro Prêto and his ministers, who had spent an
anxious night there? It was vaguely understood that the Navy Minister,
the Baron of Ladário, going to the barracks to join his colleagues, had
found the plaza surrounded by troops in rebellion, that when he was
placed under arrest he had shot the arresting officer and was in turn
wounded by him, and that troops supposedly loyal to the government
and under the command of the Adjutant General, Floriano Peixoto,
had fraternized with the rebels. Had Deodoro formally proclaimed the
Republic, or had he limited himself to deposing the Ouro Prêto cabinet? It was impossible, in the face of a number of conflicting versions,
to reconstruct the events precisely. Later, in a manifesto to the nation,
Ouro Prêto himself gave a clear account that was never contested and
that has remained as the true story of what took place.

Though forewarned by rumors of an impending military uprising,
Ouro Prêto had complete confidence in the loyalty of most of the army
and especially in that of Floriano Peixoto. The latter, either because he
was involved in the revolutionary plot and was acting out the part assigned to him, as seems likely, or because he was holding back until the
last moment, when the fate of the monarchy or of the Republic might
be decided by his attitude, was cleverly fostering the illusions of his
chief. It was only after the insurgent troops, who had marched unhindered from São Cristóvão, had posted themselves in front of the
headquarters that Ouro Prêto understood everything: the hesitancy of
his War Minister, the Viscount of Maracaju, the evasiveness of General

Almeida Barreto and the Baron of Rio Apa, and, above all, the behavior of Floriano Peixoto, who for the first time was publicly revealing his extraordinary talents for dissimulation. Refusing to be intimidated, the courageous Prime Minister ordered the Adjutant General to subdue with bayonets the rebel artillery facing the barracks. The dialogue between Ouro Prêto and Floriano is worth transcribing:

"But," I objected, "artillery can be overcome by bayonets. From this short distance, between the first and second firing of the guns, there is time to fall upon them."

"It is impossible! The guns are aimed in such a way that any sortie will be swept by shrapnel."

"Why, then, were they permitted to take up such positions? Wasn't it known what they were doing? But anyway, I don't believe in impossibilities unless they are proved by facts. In Paraguay our soldiers captured artillery in worse situations."

"Yes," replied Senhor Floriano, "but there we were facing enemies and here we are all Brazilians."

If I had any illusions left, they disappeared with that remark.

Ouro Prêto again tried to organize resistance, but the headquarters' generals asked to be excused. Beaten, he reported the facts in the urgent telegram to the Emperor, resigned as head of government, and waited for the last act of the drama. The gates of the general headquarters were thrown open for the triumphant entrance of Deodoro on horseback. A few minutes later, followed by a large escort, he entered the room where the ministers were gathered, greeting the War Minister with a quip as he passed by him. Ouro Prêto provides the following account of the final scene:

In the midst of the deepest silence, he informed me that he had placed himself at the head of the army in order to avenge the extremely grave offenses committed against it by the government. Only the army, he declared, was capable of sacrifices for the nation, and yet it was maltreated by the politicians who until then had run the country while looking out exclusively for their own personal interests. In spite of not being well, he could not refuse to lead his comrades, for he was not a man who would draw back from anything, fearing only God. He alluded to his services on the fields of battle, recalling that on one occasion he had spent three days and nights in the middle of a swamp fighting for the fatherland, a hardship beyond my power to imagine. He declared that my cabinet was deposed and that another would be organized along lines that he would submit to the Emperor. He said that all the ministers present could leave and return to their homes, except me ("an extremely stubborn man, but not as stubborn as I," thus he expressed himself) and the Minister of Justice, that both of us would be detained until our later deportation to Europe. "As to the Emperor," he concluded, "I am dedicated to him, I am his friend, I am indebted to him for favors received. His rights will be respected and guaranteed."

Having listened to him calmly and without even a gesture, I replied: "It is not only on the field of battle that one serves the nation and makes sacrifices for her. To be here at this moment, hearing your words, is not less than to spend days and nights in a swamp. I will heed what you decide concerning me. You are the winner; you may do whatever suits you. I submit myself to force."

Floriano Peixoto's personal intervention caused Deodoro to revoke the arrests of Ouro Prêto and the Minister of Justice. However, they were arrested again anyway, and the previously threatened deportation was carried out on December 21, 1889. After Deodoro's famous denunciation and Ouro Prêto's dignified answer, the Brazilian monarchy passed into history. The military chief's allusion to Pedro II was simply a last token of respect for the old sovereign. Involved as he was in the logic of events, Deodoro could not turn back now even if he wanted to. His hesitancy, even the possible misgivings of some of his civilian and military companions, could no longer hold back the republican victory.

The fate of the imperial family still had to be decided. Bewilderment became general among its members and among the members of the Council of State, called together for one last meeting to try to save the monarchy. Impractical proposals, such as the transfer of the seat of government to Petrópolis, were hurriedly suggested and as hurriedly abandoned. Ouro Prêto's suggestion that Silveira Martins, a personal enemy of Deodoro, be chosen to form a new cabinet revealed once again how little he understood the country's situation. The Emperor put aside his strange indifference, the clearest evidence of a state of affairs beyond remedy, only briefly, to reject the idea of a cabinet with Deodoro, an insubordinate military man, as War Minister. An attempt to form a cabinet under Saraiva also failed, because Deodoro would not endorse it. It was too late, the military chief said; there was nothing more to be done for the monarchy. Weary of everything, of his crown most of all, the Emperor retired from the day's tribulations.

On the following day, Marshal Deodoro sent a message informing the Emperor that his banishment had been decided upon. At the same time, while assuring him that his official stipend would be continued, he offered the Emperor transportation abroad in a Brazilian vessel and an additional subsidy of five thousand contos "for the decent maintenance of the position and establishment of the deposed monarch and his family." The Baron of Loreto wrote an answer in the name of the Emperor to Deodoro's message. The phrase the Emperor is said to have then uttered, "This is my charter to freedom," well illustrates the state of his mind.

The letter from Deodoro to Pedro II and the latter's reply, "yielding to the forces of circumstance," are two noble documents that lent to the beginning of the Republic an air of gentility and fair play that is rare in the political history of any country. To the Brazilians, however, soon to be torn by civil strife, under a permanent threat of revolution, it would seem like a vague dream of a remote past.

After protesting weakly against the order to embark late at night, saying "I am not a runaway Negro to have to embark at this hour," the old King resigned himself quietly to his fate, as so many others of his line (Charles X and Louis Philippe of France) had done before him. He departed forever from Brazil, which he had deeply loved, to go into dignified exile, and with him died the last possibility of a monarchic regime in America. His refusal of the five thousand contos (Deodoro's note offering them was handed to him on the night of departure; he apparently read it during the voyage) was his last gesture to the Republic, to him already an accomplished fact, perhaps more so than to any other monarchist.

In the chain of events we can again observe vivid reminders of contemporaneous French history, caused either by imitation or by similar psychological situations. On September 4, 1870, even after Paris knew of the disaster of Sedan and the imprisonment of Napoleon III, the republicans did not dare to go all out for the Republic. Even the ardent leftist group headed by Gambetta restricted itself to proclaiming the extinction of the Bonaparte dynasty and proposing a "committee of national defense." The tendency to temporize and compromise was always displayed by those most deeply involved in the republican cause. The fear of street rioting and the pressure of the popular masses, who were angry about the military defeat rather than opposed to the Second Empire, forced Gambetta and Jules Favre to proclaim the Republic, in keeping with the revolutionary tradition, in the city hall.

Similarly, on the afternoon of November 15, a group of young civilian republicans, journalists and men of letters for the most part, urged the people to gather at the city hall for the formal proclamation of the Republic. And similarly, the Brazilian military chiefs and civilians who joined in that day's triumphant pronunciamento decided in favor of a formal proclamation of the Republic only after the resolution was adopted by the City Council. Benjamin Constant himself, whose republican sincerity no one could doubt, replied evasively, like Jules Favre, to the questions from the townspeople who had gathered in front of Deodoro's house to hear about the City Council's vote. He would say only that what had been organized was a provisional government and

that a constitutional assembly would be called later to decide definitely
on the best permanent form of government. The tradition of half a century's loyalty to Pedro II's reign was enough to moderate the revolutionary impetuosity of the most passionate republicans.

During the evening of the same day, at the residence of Benjamin
Constant, the choice of the first republican ministry was ratified. On the
next day the new government's manifesto and first decree, constituting
the new political regime, were made public. Both documents reveal the
same temporizing and conservative spirit. The manifesto declared the
imperial dynasty deposed and, consequently, the representative monarchic system extinguished. The new government was, in keeping with
its name, provisional. Its purposes were to safeguard the integrity of the
nation, keep public order, assure the normal functioning of judicial and
administrative organs, meet domestic and foreign commitments, protect
the vested rights and benefits of public servants, etc. Though the Council
of State and the Senate with life members were abolished, the Chamber
of Deputies was merely dissolved. The first decree declared that "it is
hereby provisionally proclaimed and decreed that a federative republic
shall be the Brazilian nation's form of government." The old Empire,
"Império do Brasil," was officially renamed "Estados Unidos do Brasil,"
a choice that clearly shows the powerful influence of the North American
model. The solemn oath-taking of the Provisional Government in the
city hall was the last formal step in the establishment of the Republic.

The nation held itself in a state of sympathetic expectation. Worn out
by half a century of rhetorical and routine parliamentarism, it awaited
something new, more intense, more brilliant. Perfect calm reigned everywhere. There was no apparent change in the life of the capital and the
other big cities. Almost unanimously the feudal masters of the sugar
plantations and coffee fazendas, where the great organic strength of imperial Brazil was concentrated, were quietly rejoicing at the overthrow
of the regime that had freed their slaves and hurt their economic interests. Large numbers of persons were declaring their adherence to the
new regime. Small garrison uprisings were easily put down. The Republic was a fait accompli.

A French journalist, Max Leclerc, who arrived in Rio de Janeiro one
month after the proclamation of the Republic, sought vainly for "something tragic in the air." No outward signs of the new times were visible
in the peaceful, large, picturesque, provincial city of narrow streets, of
brightly colored façades, of sedate men wearing frock coats and high
hats in the intense heat, of ladies wrapped in heavy silks and tight cor-
sets, of dandies, loafers, beggars, market tipsters, of filthy little food-and-

drink stands, of old tilburies and diminutive mule-drawn streetcars. The citizens of Rio followed their usual restful pursuits with the carelessness of a people undisciplined by habits of work, indifferent to the ill-fortune of the Empire, so long as the Emperor was treated properly, and vaguely confident in the promises of the Republic.

5. The Provisional Government
[1889–91]

The young Republic — Composition of the Provisional Government — The United States and Argentina as models — Disappointment of the positivists — Foreign policy — The church and the Republic — Rui Barbosa's financial reform — The Encilhamento.

After the first few days, when people were naturally apprehensive, the Republic had favorably impressed not only the Brazilian people but also the foreign countries that followed Brazil's current events most closely. Some of them, mainly of America, established relations with the Provisional Government. Brazil was passing from the monarchy to the Republic by means of the most peaceable of revolutions, preoccupied by honoring her obligations to the deposed dynasty, which she felt constrained to send into exile.

Its accounts with the Empire settled, the new government began its turbulent career. Deodoro da Fonseca had filled his first cabinet with an elite of republican leaders, which gave the new state a brilliantly auspicious start. These men sincerely desired to succeed, but were without experience in public administration. They were all liberal democrats in the grand style of the century that was drawing to a close, something of political dreamers. Some of them, Rui Barbosa most of all, understood the theoretical structure of the presidential federal republic as conceived by the fathers of North American independence. Except for Quintino Bocaiúva, who was well acquainted with Argentina and who had visited the United States during the Civil War, they were all unfamiliar with the practical workings of the republican system in the United States and in Latin America. What would their influence be on the somewhat amorphous mass of Brazil, so accustomed to strong monarchic centralism? What would the economic consequences of their decisions be?

The Republic had changed from dream to reality. How to make it live, how to transform Brazil from a centralized parliamentary monarchy into a presidential republic—here was the great task confronting the Provisional Government, presided over by a brave and generous soldier, who was accustomed to military discipline but lacked political skill and experience in government, like the intelligent, sincere, and idealistic men whose help he had. However, before we analyze the work of the first republican government, we will do well to survey the personalities that made it up.

In countries like Brazil, where civic consciousness is far from consolidated, the good and bad qualities of rulers are deeply reflected in the tone and style of public life, and often in aspects of social life too. The people, politically immature, easily attach themselves to the men who personify the state. When they tire of the tutelage to which they have delivered themselves, they exaggerate their reaction, often violently. Just as the Brazil of Pedro II fondly recalled the details of his temperament and education, so would republican Brazil every four years magnify with more or less exactness the moral images of her Presidents, as they were in psychological fact or as they had been distorted by close friends and staff members who kept the Presidents, willy-nilly, from contact with the thoughts and feelings of the man in the street.

The psychology of Marshal Deodoro da Fonseca seems to have been of the least complex type: that of the impulsive, brave, generous man given to violent acts and extreme reactions. Being ruled more by emotions than by reason, he was of quick susceptibility and spontaneous frankness. He was a member of perhaps the most famous military family in Brazil. His father was a military man, and so were seven of his brothers, three of whom died on the battlefield in Paraguay.

Deodoro was born in 1827 [in the small northern state of Alagoas], and at twenty years of age entered the ranks of army officers. In 1848 he served with the government forces that put down the revolt of the Praieiros in Pernambuco. He participated in the campaigns against Uruguay and Paraguay, and was promoted for bravery from captain to colonel. The Republic found him, like his brother, a field marshal, the next to last step in his career. His oldest brother had reached the rank of marshal of the army. The atmosphere of Deodoro's family was therefore one of military discipline and loyalty to the monarchy. His warm, outgoing personality and his extreme class loyalty made him almost an idol in the eyes of his comrades. All the civilian and military conspirators recognized that without Deodoro's exceptional prestige the November 15th victory would have been impossible, or at least much more difficult.

In Deodoro's first cabinet, Rui Barbosa, whom one of his colleagues later dubbed the lightning rod of the Provisional Government, soon gained exceptional prominence. According to his own reiterated confession, Rui Barbosa joined the republicans only a few days before November 15. By temperament, by training, and even by paternal tradition, he was a liberal of the already classic nineteenth-century model. The republican idea did not especially appeal to him; like most of the lucid minds of his day, he thought a parliamentary monarchy was the least imperfect form of government. No one symbolized better than he, during the final phase of the Brazilian Empire, the typical theoretician of representative democracy. To him, the British institutions were the most ingenious creations of modern man's political genius.

At forty years of age Barbosa's erudition was enormous; an insatiable curiosity had led him to pry into all ideas and to devour books on all subjects. His prodigious memory accumulated a formidable store of facts, ideas, and reminiscences. Somewhat unimaginative and noncontemplative, he was essentially a critical and dialectical thinker, and as such could resort to sophistry without effort. As the result either of his natural temperament or of his harsh struggles, he lacked appreciation of ideas and philosophic insights. Except in the field of jurisprudence, he was rarely able to synthesize an original interpretation of facts.

His early cultural gleanings made him an excellent humanist. His wide knowledge of Latin and old Portuguese literature permanently set the pattern of his oratorical style. His harmonious prose, lengthy and somewhat monotonous (closely resembling that of Cicero, who was certainly his favorite model, and of some ancient Lusitanians), is technically perfect, judged by classical models. Distant, grave, and proud, he was not adept in the use of irony, and his sarcasm was much more aggressive than bitter. Delicacy, elegance, the light and subtle touch, rarely seem to have found expression in his nature. To the humanist in him were added the lawyer and jurist, and later, the statesman in love with the political life of the United States and England (of whose culture he had been enamored since adolescence). Perhaps no other Brazilian at the birth of the Republic was so thoroughly familiar with North American institutions. He was reminiscent of Guizot for his anglophilism, and at times of Thiers for his conceit in knowing *de omnia re*. Though his literary talent was much more brilliant than Thiers', his intuitive understanding of men and of public affairs was much more precarious than that of the old and energetic opportunist of 1870.

In the organization of the Republic, Rui Barbosa improvised successfully as he went along. Because of his superior intelligence, loftiness, and courage, traits that often showed themselves aggressively, he soon made his presence felt by Marshal Deodoro, who had first approached him

through Quintino Bocaiúva, and by his fellow ministers. Without administrative experience, therefore without having acquired through personal experience a real understanding of Brazil, he translated into action
(sometimes successfully, sometimes not) what he had learned in books:
the United States federal and presidential systems, and the financial experiments of that country and of Europe. But through all the mutations
of his ideas and plans for government that were imposed by circumstances, one cannot possibly doubt his good faith. Denied and defied, he
always struck back forcefully and brilliantly. His passion for civil liberties frequently moved him to take stands of the utmost courage.

After Rui Barbosa, the three men, of very different temperaments,
who most distinguished themselves in the Republic's first ministry were
Quintino Bocaiúva, Campos Sales [later to become President], and Benjamin Constant.

Quintino entered the government with a long record of unshakeable
republican faith. He had neither the extraordinary intellectual vigor,
the culture, nor the passion of his illustrious colleague Rui, but his lucid
mind, trained in professional journalism, readily grasped everything.
He was pleasant, urbane, and unselfish, and naturally given to temporizing. An idealist, and even somewhat of a visionary, he appears to have
been the most agreeable member of the Provisional Government. The
nobleness of his sentiments was perfect, and for that reason his attitudes
were always loyal. When his proposed treaty with Argentina was attacked, he remained unmoved in the face of impassioned street demonstrations.

Campos Sales had the keen and lively mind of the experienced lawyer;
he soon showed up in the Provisional Government as the figure of greatest political discernment, and the most intelligent after Rui. Despite his
extreme federalist leanings, so clearly revealed later in the Constituent
Assembly, and his stubborn doctrinarism, he showed more practical understanding than his colleagues of the nation's administrative problems.

Benjamin Constant was the perfect ideologist. Of a well-balanced and
speculative intelligence, he was essentially emotional or sentimental, a
man of perfect good faith whose purity of soul shone through on many
occasions. His childhood was both humble and unhappy; although he
was hard-working and self-educated, his early manhood was unremark-
able. He began as a private teacher and tried many times, unsuccessfully,
to enter the ranks of officially appointed teachers. Finally, after great
effort, he finished a course in military engineering and spent an undistinguished year on the battlefields in Paraguay.

His leaning toward mathematical disciplines led Constant (probably in 1857) to his first, hesitant contacts with positivism, which was then beginning to be vaguely known in the civilian and military academies. However, he was never able to discipline himself in the orthodoxy of Miguel de Lemos and Teixeira Mendes. He was, in sum, merely a sympathizer, and as such could not represent the purely positivist line of thought in the republican organization.

As a faculty member in the military academy, Constant greatly influenced certain future officers who would later be ardent republican plotters. His sincerity, goodness, and power of persuasion must have been his most effective weapons in the struggle for victory. He was held in high esteem by the Emperor (whose grandchildren he tutored for a while), and the most powerful military heads respected him. In the Provisional Government, he was the first Minister of War.

The Navy Minister, Eduardo Wandenkolk, highly regarded by his peers, had neither the prominence of Rui Barbosa and Quintino Bocaiúva nor Benjamin Constant's record of service to the cause. The same is true of the Minister of Agriculture, Demétrio Ribeiro, a representative of the republicans of Rio Grande do Sul and an authentic, impassioned exponent of the positivist movement.

The Minister of the Interior, Aristides Lôbo, had come into prominence during the republican campaign. A lawyer and journalist, he was noted for the sincerity of his convictions and for his radical tendencies. However, as Dunshee de Abranches pointed out, these attributes did not keep him from promoting deliberation and peaceable settlement of disputes within the councils of government on many occasions.

It was with these men, upright, sincere, keenly anxious to succeed, and of diverse origins (and because of this incapable of agreeing among themselves on interpretation of the facts), that Marshal Deodoro da Fonseca inaugurated the government of the Republic.

The ministries acted independently of one another, and Deodoro, despite his enormous personal prestige, lacked the political sense and direct acquaintance with administrative problems needed to lay out and impose a systematic program of government. Soon, therefore, he agreed to relieve himself of the sole responsibility for public affairs and to share it with the council of ministers, thus returning in a way to the practice of monarchic parliamentarism. But this kind of republican cabinet did not derive its authority from a majority in the Parliament, as, for good or ill, the cabinets of the Empire did. In short, the will of the dictator was represented by the ministers who were his assistants and closest confidants, and the legitimacy of his power rested simply on the success of the republican revolution.

Considering this, the Provisional Government's progress toward building a judicial system, mainly under Rui Barbosa's guidance, was really notable. The Republic did little to affect Brazil's social structure. It was indeed quite conservative, and insisted on respecting all the commitments of the former regime, as well as all the vested personal rights acquired under it. But the very transformation of the regime implied a series of public measures, beginning with the change from a unitary to a federative state, and the social structure had already felt the effects of the economic upheaval caused by the abolition of slavery eighteen months before the end of the Empire.

The new regime's first month was spent peacefully enough in getting acquainted with the facts. On the morning of November 15 the news of the republican victory had been flashed by wire to the whole Brazilian nation. The courts and other organs of government had openly accepted the Republic, and the provincial presidents had not attempted resistance but had handed over their control to the republicans who presented themselves or to commanders of the federal armed forces. Most of those who had been key men in the monarchy voted, in a poll taken by one of them, against any attempt at restoration. Many of them were disposed to collaborate with the Republic. To avoid anarchy was at the moment the concern of all, even the losers. The problems of new political and administrative organization could be left for later. In the meantime the inexperienced men who took on the new responsibilities would gladly follow suggestions from Rio. Instead of Pedro II, there was the dictatorial authority of Deodoro; instead of Ouro Prêto, there was Rui Barbosa, the new Finance Minister, nourishing a dream of national prosperity not unlike Ouro Prêto's.

A minority of the Empire's former politicians fell in easily with the new regime. Those who did not expressly adhere to it maintained a discreet attitude. The more realistic ones sagaciously took advantage of the trust their former high position in the politics and administration of the Empire inspired, and became businessmen, entrepreneurs, bank presidents, public-utility concessionaires, etc. By tying to its material interests a large part of the monarchy's representative men, the Republic, unknowingly following the example of Louis Philippe's bourgeois reign, was either converting them to the new order or rendering them inoffensive.

Very soon, however, the unruffled scene changed. The monarchists were said to be behind the unrest in certain army and navy headquarters. Like all governments born of revolutions undertaken to preserve threatened freedoms, Marshal Deodoro's did not hesitate to go to extremes of counteraction. On December 21, the Viscount of Ouro Prêto, one of his brothers, and Silveira Martins were sent into exile. Two days later the conspirators against the Republic and the government were indicted and held for judgment by a military commission named by the War Minister. The energetic chief of police, Sampaio Ferraz, wiped out the notorious bands of professional rioters, hired and protected by the monarchy's politicos, that menaced and brought shame to the nation's capital. With its position thus consolidated by force, the Provisional Government was enabled to pursue its great task of organization.

The defeat of the southern confederacy in the American Civil War, besides preserving national unity, marked the beginning of the central government's reaction against the excessive autonomy of the old colonies, against the weak bonds of political unity forged at Philadelphia by the constitutional convention. After the victorious revolution of November 15, 1889, Brazil attempted to follow an opposite course, that is, from the center outward, or from the old court to the new states. Her natural tendencies, living as she did in provinces segregated by geographical conditions and historical formation, had always kept alive a spirit of regionalism. However, Brazil lacked the habits of self-government that made possible the democratic and individualistic evolution of the United States. To the Brazilians, the government represented, as it still does, a form of all-powerful, all-knowing providence, outside of which it would be risky to seek solutions. Who, then, would provide the old patriarchal tutelage of Pedro II's reign? Who would replace him as the supreme arbiter?

The Republic of Argentina was another model that impressed the organizers of the Brazilian Republic. In truth, the moral distance between Brazilians and Argentines seemed much less than between Brazilians and North Americans. Brazil and Argentina had the same ethnic origin, shared the same religion, had similar habits and customs, and therefore reacted similarly to the various stimuli of community life. Nevertheless (forgetting the psychological differences between the higher levels of the Brazilian and Argentine societies, that is, between the Portuguese and the Spaniard), a thousand other factors, principally economic, had caused the paths of the two largest nations in Latin America to diverge.

Having realized the old Portuguese dream of dominion over the northern side of the Platine estuary, and having long forgotten the restless ambitions of Carlota Joaquina, the wife of John VI, Brazil had been content to immure herself within the historical borders of her own broad land, consolidated by the oneness of her language. Argentina, on the other hand, had never abandoned her dream of reconstituting the viceroyalty of the River Plate.

The early social formation of Argentina had been much more democratic than that of Brazil. There were no fabulous mines, and therefore no easy riches to attract the Spanish nobility, with its ideas, virtues, and vices, to the Platine lands—just the opposite, for example, of what happened in Peru, which during the later struggles for independence became the center of royalist reaction.

The first Argentine settlers were men of humble origin who had only their own rough labor to support them. The temperate climate and, most of all, the nature of the principal source of wealth, cattle raising, made the introduction of large numbers of African slaves unnecessary. The *criollos,* born in Argentina of Spanish descent, were the dominant class, from which arose the *estanciero* during the period of independence and the *gaucho* during the era of dominion by caudillos.

The bases for constitutional reform that would end the long struggle between centralism and federalism in Argentina were laid during Mitre's presidency [1862–68], on the eve of the war with Paraguay, and were instituted in 1880, at which time Buenos Aires, the national capital, was detached from its province and federalized. The high degree of national unity engendered by Mitre enabled his successor, Sarmiento [1868–74], to achieve a notable administrative record.

The extraordinary influx of European immigrants (about 700,000 of whom settled in Argentina between 1881 and 1890), together with the conquest of the deserts by the extermination or pacification of the Indians, the rapid building of railways (whose mileage in the same decade grew from 2,516 to 9,423 kilometers), and the growth of Buenos Aires, whose population equaled that of Rio, had altered not only the ethnic composition of the Argentine people* but the country's economic basis as well.

Agriculture in Argentina was threatening to surpass cattle raising, even after the introduction of cold storage for meat. Discounting the national prosperity, the Argentine government of Juárez Celman ventured upon a policy of inflation that culminated in a formidable financial disaster in 1890. The budget deficits averaged half the public revenues; the public debt mounted, and the commercial deficit ran to ninety million pesos.

Nevertheless, neither the specific differences between Brazil and Ar-

---

* In 1890, the population was made up of 2 million European and native whites and 1.5 million mestizos, whereas in 1810 it had been made up of 9,000 European and native whites, 420,000 mestizos, 210,000 Indians, and 20,000 Negroes. JMB

gentina nor the results of Juárez Celman's inflationism could lessen the Brazilian republicans' confidence in the miraculous power of their own new political regime. Their enthusiasm was shared in Buenos Aires, where a national holiday was declared in honor of the new Republic, preparing the climate for the approaching treaty of Misiones.

Rio de Janeiro, capital of the Republic, was becoming more absorbent than Rio de Janeiro, capital of the centralizing monarchy. The Provisional Government's policy of bold if often ill-conceived undertakings drew to the former court avid seekers after fortune and positions, whose ambitions had been whetted during Ouro Prêto's administration. Even feudal barons of the Empire left their ancient fazendas, attracted by the exciting life in Rio, where they hoped to recoup by market speculation the losses caused by abolition. The get-rich-quick atmosphere of the poorly kept city of narrow streets and primitive sidewalks, without parks or places of public amusement but overflowing with concert halls and little theaters, gave rise to extravagant spending.

The desire to efface the memory of the recent past naturally found expression in the classic manner of revolutionary demagoguery spell-bound by its own words. Physical symbols of the past were obliterated; in official greetings, passé and poorly translated terms of the French Revolution, like "citizen" and "health and fraternity," were adopted. The orthodox positivists, who had advised Pedro II to extinguish parliamentarism on his own initiative and to replace it with a "republican dictatorship, supported directly by the people," supposed that the moment to impose their ideas on the new government had arrived.

On November 17, the leading figures of the positivist movement, headed by Benjamin Constant, had gone in a body to declare their allegiance to the Republic, bearing a standard on which first appeared the whimsical legend *Ordem e Progresso,* which the new regime would adopt and later inscribe on the national flag. Some days later, the same group had presented urgent suggestions about the "political organization most suitable for the Republic." Briefly, these consisted of permanently maintaining the republican dictatorship; vesting the executive, legislative, and judiciary powers in a dictator who could choose his own successor; abolishing the parliamentary system, government-controlled education, and special privilege; deciding constitutional amendments by plebiscite; maintaining a single chamber solely for budgetary control; separating church and state; establishing freedom of religion; etc. With two of their votaries, Benjamin Constant and Demétrio Ribeiro, in the Provisional Government, the positivists believed adoption of their suggestions was possible.

But both men failed them. The first, timid and sentimental, had never been an orthodox believer; his sincerely liberal tendencies easily swung him away from an apology for dictatorship. Demétrio Ribeiro, on the other hand, with neither Benjamin Constant's record of past services to the revolution nor his personal prestige, was a fighter by nature. But he lacked the authority needed to sway a council dominated by Rui Barbosa's intellectual eminence and by the political authority of such men as Quintino Bocaiúva and Campos Sales. Marshal Deodoro, who had agreed to include Demétrio in the government, did not regard him or his ideas very highly. Floriano Peixoto was indifferent to him. Teixeira Mendes himself, in a book about Benjamin Constant, admits that the positivists obtained nothing by means of Demétrio's influence, not even so-called "spiritual liberty," the separation of church and state, or the "extinction of academic privileges." Demétrio Ribeiro, according to Teixeira Mendes, was so weak that he could not even secure the introduction of the phrase "in the name of the fatherland" into the civil wedding ceremony. Moreover, these two positivists in Deodoro's first cabinet did not get along well with each other.

Thus the Provisional Government's task of remodeling was very little influenced by positivism. Only later, in the elaboration of the constitution, do we find more active positivist influence, but even so, it came from ideas that were already before Comte a part of the political heritage from the eighteenth century. The actions of the Provisional Government were clearly inspired by the democratic liberalism derived from the new republican and federalist model of North America rather than by the old French and English doctrines, and those actions reflected the mentality and political thought of the Provisional Government's principal figures.

The first matter of major importance the Provisional Government had to deal with was the treaty of Misiones with Argentina. The Empire had developed a genuine school of diplomacy, which had made possible a foreign policy with continuity and historical significance. The old disagreements about the River Plate, dating from the colonial period, had been settled permanently; Brazil had only one preoccupation left, to safeguard her own political integrity, which was frequently threatened by disturbances in the neighboring republics. This is what brought on the campaign against the tyranny of Rosas, the Argentine dictator, and the wars with Uruguay and Paraguay, from which Brazil emerged victorious.

Nevertheless, the uniqueness of her political regime in America, the isolating effect of her language, and the bitter aftertaste of the old rivalries between Portugal and Spain all segregated her morally from the republican nations around her. The prominence of England's economic interests had given that country a leading position in Brazil's diplomatic relationships, later disturbed by the Christie incidents. Brazil carefully cultivated her friendship with Chile (a balancing factor in any possible dissension with Argentina), and gladly drew closer to the United States, in spite of small incidents concerning Confederate ships during the Civil War. In 1889 Brazil was represented for the first time at an international gathering of the hemisphere, the Pan-American Conference held in Washington at the invitation of Secretary of State Blaine during President Harrison's administration.

The Republic, mindful of the continuity of the Empire's foreign policy, supposed naturally that the alteration in Brazil's form of government would heighten continental solidarity, beginning with a closer approach to Argentina. The Second Reign had not managed to resolve numerous border problems, most of which had no immediate political or economic significance because of the enormous distances and almost inaccessible desert conditions that characterized them. The government had, however, by the efforts of Joaquim Caetano (which would later inspire the Baron of Rio Branco, son of the Viscount), reached a good agreement on the border with French Guiana. But the question of border limits with Argentina in the territory of Misiones was one that could provoke constant and disagreeable conflicts. In 1857 the Viscount of Rio Branco had been able to sign a treaty fixing the Uruguay river as the border between Brazil and Argentina, but it was not ratified by the Argentine government and the question remained unsettled. Provisional agreements had been attempted afterwards. The advent of the Brazilian Republic impressed the Argentine Foreign Minister, Zeballos, as an excellent opportunity to work out a final settlement of the dispute.

The Republic's first administrations retained not only the broad policies of the former Foreign Ministry, but also the experienced diplomatic agents and the old heads of bureaus. They were intransigent and sometimes narrow custodians of tradition, accustomed to imposing their advice on the weak and temporary ministers appointed over them by the rotating parliamentary governments. When Quintino Bocaiúva assumed the portfolio of Foreign Affairs in the Provisional Government, his sincerely pacifist and Americanist sentiments, his wish for closer relations between the two great nations, led him to accept, in full agreement with Deodoro and his colleagues in the Provisional Government, the suggestions from Buenos Aires. A few days later, accompanied by the Argentine minister in Rio, Bocaiúva left for Buenos Aires in a Brazilian warship, and there signed the treaty that divided up the contested territory between the two countries.

A violent campaign in the press turned public opinion in Rio against the treaty and its signer, who could then just barely count on the solidarity of his fellow ministers. Later, admitting that he had acted under the pressure of political circumstances of the moment, Bocaiúva himself advised the Brazilian Congress not to ratify the treaty, just as the Argentine Congress had declined to ratify the earlier Rio Branco treaty. The old question of Misiones would have to be left for the moment, and solved at a later date.

The separation of church and state, an old aspiration of the Brazilian liberals, was strongly advocated during the last days of the Empire by the positivist propaganda. Soon after the inauguration of the Republic a draft law on this point was offered by Minister Demétrio Ribeiro in behalf of his fellow positivists. It was rejected by the Provisional Government as too radical and, for that reason, unfeasible.

The law would have provided for complete freedom of religion and for absolute separation of church and state. The status of Catholic priests would have been that of public servants and their subsidies continued. The church buildings would have become public property and available for worship by any of the various religious denominations without distinction. The proposed law would have guaranteed to ecclesiastical corporations their possessions in mortmain then being held or received in the future; it would have secularized the hospitals and cemeteries, and decreed civil marriage and civil registry of births and deaths.

At the cabinet meeting of January 7, 1890, Rui Barbosa was successful in winning approval, with Demétrio's support, of the definitive draft, molded along positivist lines, for separation of church and state. It was undoubtedly one of the republican government's most worthy achievements, and received the invaluable collaboration of Bishop Macedo Soares (the same one who, with his Recife colleague, Dom Vidal, had earlier won fame for resistance to the Empire's royalism). By separating church and state, the Republic rendered religion the greatest service to which it could aspire. So pleased was the Provisional Government by the attitude of the clergy that it hastened to announce by telegram to the whole world that the Archbishop-Primate of Bahia had blessed the Republic. The matter of civil marriage was covered in another special law, which a large part of the Catholic clergy did not accept as readily as the separation of the church from the state.

The "great naturalization," that is, the conferring of citizenship on all foreigners residing in Brazil on November 15, 1889, who did not expressly protest against it, was another important legislative measure. So were the reformed mortgage law, the bankruptcy law, the penal code, and the regulation of child labor (Brazil's first attempt at social legislation except for the abolition of slavery).

In the first days of the Republic, Rui Barbosa was the one who seemed to think and act the most, extending his interests to any project that promised to reconstitute the nation. There was no coordination of the ministers' decisions, and their first meetings were not even recorded. Only after a month and a half of the Republic's existence was something like a formal cabinet set up with meetings of the whole and a secretary appointed to write up the minutes, which today make possible a more exact reconstitution of a curious period in Brazil's history.

At first there was an easy harmony among the winners of November 15; the deep sense of common responsibility for the organization of the new regime allowed them to ignore the small rivalries and constant pricks to self-esteem. Deodoro's authoritarian and impulsive temperament, habituated to a rigid notion of military discipline, frequently yielded to the counsels of his ministers, especially to those of Rui Barbosa, whom he seemed greatly to prize and to admire. The military dictator's inexperience was offset by his eagerness to do the right thing and by his intense patriotism.

The banking reform decreed by Rui Barbosa on January 17, 1890, precipitated the Provisional Government's first serious crisis. Sure of Deodoro's entire support, Rui issued the famous decree without consulting his fellow ministers, who only learned about it from the newspapers on the following day. All of Rui's fellow ministers, especially Campos Sales and Demétrio Ribeiro, showed their opposition to his plan. At one point during the argument at the cabinet meeting on January 30, Rui tendered, then withdrew, his resignation. Deodoro attempted to end debate on the subject by declaring that the banking reform was a *fait accompli,* that further argument was out of order, and that he would resign otherwise. This did not prevent some of those present from declaring themselves against the measure anyway, but the threat by the head of the government to resign so early in the life of the Republic seemed so dangerous to the opponents of the reform that they decided to accept it with some minor amendments, notably one limiting the future issuance of bank notes.

This surrender to an accomplished fact, this first "swallowing of the sword," to use a picturesque expression of the time, naturally stirred up resentment among the Republic's first ministers. The clashes resulting from irreconcilable differences in temperament, doctrine, ideas, and interests between the members of the Provisional Government multiplied. The ascendancy of Rui Barbosa was not easily forgiven. On reading the minutes of the cabinet meetings one easily senses the suspicions and prejudices dividing the ministers. Only the fear of blighting the newborn Republic kept the internal crisis from growing even worse and having dangerous repercussions in public opinion.

Demétrio Ribeiro seems to have been the most restless one, the one with the most new ideas that did not materialize, and above all, the one most adverse to Rui Barbosa. He soon dropped out of the government and was replaced in the Ministry of Agriculture by Francisco Glicério (for whom the post had first been intended), a nongraduate lawyer from Campinas, who had a long record of services to republican propaganda and was much more flexible and politic than the representative of the Rio Grande do Sul positivists. Benjamin Constant showed himself to be the most levelheaded. He was also the strongest advocate of freedom of the press; the press was then in violent opposition to the Rui Barbosa plan of reform, and its freedom was frequently threatened by Deodoro's hotheadedness.

Discussions about important legislative reforms or small matters of momentary concern filled the ministers' busy days at their headquarters in Itamaraty palace. Now and then they became alarmed over street rumors or police suspicions of a monarchist plot. Deodoro became irritated by the opposition's excesses and especially by the freedom with which military men on active duty debated political matters in the newspapers, forgetting, as do all revolutionaries who become rulers, his own transgressions. The campaign against Quintino Bocaiúva because of the treaty of Misiones convinced the government that a public statement avowing the solidarity of the ministers would be desirable. Some time later Rui Barbosa arranged for the publication of such a statement.

Aristides Lôbo became disillusioned and left the Ministry of the Interior. He was succeeded by Cesário Alvim, once a provincial president under the Empire and the first provisional governor of Minas Gerais under the Republic. Quintino Bocaiúva wanted to resign from the cabinet when the Rio chief of police, in a drive against the *capoeiras* [hoodlums], arrested the son of his friend, the owner of the republican newspaper, *O País,* of which Quintino was the chief editor.

Deodoro, impatient and self-willed, frequently threatened to resign, as did several of his ministers, on pretexts that often struck the public as childish. Benjamin Constant was transferred from the Ministry of War to the specially created Ministry of Education, Post, and Telegraph, where he could be more useful and, above all, less disturbing. The government, then anxious to assert its strength, handed the Ministry of War to Floriano Peixoto, who was regarded as a disciplinarian and was accustomed to contact with the troops. A grave personal misunderstanding between Deodoro and Benjamin Constant was resolved with difficulty. Finally, the assault on the monarchist journal, *A Tribuna,* of which a group of military friends of Deodoro were accused, prompted the resignation of the entire cabinet. This, however, did not take place until January 1891, and then on the pretext of opposing a construction contract for the port of Tôrres in Rio Grande do Sul that was advocated personally by Deodoro.

The greatest single action taken by the Provisional Government was the financial reform promoted by Rui Barbosa and decreed by him on January 17, 1890, without any prior cultivation of public opinion. The immediate reaction to it was extreme; the press and business circles started a violent campaign of opposition, in which hostility merged with sincere apprehension and threatened interests. The wreck of the Finance Minister's plans, in the sensational market boom and crash that came to be called the Encilhamento, became a millstone around his neck for the rest of his public career. Later, his policies were also blamed for causing the disaster that overtook the nation's finances.

Bookish, theoretical, intoxicated with reading, and with no practical experience in business or finance, Rui Barbosa is supposed to have drawn up his banking reform as an act of pure fantasy, completely alien to the realities of the situation it was intended to meet. He had simply depended on the judgment of a few men of affairs whom he considered expert in banking and financial matters. However, a more accurate or impartial judgment of the financial policies of the embattled Finance Minister requires (in addition to the brief summary of the Empire's finances we have made in an earlier chapter) a general survey of the conditions, principally the moral ones, prevailing when the Republic was proclaimed. If Rui Barbosa's reform suffered in part from impracticality, being the creation of his highly assimilative mind, its failure may also be explained in part by the existing conditions. It is also not correct to lay the blame for the plan's failure wholly upon its inherent flaws. Rather, the main causes of the sensational failure were the changes Rui was obliged to make during the plan's operation, and the intentional adulterations of it by his successors.

In keeping with the thought of the period, the golden age of liberal economics, the men who governed the Republic believed that state intervention in the management of public wealth might go as far as direct management of the Treasury's finances and indirect management of the currency. The modern concept of a national economy as a synthesis of state and private economies would hardly have been understood. To their way of thinking, the national economy resulted from the sum of private economic activities, just as public freedom was the sum of the individual freedoms of the people. Individual free enterprise, the free initiative of "economic man," would create material wealth and progress. By expanding both credit and currency, the state would facilitate the expansion of goods and services, from which it would collect its share by taxation. Rui Barbosa's policy was, therefore, in line with the logic of the time.

By the end of November 1889, the victorious revolution could no longer be satisfied with maintaining the status quo. Like all movements that radically transform political regimes, this one felt obliged to institute reforms and innovations in both its judicial and financial systems, toward which the example set by the Empire's last cabinets was a powerful stimulus.

Rui Barbosa, who as an opposition journalist had stubbornly fought Ouro Prêto's plans, would now as a member of the government have to attempt something different. In the beginning, however, he merely continued the policy of his predecessor and granted the right of emission to other banks in Rio and in the states, which were then under the spell of a lively federalist spirit. European circles sympathetic to the monarchy felt little confidence in the republican revolution, and this and other circumstances, such as the excess of imports and the mushrooming schemes, caused a flight of gold from Brazil that made it impossible to continue the gold-based, multiple-issue currency system.

On January 17, 1890, Rui Barbosa had Deodoro sign a lengthy and ingenious decree of banking reforms. Government bonds were to replace gold as the reserve needed to issue bank notes, as had been done in the United States by the national banks in Lincoln's time, and as had previously been suggested during the Empire.

Brazil was divided into three zones, each with a bank of issue: the northern zone, down as far as Bahia; the central zone from Espírito Santo to Santa Catarina; and the Rio Grande do Sul zone (which through a curious geographical quirk took in Goiás and Mato Grosso). Shortly afterwards, the northern zone was subdivided into three regions, and São Paulo and Goiás were joined to form a fourth zone, but Mato Grosso remained with Rio Grande do Sul.

The banks were charged with amortizing the public debt under a scheme Rui Barbosa thought both clever and original. In the first seven years interest payments would be eliminated by a yearly reduction in the interest rate. At the same time a fund would be accumulated by a ten per cent levy on the banks' gross profits, so that by the end of fifty years the entire public debt would be liquidated. The banks' notes were to enjoy the same status as Treasury bills and were to be the preferred medium of payment for all public works. The banks were to make farm loans, for which purpose the government would let them keep the interest on the national bonds loaned them as reserves against which to issue paper money. They were to redeem their own paper, as well as that of the Treasury, in gold as soon as the rate of exchange reached par.

The inflationary wave that started during the Ouro Prêto regime grew larger, and naturally stimulated speculation in the stock market. The most extraordinary enterprises for unbelievable purposes were incorporated daily, with interest payments guaranteed by the government. The speculative fever of fabulous riches, as in other countries (notably the United States and Argentina, the nearest examples), caused the Brazilian markets, in Rio most of all, to become frenzied. In his novel, *Esaú e Jacó*, Machado de Assis recalls some of its aspects: "That's right, you haven't forgotten its name, Encilhamento, the great boom of enterprises and companies of every kind. Anyone who didn't live through it hasn't seen anything. A torrent of dazzling ideas, inventions, and concessions by which one could make contos, hundreds of contos, thousands, thousands upon thousands, thousands upon thousands upon thousands of contos, poured out every day."

In the face of his original plan's failure, the Finance Minister returned to a metallic base for currency, though he had been critical of the same thing when Ouro Prêto did it. Later, confessing that the system of multiple emissions had been forced on him by pressure from the states, which were then dazzled by the federation's successes, he decided to issue unbacked currency through a single source, the Banco da República do Brasil, which was founded for that purpose. The currency already in circulation amounted to 506,992 contos, including the 285,943 contos of Treasury bills. Like all advocates of printing-press money, Rui Barbosa believed that the rate of exchange was not decisively influenced by the superabundance of paper currency, but rather that its fall resulted from deficits in the balance of payments.

In all good faith, Barbosa was convinced that Brazil had entered a period of rapid progress following the abolition of slavery, especially after the advent of the Republic. It did not seem imprudent to him to gamble on the future. Like some of the former ministers of the Empire, he was obsessed by the example of the United States, and like them, he failed to see that an incomparable growth in that country's real economic wealth had brought about its astonishing prosperity, which in turn had attenuated or canceled out the worst effects of its earlier financial experiments. The United States had made her astounding growth by means of heavy issues of currency by the banks and the Treasury. Juárez Celman's emissionist fever had precipitated the economic transformation of Argentina, modernized Buenos Aires, promoted rural industries, and intensified European emigration. The wealth potential thus created in the United States and Argentina happily proved sufficient for the redemption of their paper money.

The flow of capital and of foreign immigrants to the southern regions of Brazil, and the healthy condition of the public exchequer caused by European investments in private enterprises and loans to the government, had given the last statesmen of the Empire the illusion of an extraordinary state of prosperity. Their old physiocratic conception was evolving toward the new idea of an industrialized Brazil; São Paulo's coffee and Amazonia's rubber would finance the expected transformation. We have seen how Ouro Prêto's financial policy caused the era of speculation.

Born in this euphoric atmosphere, the Republic, guided economically and financially by Rui Barbosa's brave innovations, seemed at times to lose its sense of practical realities. Rui was designing on paper a marvelous Brazil, a sort of replica of the United States, crisscrossed by railroads and in full swing with the machine age. By extending in various ways the inflationary policy initiated by the monarchy, he unintentionally aggravated the gambling on the market and created the preconditions of the crash. However, he and Deodoro, luckier than Juárez Celman had been shortly before in Argentina, were able to survive in office. Reacting against the myth that land was the sole source of wealth, Rui converted the Empire's old revenue tariff into a protectionist one. The very change of the name of the Ministry of Agriculture, to Ministry of Industry, reflected the ideas of the time.

Nevertheless, with his high intelligence and the experience in public affairs that he gained as he went along, Rui Barbosa tried to correct many of the excesses of his original plan and to attenuate their consequences. By requiring customs duties to be paid partly in gold, he was able to stave off a disastrous drop in the rate of exchange and thus to save on the budgetary allotments that had been made to cover the balance of payments. He worked to curb and unify bank issues of currency, and to end the awarding of public-works contracts at scandalously high rates of interest, guaranteed to be paid in gold. He reduced the interest rate on a part of the internal debt and converted the banking gold reserves held in the Treasury into bonds.

The rise in the Brazilian economy after abolition was actually much more precarious than the men who were running the government during the twilight of the Empire and the dawn of the Republic realized. It is true that the stream of immigrants to São Paulo was growing, but this did not prevent the long depression from which nearly all agricultural activities were suffering. The building of public utilities, especially of railways (which did not get much beyond the drawingboard stage), brought about an excess of imports. Although the government entered the exchange market in order to support it, the gold, which had come into the country in recent years but had never really taken root there, fled precipitately. Coupled with the stock market crash, which logically followed the Encilhamento, was the disorder in the impoverished public coffers.

In long and brilliant speeches after leaving the Ministry of Finance, Rui Barbosa tried to justify his financial policy, attributing its failure to the actions of his immediate successor. It is true, as we shall see, that the reactionary steps taken by Minister Araripe in Deodoro's second cabinet could only have aggravated the mistakes that may have been made by Barbosa.

The muddle of the government in economic and financial matters was complete. The rate of exchange, which stood at 27 pence when Rui Barbosa took over and which he managed to keep from falling below 22 pence, dropped to almost nothing. The government turned again to printing inconvertible money, which, added to the Treasury's outstanding bonds, enormously inflated the amount of paper currency in circulation. The nation, which had experienced a moment of sincere hope in the Republic's work of remodeling, was left shaken by the crash and became discouraged when it did not become impatient. Thus the ground for the coup d'etat of November 1891 and for the later revolutions was prepared.

6. Establishment of the Constitution

The Constituent Assembly — The positivist influence — Political disturbances — The contest between Deodoro and the Assembly — Collective resignation of the first Republican Cabinet — The Lucena ministry — The conflict between Deodoro and the Congress — The November 3rd coup — Threat by the navy — Deodoro's resignation.

On December 3, 1889, eighteen days after the proclamation of the Republic, the Provisional Government appointed a committee of five jurists to prepare a draft of the constitution. On the 21st of the same month, it decided to convoke a constituent assembly. The committee, headed by Saldanha Marinho (a signer of the Manifesto of 1870 and a patriarch of the Republic), submitted three drafts, by Américo Brasiliense, Santos Werneck and Rangel Pestana, and J. A. Magalhães Castro, which were eventually combined into one. Rui Barbosa, charged with its editing, did not confine himself to merely polishing the document's style; in many instances he changed its substance too. Deodoro argued against several of the provisions, hostile to all that restrained authority and especially military discipline. He found it hard to accept the principle of independence between the executive and legislative branches. Trained in the parliamentary procedure of the Empire, he thought it absurd to deny the head of state the right to dissolve the Congress.

Convening on the first anniversary [November 15, 1890] of the Republic, the Constituent Assembly worked exhaustively on writing the constitution along the lines submitted by the government. Thus on February 24, 1891, Brazil came under a new constitutional regime, the dictator thereby fulfilling his promise to the nation.

The Brazilian constitution cannot be understood without an understanding also of the general conditions under which it came into being. What currents of thought controlled it? What national aspirations did it fulfill? What did the Assembly that framed it represent? How did this Assembly manage to accomplish its mission? We have seen in chapter 2 what the policies of the second Emperor were throughout his long reign. We have also recalled how disbelief in the monarchy had become general during its final phase, and how the abolitionist campaign had overshadowed the republican propaganda.

With the calling of the Constituent Assembly, Brazil was finally beginning to realize her republican and federalist dreams. The draft submitted by the government was modeled after the Constitution of the United States. It was also strongly influenced by the Constitution of Argentina and slightly by that of the Swiss Confederation. North American statesmen replaced the French and English doctrinaires of former times. As the men of 1824 believed religiously in the formulas of political liberalism, so did those of 1891. Brazil was being cast in the North American mold just as she had formerly been held within the framework of French constitutionalism. From extreme centralism to the widest federalism—this was the leap she was going to make.

Nevertheless, both constitutions were inspired by political and economic individualism, which was on the rise in 1824 and at its height in 1891. Whether at the start or the end of the century, whether in the European or the North American pattern, the controlling ideology was still that of the Encyclopedists, Rousseau, and the liberal economists. The essential difference between the monarchic and republican constituent assemblies was that the latter lacked the strong rivalries between the centralists and the federalists.

The Assembly, elected in accordance with the Cesário Alvim regulation (which repressed any possible truth in electoral campaigns as much as the electoral laws of the monarchy), was solidly republican, federalist, and presidentialist. One would have said that the entire nation had forgotten the recent Empire as if it had been a part of prehistory. Even the few monarchists who had not swung over to the Republic preferred to await its mistakes in silence.

Thus the Constituent Assembly, not being split into factions like the assembly of Bordeaux after 1870, was not forced, as the latter was, to mark time for five long years and end up giving the country a constitution of compromise. It went straight and quickly to its task, guided by the political tact and moral authority of its president, Prudente de Morais. The finished work, like the Constitution of 1824, corresponded to the best ideas of the times. Despite certain perhaps intentional overstatements or ambiguities, the document was a victory of good sense and fairness over lack of experience and the excitement caused by the novelty of the Republic.

The government's rough draft sought to preserve a sense of nationalism that would be in keeping with the principles of federalism. Though the states were given ample autonomy, the great sovereign powers belonged to the Union. The Union retained the best sources of public funds, its rights were superior to those of the states, it could mobilize the police forces of the states, etc.

In the Assembly, however, there soon appeared a strong ultrafederalist current that went even farther than the American and Argentine constitutions and would not have hesitated to convert Brazil into a confederation of twenty small nations. It became necessary for Rui Barbosa to organize resistance against what he called a "morbid superexcitement," an "insane and sickly appetite" for federalism. Although the radical federalists were mainly the delegates from Rio Grande do Sul, headed by Júlio de Castilhos and influenced more or less by positivism, they were joined by delegates from other states, including such distinguished men as João Barbalho of Pernambuco, Campos Sales of São Paulo, and Leopoldo de Bulhões of Goiás. One delegate introduced a proposal that would have forbidden a standing national army; another wanted to give each state the right to have its own navy. To the ultrafederalists (Jeffersonians more or less) the states were the reality; the Union was the fiction, and as such should have been limited, in the words of João Barbalho, to the "strict necessities for existence."

The positivist apostolate, which had had little influence on the organization of the Provisional Government, operated with greater efficiency in the Constituent Assembly, mainly in the persons of the representatives from Rio Grande do Sul. The amendments they suggested were consistent, naturally, with a republican and ultrafederalist dictatorship. Most of them were voted down, such as those suppressing the words "a perpetual and indissoluble union of the states" in the preamble of the Constitution, establishing complete freedom in the emission of currency, calling for a nonsecret, compulsory, and universal franchise that included beggars and illiterates, abolishing official education and scientific diplomas, and instituting the death penalty and hard labor in chains. Among their amendments that found a place in the Constitution were those relating to the laws of mortmain, suppressing titles and decorations, and granting the states the privilege of organizing municípios.

The articles concerning the allocation of public funds and the organization of the judicial branch offered a wider field for the clash between the radical federalists and the moderates. Opposed to the official draft, drawn up with the interests of the Union foremost in mind, stood the draft sponsored by the Rio Grande do Sul delegation, which reserved to the states, in addition to their specific sources of revenue, such as export duties, all other funds not explicitly federal in nature. The ambiguous wording of the text, finally worked out as a compromise between the two opposing drafts, caused the extraordinary confusion that prevailed in the taxing system during the whole life of the first Constitution.

The official draft called for centralization of substantive law and decentralization of adjective law (procedures and courts).* The Committee of 21, on the other hand, favored complete federal control of both the legislation and the administration of justice. They were beaten, however, in the full Assembly, which adopted the first proposal.

The ownership of unused public lands and of mines, the method for electing the President of the Republic, the organization of the Senate, the competence of the Federal Supreme Court to determine the constitutionality of laws, and, most of all, federal intervention in the states were other points of fiery debate between the major factions in the Assembly. The uncertainties and hesitancies about federal intervention resulted in the vague wording of Article 6, which later proved to be a permanent pretext for the most diverse interpretations and a motive for the most serious political incidents.

The constituent legislators also refused the opportunity (suggested earlier, incidentally, in the drafts of the Committee of Five) to revise the territorial division of the country. Thus they permitted the formation of an unbalanced federation, composed of indigent states without minimum resources for autonomous life and powerful states that would soon monopolize control of the Republic. This situation contributed to the slow but sure building-up of future revolutions, including the one that would extinguish this same Republic.

The panorama of Brazilian politics had changed greatly during the first year of the Republic. The repeated personal clashes between the members of the Provisional Government had created irreconcilable antagonisms. The departures of Demétrio Ribeiro and Aristides Lôbo from the cabinet were followed by that of Benjamin Constant, whose specially created portfolio was afterwards abolished. Deodoro, gravely shaken in health and subject to repeated attacks of dyspnea, became increasingly irritable and impulsive.

The political situation in nearly all the states became unsettled. Rio Grande do Sul was in a state of turmoil that aroused constant fears of an armed clash between the several factions. The governor of Bahia was forced to resign. In Pernambuco, Minas Gerais, and other, smaller states

---

* That is, all major legislation was to be federal, emanating from one source as during the Empire, and thus avoiding conflicting state laws. However, administration of the laws was to be largely left to the states. JLT

partisan agitations were on the increase. Still without constitutional organization, without habits of political autonomy, and without an elite of sincere republicans capable of governing them, the recently federated states were struggling in a condition close to anarchy. The Provisional Government frequently replaced their governors, without, however, managing to quiet things down. The state of the nation's finances, profoundly rocked by the Encilhamento, was lamentable.

The Constituent Assembly, which at the start had unanimously ratified the powers of the dictatorial government headed by Deodoro, turned against him. The candidacy of the old soldier to be the first President of the Republic under the new constitution seemed threatened. After leaving the cabinet, Demétrio Ribeiro plotted against Deodoro at every turn. He was aided in his efforts by General João Simeão, who had been removed from the government of Pernambuco, by Admiral Custódio José de Melo, who was dying to get into the political fray, and by Francisco Glicério.

After nearly 70 years, Brazil was repeating the drama between Pedro I and the constituent assembly of 1823, which the 1891 Assembly was like in many ways. The Assembly was jealous of its independence as a public force, and felt that it deserved the nation's gratitude for the political charter it had provided. The Assembly therefore believed itself able to stand up against Deodoro, who was as self-willed and unrestrained as Pedro I, and, like him, was supported by the great majority of the armed forces.

Marshal Deodoro did not get along well with his head ministers, who, having been elected to the Constituent Assembly, preferred to attend its sessions rather than to meet in council with their chief. They were merely awaiting the promulgation of the Constitution to abandon their posts.

The crisis suddenly exploded in a meeting of the cabinet on January 17, 1891. On opening the meeting, Deodoro declared that he would sign no administrative act until the contract for the port of Tôrres had been approved and awarded. After so many other public-works concessions had been granted, many of them senseless and suspect, Deodoro could not understand the resistance to this one he was seeking for a personal friend and considered to be in the public interest. Faced with Deodoro's ultimatum, the ministers left and decided to resign in a body. Floriano Peixoto, absent from Rio at a mountain resort, agreed by telegram with his colleagues' position.

On January 21 Deodoro was handed his cabinet's resignation, signed by Campos Sales, Rui Barbosa, Quintino Bocaiúva, Francisco Glicério, Cesário Alvim, and Admiral Wandenkolk. It stated: "The Constituent

Assembly having today approved the proposed constitution for the Republic, a circumstance that, according to our notice given at our last meeting on the 17th and motivated by our opposition to the guarantee of interest for the port of Tôrres contract, would determine the date of our withdrawal from the administration of public affairs, we await the naming of our successors." Deodoro replied immediately: "In answer to your letter of yesterday submitting your resignation, I have to say that I accept it, lamenting only that the guarantee of interest for the building of the port of Tôrres, a most urgently needed public work of great political and economic importance, and recognized as such by almost the entire ministry, should have served as the pretext for your decision."

The ministers, who had served with Deodoro for more than a year, were well acquainted with his strengths of character, his emotional weaknesses, and his political incompetence, and were leaving him exposed to a situation that could easily lend itself to malicious insinuations. Deodoro, who was without guile, made matters worse by ascribing other, more general, more serious, and less decent motives to his ministers. On the same day that he accepted his cabinet's sensational resignation he organized a new one; more correctly, he handed the job of doing so to his personal friend, the Baron of Lucena, much as it had been done in the monarchic cabinets during the era of the Emperor's exclusive personal power.

The Baron of Lucena was an old monarchist who had pursued an ordinary political and administrative career during the Empire. He had a reputation for being intelligent, obstinate, and somewhat acrimonious and, above all, for enjoying Deodoro's unlimited confidence, which caused the cabinet he headed to be characterized as his "court," a term formerly employed to condemn personal cabinets.*

Of the ministers selected by Lucena (who kept the portfolios of Agriculture and, temporarily, of Justice for himself), Alencar Araripe (Finance), João Barbalho (Interior), General Falcão da Frota (War), Admiral Forster Vidal (Navy), and Justo Chermont (Foreign Affairs), only the last had been active in the republican movement, in his northern state of Pará. Barbalho had distinguished himself in the Constituent Assembly by his exaggerated federalism. He would later distinguish himself still further by a book of commentaries (since become a classic) on the Constitution of 1891.

Alencar Araripe, a magistrate, was Rui Barbosa's immediate successor

---

* It was also referred to as "Lucena's consulate," and the Baron was referred to as "Deodoro's gray eminence" by old-time republicans who would not forgive him his title. JLT

as Minister of Finance. He was much less experienced than Rui, and was far from distinguishing himself. Indeed, at no time did he show any interest in the affairs of his department. Wishing to recast the policies of his predecessor, who had become the target of every kind of criticism, made in good faith and bad, he compounded Rui's possible errors to the extreme. He was easily manipulated by market speculators, shady promoters, and organizers of absurd enterprises, who abounded in all the country's cities, especially in Rio. The rate of exchange kept dropping. The banks kept issuing currency without even bothering to print paper bills, using instead those of the Treasury, on which they simply imposed their own imprint. Bankruptcies followed one after another, and security values dropped. Public confidence was badly shaken.

Lucena, the *de facto* head of government, took over the Ministry of Finance, but did not improve matters. He canceled the payment of customs duties in gold and sold or loaned the Treasury's gold to more or less insolvent banks. In a bitter fight with Congress, he insisted upon a banking reform that was rejected as scandalous. This was one of the factors that would lead to the dissolution of Congress by Deodoro on November 3. The merger of the Banco do Brasil with the Banco dos Estados Unidos do Brasil (both in bad shape), the issuing of 100,000 contos in Treasury bonds for "national industries," the reorganization of the Banco da República with permission to issue up to 600,000 contos, and the failure of the General Railroad Company with liabilities in excess of 300,000 contos were the chief fiscal events of the Lucena government's time in office, events that reveal the enormous confusion in which Brazilian politics and the administration were struggling. All this, however, did not keep Lucena from asserting in a telegram to the Rothschilds a few days after the November 3rd coup that there was neither a political crisis nor a financial one in Brazil, a statement that the English bankers bluntly contradicted while they summarized the financial debacle of the Republic.

The resignation of Deodoro's first cabinet put new life in the campaign being waged to prevent his election to the constitutional presidency of the Republic. A group of military delegates, allied with civilian politicians, nominated Floriano Peixoto, former Adjutant General of the army, to run against Deodoro. This was soon changed, however, to a nomination of Prudente de Morais for President and of Floriano for Vice-President. Prudente de Morais, by not declaring himself clearly, aggravated the crisis, forcing the São Paulo delegation to support him despite Campos Sales's and Bernardino de Campos's repeated efforts to temporize. It was stated openly everywhere that if Deodoro were defeated, the military would proclaim his dictatorship and dissolve Congress. Unwilling to place himself in opposition to his fellow officer, Floriano Peixoto recommended Deodoro's election.

On February 24, 1891, the "representatives of the Brazilian people, gathered in a Constituent Assembly to organize a free and democratic method of government, established, decreed, and promulgated the Constitution." In closing the Assembly, Prudente de Morais congratulated his colleagues on the work accomplished in only three months and a few days, saying:

The Assembly strove to introduce all the cardinal principles of the federal republic into the fundamental pact with which it has endowed the nation. . . . We have fulfilled our duty. The Assembly, in adjourning, may take satisfaction in reflecting that despite the unfavorable public opinion and prejudice it initially encountered, it so proceeded as to destroy, or at least diminish, this prejudice, and to win the public prestige and confidence that now surround it as it ends its task.

If the Constituent Assembly, ill-received indeed by the conservative opinion of a nation that feared its inexperience and, above all, its positivist and radical tendencies, was really able to reconcile itself with that nation, it did not maintain its solidarity and harmonious collaboration with Deodoro's government.

On February 25th, Deodoro was elected President of the Republic by 129 Assembly votes, only 32 more than the 97 cast for Prudente de Morais. Having shown a lack of enthusiasm for Deodoro, the Assembly underscored its prejudice by electing Floriano Peixoto Vice-President by 153 votes, 96 more than the 57 cast for Admiral Wandenkolk, who had been suggested by the government to flatter the navy.

On the day of his inauguration, Deodoro was coldly received in pointed silence by a small committee of the Congress, but Vice-President Floriano was escorted to the head table amid wild applause. The politically acute no longer had any illusions about how near an outbreak of violent conflict was.

Once the Constitution had been promulgated, the Constituent Assembly changed itself into an ordinary legislature, with a separate Senate and Chamber of Deputies. The fight between the Republic's two powerful political factions was no longer disguised, and erupted with more force in the Chamber than in the Senate. The grave state of Deodoro's health raised the hopes of his adversaries. Some long-time republicans made final, futile attempts at reconciliation with the government.

The fight between Deodoro and the Congress (which in some ways was like the tragic dissension between the Chilean Congress and President Balmaceda) became more impassioned day by day. The Marshal became convinced that the opposition in Congress would not only refuse to approve his budget requests, but also override his veto of the law of presidential responsibility, in order to be able to start impeachment proceedings against him later. The virulence of his opponents' language annoyed him extremely. Accustomed to the military hierarchy and to the respect he had always inspired, he found the insults they hurled at him intolerable. A motion headed by Quintino Bocaiúva's signature was passed in Congress the day after the presidential election. Solemnly declaring Benjamin Constant, three days dead, as the founder of the Republic, as "a republican without blemish," and as "a splendid model of virtue for its future rulers," it must have wounded Deodoro deeply. Naturally, many of his intimates urged him to dissolve Congress. The Baron of Lucena himself, who claimed to have done everything to avoid it, confessed later that he had recommended dissolution when the Constituent Assembly changed itself into a legislature.

According to his testimony (as reported by Tobias Monteiro), the Baron of Lucena had intervened directly to keep Prudente de Morais from including in the Senate's order of the day bills that had not been previously sanctioned and that might have set off the final explosion of the crisis. He also offered to try to persuade Floriano Peixoto to preside over the Senate.

Deodoro's reply to his minister's proposal reveals the President's opinion of his Vice-President. "Don't do it," he said. "You don't know Floriano. I won't say that he is a coward, for that would be doing him an injustice. But he is wholly passive, and, though he has group courage and fulfills his duties well, he does not have individual courage. You may be sure that if he becomes convinced we need his support, he will openly throw himself into the arms of the opposition."

To this, Lucena replied, "I cannot put up with this Congress any longer. It must disappear for the good of Brazil. Draw up a decree dissolving it, and don't further concern yourself with Floriano."

Nevertheless Lucena went to Floriano's house to insist that he assume the presidency of the Senate, as its president by law. The Vice-President, whose nose was "red and inflamed," and who was the recognized leader of the conspiracy against Deodoro, began by protesting his loyalty. If he received plotters in his house, he explained, it was to counsel them in the direction of tolerance and moderation. He agreed with Lucena that there might be monarchist plots supported by the navy, but he refused to preside in the Senate. He ended the interview with these words, in which he revealed his extraordinary capacity for dissembling: "I have not been a friend of Marshal Deodoro since the day he doubted my loyalty, but I am his comrade, I am a military man, and I am above all a Brazilian. You may assure the Generalissimo that he will always find me at his side in any emergency. I am like the ram [mascot] of a battalion's band; wherever the band goes, there goes the ram."

Finally, on November 3, 1891, the government, sure of the support of the greater part of the army and sure of the indifference of the country at large, issued two decrees: one dissolving Congress and the other proclaiming a state of siege. The Senate and Chamber buildings were surrounded by military forces. Most of the legislators returned to their states, more or less resigned to the situation, but a more active and bolder minority, including the deputies from São Paulo, who counted on Floriano Peixoto's complicity and the navy's sympathies, intensified the conspiracy.

Deodoro's manifesto to the nation, justifying the revolutionary step, was largely a recapitulation of the disagreements between Congress and the administration. In it he accused Congress of factiousness and of intending to restore old parliamentary practices. The laws of presidential responsibility and ministerial incompatibility, the refusal to approve budgetary appropriations, the campaign against the commercial treaty signed with the United States, the suppression of the legation to the Vatican, and the opposition to Lucena's financial reforms were the principal items in Deodoro's list of accusations. In the same acrimonious and polemic tone, Campos Sales drew up Congress's answer, which was later secretly printed.

Brazil's nonpolitical classes received the news of the dissolution of Congress with their customary indifference. Deodoro had merely acted like the Emperor during the latter's reign of exclusive personal power. The public feared only the possibility of armed conflict.

In the political world, however, the commotion was great. The governors of the states applauded the dissolution with more or less ardent enthusiasm. Only the young officer Lauro Sodré, governor of Pará (and looked upon as Benjamin Constant's favorite disciple), courageously opposed it. There was no lack, either, of those who had a clear vision of the future. Brazil was beginning, with the mutilation of the Constitution promulgated less than a year before, a long revolutionary phase in which the fate of the Republic itself would hang in the balance.

The political atmosphere had been greatly poisoned by suspicions about shady deals that had been made easy by the Encilhamento. It was said at the time that the November 3rd coup had been more a stock-market solution than a political one. On entering the government, Lucena had ordered the signing of the port of Tôrres contract, and this made a grievous impression on the public. Other large concessions, such as the one for the General Railroad Company, occasioned the most serious accusations. The reform of the Banco dos Estados Unidos do Brasil (doggedly combated in Congress and in the press) was described as what would later in France be termed a "Panama," a scandalous enterprise in which men of affairs, politicians, and influential legislators would become involved.

In Rio Grande do Sul, where civil war was expected at any moment, some of the federal armed forces teamed up with members of the opposition, deposed Governor Júlio de Castilhos, who had supported Deodoro's coup, and set itself up as a governing junta, picturesquely nicknamed *governicho* [phony little government]. An analogous situation prevailed in Paraná, and apprehension was felt in the other states in spite of optimistic reports from their governors. In Rio, Admiral Custódio José de Melo, whose political ambitions, resentments, and personal vanity were easily exploited by the politicians, placed himself in the forefront of the reactionary movement. His navy comrades, long-time rivals of the land forces and relegated, but not resigned, to a secondary position, were stimulated to action.

On November 15th, Lucena called on Floriano again, bearing an invitation from Deodoro to join him to review the parade celebrating the Republic's second anniversary. Floriano was not at home, and replied at the last minute to Deodoro's invitation, excusing himself "because the uniform I have is not fit to wear."

The plotters met in Floriano's house, he being Deodoro's constitutional substitute and the recognized, though not openly admitted, leader of the revolutionary movement. In the beginning, Deodoro appeared to accept the challenge. He prepared his defense and ordered the arrest of the highest-ranking conspirators, including the two admirals, Wandenkolk and Custódio de Melo. The latter managed to escape arrest and to incite to mutiny nearly all the war vessels (many of them of doubtful efficiency) anchored in Rio's harbor.

On the morning of November 23, the mutinous squadron, with the flag of its commander, Custódio de Melo, raised on the battleship *Riachuelo,* was ready to begin hostilities when it received the news of Deodoro's abdication. Only one shot of the planned bombardment was fired, and that, because of poor marksmanship, hit the dome of the Candelaria church [in downtown Rio] and panicked the city's peaceful inhabitants.

Though he could have counted on the support of most of the military garrison, Deodoro backed away from the fight, sacrificing his traditional bravery for fear of throwing the country into civil war. Surrounded by desolate friends who did not acquiesce in his resignation, he sent for Floriano and turned over the reins of government. "I sign the manumission of the last slave in Brazil," he is reported to have said, a phrase similar to the one attributed to Pedro II. On the following day he applied for retirement from active military service. Only a few days later Pedro II died in Paris. In August of the following year Deodoro died. He was buried, at his wish, in civilian clothes and without military honors.

In the two years of his government, Deodoro had always fully revealed his bravery, generosity, and impulsiveness. He acquired neither administrative nor political experience. He made abundant mistakes, in spite of being amenable to the good advice of those who knew how to handle him. Intensely patriotic, of unassailable integrity, he did not know how to dissemble, to bide his time, to sidestep, to protect himself against treachery. Like all free and open souls, Deodoro had trusted others too much and, because of this, suffered greatly when those he believed to be his friends betrayed him. He was an old-fashioned soldier, unsuited and ill-prepared for public life, perhaps unable to cope with life's recurring problems except in terms of the battlefield.

In Deodoro's immediate successor, also a soldier, also born in the same small province of Alagoas, Brazil would soon come to know a man from the opposite moral pole: taciturn, coldly courageous, almost morbidly impassive, of never-ending dissimulation and distrust, of peasant shrewdness, of disdain for all outward appearances, of invincible tenacity and indomitable energy disguised as discouragement and laziness, and with a lust for power.

7. The Era of Floriano Peixoto
[1891–94]

*Portrait of Floriano Peixoto — The center and the states —
An interpretation of the Constitution — The officers' manifesto — Floriano's reaction — Support and opposition — Financial problems—The PRF.*

Deodoro's resignation raised his constitutional successor and fellow soldier from the days of Paraguay, General Floriano Peixoto, to the presidency. Who was this man? What did he inherit from his predecessor?
How would he fulfill the mission events had thrust upon him?

No figure in Brazilian history has been discussed more than Floriano.
He inspired either rabid zeal or intense hatred. Even now, more than
half a century later, it is not always easy to judge him dispassionately.
More time will be needed to wipe out the extremes of feeling he aroused.
In this aptitude for inflaming the passions of his contemporaries and
even of those who view him in historical perspective, one sees the first
indication not of his superiority but of his uniqueness. There is no mis-
taking his mysterious personality, which defies psychological penetration
by critics and biographers. Euclides da Cunha popularized his nickname,
The Sphinx, and those who sought to decipher his riddle were coldly
destroyed, like all who, according to the legend, pry into such mysteries.

Floriano was not distinguished by any masterful outward signs. He
was careless of his personal appearance; his face was ordinary, somewhat
inexpressive, and sickly. He did not have, for example, Deodoro's military bearing, élan, or flashing look. His voice, with the drawl of the
northern *caboclo* [peasant], was never raised; he never showed annoy-
ance at the gestures or attitudes of others. His perfect impassivity, as well
as his other virtues and faults, remind one of Benito Juárez, the Mexican
national hero, who came from the same Amerindian stock.

Floriano was not intellectually brilliant. His skimpy education was
almost entirely in the usual techniques of his profession. He displayed
no intellectual curiosity, inner doubts, or conflicts. He despised money,

and was completely indifferent to material comforts. He held mankind in contempt, and therefore found it easy to reduce everyone to a common level. He mixed easily with the crowds in the streets, but remained aloof from any intimate contacts. His petty bourgeois family took up perhaps his entire capacity for affection.

Like other caboclos, Floriano was incurably suspicious and impassive. Though plain and accessible, he was incapable of impromptu familiarities, of coarse and funny jokes, which Deodoro always indulged in so easily. Basically he was an unhappy person. In his irony, which runs through the vast collection of anecdotes about him, there was always something of the coldness and cruelty of a resentful and embittered nature.

But in spite of all his faults, Floriano, more than any other Brazilian, could arouse vibrant enthusiasms, often with overtones of mysticism. To most of the Brazilian elite, Floriano embodied the most savage forces in the soul of the nation, a sort of throwback from the crust of the coastal civilization. That is, he exemplified what the rough frontiersman Jackson represented to the North Americans who believed Washington, Jefferson, and Hamilton to be model statesmen. To the vast majority of his contemporaries, however, he embodied precisely what to them seemed the deepest, the sincerest, and the most earthy elements in their nationality. In spite of outward appearances, Brazil, ill-adapted to alien patterns, established perfect rapport with the cold, calculating, and indomitable psyche of her caboclo hero. Thus, he long remained, and to some extent still remains, a symbol of the real nation, the nation of immense and brutal backlands, which was opposed to the artificial nation of the cities that the Empire had fostered and that the "doctors" and journalists of the Provisional Government had supposed untouchable.

In Brazil's gallery of political figures, Floriano's type was until then unknown. Early in her independence there had flourished a few men, such as José Bonifácio, Feijó, and Bernardo de Vasconcelos, whose powerful wills left their marks on her. In the Second Reign other statesmen, such as Paraná, Olinda, and Ouro Prêto, distinguished themselves by their authoritative energy. The wars of the River Plate and Paraguay developed arrogantly brave military heroes, such as Osório, Barroso, Tamandaré, Pelotas, and Deodoro. In Caxias, military genius was singularly joined with a sense of political moderation, which helped him placate the fratricidal hatreds in Rio Grande do Sul. But there was nothing enigmatic about any of these figures; they all revealed themselves clearly from their first participation in the events of their time.

Floriano was a psychological surprise. In the atavism of his ethnic origins, he reproduced the caudillo characteristic of Hispanic America, perhaps one of the purest subspecies: taciturn, withdrawn, double-dealing, disdainful of outward show. Loving power as a form of self-projection, he did not stop at violence and even cruelty when he judged them useful or necessary. But he was careful to observe certain regulations and bureaucratic formalities, as military men often are even when in revolt against the constituted order.

Until the advent of the Republic, there had been nothing unusual in Floriano's career. He was born in Alagoas in 1839 on a sugar plantation near Maceió. His family, modest planters, had none of the vainglorious and lordly habits of the great landowners in the Northeast. Poor and overburdened with ten children, they gave him into the keeping of a more prosperous uncle, who owned a sugar mill and was involved in the tempestuous partisan struggles in the province. On completing in a Rio school the secondary course, as the preliminary instruction in the humanities was then called, he enlisted in an infantry battalion. In 1861 he matriculated in the Military Academy. He distinguished himself not by his studies, but by his physical strength and agility and by his fondness for painting the scenery of the school's little theater.

In 1861 Floriano obtained his first promotion, to second lieutenant in the artillery. In 1865 he joined the campaign against the dictator of Paraguay, in command of a small river squadron at Uruguaiana that kept two enemy units from joining forces. He became noted at once for his phlegmatic bravery and was promoted to the next higher rank. He took part in several of the big battles, such as Tuiuti, Itororó, Lomas Valentinas, and Angustura. His cool contempt for danger was constantly discussed by his companions. On one occasion he is said to have calmly exposed himself to enemy fire in order to set an example of courage for his frightened men. He did not return to Brazil until the death of López ended the war. By then he was a lieutenant colonel, covered with military honors.

With the return of peace, Floriano's career turned bureaucratic, like that of so many other officers. He served on various unimportant commissions and enjoyed frequent vacations on his uncle's sugar plantation. Here he also married one of his cousins. On behalf of the central government, Floriano undertook an investigation and housecleaning of the scandalous school-examination situation in Maceió in 1882. In the following year he was promoted to brigadier (equivalent to today's brigadier general). While commandant in Pernambuco and Ceará he must have discreetly endorsed the campaign for abolition of slavery, for he was proclaimed an honorary member of "Ceará Livre," the abolitionist club of Recife.

In 1884 Floriano was named president and military commandant of Mato Grosso province, and became interested in developing the *herva mate** industry. He tried to repress the wild Indians (who frequently menaced the town of Cuiabá) by the same violent methods used by the pioneers in the United States and by the caudillos in Argentina. He also became attracted by political issues, joined the Liberal party, and took a more positive position in the abolitionist movement.

In his private correspondence, Floriano's allusions to politics, which he thought of only in terms of party rivalries, are vague. The military question, which had so stirred many of his colleagues and had ended by converting Deodoro to the republican revolution, did not disturb him. Nevertheless, in an intimate letter to a friend written from Alagoas in July 1887, he remarked briefly:

I saw the solution offered to the military question; without a doubt it goes beyond everyone's expectations. This fact alone demonstrates overwhelmingly the rottenness that pervades our poor country, which stands in great need of a military dictatorship to clean it up. As a Liberal, I cannot wish government by the sword for my country; but there is no one who doesn't know, and the examples are there, that it can purify the blood of a corrupt social body such as ours.

In the light of his own later dictatorship, a prophetic significance could have been attached to these words. Floriano was describing the path he himself would follow. But in the context of his correspondence, two and a half years before the Republic, his words indicate merely a passing irritation, a venting of feelings. He continued peaceably serving the Empire.

At one time Floriano considered retiring from the army in order to take on the operation of the sugar plantation in Alagoas. But while he was in command of the Second Brigade, stationed in the imperial capital, he was named acting Adjutant General of the army. With the inauguration of the Ouro Prêto cabinet, he achieved the third highest military rank, field marshal, and his appointment as Adjutant General was made permanent. The coming of the Republic found him at the peak of his military and administrative careers.

What was Floriano's attitude toward the new regime? As in everything relating to him, a clear-cut answer is difficult. In the minds of his early fellow partisans, he had long been in favor of the Republic; he was

---

* *Herva mate—yerba mate* in Spanish, and Paraguay tea in English—is an evergreen shrub or small tree (*Ilex paraguayensis*) from whose leaves is brewed an aromatic beverage, high in caffeine, popular in much of southern South America. JLT

discreetly involved in the military conspiracy that toppled the throne of Pedro II. But the head of the monarchy's last cabinet, Ouro Prêto, believed absolutely in his loyalty to the old institutions. His comrades, as well as the civilians who won Deodoro over to the republican movement, were not sure of the reception they would get from the Adjutant General, upon whom rested the immediate responsibility for the defense of the beleaguered general headquarters and of the ministers gathered within its walls.

It would appear that Floriano, always inclined to ambivalence, was basically indifferent to forms of government. As a cold realist and political opportunist, he did not decide until the last minute, and then decided that neither Ouro Prêto nor the Empire seemed worth the lives that would be sacrificed by throwing the headquarters reserves against Deodoro's insurgent troops. He declared for the Republic probably without anything like Deodoro's scruples.

On the eve of November 15th, holding the most responsible post in the army, he appeared to be a perfectly loyal and trustworthy soldier. On the 13th he had thanked Ouro Prêto for some small favor, adding that the head of government "must have heard that some sort of plot was being hatched on the outside, but give it no importance and depend on the loyalty of the military chiefs, who are on the alert." Two days before he said this, Floriano supposedly had a personal meeting with Deodoro in which he offered to be a go-between for any conciliatory solution. Finally, when he saw that agreement was impossible, he declared in one of his picturesque and cryptic phrases: "Well, if the thing is to be against the *casacas* [frock coats], I've still got my old gun." He then asked to be relieved of his post as Adjutant General or to be retired from active service, but was dissuaded from insisting on either step. In chapter 4 we described his behavior on the morning of November 15th, and his short dialogue with Ouro Prêto.

During the first phase of the Provisional Government, Floriano, still Adjutant General, gave others little cause to talk about him. The monarchists did not forgive what they termed his betrayal of the Empire; the republicans extolled his siding with the revolutionary forces and thereby preventing a fratricidal war. On May 19, 1890, Floriano replaced Benjamin Constant as Minister of War; on August 19th he replaced Rui Barbosa as vice-chief of the Provisional Government.

In the council of ministers, Floriano's attitude was always discreet. In the most serious clashes with Deodoro, such as that over the raid on the offices of *A Tribuna,* he stood solidly with his colleagues. When the entire cabinet resigned, he was appointed minister of the Supreme Military

Tribunal, at the same time occupying a chair in the Constituent Assembly as a senator from his native state, Alagoas. After Congress elected him Vice-President of the Republic, he seemed to withdraw from political activity. When he returned to Rio after an illness in Minas, he did not once preside in the Senate as he was supposed to under the Constitution. His poor health was always a pretext for his withdrawing from situations or turning aside conversations that did not suit him.

Clearly he was a man biding his time, meanwhile moving tenaciously in the shadows. He understood, perhaps better than any professional politician, the rapid disintegration of Deodoro's government under the Lucena ministry. In the fight between Congress and Deodoro, Floriano stood on the sidelines, knowing that he was indispensable to the final decision, as he had been on November 15th. If Deodoro did not have much faith in Floriano's loyalty (as his remarks to Lucena indicate), nevertheless he could not treat him as a declared enemy. The Congress, on the other hand, thought him an easy tool in its fight against Deodoro. It soon did penance for its ingenuous mistake.

Deodoro's abdication could not have surprised Floriano much. On November 23rd he received with perfect impassivity Deodoro's War Minister, who called to invite him to assume the presidency of the Republic. In the government palace, where he witnessed the emotion of the Marshal and his dedicated friends, Floriano did not for an instant lose his self-control. He appeared to be the most distant, the most indifferent of men. "May it please Heaven that you will be more fortunate or better understood than I," said Deodoro, emotionally upset. Floriano replied with barely a vague word of praise for his old comrade-in-arms. His first concern was to get word to the commander of the naval squadron in revolt that the victory had been won without a struggle. Then, in a manifesto to Brazil that was somewhat an answer to Deodoro's, he explained his taking over the government.

In justifying his abdication, the founder of the Republic had once again poured out his woes. To save Brazil, he had been compelled to dissolve the Congress, but "the situation in which the nation, in these latter days, finds itself, the ingratitude of those for whom I sacrificed myself the most, and the desire not to let civil war break out in my beloved land move me to hand over the power to the functionary [sic] who must replace me."

The tone of the document signed by Floriano is different:

The navy, a large part of the army, and citizens of various classes brought about by force of arms the reestablishment of the Constitution and of the laws suspended by the decree that dissolved the national Congress. History will record this civic deed by the armed forces in behalf of law, which cannot be replaced by force, but at the same time it will recall also the act of abnegation and patriotism of Generalissimo Marshal Deodoro da Fonseca. . . . To obey fundamental law and to fulfill the intention of this triumphant revolution, I must regard as null and void the act by which the Congress was dissolved on the 3rd of this month, raise the state of siege in this capital and in Niterói, and reestablish all constitutional rights and safeguards. The administration of fiscal affairs will be one of my major concerns.

Later, he described his concern in a more explicit phrase: he was the "sentinel of the Treasury."

Floriano brought some outstanding personalities into his first cabinet, including the jurist José Higino Duarte as Minister of the Interior and Justice, and the Conselheiro Rodrigues Alves (a carry-over from the monarchy who had discreetly accepted the Republic) as Finance Minister. The military portfolios were allocated, naturally, to Admiral Custódio José de Melo and General José Simeão de Oliveira, the top conspirators against Deodoro.

Following its dreadful apprehensions over the coup d'etat and the navy's revolt, the nation trustingly accepted Floriano's accession. The law had triumphed; the constitutional regime had been fully restored. The reinstated Congress supposed itself the big winner. The impression created abroad was sympathetic.

The peaceful atmosphere lasted only a few days. The state governors who had supported Deodoro's coup, though they were quick to jump on Floriano's bandwagon, were deposed by the opposition factions allied with the army and navy and prevented from transmitting their governments to their legal successors. Few of them offered any resistance. On the contrary: the governor of Ceará, among others, forgetting the solidarity he had warmly expressed to Deodoro the day before, had enthusiastically gone over to Floriano. In a famous telegram, which can be quoted as a specimen of the style of the period, the governor exclaimed: "All of Brazil is exultant, and reposing confidence in the profound wisdom of her valorous soldier, her chief magistrate, turns to you and remains tranquil. Ceará is with me and therefore with you." He subsequently had to be deposed by force. In Rio de Janeiro and São Paulo a show of military strength also proved necessary to force the governors out of office. In Rio Grande do Sul, where Júlio de Castilhos had been ousted shortly after November 3rd, a great revolutionary movement was openly prepared.

In Pernambuco, where the Baron of Lucena was striving to strengthen his party, public passions rose to extreme heights. The governor, who had fallen over himself in praise of Deodoro, handed his office over to his successor, who then was ousted by an armed attack on the palace. Shortly after, when asked to choose a new governor for the state from a list of three names, Floriano suggested a young military man, Alexandre José Barbosa, whose name was not on the list.

The occurrences in the other states did not differ much from those in Pernambuco: threatened revolution, isolated riots, general confusion, and, finally, direct intervention by the Union government. The Navy Minister, Custódio José de Melo, at the peak of his political influence, worked alongside the Vice-President as a sort of high constable of the nascent dictatorship. He had friends and fellow partisans everywhere whom he felt he had to protect, in the sincere desire, perhaps, to lessen the tensions. In his native state of Bahia he worked to secure the governorship for Conselheiro Saraiva, the former Nestor of the Second Reign, who had lived through the republican Constituent Assembly in a state of shock.

In far-off Mato Grosso the federal forces, split between dissident parties, provoked armed clashes that spread to the various towns. In nearly all the states the local assemblies and magistracies were dissolved, or, as the opposition deputy [later Brazilian President] Epitácio Pessoa described it, "side by side with one large coup d'etat there were twenty smaller ones."

In the general disturbance Floriano went about placing persons who had his immediate confidence, usually young military officers, in charge of local governments. His ministers resigned one after another and were replaced without trouble. Skeptical about men's worth, Floriano attached little importance to any special aptitudes that they might reveal. His assistants were kept in a constant square dance, moving from one portfolio to another, and at times holding down two or more at once. He alone was the government, with his suspicious vigilance and his disguised will to power.

The turmoil in the states reflected itself immediately in national politics. The majority in Congress, who had supported Floriano in order to get rid of Deodoro, broke away from him. Defense of state autonomy or of the federative principle was the pretext for the new opposition. The Navy Minister, Custódio José de Melo, thinking of himself as the leading national figure of the November 23rd movement, sought to interfere in all political and administrative affairs, assuming his authority to be equal to that of Floriano, who temporized and awaited the right moment to obliterate him.

Rui Barbosa, who in the last session of the dissolved Congress had vehemently criticized the financial policy of the Baron of Lucena, renewed his parliamentary activity by denouncing the dismissal of the state governors. A few days later, in a manifesto renouncing his Senatorial seat, he declared: "Between a dictatorship that in dissolving the Federal Congress depends upon the weakness of local governments, and another that dissolves the local governments, basing its support on the reinstated Congress, there is no appreciable improvement." Not only in the Senate but in the *Jornal do Brasil* (whose management he had undertaken) and before the Supreme Court, Rui Barbosa was the major voice of the opposition, fearlessly defending Floriano's opponents.

In the Congress and in the press, the campaign against the dictatorship of the former Vice-President was even more violent than against Deodoro's. Some young deputies, such as Epitácio Pessoa of Paraíba, José Mariano of Pernambuco, and J. J. Seabra of Bahia, were the most ardent fighters. Deodoro's military and civilian friends, and all who felt that their political machines had been ruined by the wholesale dismissals, were drawn to them.

On the other hand, the republicans of São Paulo, anxious only to avoid new civilian conflicts, frankly supported Floriano, as did the main body of positivists, who wielded great influence in military circles. In Rio Grande do Sul the political confusion was extreme; in spite of their endorsement of Deodoro's coup, Júlio de Castilhos and his supporters inclined toward Floriano, whose government suited their ideology in many ways. Most of the men of letters, who since the advent of the Republic had become more involved in politics, were openly hostile toward the caboclo from the North, though later some of them would be among his most fanatic followers. They were especially hostile toward Admiral Custódio José de Melo, the favorite butt of their satires.

The campaign of political opposition found some sympathy in certain military circles. On January 19, 1892, under the leadership of a Sergeant Silvino de Macedo, the fortress of Santa Cruz rebelled; it was shortly backed up by the Laje fortress [both are in Guanabara Bay]. Congress voluntarily adjourned on January 22 to allow Floriano to restore order. The government was unable to pin the blame on those most responsible, but the speed, decisiveness, and cold-bloodedness with which Floriano repressed the rebellion gave the people their first taste of the fighting ability of the man who ruled them. This taste was not enough, however, to intimidate his adversaries.

In the press, there appeared the suggestion that he call for a new presidential election. Deviating on this point from its North American and Argentine models, Article 42 of the Constitution provided that "if there is a vacancy from any cause in the presidency or vice-presidency, and less than two years of the presidential term have elapsed, a new election shall be held." Since Deodoro had renounced the Presidency during the first year of his term, it was incumbent on Floriano to carry out the provisions of the Constitution.

Those who wanted to keep the Vice-President in control of the government at all costs, and those who in good faith feared the dangers of a new presidential election, got around Article 42 by falling back on the Transitory Dispositions. In the permanent text, the Constituent Assembly had fixed the rules for future presidential and vice-presidential elections by popular and direct vote. In the Transitory Dispositions it had determined the rules for the first election, and had prescribed further that "the President and Vice-President elected in accordance with this article (that is, by the Congress) shall occupy the presidency and vice-presidency of the Republic during the President's first term of office." According to this, new elections could not be held during that period.

A lengthy opinion that had been rendered by the Committee on the Constitution and Justice of the Chamber of Deputies, which, like the Senate, had been called upon to express its views on the controversy, went further. It stated that there had been an evident misprint in the text of the Constitution, namely, the use of the disjunctive *ou* [or] instead of the connective *e* [and]. In other words, a new election was to be held only if both offices, of the President *and* the Vice-President, fell vacant during the first two years of the presidential term.

Supported by a questionable legal technicality, the result of an interpretation seemingly much more political and opportunistic than judicial (Rui Barbosa, in reply to a letter from the man of letters Pardal Mallet, called it absurd), Floriano kept himself in the presidency. He insisted, however, on retaining the title of Vice-President. His adversaries, civilian and military, redoubled their revolutionary plotting.

On March 31, 1892, thirteen general officers of both the army and the navy sent him a short message urging him to order a presidential election:

The undersigned general officers of the army and navy, not wishing by their silence to share in the moral responsibility for the disorganization the states find themselves in because of undue armed intervention in the ousting of their governors, which in turn brought about the deaths of innumerable citizens and the implanting of terror, doubt, and sorrow in the hearts of families, appeal to you, Marshal, to put an end to so lamentable a situation. If this state of general disorganization continues much longer, the achievement of November 15, 1889, will be converted into the most complete anarchy. The undersigned believe that only by means of an election for the presidency of the Republic, to take place at once as provided in the Federal Constitution and electoral law, and to be held freely and without pressure, can the confidence, quiet, and tranquility of the Brazilian family, as well as the good opinion of the Republic held abroad, which is now so badly shaken, be restored. We hope and expect that you will issue your wise orders for this election, and that you will not shrink from adding this important civic service to the many you have rendered the nation on the field of battle.

Heading the list of signatures on this document were those of Marshal Almeida Barreto, who on November 15th, while in command of the loyalist forces at the general headquarters, had joined the republican revolution, Admiral Wandenkolk, former Navy Minister under Deodoro, and General João Severiano da Fonseca, an army doctor and one of Deodoro's brothers. At Itamaraty palace Floriano received the threatening manifesto with his usual serenity. That same evening he deprived the signers of their military commissions and sent them into retirement.

Addressing the nation in his turn, Floriano criticized those who arrogated to themselves the right to be

supreme interpreters of the Constitution, [and who,] though invested with high-ranking commissions to watch over and defend the honor of the nation, the integrity of its territory, and its internal order, are the first to encourage disorder in the country and to lend discredit abroad, where it might be falsely believed that the Brazilian Republic had reached a disastrous period of pronunciamentos and of complete ruin.

He pointed out that several of the signers of the manifesto had been ardent supporters of the November 3rd coup, and he severely censured their undisciplined spirit.

One general and one admiral expressed regret for signing the manifesto; the others stood by their decision and protested against being forced into retirement. The Military Club endorsed the proposal by two young officers, Ximeno de Villero and Tasso Fragoso, to "eliminate from their midst the signers of the manifesto." Thus Floriano revealed again to the nation the implacable energy hidden under his tired and listless appearance.

The Congress being adjourned, Floriano was fully aware that he was heading rapidly and securely toward dictatorship. All the powers of the state were centered in him. The positivists, who had not succeeded in converting the impulsive Deodoro into the Republic's ideal dictator, now began to idolize his successor. The students in the military and civilian schools were filled with their first, hot enthusiasm for the future Iron Marshal. Patriotic battalions increased in numbers. Brazil, peaceful and sleepy during the Second Reign, appeared to arm herself for vigilance. The more impressionable republicans imagined that the fate of the political system depended on defending the legality of Floriano's power.

Driven to desperation in their fight against Floriano, the plotters tried to regalvanize Deodoro's prestige. Ten days after the generals' manifesto, they staged a great public demonstration in honor of the former head of the Provisional Government, whose resignation, they said, had not been expressly accepted by Congress. Because of illness, Deodoro could not receive the demonstrators, but the pretext for street riots had been found. Excited groups filled the city; the bolder ones tried to reach the presidential palace. Floriano calmly arrived by train from his modest residence in a distant suburb and personally arrested the men he considered the most dangerous. On the following day he deported them to unhealthy and almost inaccessible regions on Brazil's northern frontiers. In the gangs of deportees to the upper reaches of the Amazon and among the prisoners in the forts, there were military men, journalists, men of letters, and members of Congress, the last despite their Congressional immunity.

The Vice-President's dictatorship was now a dangerous reality for his adversaries. They began to realize that the game with the dissembling, inflexible Floriano was becoming infinitely more difficult than it had been with the impetuous Deodoro, that no one would be able to drive him into resigning by threats of civil war. He was reported to have said that only the law or death could remove him from office, that he was convinced of the legality of his government, and that he had never feared death. Because of this, the approaching revolt led by Admiral Custódio José de Melo would not limit itself this time to maneuvers of war vessels in Guanabara Bay, or to pot shots at the dome of Candelária church.

The situation in Rio de Janeiro was one of constant alarms and daily rumors of new revolts. The plotters of April 10 had hardly been granted amnesty before they returned to engage in new revolutionary conspiracies. The opposition press, whose freedom had been spared by the state of siege, openly preached revolution and even the personal elimination of the head of government. Distinguished for their virulent language were the two newspapers *O Combate,* published by Pardal Mallet, and *A Cidade,* belonging to the famous abolitionist orator José do Patrocínio. The most passionate and impetuous of Floriano's champions was also a writer, Raúl Pompeia, whose high intellect and morbid sensitiveness made a most interesting contribution to Brazilian letters.

Almost simultaneously with subversive movements in Rio Grande do Sul and Minas Gerais, there appeared signs of a conspiracy in São Paulo to unseat the governor. Shortly thereafter, a plot developed in Minas to create a new federative unit by cutting off a southern section of the state. Floriano's government put out the fires, without, however, being able to prevent the outbreak of others. The Republic, proclaimed in a bloodless revolution, was beginning to pay its delayed toll to the chronic caudillism of the continent. Deodoro, with the dissolution of Congress, had inaugurated a period of unrest for Brazil that was like the regency, but without its patriotic ideology. Rule by pronunciamentos, which Floriano had described as the greatest calamity that could befall the nation, had begun.

The young military, imbued with the positivist ideology and believing that dictatorships were needed to restore corrupt social organisms, were persuaded that the fate of the Republic depended on them. The more educated elements of Brazilian politics and society, who had lived in the orderly climate of the Empire and had applauded the liberal legislation of the first phase of the Provisional Government, found the new procedures profoundly repugnant. Being incapable, however, of organizing themselves into a great party of reaction that could bring out the latent strengths of the middle class, they withdrew into self-seeking or defeatist attitudes, or tried, in their turn, to gather around representatives of the armed forces.

In reinstating the dissolved Congress, Floriano had appeared to be the embodiment of law and order against anarchy and militarism. The richest communities in Brazil (and so, by definition, the most conservative), such as São Paulo and Minas, hastened to pledge support to Floriano's government, whose legality the Congress had expressly recognized. In the name of the Paulista republicans, Campos Sales once more undertook to reconcile rancors and injured pride, notably that of Admiral Wandenkolk.

Soon, however, Floriano shattered the last illusion that he might be a tool of political eggheads or of their attempts at pacification. Because of his authoritarian temperament, or because he was sincerely convinced that the great constitutional crisis of the Republic could not be resolved by the old panaceas of appeasement and hesitant liberalism, Floriano imposed his dictatorship over the torn and bleeding body of the Constitution.

The economically ruined and conservative masses of the nation became fearful and silent. The Congress fought hard to maintain its prestige as a political force. Rui Barbosa became the most intrepid defender of civil liberties. Having been the statesman most responsible for transplanting North American political institutions into Brazil, he naturally became their greatest theoretical interpreter, a sort of Chief Justice Marshall of the new Republic. Despairing of his campaign in the press and in the Congress, he resorted to the law. But the Federal Supreme Court, which he had imagined to be a perfect emulator of the Supreme Court in Washington, denied his petition for a writ of habeas corpus for political prisoners. As an example of Floriano's coldly ironic remarks, he is reported to have said at the time that "if the judges of the Court grant the politicians habeas corpus, I wonder who will grant them the habeas corpus they in their turn will need tomorrow."

Congress reconvened in ordinary session on May 3, 1892. The opposition did not lack grounds for vehement criticism: the ousting of the state governors, the arrest and exiling of members of Congress and military men, the failure of the courts, the disarray of public finances.

The Empire had lived peaceably owing to the rivalry between the two artificial parties whose stays in power Pedro II arbitrated. The Republic had not been able to improvise a political equilibrium to replace the one its revolutionary advent had upset. The political administration of the federated states had had to be placed in the hands of new figures, most of them young military men, with no experience in political affairs and, in the final analysis, subordinated directly to the central government.

Quickly, however, most of the monarchy's politicians, tacitly accepting the Republic, resumed their party politics, with the best wishes of the nation's conservative classes, who esteemed their experience in public affairs and who saw in them, above all else, a shield against military tyranny. But the lack of any discipline splintered them into numerous groups engaged in passionate contests for local office.

In order to exist, the federal government felt it had to compromise with the state factions. The constant temporizing and balancing of interests of every kind were reflected in the Congress, and understandably enough absorbed most of the President's time and attention.

In spite of the revolutionary movements, the strong tradition of individual civil rights inherited from the Empire had not yet been lost. Public administration was forced to yield at every turn to the demands of single persons or of powerful groups protected by the formalism of the law. The Encilhamento created a class of businessmen, of adventurers, of gamblers and speculators in the market and in foreign exchange, who directly or insidiously sought to interfere in public affairs, especially by means of Congressional influence. Thus Brazil had a sample of what the North American political rings and lobbyists were like.

The dissolution of Congress increased the political confusion. Obliged to defend the public order and to cope shortly thereafter with great subversive movements, the President had not been able to tackle any administrative problems. And if the routine business of the government was in chaos, its public finances looked like nothing short of ruin.

The heritage Floriano's government received was most burdensome. The financial crisis clearly revealed itself by the steady drop in the rate of exchange, in the value of securities, and in public revenues. The insecure political situation and the cleaning-up of the aftermath of the Encilhamento, which had devalued the money without creating any new sources of wealth, rendered even more delicate the task of the new government, whose public finances had been entrusted to the clear-sighted and balanced judgment of Rodrigues Alves [later President of Brazil].

The consequences of abolition, decreed with no economic preparation, were making themselves felt in the shortage of farm labor, and in the coincident high wages for free agricultural workers (especially in São Paulo) that only added to production costs without improving the extremely low purchasing power. The great sugar industry in the North, which, unlike the coffee industry in São Paulo, could not use immigrants to replace the slaves, was on the downgrade, impoverishing the already precarious local economy even more. The state of Rio de Janeiro, the center of the old and opulent latifundian barons of the monarchy, began a rapid decline. The gross national product, already very small, became noticeably smaller.

Discarding the bold plans of the Provisional Government, Brazil found herself, perhaps not poorer, but besieged by apprehensions and anguish, weakened by habits of gambling and risky ventures, and reduced to political and administrative anarchy. The income of the Union [during Deodoro's last fiscal year] was 208,000 contos, only 50,000 more than during the last fiscal year of the Empire. The paper currency in circulation, which on November 15, 1889, had stood at 200,000 contos, had increased to 514,000, that is, more than double the federal income, something which apparently has not happened at any other time in the financial history of Brazil.

The Republic had not obtained any foreign loans, being satisfied with the 29 million pounds sterling inherited from the previous regime. The consolidated internal debt amounted to almost 400,000 contos. The exportation of coffee and of native rubber, holding more or less steady at the 1889 level of 22 million pounds and 5½ million pounds, respectively, barely sustained the national economy. Attempts to start a manufacturing industry had not had time to show appreciable results. Brazil continued to be restricted to her old economic role of exporting a few agricultural products and raw materials, and importing everything else for her minimum needs.

On taking charge of the government, Floriano seemed especially preoccupied with eliminating scandalous deals. The program of his Finance Minister was modest and cautious: economies in the administration, expropriation of the banks of emission, and gradual redemption of the excess paper money. The Congress, battered by conflicts of interest between groups tied to the old inflationist policy, had no well-defined course, and tried to reconcile those favoring and those opposing issuance of paper currency.

The pleasant dream of the Provisional Government, to promote urban industries by credit inflation and protective tariffs, had quickly vanished. The tax system, based on import taxes, placed the government in a vicious circle: if imports were not restricted, the outflow of gold was increased; by restricting them, the government reduced the revenue on which it depended for the expenses of its administration. The Finance Ministers, trying vainly to bring some kind of order to the financial situation, followed one another in and out of office in rapid succession, sometimes going from their offices to prison.

Forced to forget his earlier intentions to economize, to be a "sentinel of the Treasury," Floriano turned to every possible source of money. The Congress was deeply divided on the financial issue. Under Lucena's ministry, the majority in Congress had fought uncompromisingly against the system of emission of banknotes. The Chamber of Deputies had finally succeeded in passing by a large majority a plan under which the total emissions were to be limited to the outstanding volume; the banks in the meantime were to restore their gold reserves to pay off their banknotes within five years. The *papelistas* [paper advocates] had just started their opposition to the plan with a long and fiery speech by Rui Barbosa when the November 3rd coup took place.

Under Floriano's government the financial policy underwent new changes. The papelistas, led by Senators Rui Barbosa and Amaro Cavalcanti, insisted on maintaining the banks' old privileges. The most influential of the government's supporters radically opposed them, and favored the Treasury's expropriation of the banknotes as recommended by the Finance Minister, Rodrigues Alves. The government obtained a loan of one million pounds sterling from the Rothschilds, repayable in 18 months. The foreign exchange rates, worsening steadily, consumed more than a third of the federal revenue (then about 300,000 contos).

Not having received Floriano Peixoto's full acquiescence to his plan for expropriating the currency issued by the banks, and thus cleaning up the aftermath of the Encilhamento, Rodrigues Alves resigned as Finance Minister and was succeeded by Serzedelo Correia. In Congress plans for monetary reform multiplied, often in disharmony with the government, which found itself unable to establish any firm policy. The political faction headed by Francisco Glicério proposed a merger of the Banco do Brasil with the Banco da República, the new bank to be charged with substituting within two years its own emissions for those of the other banks and of the Treasury. Thus there was a return to Rui Barbosa's policy, which he had changed during the Provisional Government to emissions by a single bank instead of by more than one. The Glicério bill was approved by the Chamber against the government's wishes, though there had not been time before the adjournment of Congress [on January 22] to debate it in the Senate. During the Congressional recess, Serzedelo Correia decreed the merger of the two banks. The new Banco da República dos Estados Unidos do Brasil was given the right to issue currency up to twice the value of its gold reserve. Thus satisfying the partisans of bank emissions, the government's decree also satisfied the opposite doctrinaire line of thought by permitting the issuance of 100,000 contos in Treasury bonds to meet the needs of agriculture and industry. In addition, the government took possession of a foreign loan of four million pounds sterling granted to the Minas Railroad Company, and put back into circulation the amount of currency that had been redeemed.

All these contradictory measures only worsened the public finances. In impoverished Brazil, where the establishment of the most rudimentary economic policy was not even attempted, the mass of inconvertible paper rose from 192,000 contos in 1889 to 712,000 in 1894, of which 370,000 (not counting Treasury bonds) had been issued directly by the government, even as the sterling rate of exchange dropped from 27 pence to 10 pence to the milreis. The foreign banks speculated freely on the rate of exchange, causing it to rise or fall as they wished.

Because of all this disorder, the Federalist revolution in Rio Grande and the navy's revolt in Rio gave rise to a temporary realignment of political forces strong enough to assure the government a parliamentary majority. Francisco Glicério, an old propagandist for the Republic and its Minister of Agriculture in Deodoro's cabinet, headed the new party. It was a most diverse assemblage: old-time republicans, ex-monarchists, moderate Liberals, old-fashioned Conservatives, federalists, centralists, hotheaded Florianistas or "loyalists," intransigent Jacobins, positivists, intractable presidentialists, and even sympathizers with Custódio de Melo's revolt.

"A cathedral open to all creeds" was the term used by one deputy to describe the new party, which took the name of Partido Republicano Federal [hereinafter PRF]. Enjoying the personal esteem of Floriano Peixoto, Francisco Glicério, who [as a poor young man] had ably forged ahead on his own in the rural plutocracy of São Paulo, had the qualities needed to direct, amid a thousand daily difficulties, the catchall party he had built.

Preoccupied with his government's fight for survival, Floriano gave his leader a free hand in political and parliamentary matters. Among other things, Glicério became the general of the "21 brigades" (the representatives in Congress of the twenty states and the Federal District), and thus justified, for the first time, the gold braid of an honorary general with which the Provisional Government had rewarded him and the other ministers.

An atmosphere of apprehension, and very often of distress, prevailed throughout all of 1892. Political hatreds were dominant in everything. No one doubted the imminence of a revolution, whose explosion Floriano only awaited to put it down and to impose the rule of his executive authority. The monarchists had moved to the larger centers of Europe and the River Plate, where they carried on a strong campaign to discredit the Republic. The fanatic nationalistic sentiments of the young people who followed Floriano turned into aggressive xenophobia. The government, obliged to defend itself on all sides, lived from day to day on expedients advocated by its informal counselors and its transitory ministers.

8. The Crisis in Rio Grande do Sul

Special case of Rio Grande do Sul — Psychology of the gaúcho people — Júlio de Castilhos and Silveira Martins — Early warning signs of the Federalist revolution — Floriano's attitude — Ministerial crisis.

It was toward Rio Grande do Sul that the fondest hopes for rebellion against Floriano's dictatorship turned. The navy (another great force still almost intact), having compelled Deodoro to resign on November 23rd, might repeat the same feat against the Vice-President, or at least force him to generally reconstruct national policy. Rio Grande do Sul and the navy—here were the two great supports of Floriano's adversaries, the monarchists who still longed for the *ancien régime,* and the liberal minorities that wanted Brazil to resume her peaceful growth under the Republic.

Rio Grande do Sul was wholly unlike any other region of Brazil. Because of its physical geography, its ethnic and social background, its economic activities, its conditions as a frontier province, and its political habits and customs, Rio Grande do Sul had always been given special attention by the rulers of Brazil. Its peculiarities kept it from blending easily with the rest of the country. Its vast and monotonous grasslands have little contact with the ocean, despite its extensive, flat, low-lying Atlantic seaboard, which is devoid of natural harbors,* a loss its great inland lake, Lagoa dos Patos, could not replace. Rio Grande do Sul, in a permanent state of alert on its frontiers with foreign countries, therefore had to develop in greater isolation from the rest of Brazil than the other provinces. Its plains and foothills were originally crisscrossed and settled by Paulista pioneers, by those who had braved jungles and over-

* The state's only harbor of any consequence (Rio Grande) lies at the southern end of Lagoa dos Patos, at whose northern end the capital, Pôrto Alegre, is situated. JLT

run the Jesuit Indian compounds, and by adventurers from the North, Spaniards from the River Plate, and Portuguese from the Azores.

Rio Grande do Sul, the last region to be brought into the national community, had not undergone the hierarchical formation that the rest of Brazil had. Cattle raising on unfenced plains obviated the system of latifundia, and thus there rose no rural aristocracy jealous of its privileges and civilization as happened everywhere else in the country. Although close commercial ties with Uruguay and Argentina gave the Rio-Grandenses a psychology rather different from that of other Brazilians, this foreign trade also heightened their instinct for national defense.

The life of the plains and the herding of cattle gave the gaúcho* of Rio Grande do Sul (like his counterpart in the River Plate countries) the habits of horsemen and herdsmen, and thus of adventure, fighting, and guerrilla warfare. The long civil war of the Farrapos had aroused his old martial instincts, although the mollifying policies of the Second Reign later subdued them. The growth of German and Italian settlements in the hill regions of the province had brought its primitive, exclusively pastoral economy other sources of wealth and had somewhat modified its social type. The very system of small-scale agriculture in the foreign settlements also helped differentiate Rio Grande do Sul from the predominant pattern of Brazilian society, which was defined by the sugar baron of the Northeast and the fazendeiro of São Paulo and Rio de Janeiro.

Like all peoples who lack the traditional discipline of a class society, the Rio-Grandenses always leaned toward a strong state or toward state-controlled organizations. In no other Brazilian province did the political parties put down such deep roots or the individual leaders attain such great influence. With a sense of individual freedom and equality perhaps greater than that of any other Brazilian, the gaúcho of Rio Grande do Sul was at the same time more prone to join parties, a fading memory perhaps from the dim past of clans or nomadic tribes.

During the last phase of the Second Reign, the Liberal party, dominated by its leader, Conselheiro Gaspar da Silveira Martins, had virtually monopolized political control of Rio Grande do Sul. A gaúcho of the purest stripe, Silveira Martins added singular virtues to the common qualities and faults of his people, which made him stand out in bold relief in the Brazil of the late 1880s. Everything about him seemed far above average: his physical strength [Joaquim Nabuco referred to

* *Gaúcho:* formerly a cowboy or herdsman, nowadays a native or inhabitant of Rio Grande do Sul. The pronunciation in Portuguese is *gah-oo-shoo*. JLT

him as the "Samson of the Empire"], his passions, his dazzling intellect, his torrential eloquence.* Thus he seems to have been one of those few men who, by throwing themselves violently into whatever they do, are capable, if circumstances permit, of brutally changing the peaceful course of events, a type of which Mirabeau was the highest model, of which Danton and Gambetta were more vicious imitations, and of which Kemal Ataturk is the perfect contemporary example.

Often implacable in his condemnation of the Empire, frequently wrong in his judgments and attitudes, proud, fearless, and feared, Silveira Martins was approaching his political apex in the twilight of Pedro II's reign. He was president of his province and a life Senator of the Empire, and despite the fears he aroused, he was ripe for the presidency of the Council, a post no Rio-Grandense had held until then. On November 15, 1889, Ouro Prêto considered him the only politician capable of successfully counteracting the republican coup. But the Republic arrested him as he was en route from Rio Grande do Sul to Rio de Janeiro and exiled him to Europe, for of all the monarchy's political chiefs, Silveira Martins was the one with the greatest popular appeal in his war-hardened province and the only one with the daring needed to attempt a counterrevolution.

With its great Liberal chief in exile, Rio Grande do Sul was taken over by the small group of long-time republicans. Among them was Júlio de Castilhos, who soon came to the fore with growing authority. Castilhos had been born in 1860 on a cattle ranch in the interior of the province. His childhood, therefore, had been spent in typical gaúcho surroundings, frugal and rugged, in which the old civil wars and the federalist and republican aspirations had not been forgotten. From 1877 to 1881, he attended the law school in São Paulo, and while there he was attracted by the republican propaganda initiated by the Manifesto of 1870. He tried his hand at political journalism and became infected by the positivist doctrine, whose spread in certain intellectual centers of Brazil was intensified after the philosophical movement led by Teófilo Braga in Portugal.

Returning to Rio Grande do Sul, Castilhos joined Venâncio Aires in organizing republican propaganda there. When the republican newspaper *A Federação* was founded in 1884, he became its editor-in-chief. In journalism his love for polemics, so often personal and aggressive,

---

* He was described by another writer as "Brazil's most famous orator, whose speeches were compared to a great blaze, a flame, a fire, a volcano, an earthquake, thunder and lightning." JLT

merged with his devotion to doctrine. Through the press he maintained a stubborn campaign against the Empire, against slavery, and against Silveira Martins. His positivist leanings turned him away from the liberal republicans in São Paulo, and he became identified with the young officers who were disciples of Benjamin Constant. When the Republic was proclaimed, he was one of those who nominated the Viscount of Pelotas for state governor.

Pelotas, an old soldier-hero of the war with Paraguay, and a Senator of the Empire, had played a leading role in the "military question." Appointed a secretary in Pelotas's government, Castilhos assumed in fact the political and administrative direction of the state. He had a falling-out with Pelotas soon after and retired from the government. The old general himself did not linger long, either. Nominated to replace him, Castilhos refused, but submitted the name of General Frota. Before long, dissenting from Deodoro's financial policy, especially the founding of the Banco Emissor do Rio Grande do Sul, General Frota and his Castilhista friends renounced their posts. Various ephemeral administrations were then appointed until Castilhos was finally elected the constitutional governor [in 1890].

At the time he became head of the state government, Castilhos no longer enjoyed the unanimous backing of his old republican companions. The disaffection of Demétrio Ribeiro, Assis Brasil, Barros Casal, and Antão de Faria established an opposition party within the body of orthodox republicans, and swelled the numbers of his stubborn and resolute enemies. As a result, just before the outbreak of the revolution of 1893, two big parties were competing for power: the Republican party headed by Castilhos, and the Federalist party, in which the various oppositionists united under the supreme leadership of Silveira Martins to fight what they called "the positivist dictatorship, an offense to the Federal Constitution." The old warring impulses of frontier caudillism, dormant for nearly sixty years, were aroused once more to begin the cruelest of Brazil's civil wars.

As head of his delegation to the national Constituent Assembly Castilhos set himself up as champion of the ultrafederalist and positivist stream of thought. Everything that he failed to get into the Federal Constitution was later included in his state's constitution: a single chamber exclusively budgetary in action, appointment of the vice-governor of the state by its governor, reelection of the governor, free education, etc. This positivist constitution was the grand pretext for revolutions during Castilhos's era and, during the thirty-year governorship of his successor, Borges de Medeiros, the permanent cause of bitter partisan fights.

When Floriano Peixoto assumed the presidency of the Republic, Júlio de Castilhos had already been deposed from the government of Rio Grande do Sul. In not openly opposing the November 3rd coup (for the sake of maintaining public order, though he disapproved of it), it would seem Castilhos was self-condemned. But, on the contrary, Floriano's whole personal policy was aimed at accommodation with the Castilhistas, who were closely tied to the young positivist officers who surrounded Floriano. With his extraordinary capacity for covering up and temporizing, Floriano managed to gain time and prolong the confused state of affairs in Rio-Grandense politics to the point that the return of Castilhos's strong rule would later be imperative for the defense of the Republic.

Custódio José de Melo later related in his book about the navy's revolt that Floriano had made believe he sided with Castilhos's adversaries (among whom was Custódio himself) even as he prepared for their sure and final defeat. The wary President of the Republic foresaw more clearly and acutely than the republican politicians, broken into numerous factions, that the parade of passing figures and perturbing events in Rio Grande do Sul presaged a decisive showdown between Castilhos and Silveira Martins, who were perhaps symbols of two great undercurrents of ideas and sentiments in the life of Rio Grande, possibly of the entire nation. Without Castilhos's presence there, dominion over Rio Grande do Sul would sooner or later fall into the powerful hands of Silveira Martins. How much might the victory of the former Liberal leader menace Floriano and the Republic?

On his return from exile [probably early in 1890], Silveira Martins had accepted the Republic as a *fait accompli,* as had the great majority of monarchists. Nevertheless, direct contact with the immense disorder that prevailed in the country during the first two years of the new regime convinced him (as it did all conservative men) that, in order to save itself, the Republic would have to travel another road. In particular, a strife-ridden Rio Grande do Sul poised for civil war and under the sway of Castilhos's positivist constitution probably aggravated his fears. Parliamentarism was the possible rallying point. He assumed the spiritual leadership of the oppositionist elements that General Silva Tavares had congregated. An old political strategist, he tried at the start to separate the local problem from the general one: fight the Castilhista positivism, not Floriano.

The Republicans, under the leadership of Júlio de Castilhos, had refused to resign themselves to the loss of their power, which had been snatched from them by surprise even before November 23rd. The junta that had replaced Júlio de Castilhos lasted only a short while, poisoned to death by its own inner rivalries, and the governorship of the state passed to General Barreto Leite. A few days after the uprising in the Rio fort of Santa Cruz, Júlio de Castilhos (claiming the title of rightful governor) and his friends took over a public building in Pôrto Alegre. In it they installed the seat of government, and they forced General Barreto to take refuge on the gunboat *Marajó*. The sedition spread to other parts of the state, where the caudillism of frontier days, almost forgotten since the war of the Farrapos, sprang back to life in the service of the warring parties. Urged by Custódio de Melo, Floriano sustained General Barreto's precarious authority by naming him commandant of the military district, from which he removed the undependable General Barcelos. The "Castilhistas" desisted from their first revolutionary attempt, only to return at a later date with Floriano's full blessings.

The Federalist convention, which met in Bagé in June 1892, adopted the party's resolutions against the regime in Rio Grande: to replace the state's positivist constitution by a representative republican one based on the parliamentary system, to forbid reelection of the governor, to institute a legislative (rather than merely budgetary) chamber, to establish the autonomy of the municípios, etc.

Silveira Martins' apparent sincerity notwithstanding, all the political forces opposed to Floriano soon grasped the real significance of the Federalists' move. The destinies of Floriano and Castilhos were being united. A parliamentary republic might be no more than a cloak to attempt restoration of the monarchy, which future events could very well have led Silveira Martins into trying.

In historical perspective, therefore, Floriano's apparently dubious attitude seems perfectly logical. In depending on the Castilhistas for support and by violently replacing the governor and vice-governor of Santa Catarina with men whom he trusted, he was bolstering the defense of his government. Since it did not suit him to take direct action in the states, he used emissaries, disguised more or less as observers or pacifiers, among them the commandant of the military region, General Bernardo Vasques.

The ruling junta, or governicho, that had deposed Castilhos was unable to keep itself in power, and the governorship of the state was returned to the Viscount of Pelotas. With no heart for the inevitable struggle, unable to depend on the federal garrison, and unsure of his own police force, Pelotas delegated his power to the vice-governor, whom he himself chose, namely General Silva Tavares, the bravest of the Federalist chiefs, who had turned the town of Bagé into the main center of oppositionist strength.

The Republicans, with Júlio de Castilhos at their head, precipitated the action, and on June 17, 1892, Pelotas was deposed. Once more in power, Castilhos, in order to get himself reelected governor by popular vote, resigned his office in favor of a hand-picked vice-governor. General Silva Tavares, commanding strong forces in Bagé, could have begun the fight at once. But in deference to an insistent telegram from Silveira Martins, he retired from the town, menaced by the Castilhistas. The telegram read:

As head of party I counsel you, as fellow partisan I ask you, as a Rio-Grandense I implore you: no civil war. It is not needed to win power and to contain the federal government. Difficulties of every kind, natural mistakes in government, a free press, public opinion can do what violence cannot. Only circumstances beyond my control prevent me from being there with you to drive home the need to avoid civil war at all costs.

Castilhos, again governor, must have felt certain that any reconciliation between his followers and the Federalists was impossible. The hatreds, built up over a long period and barely held in check, were beginning to break out in violence of all sorts; the atmosphere was one of continual turmoil. Among a people as proud and dauntless as the Rio-Grandenses, the strife would inevitably lead to civil war.

The illusion inherent in Silveira Martins' telegram was short-lived. Entering the town of Bagé, which had been evacuated by General Tavares on the advice of Silveira Martins, the irregular troops in the service of the Republican party failed to respect the customary rights of unarmed foes. Other acts of despotism occurred elsewhere in the state.

The destructive instincts of fratricidal warfare were being awakened. From the frontier zones, from the farthest parts of Uruguay and Argentina, the dangerous elements of armed caudillism, elements that are always ready for fighting, revenge, and crime, headed toward the arena of the approaching conflagration. The two governors who had served before Castilhos's return to power had gone to Rio and were unable to restrain the outrages in which the Republicans and the Federalists were trying to outdo each other.

Under the command of Lieutenant Santos Lara and directly inspired by Barros Casal, who had taken refuge on a small gunboat, a flotilla in Pôrto Alegre revolted [in July 1892], senselessly bombarded the city, then surrendered a few days later. This marked the first armed clash between the navy and the army, and was a portent of the war to come.

However, before we discuss the revolution itself, we should review the repercussion that the happenings in Rio Grande do Sul had on the country's politics in general.

The opposition in the Congress became more violent. A deputy from Ceará, Justiniano de Serpa, offered a bill authorizing the government to intervene in Rio Grande in order to prevent civil war and ordering the municípios that predated the Republic to elect a provisional junta that would reorganize the state in keeping with the precepts of the Federal Constitution. The Serpa bill (defeated by only 16 votes out of 128 cast) provoked a most heated debate and rejection by the members from Rio Grande, for it obviously condemned the constitutional system favored by Júlio de Castilhos. New agitation was created by a motion by Demétrio Ribeiro blaming the events in the far South on the Floriano government.

A few days later the deputies J. J. Seabra, Jaques Ourique, and Vicente Antônio of Espírito Santo (the last two being military men) asked Congress to impeach the President. Among the list of charges were the retirement of army and naval officers by arbitrary executive order, the discharge of teachers with life tenure, the decree merging the Banco da República and the Banco do Brasil and controlling the emission of currency, the forced military draft, and interference in the private affairs of Rio Grande do Sul. The Chamber rejected the impeachment and approved a long report by its Committee on the Constitution and Justice, whose chairman was a deputy from São Paulo, a state always ready to uphold the authority of the President.

Meeting in Uruguay, the Federalist leaders decided on revolution, just as the Republicans ousted from the government had at an earlier meeting [late in 1891] in Monte Caseros, Argentina. In a manifesto calling on the people of Rio Grande to rally to them, the Federalists held themselves to the Bagé plan: they did not intend to restore the monarchy or to overthrow the federal government; they proposed merely to "liberate Rio Grande do Sul from the tyranny of Castilhos." Silveira Martins, a refugee in Uruguay, accepted the supreme moral leadership of the fight, despite the dangers he had forecast in his telegram to General Silva Tavares.

The history-making events in the offing would turn the plains of Rio Grande do Sul into a testing ground of the Republic. Because of Rio Grande's special conditions, this great southern state had to be the battlefield in Brazil's new regime. Proclaimed in a bloodless coup, in an atmosphere of vague indifference, in a large, neglected, and lazy cosmopolitan city of businessmen, the Republic would prove here whether or not it could survive.

In various ways the drama of the Farrapos would be repeated. In their struggle for local freedom or for federation, the revolutionists of 1835 could have gone as far as secession. In taking up arms against Castilhos's extreme presidentialism and for republican parliamentarism, the revolutionists of 1893 could have been driven to a restoration of the monarchy or to a vast and dangerous national convulsion. Brazilian unity had been consolidated in 1845 by the victory of the centralizing monarchy; the victory of Castilhos would consolidate the federative Republic. Although the parliamentary monarchy lived for half a century on the success of its arms, the constitutional Republic of 1891 survived for just forty years.

After the outbreak of the revolution, Floriano Peixoto, who had been inclined all along to support Castilhos, no longer hid his intention of doing so. He intervened directly in Rio Grande in the name of constitutional precepts to reestablish order and public tranquility.

During the political crisis in Rio Grande do Sul that preceded the revolution, Custódio had set himself up as the leader of the opposition to Castilhos. The telegram with which he answered the communication from the vice-governor (appointed by Castilhos) announcing his assumption of the state government is a perfect example of the Admiral's habitual tone and political attitude while he was Navy Minister:

I have noted that you are now vice-governor of your state. Permit me to tell you that I do not agree on the constitutionality of the authority you say appointed you to that office. If we were to accept such a doctrine, we would undo the work of November 23rd, which you so greatly upheld and applauded, and reinstate the government of Marshal Deodoro, who must be in your view the constitutional President.

These expressions of Custódio's stand out all the more when compared with Floriano's reply:

Having noted what you inform me of in your telegram of today, I hope you will have the glory of achieving what your predecessors could not: complete triumph of the republican idea, a calming of partisan passions, peace and tranquility for the Rio-Grandense family. For the achievement of so great a good, you can count on my cooperation, in the assurance that it is one of my own principal preoccupations.

This brief recapitulation of the political events of the year 1892 shows, then, how Brazil was rapidly heading for civil war. With a submissive Congress and judiciary and a disaffected navy, Floriano's government had all the well-known earmarks of the Hispanic-American dictatorships. To complete the analogy between Brazil and her neighbors, there was even the same language between the quarreling factions, the same sort of personal hatreds, and the cruelty of the first armed clashes. The Rio-Grandense revolution at the beginning of 1893 and the later revolt of the navy were, despite their stated motives and the final distortion of their purpose, largely the reaction of the nation's civilian culture and liberal traditions against the tyranny of one man, who had turned out to be an agonizing surprise to his own followers.

9. The Naval Rebellion

The first Federalist invasion — Guerrilla incursions — Wandenkolk's adventure — Revolt of the navy — Two parallel revolutions — Intervention by foreign squadrons — The admirals' mistaken political and military strategy — Specter of restoration — Victory of legality.

The first invasion by the revolutionary Federalists started on February 9, 1893. Under the command of the civilian caudillo Gumercindo Saraiva, they crossed the border from Uruguay. Their first armed clash with the legal forces took place a few days later.

In both opposing camps, civilian caudillos, all intrepid plainsmen and many of them veterans of guerrilla warfare in Uruguay and Argentina, appeared at the side of regular army troops and Rio Grande police forces. Again, as in 1835, the caudillos on both sides felt more solidarity (born of many affinities, including blood ties) with each other than with their allies. Uruguayans and Argentines also joined the Brazilian columns on both sides. In certain parts of the two River Plate republics, revolutionists gathered and prepared to invade Brazil. Argentina at that time was beginning her return to prosperity under Vice-President Pellegrini, who was fighting to correct the financial disasters brought about by his predecessor, Juárez Celman. Uruguay, however, under the Colorado [a political party] rule of Herrera y Obes, was struggling in the early stages of a grave economic crisis that would later trigger the revolution against President Idiarte Borda. In such an atmosphere, the Brazilian revolutionaries easily got help and support, even from the Uruguayan authorities.

Gumercindo Saraiva's group invading from Uruguay was soon joined by several larger forces, and [Colonel João Nunes da] Silva Tavares assumed supreme command of the Federalists. The whole of the frontier with Uruguay quickly entered a state of guerrilla warfare. The rebel forces numbered about 3,000 men, excellent horsemen and lancers, but poorly armed and precariously disciplined. Victorious in their drive on the town of Dom Pedrito, which surrendered to them, they marched on Santana do Livramento (separated by the width of a street from the Uruguayan town of Rivera). With the approach of Republican army forces in defense of the town, the revolutionaries called off their attack and moved to the outskirts of Alegrete, where they defeated the enemy. Their advance continued to Quaraí, where they received armaments. Oliveira Salgado, an army colonel, defected to the revolutionaries and took over the supreme military command from Tavares. The federal forces, better armed and supplied, hastened to meet the rebels, and beat them on the banks of the Inhanduí arroyo. In this scrap, Pinheiro Machado, a Senator of the Republic, revealed the military qualities that would distinguish him as the most brilliant of the Castilhista caudillos. The state government celebrated the Inhanduí battle as a great victory. General Hipólito Ribeiro, Rodrigues Lima, Pinheiro Machado, and Fernando Abbott said in a boastful telegram to Júlio de Castilhos: "The glories of Inhanduí, made famous by the Farrapos, were revived yesterday. Revolution strangled. Long live the Republic."

The good tidings were somewhat premature. Most of the revolutionary army, without arms or supplies, ill-fed, poorly protected against the cold, and persistently pursued by the legal forces, took refuge in Uruguayan territory. In agreement with Castilhos, Floriano sent his War Minister, General Francisco Antônio de Moura, to Pôrto Alegre to direct the military operations from there. But although Colonel Tavares and Colonel Salgado desisted temporarily from fighting, Gumercindo moved around inside the state in a series of guerrilla hit-and-run maneuvers that wore down the regular forces and kept the hopes of the revolution alive. Thus the first revolutionary invasion ended without success. Castilhos's vigorous resistance and capacity for quick decision solidified his authority and his public image.

Admiral Wandenkolk, one of the signers of the manifesto of the thirteen general officers, had, in his injured pride, never forgiven Floriano. On July 6, 1893, after issuing a challenge to Floriano from Buenos Aires, Wandenkolk boarded the merchant vessel *Jupiter,* which was loaded with arms and munitions for Rio de Janeiro, and persuaded the captain to sail to Rio Grande do Sul instead. In the seaport town of Rio Grande [at the far southern end of Lagoa dos Patos], he gathered some followers and published a manifesto urging a revolt against Floriano and Castilhos. On failing to receive the backing by the navy or the help from Gumercindo's troops on which he had counted, he abandoned the venture and gave himself up in Santa Catarina's waters to the commander of the cruiser *República*, which had been sent after him from Rio. Since he was a Senator of the Republic, after his arrest Rui Barbosa obtained a writ of habeas corpus for him from the Federal Supreme Court. Floriano, who had honored the court with some eminent judges, later appointed two military men and a reliable physician to it. However, the worsening of the bitter rivalry between the army and the navy, which would climax in the September uprising, resulted more from Wandenkolk's frustrated attempt at rebellion than from Floriano's contemptuous appointments.

The Rio-Grandense revolution aggravated the already chronic unrest throughout the country. In the North, Pernambuco appeared to be the most dangerous center of agitation and was proclaimed to be in a state of siege by Floriano. Paraná constantly expected war. Minas remained relatively quiet and became a refuge for persons threatened, or who believed themselves to be threatened, by the government's repressive measures. São Paulo remained faithful to Floriano, and was kept busy defending its southern borders and trying to secure the presidential succession for one of its own republican leaders.

In Santa Catarina, events were more tragic. Floriano suspected the acting governor, Machado, of sympathy with the revolutionary cause, and had him removed from office. The vice-governor who replaced him was subsequently ousted by a coup that took some lives.

In Rio the opposition in Congress and in the press daily reviled the President, who also had the city's most cultured and independent elements against him. The Paulista deputy, Francisco Glicério, managed with difficulty to keep the Congressional majority under control and allow the government to carry on its public administration.

The most serious problem, however, was the navy. The rivalries between the army and navy had been carried over from the Empire, which had never tried to dissipate or attenuate them. Profoundly civilian in temperament, Pedro II had no special liking for the armed forces. If he had any preference, it was probably for the navy. An admiral's uniform perhaps impressed him more than that of a marshal.

The aristocracy of the Empire had encouraged their young men to seek careers as naval officers. Their top-ranking position in South America, the glories of the war with Paraguay, their constant voyages abroad, and their fondness for worldly living lent the navy's staff officers a certain aristocratic coloration. Admiral Luís Filipe de Saldanha da Gama, for example, of noble ancestry, brave, cultured, widely traveled, elegant, worldly, and highly esteemed by the court, was the navy's grand representative.

The republican propaganda aroused little enthusiasm in navy circles, and barely touched the youths in the Naval Academy. The Republic was accepted as an accomplished fact by the navy in a spirit of discipline and patriotism that was still tinged with discontent over the supremacy of the army in the establishment of the new regime.

The army was more democratic. As a rule, its officers came from the lower-middle class, mainly from Rio Grande do Sul. Several generations of military families followed one another, like the Fonsecas, the Mena Barretos, the Fontouras, and the Câmaras. The officers, with small salaries and no personal wealth, lived in the most modest economic situations. The abolitionist and republican ideas of freedom, therefore, found much more fertile ground in the army than in the navy.

Deodoro da Fonseca brought the military with him almost unanimously in the November 15th overthrow of the Monarchy. Later the army was divided between Deodoro and Floriano without a break in its republican faith. When the Republic encountered its first great challenge on the plains of Rio Grande, the majority of the army officers regarded their fate as one with that of the President.

The navy, on the other hand, or at least its highest-ranking officers, became suspect. Admiral Custódio José de Melo, who seemed to act in its behalf, did not have the foresight to keep the navy out of political strife, as a base of moral strength that could pacify the nation. Admiral Tamandaré, an impenitent monarchist, was a relic of the past. Jaceguai retired from active service. Wandenkolk ruined himself by his own imprudence. Saldanha da Gama, with exceptional prestige among his peers after Deodoro's resignation (which he worked hard to prevent), kept himself aloof from the intrigues, absorbed in directing the Naval Academy. Inwardly unhappy over the republican disorders, his hierarchic and aristocratic view of life offended, he later committed the great error of believing it possible to restore the monarchy.

Harassed by implacable foes, Floriano, who had an abundance of those political talents that Custódio, Wandenkolk, and Saldanha lacked, was not interested in dissipating the navy's prejudices. With the fate of his administration tied to the Rio-Grandense Republicans, supported enthusiastically by his army companions, he might have found navy support embarrassing.

The rivalry between the two military branches became so bitter that it frequently exploded in the streets. The progovernment papers were unsparing in their criticism of the "monarchic" navy. The opposition press in turn persisted in defending the navy and in underscoring the government's hostility toward it. When Wandenkolk left Buenos Aires for his adventure at the port of Rio Grande, the Navy Club elected him its president. Floriano's adversaries, including the old monarchists, did not conceal their sympathies for the Federalists and the navy, nor did the foreign colonies in Rio, especially the Portuguese, which added to Florianista xenophobia.

The Castilhista Republicans carried on a stubborn propaganda campaign, accusing their enemies of plans to restore the monarchy. These plans were allegedly inspired by the ex-monarchist Silveira Martins. Although the various oppositionists shared their hatred of Floriano, they had no such uniform plan of action. Their personal and regional rivalries made their efforts largely useless. Their much-debated objectives tended to isolate the revolution from the rest of Brazil and win merely sentimental support.

The partisan quarrels in Rio Grande do Sul were reflected also in Floriano's own cabinet. Although the Finance Minister, Serzedelo Correia, a young military man with positivist learnings, was an ardent Florianista, he was, like Admiral Custódio de Melo, opposed to the President's personal policies in Rio Grande do Sul. Alleging great problems in the Federal Treasury, he insisted on a direct agreement with General Silva Tavares, chief of the Federalist army, to end the civil war. When his request was denied, he used disagreements with Floriano over the auditing office as his pretext for resigning his ministry on April 27, 1893, at the same time that Custódio, the Navy Minister, resigned his. If Serzedelo Correia limited his letter of resignation to defending the auditor's fiscal prerogatives, Custódio went much further. He severely criticized Floriano, accusing him of having provoked and maintained the civil war in Rio Grande do Sul, and, furthermore, of having done so through his own War Minister.

The President willingly accepted the resignations of his two vexatious ministers, who had been the principal targets of Congressional and press opposition. But if he found it easy to replace his Finance Minister, the appointment of his Navy Minister's successor involved the delicate problem of the rivalry between the nation's two military classes. The highest-ranking officers in the navy, including Admiral Saldanha da Gama, declined the post. Distrusting the politicians and the naval officers, Floriano was seeking security for his hard-pressed government in the enthusiastic dedication of the young army men and in the extreme radicalism of the populace.

The attitudes of the three most prominent admirals at the time, Custódio de Melo, Wandenkolk, and Saldanha da Gama, naturally had increased Floriano's apprehensions. If Saldanha da Gama held himself disdainfully aloof, and Wandenkolk was lessening his prestige in abortive ventures, Custódio de Melo, who had grown ever more demanding, was being credited with authority equal to that of the President.

In preparing a new naval revolt, Custódio José de Melo appeared to have no intention of allying with the Federalist guerrillas, and no political program. The Rio Grande revolution and the naval revolt were to become two parallel but separate movements against Floriano's government. Only at the last minute, when Saldanha da Gama assumed command of naval operations, did Custódio try to establish closer moral and tactical contact with the Federalists, and in doing so he became deeply suspect to sincere republicans. Floriano and Castilhos could only gain, naturally, by the scattering of their common enemy's efforts.

After noisily resigning as Navy Minister, Custódio could not return passively to his professional duties. Like Wandenkolk, he could not forget his grievances, nor could he accept the lesser position in political affairs into which Floriano had maneuvered him. The navy's constant state of irritation, the burning political questions of the time, and the revolution in Rio Grande all created a favorable climate for a new insurrection by the navy. The easy victory on November 23, 1891, when a simple show of force by a few vessels in Rio's harbor had sufficed to make Deodoro resign, had increased Admiral de Melo's confidence in himself and in the mission to which he felt predestined. A poor psychologist, he did not see how different in temperament Deodoro was from Floriano, about whom Admiral Saldanha, who was a better judge of men, used to say, "The game will be tougher."

Custódio hesitated a long time before taking the lead in the insurrection. Finally, however, after Jaceguai and Saldanha had refused to, he took the fateful step. Even then, though he was in command of the navy in revolt, he did not seem to have a clear idea of what he wanted. His manifesto became lost in the usual verbiage of such documents. He proposed to "restore the supremacy of the Constitution," which Floriano had torn to pieces many times while praising it.

On September 6, 1893, Custódio raised the white flag of revolt on the battleship *Aquidabã*,* which he had boarded the night before with some naval officers and Federal Deputies. Soon all the other Brazilian ships in the bay of Rio de Janeiro joined the insurrection. The rebellious squadron consisted of sixteen war vessels and eighteen merchant steamers and tugboats. Even the former were militarily inefficient, and most of them

---

* Named to commemorate the battle of the Aquidaban (a small river in northern Paraguay), during which the Paraguayan dictator, Solano López, was killed, thus ending the war, in March 1870. JLT

were old and practically useless. They included steelclad battleships, wooden cruisers, armed lighters, and old sidewheelers left over from the war with Paraguay. Only five of the vessels could sail under their own power; the others, some with good, modern guns, had to be towed.

Floriano had not been caught by surprise. He had prudently sent his best ship, the *Riachuelo*, to Europe, supposedly for repairs. He had also removed some essential parts from the *Aquidabã;* they had to be replaced by improvisation. However, the bay fortresses, which to Custódio's surprise remained loyal to the government, were in no better shape than the rebellious naval vessels, which were thus able to dominate the harbor completely.

Since Custódio was untouchable at sea, one would think his first concern would have been to gain a foothold on land by taking, for example, the town of Niterói, which lay across the bay from the capital and was totally unarmed. He did not do so, however, under the delusion that the rebellion would find immediate support in Rio. His strategy, which was really both intelligent and logical, was instead to attack the port of Santos [about 200 miles down the coast from Rio], invade São Paulo, and establish there the headquarters of his rebel government. The Federalists, by then already in Santa Catarina, were to be his invaluable allies. Thus the navy's rebellion would eventually absorb the Rio-Grandense revolution, which was more regional in character though it had much more clearly defined political objectives.

But Custódio did not carry out this plan. Though he could have broken out to sea with the greater part of his squadron (as some of the vessels did singly later), Custódio chose to stay inside the harbor. Cruel disappointments came from all sides. In the North, the country remained relatively quiet, including Bahia and Pernambuco, on whose governor, it seems, Custódio had counted. He made no attempt to join the Rio Grande revolutionaries, in spite of an appeal from Silveira Martins. São Paulo, under Governor Bernardino de Campos, was preparing its own defenses.

Certain of the army's support, Floriano did not for an instant lose his serenity or his determination to fight. The navy's revolt was in a way rendering him a great service. His government, unpopular with or at least distasteful to the more cultured and independent classes, rapidly gained their good opinion, which Floriano and his followers had not been at pains to cultivate. His message to Congress informing it of the navy's insurrection is a model of terseness: "I must report to you and the other members of the Chamber that early this morning the Navy Minister advised me that a part of the navy has assumed a position of rebellion and open hostility against the legal government. The government believes its duty is to bring this fact to your knowledge, with the assurance that it feels strong enough to maintain public order. Health and fraternity." The city remained calm. Floriano stayed on the alert, but took no repressive measures.

Meeting Floriano's wishes, Congress authorized him to extend the state of siege to as much of Brazil, and for as long a time, as he deemed necessary. The youths in the military and civilian schools enthusiastically volunteered their services and formed patriotic battalions. Suspicion that the rebellion was an attempt at restoration (a suspicion later reinforced by Saldanha da Gama's adherence to it) caused the republicans, including those who were averse to Floriano, to rally around him.

Patiently, methodically, Floriano strengthened the city's defenses by emplacing guns in the surrounding hills, setting up strong points on the seashore, and reinforcing the garrison at Niterói. With the exception of the fortress of Villegaignon,* which declared itself neutral, all the others remained loyal to Floriano. Saldanha da Gama, who had taken no part in the preparations for the revolt and had tried futilely to prevent it, also declared his neutrality. His concern was to safeguard the Naval Academy, which he directed, as a nucleus for rebuilding the navy.

The insurrection of the navy in an open city like Rio de Janeiro, whose commerce was largely in the hands of foreigners, inevitably gave rise to highly irritating diplomatic incidents. Brazil, during Pedro II's time, had been able to instill a certain respect in the great powers, who, seeing only her orderly and tranquil surface, supposed her forever immune to the habitual political convulsions of Latin America. The financial collapse under the Provisional Government, the partisan agitations that had culminated in the dissolution of the Congress, and the Rio Grande revolution changed their opinions. The Portuguese- and Spanish-speaking American republics were not so different after all: semi-barbaric nations given to financial adventures, pronunciamentos, tyrants, and caudillos.

The navy revolt did not, therefore, greatly surprise the European powers or the United States. They were concerned only with protecting their business interests in the distant, tropical land torn by civil war. Portugal alone, tied to Brazil by moral affinities, by a common language, and by the vast Portuguese colony in Rio, completely integrated into

---

* The fortress is situated on an island well inside the harbor and very close to the city. It is now connected to the mainland by a strip of filled-in land on which the Santos Dumont airport was built. The island was named for the French admiral Nicholas Durand de Villegaignon, who founded a short-lived colony there in 1555. JLT

the life of the city, could feel in Brazil's tragedy something more than a threat to her immediate interests. To the United States the Brazilian revolt became important only when it apparently became an attempt to restore the monarchy, that is, European hegemony, in a part of the South American continent, which under the primitive, unilateral, and vaguely contemptuous Monroe Doctrine she had committed herself to protect.

To all of Custódio's other troubles was now added the decision of the foreign war vessels anchored in the harbor to afford their nationals whatever protection they might need. As soon as the revolt was declared, the naval units of England, France, Italy, Portugal, and the United States that were there at the time decided to act in concert, alleging humanitarian reasons, to keep the contest from disturbing foreign trade or reaching the point of bombarding the city. On October 5th, they declared Rio an "open city." Only the commander of a German unit refused to take part in any collective action, limiting himself to defending the special interests of his country. To Floriano's government, at first powerless against the rebellion, this agreement formally entered into by the foreign naval commanders (an agreement Floriano himself had solicited through his navy's chief of staff) represented an extraordinary advantage.

Prevented from engaging in any acts of violence against the city (sometimes the foreign commanders' friendly suggestions changed to insults and threats), Custódio insisted on remaining inside the harbor to carry out the futile, daily artillery duel with the loyalist forts permitted under the rules and the frustrating attempts to land in Niterói. From time to time, graver threats or stray shells created panic in the city and precipitated a wild rush to the suburbs or the interior. But as a rule the populace enjoyed watching the daily spectacle of the bombardment, more saddening than effective, between the forts and the insurgent vessels.

Frequent quarrels arose between the foreign vessels, the insurgent squadron, and the legal authorities. The press favorable to the government, overlooking the indirect benefits provided by the ships' presence in the bay, showed itself hostile to them, considering their actions favorable to the rebels. The posture assumed by the foreign fleet, which both the legal government and the rebellious admiral had willingly acquiesced in at the start, began to strike them as impertinent. The insurgents complained of hindrances imposed upon them; Floriano's government felt that the foreigners, especially the Europeans, were aiding the revolt. Both sides had had their patriotic pride hurt by the foreign interference in their domestic quarrel. Although the insurgents disguised their feelings, the loyalists gave vent to theirs with increasing vehemence.

The Portuguese commander Augusto de Castilhos, whose small and almost unserviceable corvettes, the *Mindelo* and the *Afonso Albuquerque,* were a constant reminder of Brazil's former colonial status, was the favorite target of xenophobia. He had been practically abandoned by the Portuguese diplomatic corps, which had fled to Petrópolis. In striking at this brave and serene man, who was doing his best to carry out his difficult assignment, the Brazilians' hatred of foreigners seemed to be concentrated on the very ones who were closest to themselves. Monarchic Portugal, with its royal ties to Brazil's former rulers, was a prime target for republican sniping, and the Portuguese colony in Rio was regarded with suspicion by aggressive xenophobes.

By his earlier incisive protest to the British and French legations against their insolent decision to land sailors from their warships in order to protect their nationals in the city (which they said was threatened with anarchy), Floriano won open support from some members of the South American diplomatic corps. (Whether it was true or not, Floriano was credited at the time with threatening to shoot any foreign troops that were landed.) Already the embodiment of republicanism in Brazil, Floriano made himself its great symbol in the rest of the continent, which was always wary of Europe's expansionist policies.

Immobilized within the harbor and without any consequential support from public opinion, the rebels were naturally suffering from the demoralizing effects of this situation of their own devising. They were beginning to feel the lack of the essentials for carrying on the fight. At the beginning of October, the fort of Villegaignon joined their cause. But the intervention of the foreign squadron, which applied to the fort its agreement to protect the city, largely canceled out its military potential.

Saldanha da Gama lived out his own drama in the midst of the larger drama that was ruining the navy. His neutrality, absurd in so many ways, became unbearable. He could not declare himself for Floriano and legality. The newspapers backing the government insulted him daily. He felt that he must join the revolt, but in order to give it another direction and meaning.

Custódio and Saldanha did not understand or like one another, though both were from the same origins. Both were heroes of the war with Paraguay, and both were intelligent, cultured, and brave to the point of folly; they enjoyed equally enormous prestige among their fellows. Both had been loyal servants of the Empire. Custódio had seemed to enjoy the special confidence of the small court of Princess

Isabel; the advent of the Republic had found him on a cruise around Asia with one of her young sons on his staff. Restless and full of political ambitions, Custódio had easily accepted the Republic. As the principal author of the November 23rd countercoup, he had never been willing to play a secondary role. His enemies declared that he had revolted merely to replace Floriano's dictatorship with his own.

Saldanha, on the other hand, had been perhaps more esteemed by Pedro II. He was resigned to the Republic as an accomplished fact, but he had never renounced his loyalty to the monarchy. It was only his respect for and confidence in Deodoro that had made it possible for Deodoro to win him over. On November 23, 1891, Saldanha wanted to frustrate Custódio's first insurrection, and insisted to Deodoro that they fight back. Floriano aroused his instinctive antipathy and filled him with a certain dread. Custódio he dismissed as a hasty hothead and inconsequential "improviser of legality."

When he decided this time to join Custódio's revolt, Saldanha could not doubt that he was casting his lot with a lost cause. Only immediate alliance with the revolutionaries in Rio Grande do Sul might give the revolt a chance of success, and a remote one at that. In his manifesto to the nation on December 7, 1893, one detects a note of melancholic fatalism:

Accepting the situation [the revolt] that is imposed on me by patriotism, without conspiracy, in the full light of day, and aware of the responsibilities, I rejoin my brothers who for more than a year on the plains of Rio Grande and for three months in the bay of this capital have been valiantly fighting to liberate the Brazilian fatherland from militarism, the concubinage of sectarianism [i.e., positivism], and the most unbridled radicalism. As a naval officer, I will use my sword to fight the militarism that all my life I have condemned. As a Brazilian, I intend to contribute my efforts to ending this terrible time, in which the country has been thrown into anarchy, into dishonor, and into the asphyxiation of all her liberties. . . . Logic and the justice of the matter authorize me to seek by force of arms to return the government to the position it occupied on November 15, 1889, when in a moment of surprise and national stupefaction it was overcome by a military revolt of which the present government is only a continuation.

Sincere with himself, or deluded about most Brazilians' sentiments, Saldanha dreamed openly of restoring the monarchy. He and Silveira Martins, chief of the revolution in Rio Grande, called for a plebiscite (such as had twice solidified the Bonapartist monarchy) and agreed to unite their forces. But this meeting of the two subversive movements came too late. Condemned to failure by their clearly monarchic intentions, they lost their drive, and, perhaps without illusions, went down to defeat.

The agreement between the two old monarchists did not unite all the forces opposing Floriano. Some of Custódio's early companions publicly abandoned the cause when it apparently turned toward restoration. The exiled imperial family seemed to hold itself completely aloof. Important opponents of the government, such as Rui Barbosa (who, fearing reprisals by Floriano, had fled first to Argentina and then to Europe), had not been consulted. On being sounded out by some army monarchists, Saldanha refused to have anything to do with them. Custódio himself only learned of his new ally's manifesto days after its publication.

Having set off the rebellion to defend the Constitution, could Custódio now agree with the new direction in which Saldanha was heading it? Was not a plebiscite an indirect way to restoration? Might Saldanha not take it upon himself to play the king-making role of Monck,* a role which monarchists of all lands and periods, when overcome by republican revolutions, always assign to insurgent generals? In the general confusion, no one could answer these questions. In its new phase, therefore, the revolution remained an uncertain adventure against an ever-stronger government, which had put aside earlier scruples and was fighting back by every means, legal and extralegal, humane and inhumane.

In November 1893 the rebel squadron lost the ironclad *Javari,* which was sunk by the guns of the loyal forts. The powder magazine on Governador Island had blown up, and the attempts to reach the supply depot in Niterói had been frustrated. Custódio decided to separate the naval forces into two groups: one to operate in the South in direct contact with the Rio Grande revolutionaries, and the other to carry on the struggle inside the harbor of Rio. On December 1st, the *Aquidabã,* under the command of Alexandrino de Alencar and with Custódio on board, put out to sea under fire from the forts and sailed for Santa Catarina.

Saldanha seized control of the ships in the bay and tried to step up the campaign, but had nothing but bad luck. The loyalist forces took the rebel squadron's supply center on Governador Island in the middle of the bay, the town of Magé on the mainland [at the northern end of the bay], and the small island of Mocanguê Grande [across the bay from Rio].

The attitude of the foreign vessels became even more annoying. The revolt had at first inspired some sympathy from the European powers, but, convinced it had failed, they were reducing the number of their units in Rio, leaving the United States, which increased its forces, as the main spectator. The possible restoration of the monarchy had somewhat

---

* A former lieutenant general under Cromwell, he was largely responsible for the restoration of Charles II in 1660. JLT

alarmed Cleveland's government. Five large American warships kept a close watch on the developments of the revolt, determined to intervene directly if necessary.

The commander of the *Newark,* who on entering the bay had ordered a salute to Admiral Custódio's flag, was recalled. He was replaced by Rear Admiral Benham. The New York press said the action demonstrated the United States's unequivocal sympathy with Floriano's loyalty to the Republic. When an incident took place between American merchant vessels and the insurgent squadron, Admiral Benham maneuvered his warships into battle position, thus threatening to sink the small and weak Brazilian ships.

Made desperate by immobility (like Custódio before him), Saldanha attempted to capture Niterói on February 9, 1894. The invading force of about 500 men was led by Saldanha himself and was covered by units of the squadron. Victorious in their first clashes on the beaches near Niterói, the rebels marched toward the center of the town, which was being defended by regular army troops, military police, and battalions of patriots under the command of Colonels Fonseca Ramos and Argolo. Thrown back, the rebels made a stand on the point at Armação, which was then attacked by the loyalists. After a violent and bloody encounter, during which both sides fought bravely and Saldanha was wounded, the rebels abandoned the venture. A few days later, the *Aquidabã,* with Alexandrino de Alencar commanding [having returned to Rio after leaving the other vessels and Custódio in Santa Catarina], again broke out of the bay under concentrated fire from the defending forts [and returned to Destêrro].

The revolt in the bay of Rio de Janeiro was nearing its end. Free to move in any direction, with the resources of the Treasury and the nation's credit (precarious though they were) at his disposal, Floriano had consolidated the defense of his government on all sides. Little by little, with ships obtained in Europe and America, he had formed a small mixed squadron, based in Pernambuco and commanded by Admiral Jerônimo Gonçalves, a retired veteran of the Paraguayan war.

Shortly before the expected arrival on March 11th of this loyalist squadron in Rio, the government notified all the diplomatic corps that within forty-eight hours (postponed twice, incidentally, at the diplomats' request) final land and sea operations would begin against the insurgent ships. However, before the end of that time limit and before panic in the city became extreme, Saldanha da Gama and his followers took refuge on the two Portuguese ships, perhaps, as Joaquim Nabuco justly commented, the only ones able to make the sacrifice needed to give shelter to the vanquished Brazilians. On March 13th, Admiral Jerônimo Gonçalves' loyalist squadron entered the Rio harbor, which was now free of revolutionaries and had republican flags flying above the old forts and rebel ships.

Poisoned by Jacobinic passions and cries for vengeance, Floriano's government could not understand Commander Castilhos's generous gesture. Rejecting the conditions for surrender proposed by the insurgents, it demanded that they be handed over for trial, alleging they were not political criminals but deserters, and guilty of common crimes. The Portuguese government denied the request. There followed repeated exchanges of diplomatic notes. The British government was approached to intervene in the dispute, but refused, since it agreed with the Portuguese position. Finally, one day before the negotiations had terminated, the *Mindelo* and the *Afonso Albuquerque* put out to sea from Guanabara Bay with about 500 defeated Brazilians on board.

Both ships were unseaworthy, without minimum accommodations, and with doubtful sanitation. The fear of yellow fever among the crew members and refugees and the unfitness of his small vessels to attempt the Atlantic crossing forced Commander Castilhos to steer south to the River Plate. His decision was taken by Floriano's government as an unpardonable affront, and it was answered by breaking off diplomatic relations with Portugal. Besides refusing to hand over the refugees, Floriano charged, the Portuguese chancellery had permitted them to be transported to the River Plate, from where they could easily join the revolutionaries in Rio Grande do Sul. In fact, about half the refugees on the two ships, including Admiral Saldanha, did evade the dubious vigilance on board and escape in Montevideo and Buenos Aires to take up the fight against Floriano once more.

But regardless of this, the navy's insurrection inside Rio's harbor had ended. The government and its ardent followers noisily celebrated the triumph, which was a victory for the Republic also. The Brazilian navy came out of the ordeal shattered and embittered by a defeat its bravery had not been able to prevent.

10. The Civil War

On September 17, 1893 (a few days after the navy's revolt had begun), Admiral Custódio de Melo ordered Captain Frederico de Lorena, commanding the cruiser *República,* to proceed to Santa Catarina with one of the insurgent squadron's torpedo boats. Lorena was to set up the seat of the rebel government at Destêrro, the capital of Santa Catarina. However, Custódio still did not plan to coordinate his own efforts with those of the Federalist forces [who were only trying to oust Castilhos].

The purpose of the government at Destêrro* was to justify before the foreign powers the rebels' claim to a state of war, which would oblige them to assume neutrality and thus impede the supplying of arms and ships to Floriano's government. Composed of second-rate figures, the insurgent government was soon torn by personal quarrels. The high positions that positivist dissidents from Rio Grande do Sul had in it rendered it profoundly antipathetic to the Federalist revolutionaries. Silveira Martins refused to act as its representative in Buenos Aires.

Gumercindo Saraiva had stayed in the interior of Rio Grande do Sul and engaged in a series of skirmishes, stimulating new foci of rebellion. Colonel Salgado, who had fled to Uruguay, had come back across the border in August 1893. Joining forces, the two Federalist chiefs fought with uncertain success against the legal troops and Republican caudillos, who pursued them relentlessly. Riots, attacks, and crimes of all sorts

* After the revolution, the town was renamed Florianópolis in honor of Floriano Peixoto. It is situated on an island, which is now connected to the mainland by a modern suspension bridge of some renown in engineering circles. JLT

increased. Rio Grande was devastated by the merciless guerrillas. The
peaceful populations, in constant panic, fled to the hills and woods
when they could not emigrate to the neighboring republics. The classic
picture of South American civil wars was reproduced in Brazil: exploits
and cruelty, heroic charges by lancers, barbarous beheadings of prisoners, enemies, and even simple suspects. The heightening of fratricidal
hatred, the delight in blood and death aroused by armed combat, wiped
out all humane sentiments. The civil war, like all of its kind, became
implacable.

In Rio Grande's northern zone of foreign settlers, where the prevailing type differed in certain ways from the typical gaúcho of the frontiers, and in the hill country, *banhados* [evergreen slopes], and *cochilas*
[rolling plains], the civil war, though less intense, was no different from
that which scourged the southern part of the state. The governments of
both the Union and the state had to defend themselves everywhere from
the same roving guerrillas, the same cavalry incursions, and the same
outbreaks of rebelliousness.

Extending their field of action to the old Jesuit missionary zone between the Quaraí and Uruguay rivers, and to the hill country in the
north, the revolutionaries won the battle of Sêrro de Ouro in the município of São Gabriel. They captured the towns of Alegrete and Itaquí (the
latter on the east bank of the Uruguay), where a federal government
flotilla declared itself neutral.

Hard-pressed by the Northern Division of the legal forces, in which
Pinheiro Machado showed his remarkable fighting ability, Salgado and
Gumercindo began their extraordinary march of nearly 200 leagues [750
miles] to Santa Catarina, which they supposed was controlled by the
navy rebels. In constant skirmishes through forests and over ranges,
fording rivers, capturing and losing towns and villages, the two caudillos
cut across the entire northern region of the state, from the Uruguay
river on the Argentine border almost to the Atlantic. In early November
they crossed the Pelotas river, which divides Rio Grande from Santa
Catarina.

Salgado headed toward the Laguna rail center on the coast and occupied it. Fearful, however, of a clash with the Central Division, which
under General Artur Oscar had moved up the coast and also entered
Santa Catarina, Salgado entrained for Destêrro. Meanwhile, Gumercindo moved north to Lajes, and then, meeting no resistance, to the region
of the German colonies in Santa Catarina, where insurgents from Rio
de Janeiro were operating. The civil war had transferred its major thrust

from Rio Grande do Sul to Santa Catarina, thereby acquiring a new aspect.

Colonel Silva Tavares, reanimated by the revolt of the navy, came back across the border of Rio Grande do Sul. After the capture of Quaraí by one of his caudillos he won a battle at Rio Negro, capturing the commanding general of the loyalist forces. The barbarous decapitation of prisoners at Rio Negro marked the episode as the most brutal of the civil war. After this dreadful atrocity, the revolutionaries marched on Bagé and besieged it. The town's garrison, commanded by General Carlos Teles, held out from November 24, 1893, to January 8, 1894, when the Federalists abandoned the siege and broke up into several columns, which were then pursued and beaten by the government troops.

Repeated clashes occurred between the governicho in Destêrro, the Federalist politicians, and the caudillo forces. Nevertheless, the naval units Custódio had brought [from Rio] to Santa Catarina in December 1893 reinforced the gaúcho guerrillas who had come up from their home state. Their troop movements made easier by sea transportation, the Rio Grande rebels engaged in constant skirmishes in the colonial or coastal region of Santa Catarina. They were beaten in Itajaí by the loyalist Northern Division, which had pursued them all the way from Rio Grande do Sul. Colonel Silva Piragibe took top command of the revolutionary troops, which had been weakened by personal rivalries among their chiefs. He set up his headquarters in the town of Rio Negro in Paraná. Gumercindo Saraiva persisted in his march on Paraná and São Paulo, from where he could threaten the federal government more directly.

After the port of Paranaguá had been taken by the insurgent squadron, the revolutionaries [presumably including Gumercindo] felt strong enough to begin an offensive that carried them to Curitiba [capital of the state of Paraná]. There Custódio established the state government of his followers, and once more enjoined Floriano Peixoto to relinquish the government, a demand that naturally received no response. The town of Lapa held out against the rebels for twenty-six days and surrendered only after the death of its brave commandant, Colonel Gomes Carneiro, who had been wounded in the fighting. Lapa became an outstanding page in the military history of Brazil and in the history of the consolidation of the Republic.

The control of Paraná by the revolutionaries was short-lived. The navy's revolt in Rio having been crushed, the federal government was free to pursue its enemies. The army, the local police, the volunteer bat-

talions, the national guard, in short, all available forces, prepared themselves for the fight. Gumercindo Saraiva gave up his plan to invade São
Paulo, where the government of Bernardino de Campos maintained
constant vigilance, and began his heroic return march to Rio Grande
do Sul.

The surrender of Saldanha da Gama in Rio de Janeiro had to be offset
by a great naval feat capable of reanimating the revolt. On March 28,
1894, Admiral Custódio de Melo embarked from Paranaguá with some
rebel contingents. In Destêrro his squadron, which consisted of the
cruiser *República* and four armed merchant vessels, took aboard the
forces under Colonel Salgado, who had been prevented from returning
overland to Rio Grande do Sul, which he had wanted to do, by intervening federal forces. With a total landing force of about 2,000 men, the
squadron headed for Rio Grande, at the same time that Gumercindo
began his retreat back from Paraná.

After crossing the dangerous bar at the entrance to the harbor under
the uncertain fire of some land batteries, the rebels prepared to assault
the town of Rio Grande.* But the federal government and Castilhos's
government were not to be taken by surprise; the defense was waiting
for them. The chronic dissensions between the chiefs of the invading
troops, a mixture of navy contingents and civilian guerrillas, made
things easier for the loyalist forces.

In the meantime, the fleet Floriano Peixoto had improvised and
turned over to Admiral Jerônimo Gonçalves arrived in the bay of Santa
Catarina [on April 16, 1894] and torpedoed the ironclad *Aquidabã*.
Her commander, Alexandrino de Alencar, managed to save himself and
his crew and to reach the mainland, where they joined the remaining
revolutionary troops.

Defeated in Rio Grande, in danger of being caught between two fires,
the invaders withdrew. To save the last remnants of his followers, and
avoid at the same time a duel with Admiral Gonçalves, Custódio decided to land them on the coast of Uruguay. When the Uruguayan
authorities put a stop to the landing (which had already begun), Custódio took shelter in Buenos Aires, appealed to Argentina for asylum,
and turned the remainder of his fleet over to her.

The Rio-Grandense Federalists who had fled into the Argentine
Misiones district on the west bank of the Uruguay river had not been
entirely inactive. They crossed the river on several occasions and engaged
in skirmishes of little consequence. They easily took and just as easily

---

* They could then have moved up the Lagoa dos Patos all the way to Pôrto Alegre. JLT

lost the município of São Borja, and kept the whole missionary zone in a state of alarm until they joined up with the forces of Gumercindo and Prestes Guimarães, which had made the return march from Paraná in circumstances calling for extreme boldness. Maneuvering and fighting with his small, ill-munitioned army, Gumercindo was mortally wounded in a skirmish on August 10, 1894.

With the death of Gumercindo, whose body his enemies desecrated and whose memory they insulted, the second invasion of Rio Grande do Sul was practically at an end. The forces of General Rodrigues Lima, Pinheiro Machado, and Manuel do Nascimento Vargas beat the last revolutionary remnants of Aparício Saraiva, Prestes Guimarães, and Dinarte, which had been making unsuccessful incursions in the South, and forced them to seek asylum in the neighboring countries. The three southern states were now therefore free of the guerrillas who had devastated them for so long. With the internment of about 2,000 revolutionaries in the two Platine republics, the triumph of Floriano Peixoto's government became complete. Going as they did from one mistake to another, Floriano's adversaries, unable to discipline or coordinate themselves, only contributed to his glory as the consolidator of the Republic.

Custódio José de Melo, like all losers, would not be easily forgiven. The great many apparent facts about him even now cannot be fully interpreted, which makes it hard to judge his record impartially. It would seem that the revolt, into which he had led most of the Brazilian navy, was lost because of his lack of a clear purpose, his petty ambitions, and his personal vanities. And yet his obvious intellectual qualities make us hesitate to pass final judgment on his political inconsistencies and strategic mistakes. He may have been a victim of the hopeless dissensions among his companions. As the head of a revolt in which the most diverse groups barely got along with one another, Custódio had not been able to assert any supreme authority, unlike Floriano and Castilhos.

Floriano, who had proved his indomitable energy during the struggle, did not know how to be, or perhaps how to prove himself to be, generous in victory. The great example of Lincoln, who on the day of victory put aside the differences that had driven his nation into the most prolonged and devastating of civil wars, was not followed in Brazil. The revolution in Rio Grande do Sul and the navy's rebellion had only deepened the discord among the country's ruling classes.

Memory of the danger the Republic had been in and concern over those who might still threaten it exacerbated the passions of the most ardent republicans, especially of the young men in the military and civilian academies. Alongside these sincere elements there swarmed, as after all victories, various opportunists, men who had probably avoided any personal risk in the warfare.

The message with which the President informed Congress of the end of the revolt, despite the coldness of the wording, tended to aggravate the prevailing prejudices:

At first I feared that cosmopolitanism, dissolved in the soul of the nation, had weakened its cohesion and civic virtues. However, I soon convinced myself of the contrary, for from north and south, from all points of Brazil, patriotism revealed more than enough strength to safeguard the seriously menaced Republic. From the schools and the shops, from agriculture and commerce—in a word, from all social classes—men hastened to take up arms, thus magnifying the nation's determination to support the government and uphold the law.

The repressive measures taken by some of the government's agents, such as General Quadros in Paraná and Colonel Moreira César in Santa Catarina, took cruel forms, needlessly staining the republican victory. The summary executions of Commander Lorena and his companions in the rebel government of Santa Catarina, and of other worthy persons, such as the Barons of Batovi and Sêrro Azul, who had had little to do with the revolt, created an atmosphere of apprehension, repression, and silent fear. Floriano had to intervene directly several times to prevent new atrocities. During the war of the Farrapos an old law had subjected military and civilian revolutionists to courts-martial and the death penalty. Abolished by the Federal Constitution, it was now being reinstituted.

Jacobinism was rampant. The enthusiasm for the Iron Marshal was changing into fanaticism. By crushing the revolt, Floriano had in fact made an end of pronunciamentos and consolidated the Republic. He was showing, as Thiers had in suppressing the Paris Commune, that the new political regime was quite capable of imposing physical order. But it was incapable of going further and imposing moral order, or of appeasing emotions. The *exaltés,* drunk with victory, saw monarchic plotters in every corner. A ferocious intransigence afflicted the nation. The Florianistas and the Jacobins thought that they themselves were the only republicans and the only patriots.

Floriano, always relentless in defending his authority against his fellow officers and politicians, seemed unaware of the indiscipline and fanaticism of his partisans. Everything was condoned, even their opposition to the plan suggested by nonsuspect friends of the government that would have eliminated the positivist legend [*Ordem e Progresso*] from the national flag.

Floriano had triumphed, but above all there had triumphed Júlio de Castilhos's unbreakable will. Floriano's term of office was nearing its end. The navy's rebels had been put down. The Republic had been consolidated, despite the immense disorder in its finances and administration. But the hatreds had not cooled down. During President Prudente de Morais's administration, the Federalists and Saldanha da Gama would try a third invasion of Rio Grande do Sul.

Even before the outbreak of the navy's revolt, Francisco Glicério had tried to consolidate enough political strength to allow a successor to Floriano (who apparently refused to take a hand in the matter) to be chosen peacefully. On the eve of the political convention that ratified the nomination of Prudente de Morais, Glicério pleaded with the President once more, explaining the motives that had caused Prudente to be chosen.

Again refusing to make a direct statement, Floriano is alleged to have said, after stressing Prudente de Morais's qualities and services, "Under Prudente de Morais I foresee persecution of our friends. Even you will not be spared; you will suffer a great deal. You will tell me later whether I was right or wrong, but of one thing you may be certain: I will install in power whomever the Congress elects and proclaims."

However, Floriano's sincerity is questioned even today. He was said to have had a private conversation with a political boss from Rio's suburbs about an extension of his mandate. This rumor was publicly denied by the governor of Alagoas, Colonel Gabino Besouro. Floriano must also have been aware of the initiative one of his private secretaries took to launch Lauro Sodré's candidacy. After the navy's rebellion had been crushed, rumor also had it that cautious plans were being laid for a coup d'etat that would deliver the dictatorship to Floriano, but his poor health and the opposition encountered by some of his radical partisans caused the plan to fall through.

Victorious over the navy and the Federalist revolutionaries, Floriano had extraordinary prestige with the army, and the fanatical dedication of the radical republicans, who were ready for anything. Even on the day power was transferred to his successor, he could have tried, and probably could have carried off, the dreaded coup, had he not been more inclined to stubborn resistance than to bold ventures. The nation, severely shaken, did not have the strength to deny him. Though he could have successfully imposed on his supporters the candidacy of one of the earlier Paulista Republicans, for example, or Lauro Sodré, or anyone with his immediate confidence and sympathy (Júlio de Castilhos had not yet reached the constitutional age of 35), he resigned himself to the nomination of Prudente de Morais, whom he did not like. Over and above the conjectures about his attitude toward being succeeded, the historical fact stands out that the succession took place peacefully and in the manner provided by the Constitution.

To underline once more his singular and rather contemptuous indifference, on the day [November 15, 1894] the nation's first civilian President took office, Floriano left the government palace and retired to his modest bourgeois residence. On entering the Itamaraty [palace], the new President found only one of Floriano's ministers present to carry out the formalities of the transfer of power.

A few days later, Floriano, whose continually precarious health had become much worse, moved to a spa at Cambuquira and from there to a fazenda in the município of Barra Mansa, state of Rio de Janeiro. On June 29, 1895, his arduous life came to an end. The Republic honored him with a funeral of great pomp.

The psychological enigma of Floriano would continue to challenge the acumen of his friends, of his foes, and of all who, nearly half a century later, would try to decipher his meaning. His name became a kind of alarm signal for fanatical Jacobins. Speaking to a group of young men who had called on him, Floriano had urged them to be always alert in the defense of the Republic: "They say, and they repeat, that the Republic is consolidated and in no danger. Don't depend on it, and don't let yourselves be taken by surprise. The ferment of restoration works quietly but constantly and relentlessly. So be on your guard." This political testament explains the revival of Jacobinism and the consequent difficulties of the population.

11. Prudente de Morais
[1894-98]

*Political lull — Biographical sketch of Prudente de Morais —
The PRF and Francisco Glicério — The last Federalist incursion — Death of Saldanha da Gama — Pacification of Rio
Grande do Sul — Administrative disorder — Diplomatic incidents.*

With the inauguration of its first civilian President, the Republic
could pause, with a general feeling of relief, to take stock of its five
years of existence. After an all too brief initial period of order, tolerance, and peace, the struggles that had convulsed the two military
governments had created physical and moral fatigue, occasionally discouragement and despair, among the orderly classes. After losing the
peaceful traditions of the Second Reign, Brazil became permanently
contaminated with the morbid, revolutionary predisposition of the rest
of Latin America. Floriano Peixoto's defense of his much-controverted
legality had shown the new regime's ability to affirm itself by force. The
task of consolidation that Floriano had not been able to finish devolved
naturally upon his peacefully elected successor.

The last Federalist revolutionaries, who had been given asylum in
the Platine republics, would certainly accept the first honorable opportunity to stack their arms. The political party Francisco Glicério had
put together, despite its heterogeneous opportunism, was strong enough
to assure the federal government of the support of majorities in the
states and in Congress. Prudente de Morais's victory gave him extraordinary prestige. The sincere Republicans, who felt they had been mainly
responsible for the institution of the Republic, did everything they
could to raise it in the public's esteem, now that peace and prosperity
had returned and the revolutionary trials could be forgotten.

Nevertheless, beneath the surface appearances that augured complete
success for Prudente de Morais's administration, the passions aroused

by the civil war were still boiling. Suspicions divided the politicians, and the fanatic Florianistas would not tone down their demands. Financial difficulties and economic depression were ruining the country. Administrative disorder became extreme. The PRF, which had endorsed Prudente de Morais's candidacy, was held responsible for his administration by Floriano's friends. On the other hand, the various elements of the opposition felt themselves strong enough to demand full reinstatement in political affairs after the amnesty. The victory of the civilian presidency, they said, was essentially their doing; without the armed resistance of the Federalists and the navy, the Republic would have gone the way of military dictatorships.

Inside the PRF itself, three currents were forming: the fanatic Floriano worshipers, who would not or could not forgive, and who, in keeping with their idol's political testament, considered the Republic to be in permanent danger; the reactionaries, who would have liked to eliminate the intransigent and disturbing Jacobinism once and for all; and the moderates, who were trying to balance the extreme groups. Did Prudente de Morais have the qualities needed to rule the country in such an atmosphere, to pacify it, and to restore financial and administrative order?

Prudente José de Morais e Barros was born in 1841, on a fazenda in São Paulo. On graduating as a lawyer, he joined the Liberal party, and became the president of the chamber of the município of Piracicaba and a provincial deputy. Soon, despairing of the monarchy, he joined the republican movement set off by the Manifesto of 1870. In 1873, he was at the Republican convention in Itu, along with other Paulista personalities such as Américo de Campos, Bernardino de Campos, Francisco Glicério, and Cesário Mota, who would later distinguish themselves in the Republic.

From the very start of his public life, Prudente de Morais was known for his willpower, wisdom, and austerity. He was the respectable man par excellence: authoritarian, reserved, distant, and of rare moral courage. Few public men in the Republic would prove to be so close to the worthy type of politician developed during Pedro II's reign, marked by a balanced intellect without brilliance, by perfect integrity, and by a somewhat formal gravity, proud, civic-minded, and invincibly averse to any shadow of militarism. However, Prudente de Morais, cold and circumspect, would always lack eloquence and personal warmth.

In 1885 the Republican Party of São Paulo elected Prudente de Morais and Campos Sales to the monarchic Parliament, which received Republican deputies for the first time. Minas Gerais had elected another

Republican, Alvaro Botelho, to it also. Prudente de Morais did not hesitate to support certain measures of the Dantas cabinet.

When the Republic was proclaimed, he, General Murta, and Rangel Pestana made up the governing junta of São Paulo. A few days later his two companions resigned and Prudente de Morais assumed the provisional governorship of the state. He worked hard to maintain order during the difficult transition and to establish the basis for republican organization. For his efforts he won general praise, including that of the monarchists.

Prudente resigned the governorship of São Paulo to exercise his mandate as a delegate to the Constituent Assembly. He was elected President of the Assembly over the old Republican Saldanha Marinho, who had been the first to sign the Manifesto of 1870. He quickly established his authority by his dedication to his duties, by his sense of fairness, and by his personal austerity. Campos Sales said of Prudente de Morais what Gabriel Hanotaux had said of Jules Grévy, President of the Bordeaux Assembly and later of the French Republic: "His cold, impassive, wisely impartial attitude had won the good will of all, and was quickly preparing the way for the realization of heavily veiled and very stubborn ambitions."

In an assemblage of inexperienced men, somewhat stunned by the Republican victory and uncertain of the nature of the task to which they had been called, Prudente de Morais's talents were invaluable. He was considered when those who resented Deodoro da Fonseca, or who honestly feared his impulsive temperament, speculated on nominating a civilian to oppose the Marshal's candidacy for the first constitutional presidency of the Republic. Prudente de Morais's foes later attributed his running against Deodoro to vanity. In agreeing to challenge Deodoro for the presidency, he was probably obeying his aversion to an extension of a military government that he judged could be easily turned toward dictatorship. The votes he received in the Constituent Assembly reflected, perhaps, the nation's currents of civilian and conservative opinion. But more than that, they were also the first formal reconnaissance of the road that less than four years later led him to the highest office in the land. From this first contest grew the incidents that led to the dissolution of the Congress and to the later struggles of the Republic.

Elected Vice-President of the Senate, over which he presided during the systematic absence of Floriano Peixoto (Vice-President of the Republic), Prudente maintained his traditional authority, a virtue stressed by Quintino Bocaiúva, as spokesman for a group of Senators gathered to do him honor. No other man in public life acquired greater personal authority than Prudente.

Brought up under the patriarchal tutelage of the Empire, Brazil was unable to adapt herself to the new constitutional forms, so ingenious on paper and so foreign to her lifelong habits. In spite of their rhetorical declarations and their sincere desire to swing into step with the new political order, the ruling elite of the young Republic could not free themselves of their old tendencies toward centralized government and parliamentary rule. State politics, which until then had not been organized and in which the future oligarchies had not yet taken hold, revolved around the Union's likes and dislikes. Congress was an independent and often rival force, without whose willing cooperation the government could not continue to exist.

Having organized a vast, mixed political party [the PRF] despite Floriano's indifference, Francisco Glicério was looked upon by the new President of the Republic as the incarnation of the sovereign power of Congress. In order to pacify the nation, split between arrogant winners and unresigned losers, and put public affairs in order, Prudente de Morais had to rely on the Congressional majority of the PRF. His close personal ties to Glicério, an enthusiastic supporter of his candidacy, seem to have made it easier to create close relations and harmony between the executive and legislative branches.

Prudente de Morais at first seems to have taken an excessively non-interventionist position. Refusing to express his opinion on current legislation, he confined himself narrowly to his immediate functions, sacrificing the collaboration between himself and Congress that the country's needs demanded. Autonomous in his direction of the "21 brigades" in Congress, the head of the PRF became a sort of high constable of the Republic. His friends and foes, for different reasons and purposes, exaggerated his influence on Prudente de Morais. However, the loose discipline and deep-seated antagonisms within the PRF made its leader's prestige seem much more brilliant than his effectiveness warranted. Though able in bringing men together and tactful in dealing with their vanities and petty personal interests, Glicério was not leader enough to impose his will on them at decisive moments.

The Florianistas who made up the radical core of the PRF received Prudente de Morais's government with ill-concealed mistrust: would it or would it not cater to their passions? This attitude naturally impelled the former revolutionists and the anti-Jacobins toward the government. Congress became the battlefield on which the two large groups struggled to control the government.

Although he avoided any interference in the decisions of Congress, Prudente de Morais nevertheless demanded a free hand in state politics. Thus the tendency of Congress to override the Executive, and the latter's tendency to control absolutely the states' politics and administration, were clearly complementary manifestations of the parliamentarian and centralizing habits of the Empire. It was not possible to harmonize them with the spirit of the new regime, especially amid the still-hot passions of the civil war. The dissensions that would agitate Prudente de Morais's four-year term, and render his efforts at financial and administrative reform largely ineffective, grew worse.

To bring the revolutionary phase to a close, Prudente de Morais had to carry out two big preliminary tasks: to return the military gradually to their normal functions, thereby definitely removing them from their bitter partisan contests, and to pacify Rio Grande do Sul, which the navy's revolt had kept Floriano from doing. The President's inflexible nature was perhaps not ideally suited to the first task. The military chiefs, understanding his motives, loyally cooperated in restoring discipline and withdrawing their comrades from political activities. On the other hand, the young officers, in their blind devotion to Floriano, discovered intentional spite in the government's every move. His republican sincerity notwithstanding, Prudente de Morais was in their view making himself a tool of the reactionaries.

In the press and in Congress, the oppositionist attacks became more rancorous than they had been during even the most furious phases of the Deodoro and Floriano administrations. The dedication of his friends in the PRF could not begin to equal the vehemence of the President's adversaries. And while he was not able to please the radical elements, Prudente de Morais was also not able to inspire the complete confidence of the Rio Grande Federalists.

These revolutionaries, though beaten back after their second invasion of the South, had not completely laid down their arms. Within the state and along the frontier with Uruguay and Argentina, they kept themselves ready for a new call to rally. Saldanha da Gama, to whom Silveira Martins had turned over the leadership of the revolution, was on the River Plate organizing a new incursion. He expressed his views in a letter to the monarchist chief Andrade Figueira: "If Floriano remains in the presidency by means of another coup, the revolution will redouble in vigor and will end in absolute victory. The same will occur if the government passes to Prudente and he is unable to maintain himself in office. If Prudente manages to solidify his authority, a new situation will be created that will have a strong political bearing on the armed contest and on the revolution itself." Months later, after Prudente de Morais was already in office, Saldanha da Gama wrote to *La Prensa* in Buenos Aires:

Floriano Peixoto was obliged, finally, to yield his office, leaving the revolution unabated. Prudente de Morais's government, by showing us in its turn an intentionally aggressive attitude, is giving us reasons for carrying on the armed struggle.... The revolutionists would not be unwilling to lay before the altar of the mother country their arms, their just complaints, and their high purposes; only it does not behoove them to be the first to hold out the olive branch.

To take the initiative toward pacification was precisely Prudente de Morais's greatest concern. But to do so he had to have time to let the passions cool down. In his message to Congress he had said that pacification would depend upon prior disarmament by the revolutionists. But it was now clear that in making this restriction he was trying to gain time without openly going against the more uncompromising elements.

Júlio de Castilhos, despite his earnest desire to end the contest that was ruining his state, could not have the same charitable feelings toward his long-standing foes that animated the rest of the Brazilian community. Not having joined Glicério's PRF, the gaúcho Republicans enjoyed greater freedom of action in national politics, and were zealous above all in defending their state's autonomy and their political principles. Even more than the Federalists, they distrusted the impartiality of Prudente de Morais, who was under attack, justly or unjustly, by the Florianistas.

To deal with the problem of pacification, Prudente de Morais sent General Francisco Moura to Rio Grande do Sul, with orders to move the headquarters of the military district away from the state capital, where he might come under the influence of the local government. When he insisted on staying in Pôrto Alegre, he was replaced by General Inocêncio Galvão de Queirós. Before leaving Rio, General Galvão invited Colonel Silva Tavares, to whom he wrote about the mission with which he had been charged, to come to his future headquarters in order to discuss peace terms.

Without even consulting Silveira Martins and Saldanha da Gama, both of whom were under suspicion of plotting restoration, Colonel Silva Tavares agreed to an appointment with General Galvão. On June 8th General Galvão arrived in Rio Grande do Sul and set up his headquarters in Pelotas. He was disposed to make peace without the consent and approval of Júlio de Castilhos's government, and in fact to exceed his instructions from the federal government.

Before General Galvão's peacemaking steps could be taken, however, the Federalists invaded Rio Grande do Sul for the third time. In a desperate last effort Saldanha da Gama, who had the support of some local authorities in Uruguay, had succeeded in reviving the revolt. The Federalist bands crossed over the frontier and resumed their guerrilla tactics on Rio Grande soil. But their fighting spirit had slackened, whereas the government troops performed with greater skill, sure that final victory would be theirs.

Beaten at every turn, abandoned by public sympathy, those who did not take refuge on foreign soil dug in at strategic points to await the promised armistice. The beleaguered troops were forced to move by the government of Uruguay, which at the insistence of Brazil had ordered their internment. Saldanha crossed the Quaraí river and camped near Osório with about 700 men, including 150 navy riflemen. This small contingent was reduced even further by a number of platoons sent off to aid Aparício Saraiva.

Attacked on June 24, 1895, by the much larger forces of Hipólito Ribeiro, the rebels fought bravely until Saldanha was pierced by a lance and killed. An official autopsy later confirmed the mutilation of his body by the victors. In sacrificing himself for a lost cause even as peace negotiations were in progress, Saldanha da Gama seems to have committed a gallant suicide that would exalt his memory and bring his comrades-in-arms an honorable peace.

On July 1, 1895, Colonel Silva Tavares negotiated the armistice after a full understanding with Silveira Martins. He also met with General Galvão in Piratinim, a short distance from Pelotas, on July 10. In the draft memorandum of their meeting, Silva Tavares declared that he had never fought against the Republic and the federal government, but only against the government of Júlio de Castilhos. The rebels agreed to surrender their arms to the federal government if the latter would guarantee them all their rights and would proceed to reconstitute Rio Grande do Sul in keeping with the Federal Constitution.

By endorsing this last condition, Galvão went far beyond the authority vested in him. The Minister of War, General Bernardo Vasques, informed him that the clause about the constitutional revision of Rio Grande do Sul was unacceptable, since it was a matter to be decided solely by Congress. However, in the final draft of the agreement, which deleted the clause, General Galvão committed himself to address an appeal to the Union government "requesting a study of the constitution of the state of Rio Grande do Sul, which is contrary to federal law." The

President of the Republic and the War Minister telegraphed Galvão ratifying the final draft of the agreement. The loyalist general and the rebel colonel appealed directly to Congress, which, through Francisco Glicério, rejected the suggestion.

Júlio de Castilhos, who had congratulated General Galvão on his success as a peacemaker, severed official relations with him on learning the details of the agreement. On his own authority and in opposition to the radical faction in his own party, Castilhos reestablished public order and reopened the territory of Rio Grande do Sul to his former enemies. Silveira Martins and other revolutionary chieftains were free to return to the state and renew their press campaign against its government.

In March 1895 the students at the Military Academy, located not far from the center of Rio, had risen up against its commandant, whom they suspected of being anti-Florianista. The government reacted vigorously, arresting the insubordinates and discharging them from the army, but it did not succeed in imposing unconditional respect for its authority and in extinguishing the undisciplined ferment. From then until the signing of the peace treaty in Rio Grande do Sul in July 1895, there was a lull in partisan agitations.

On the initiative of Campos Sales, Congress voted a general amnesty on October 11 after a series of parliamentary incidents. Thus the long and painful chapter of the Rio Grande revolution, which for two years had laid waste the south of Brazil, impoverished the entire nation, and kindled immense resentments, was finally concluded. Prudente de Morais had attained his greatest objective: he had brought the armed struggle to an end. However, he still had to reestablish tranquility and restore financial and administrative order. These two tasks were to prove much more arduous.

The terms on which the government had put a stop to the civil war had not pleased the radicals. The discussion about the amnesty aroused strong feelings and opposition in Congress. Within the PRF there developed a strongly dissident faction of "moderates," composed largely of conservatives and former monarchists, whom the pure Florianista "loyalists" lumped together as "reactionaries." Taking advantage of the radicals' prejudices against Prudente de Morais, the moderates swung closer to the government, for which they would provide the nucleus necessary for future resistance to the PRF.

Júlio de Castilhos's political authority had been increased enormously by his long and stubborn campaign against the Federalists. He became, willingly or otherwise, the figure around whom the foes of the President would rally. Castilhos had not spared the President in his messages to his own state's assembly. The Florianista zealots, the positivists, the various intransigents and radicals, elevated him into a successor to Floriano Peixoto.

The years 1895 and 1896 passed in an atmosphere of rancorous discontent, veiled threats, and indecisive political plottings. Francisco Glicério, an extraordinary compromiser and strategist, strove to avoid a formal break with the government, though he was the one most aware of the President's efforts to free himself from the tutelage of the PRF. Prudente kept the support of his dedicated friends in São Paulo, and, winning strong political support in other states such as Maranhão and Pernambuco, where the leadership of the progovernment party had passed to Conselheiro Rosa e Silva, a former monarchist, he paved the way for his future split with the PRF.

Rui Barbosa, although maintaining his independence from the federal government, was an unrelenting foe of the Jacobins. Campos Sales, governor of São Paulo since May 1896, considered himself exempt from the discipline of the PRF. The Vice-President of the Republic, Manuel Vitorino of Bahia, gradually withdrew from Prudente de Morais, and later became one of the extremists.

In March 1895 Brazil had resumed diplomatic relations with Portugal, which had been broken off by Floriano when the navy rebels had been given asylum on the Portuguese corvettes. The British government was the friendly arbiter of the negotiations between the two countries. That same British government soon gave Brazil grave cause for displeasure, when in July 1895 it occupied the island of Trinidade,* from time immemorial a Brazilian possession. Though the desert island in the Atlantic was of no economic importance to Brazil, the occupation was a slight to her sovereignty, and could have signified the installation of a strategic base at a relatively short distance from her shores. The Foreign Minister, Carlos de Carvalho, protested vigorously against the attitude of Salisbury's cabinet (then heading toward Joseph Chamberlain's imperialism) and refused to arbitrate. A year after its improper occupation, the island was peaceably restored through the good offices of the Portuguese government. For Prudente de Morais's government the incident with England created new domestic difficulties and inflamed nationalistic passions once more. However, just at this point

* This islet lies hundreds of miles off the coast of Brazil, opposite Vitória, and is not to be confused with the former Crown Colony of the same name in the British West Indies. J L T

two great diplomatic victories strengthened the President's hand, and marked the beginning of the triumphant career of the Baron of Rio Branco, whom Rui Barbosa called "a god of Brazil's frontiers."

Quintino Bocaiúva's agreement with Argentina in the early days of the Provisional Government not having been ratified, the old Misiones question was submitted to President Cleveland of the United States. The notable defense by Brazil's advocate, Rio Branco, soon resulted in full recognition of her claims. After clashes between Frenchmen and Brazilians in the region of Amapá, on the border with French Guiana, the two countries submitted the question to arbitration by the President of Switzerland. A new and brilliant success by Rio Branco put an end to the irritating frontier question in this area, which had dated from colonial times.

In November 1896 Prudente de Morais, his waning health grown worse, took a leave of absence and journeyed to a mountain resort. On assuming the presidency temporarily, Vice-President Manuel Vitorino did not restrict himself to handling routine matters. He had his own policies and ideas of government. Vitorino began, though apparently in agreement with Prudente de Morais, by reorganizing the cabinet. Bernardino de Campos left the governorship of São Paulo to replace Rodrigues Alves as Finance Minister. Joaquim Murtinho became Minister of Transportation. The Army and Navy Ministers were replaced also. The old Florianistas, as well as all the malcontents who opposed Prudente de Morais, naturally flocked to the Vice-President, who conceivably could become the actual President for the remainder of the four-year term.

A November 15th republican, an eminent physician, a brilliant orator, and an idealist, Manuel Vitorino could not exercise the cold judgment needed to resist the pressures of the radicals and the extremist upholders of the regime. He let himself become involved with them, which led to incompatibility and conflict with the President. Whether he willed it or not, he was being transformed, like Júlio de Castilhos, into a symbol of republican exaltation, opposed to the various reactionaries who found shelter under the wing of Prudente de Morais. The Canudos outbreak, coming as a painful surprise to the whole country and causing already heated passions to boil over, developed into another dangerous test for the Republic.

12. Canudos and Its Consequences

The Canudos affair — Euclides da Cunha's Os Sertões — The Vendée of the Republic — The PRF splits — Victory of the legal forces — Attempt against the President's life — The sacrifice of Marshal Bittencourt — Anti-Jacobin reaction — President Morais's succession — Bankruptcy and the funding loan.

After Canudos had been wiped out and the passions the affair aroused had subsided, it became easy for Brazilians to see through the tragic error, which was made amply clear in Euclides da Cunha's *Os Sertões*, a masterpiece in spite of its dramatic staging, exhaustingly pompous style, and arbitrary ethnographic and sociological conclusions.* Both before and after Canudos, Brazil experienced similar outbreaks of fanaticism among the ignorant backlanders, and even among the German colonists.† But at a time when Brazil was still stunned by the civil conflicts, Canudos took on an unexpectedly dangerous aspect.

The Canudos campgrounds had been set up some years previously in a spot between the railroad and the São Francisco river about 200 miles north of Salvador, capital of Bahia. If the region, as Euclides da Cunha said, portrayed on a small scale the general physiography of the scorched backlands of the Northeast, the people who occupied Canudos were characteristic of the Northeastern *sertanejos* [backlanders], cut off from the Atlantic seaboard and centuries behind its contemporary civilization.

Canudos was founded by a poor and primitive mystic, Antônio Conselheiro, who had come down from Ceará, harried by partisan persecutions in an area where the fanaticism of the *afilhados* [foster-children]

---

* Translated by Samuel Putnam as *Rebellion in the Backlands,* University of Chicago Press, 1944. JLT
† In Rio Grande do Sul in the 1870s a sect called the Muckers had had to be quelled by force. JLT

of Father Cicero would later flourish. Large numbers of the faithful soon gathered around the strange, half-crazy, sixty-year-old ascetic. In a desolate landscape beside a river that had water in it only during the rainy season, Canudos grew into a sprawling mass of tumbledown shacks without plan or order, with churches as the centers of the community's moral life. Monstrous and harmless, an expression of the bigoted caboclos, of the stoicism, backwardness, and poverty of the backlands, it grew and would have survived until a wave of civilization from the seaboard swept over it and transformed its collective soul.

Conselheiro's stolid devotees knew nothing about the world at large and cared less. About Brazil they understood vaguely that it was a republic of Masons and atheists who had expelled the old Emperor and instituted civil marriage, acts that struck them as displaying unpardonable irreverence. In their ambitionless, otherworldly lives, they cared only about their simple-minded, visionary religion, a crude mixture of Catholic rites, African witchcraft, and Indian superstition.

Some cheap building materials for a church provoked the first clash between the "prophets" of Canudos and the public authorities. The governor of Bahia decided to punish the fanatics who dared to oppose a government order, and sent out a small police force. Surprised by Conselheiro's zealots, who were armed with old blunderbusses, crude work tools, and rosaries and amulets (as outward signs of their devotion), the governor's expeditionary force was easily routed. In an environment where nervous tension had long been near the breaking point, the enormous publicity given to this trivial incident in the policing of the backlands inflated it out of all proportion. Unsure of what to do next, and not understanding the potential significance of Canudos, Governor Luís Viana asked for help from the federal government, which was then under the temporary administration of Vice-President Manuel Vitorino. An expedition of 543 men, consisting of federal and state forces under the command of Army Major Febrônio de Brito, was sent to Canudos. Even before they reached the town, the fanatics attacked and routed them disastrously. The outcry against the failure of the second expedition was enormous.

Only recently saved by Floriano Peixoto's victory of legality, the Republic felt itself once more to be in peril. On Rua do Ouvidor, an epitome of Rio de Janeiro and a garish, if false, image of Brazil, the Jacobins once more voiced their hatreds and patriotic threats. They blamed the uprising on Prudente de Morais, saying that by precipitating the pacification of Rio Grande do Sul, he had left the way open for a new blow by the reactionaries. Conselheiro's fanatics fought crying out against the Republic, against atheists and Masons; the monarchists must be behind these rebels, the Jacobins said. Patriotic battalions sprang up as in Floriano's time.

Canudos, as Euclides da Cunha was to say, was the Vendée of the Republic. In Antônio Conselheiro's miserable shantytown deep in the backlands of Bahia, the Republic, founded by Deodoro and consolidated by Floriano, was battling against desperate reactionary opposition, even as the armed forces of the French Revolution, victorious on all European fronts, had hurled themselves against the Chouans of Brittany. As a matter of fact, the Canudos affair, though the men of the period did not think so, was much more modest. The differences between the Catholic, realistic Chouans and Conselheiro's fanatics were as great as those between the physical geography of the Vendée and that of the backlands of the Brazilian Northeast.

A new military expedition under the command of Colonel Moreira César, this time a thousand men with a squadron of cavalry and a battery of artillery, was sent to Canudos by the Vice-President. On February 21, 1897, the column was routed and its commander killed. No one could understand or explain the disaster. With extremely poor services in their rear, operating in an unfamiliar terrain of scorched backlands, thorny vegetation, and very high temperatures, the troops, raw or only used to the southern plains, were victims of their own folly.

When news of the calamity reached Rio on March 7th, the Jacobins went wild. The monarchists would pay with their lives for the defeat of the Republic's arms. While the police stood by, powerless if not in connivance, the offices of three monarchist newspapers were attacked and destroyed. On the following day, in the station of the Rio-Petrópolis Railroad, the capitalist Gentil de Castro, principal owner of two monarchist newspapers and an intimate friend of the Viscount of Ouro Prêto, was murdered by the mob. The Viscount and one of his sons, Afonso Celso, were with Gentil de Castro at the time, and barely escaped a similar fate.

Three days before, Prudente de Morais had returned unexpectedly from Teresópolis and, without formalities of any kind, resumed his duties as President in Catete palace. Since the Vice-President had spent the night away from the palace, the President limited himself (as Floriano would have done) to sending him a written notice that his provisional occupancy of the office had ended. Under Prudente the drama of Canudos would be brought to a close.

On resuming his duties, Prudente de Morais faced perhaps the greatest degree of unpopularity ever suffered by any Brazilian statesman. Isolated in Catete palace, he was not sure even of his personal security. There was the ever-present possibility, considering the growing Jacobin boldness, of an attempt to assassinate him. One would have said that the police had lost control of the city, and that the government was no more than a shadow of power.

The vandal attacks on the monarchist newspapers had gone unpunished, as had the persons implicated in the murder of Gentil de Castro. The monarchists, who had been organized into a political party in 1896 by Ouro Prêto, fearfully kept out of sight, or fled to Europe. Incendiary public meetings were held daily in the centrally located Largo de São Francisco, the traditional gathering place for popular demonstrations. The Jacobin chieftains and patriotic battalions overrode the legal authorities in a latter-day aping of the French Revolution, whose demagogic utterances they also adopted.

Some months later Rui Barbosa analyzed in a speech to the Senate the white terror that stalked the city of Rio during the somber year of 1897: "Because of the prudence of his acts, the mildness of his habits, and the reticence of his attitudes, there has grown up around the President an aura of weakness that has encouraged a certain audaciousness, a certain daring aggressiveness, which always runs riot whenever it does not expect to meet strong opposition."

In Congress, the radicals, Jacobins, and fanatics were warmly applauded. Still under the influence of the Empire's parliamentary tradition, the republican legislators demanded the upper hand in political matters, which was contrary to the nature of the regime. Fundamentally, it was the same sort of contest as had occurred between the French Parliament and MacMahon, and was repeated in other phases of the Third Republic's history.

The separate powers of the President and Congress were in harmony only in the articles of the Constitution; in actual fact, they would never be harmonized. In spite of Glicério's political machine [the PRF], which was supposed to keep the parliamentary majority in line, Prudente de Morais's government, the daily target of oppositionist insult, felt its lack of sufficient support. Little by little, however, the President worked to bolster his authority by painful concessions that won him the dedication of a few military chiefs and the sympathy of the conservative elements. He replaced the capital's chief of police by a more vigorous man. The Minister of the Interior, Amaro Cavalcanti, went personally into the streets to direct the countermeasures against new threats of assaults and depredations. But the President's biggest political stroke was emancipating himself from the tutelage of the PRF.

On May 26, 1897, the cadets of the Military Academy in Rio, inflamed by the passions of the times and spoiled by the acquiescence of the republican governments, declared mutiny—sure in their own minds, naturally, that the other military forces and the politicians would support them. The government surrounded the Academy with land and sea units, and forced its surrender without a fight. The insubordinate students were discharged. Seizing the opportunity, the government took similar action at the Military Academy in Ceará, and dissolved the civilian patriotic battalions. With the taking of these measures, Rio breathed easier.

On the following day, Deputy J. J. Seabra (at one time under proscription by Floriano Peixoto) proposed to the Chamber that a committee be appointed to congratulate the President on having "safeguarded the order and prestige of the civilian Republic." The meaning of this maneuver was clear; it was designed to discredit the government's parliamentary leader, who lacked the President's confidence.

Glicério tried to ward off the blow. "The Military Academy was the fortress of Brazil's glories. The President of the Republic was unaware of the Seabra proposal,* whose sole purpose was to divide the political forces that upheld the government." The Chamber rejected Seabra's proposal by a vote of 86 to 60. On the following day, the *Jornal do Comércio* published a government-inspired statement declaring that Francisco Glicério was not an interpreter of the government's thinking. The split that had lain hidden for so long widened.

Artur Rios, a deputy from Bahia, resigned the presidency of the Chamber for having voted with his colleagues from that state in favor of the Seabra proposal. Four days later Glicério volunteered to fill the vacancy himself, and was defeated by Artur Rios by a vote of 88 to 66. In his reaction against his old companion in the republican movement, Prudente de Morais received his principal support from representatives of Bahia, Pernambuco, Minas Gerais, and São Paulo. Glicério had on his side the combative Castilhista Republicans.

During Manuel Vitorino's interim presidency, still another military expedition had been organized against Canudos under the command of General Artur Oscar, a "red Florianista," who had distinguished himself in the campaign against the Rio Grande rebels. The force consisted of almost 6,000 men in five brigades made up of state police and army battalions. In spite of the previous disastrous experiences, the services of the rear had not been improved.

---

* On the contrary, he had been advised of it by Seabra himself. JMB

Euclides da Cunha, who had once been a military cadet, accompanied the new expedition as a correspondent for a São Paulo newspaper. He was outspoken in his criticism of the expedition's deficiencies. The dubious contest against the rude fanatics in the backlands of Bahia was not one to arouse enthusiasm. Nevertheless, the suspicion, which even Euclides da Cunha could not rid himself of until much later, that the fanatic uprising was inspired, aided, and abetted by the monarchists, acted as a spur against discouragement, especially among the young republican officers. If the highest ranks dodged the distant campaign, the lowest ones gallantly sacrificed themselves in what they supposed was the defense of the Republic.

General Artur Oscar seemed to have the same delusions about the defensive strength of Canudos as the commanders of the previous expeditions. With no knowledge of the terrain or of the psychological factors involved in a fight against fanatic backlanders, he thought it possible to use tactics from the Rio Grande guerrilla warfare. The first clashes with the fanatics rudely awoke him to his mistake.

On attacking the rebel camp with a part of his forces, he was completely surrounded and lost nearly all his reserve supplies. General Savaget's column came to his aid from another direction, and saved him from the fate of the Moreira César column. But without food or water General Oscar's forces could not even hold their supply base at Monte Santo.

Skilled in fighting and now armed with munitions captured from the previous expeditions, the fanatics fought bravely, in bold assaults that wore out and decimated the regular troops. The government sent a new brigade to the rescue, but it exposed itself carelessly to the fire of the backlanders, and was forced to retreat in disorder with the loss of its baggage train. Hunger, thirst, heat, and irritation over their inability to reduce the miserable stronghold of the fanatics created extreme tension among the government troops.

Susceptible to the political maneuvers of the President's foes, General Oscar helped lend the Canudos affair a meaning it could not have had. He did not hesitate to declare that the backlanders were equipped with the latest types of arms, probably bought in Europe and transported across the deserts by the monarchists, etc. In the impassioned atmosphere any story could spread unchallenged. Going over the head of the government, the commanding general addressed himself directly to the politicians and newspapers of the opposition in Rio, describing the events in the fighting and giving his political interpretation of them. The more fanatic Jacobins might discover in the general of Canudos the successor to Floriano. Meanwhile, the disasters he did not or could not avoid diminished the general's prestige.

The President replaced the Minister of War, who impressed him as too complacent about the political maneuverings of the opposition. The new minister, Marshal Machado Bittencourt, a veteran of the war with Paraguay, brave and austere, went to Bahia with fresh troops. He was determined above all to organize the services of transport and supply.

The campaign took a new turn. Attacked by regular troops and shelled by field artillery, Canudos did not hold out much longer. The fanatics defended their position house by house, foot by foot, displaying a resistance that was not only heroic but fantastic. Assaulting waves, one after another, were destroyed by the fire of the famished, thirsty, and ragged fanatics. On October 5, 1897, the last smoking huts were finally taken.

Not a sound, not a cry was to be heard, nor any sign of life to be seen. Antônio Conselheiro had been dead for some time, and so were the principal figures of his general staff. The strange citadel was a shambles. The government troops found no one alive to take prisoner; "a unique case in history," declared Euclides da Cunha. If any wounded fighters remained alive, they died in the fire that was set by some of the victors, who thought thereby to wipe out the stain of Canudos forever. The army and state police lost nearly 5,000 men in the year-long campaign.

The victory of the legal forces over the fanatics of Canudos did not add to the prestige of the government in the eyes of the radicals. The campaign against the President, born inside the PRF and supported by the legislative minority, grew in virulence. Vice-President Manuel Vitorino, now definitely separated from Prudente de Morais, became by force of circumstances a natural leader in the campaign. A group of young legislators and republican journalists formed the vanguard of the political contest, a contest that could only end by confronting the government with an intolerable choice between quitting and an act of violence of some sort. The November 5th attempt on the President's life saved his prestige and unexpectedly bolstered his authority.

On that day in 1897 some battalions returning from Canudos were disembarking at the old arsenal in Rio. After a brief visit on board the ship that brought them back, the President and his War Minister, Machado Bittencourt, went to await the returning veterans in the courtyard of the arsenal in spite of the high state of public excitement and warnings against doing so. Above the acclamations given him could be heard angry shouts and invocations to the memory of Floriano Peixoto. According to Rui Barbosa's speech before the Senate, a military deputy on the ship had incited the soldiers to show disrespect to the President.

As he crossed the courtyard of the arsenal, between his military aide and the War Minister, the President was attacked by Marcelino Bispo, a young half-breed soldier from the North, who leveled his pistol at him. The gun misfired and the President instinctively knocked it aside with the tall hat he held in his hand. The President's aide, Colonel Mendes de Morais, Marshal Bittencourt, and others seized and tried to subdue the struggling criminal. The President and the War Minister shouted to them to spare his life. Freeing himself for a moment from the hands of his captors, Marcelino stabbed Marshal Bittencourt several times, and also wounded Colonel Mendes de Morais and another officer. The President had already been led away from the arsenal. The Minister died shortly afterward, having bravely sacrificed himself to protect his chief.

The consternation in the capital and throughout the country was enormous. Brazil was not in the habit of settling her political dissensions by assassination. As a result of the tragedy, Prudente de Morais acquired the popular prestige he had previously lacked. The progovernment newspapers branded the crime as infamous, and described it as clearly political. The opposition press also condemned the crime, but as the act of a madman.

Congress became extremely excited. In a vehement speech to the Senate, Rui Barbosa analyzed the antecedents of the crime and called on the government to take stronger measures. Quintino Bocaiúva, despite his party connections with the opposition, also supported classifying Marcelino Bispo's crime as political.

Marshal Bittencourt's funeral was an apotheosis; the President, there in person, received enthusiastic acclamations. On November 6, the *Diário Oficial* published a short manifesto to the nation. It was signed by the President of the Republic, who, after exalting Marshal Bittencourt's sacrifice, declared that he depended on the support of the Brazilian people to uphold the authority vested in him by their free and spontaneous votes. In concluding he said, "The law will be respected, as the honor of the Republic requires it to be."

Fortified by the state of siege that Congress had finally granted him, Prudente de Morais initiated a reaction that often went beyond legal limits. The domination of the streets passed from the Jacobins to the reactionaries. The opposition newspapers were cowed into silence. The police investigation listed among the accomplices to the political crime some of the more ardent congressmen, such as Pinheiro Machado, who was arrested on board a warship, Barbosa Lima, former governor of Pernambuco, and Alcindo Guimarães, a journalist who was shortly deported with other prisoners to the island of Fernando de Noronha.* Congressional immunities were worth as much as they had been during Floriano's era. Francisco Glicério took refuge in São Paulo. Vice-President Manuel Vitorino was also denounced, but the charge was later withdrawn. The government closed the Military Club.

After three years of struggle against the impassioned Florianistas, the Jacobin agitators, and the politicians in Congress, Prudente de Morais finally succeeded in establishing the supreme authority of his office. He had tried several times, unsuccessfully, to set practical limits to federal intervention in the states, and to free himself from political subordination to the majority party in Congress [the PRF]. The attack on November 5th gave him the base that he had vainly sought. The presidential system adopted on November 15, 1889, was revealing the tremendous powers that the Constitution allowed to be placed in the hands of the President, a lesson not lost on his successors, who would take the greatest advantage of it.

Many of the politicians committed to the PRF took the opportunity offered by the November 5th crime to draw closer to the government. Rid of the Jacobin public meetings and constant threats of disorder, the city quieted down. The assassination of Marshal Bittencourt had stimulated the army to avoid contamination by partisan politics and to tighten up its discipline. The government of Prudente de Morais could therefore devote its last year to the problems of public administration.

Soon after the split in the PRF, the members who had sided with the government formed something of a coalition and took up the problem of the presidential succession. Bernardino de Campos, the Finance Minister, and Campos Sales, governor of São Paulo, were among the republicans with the best chance to be nominated. Prudente de Morais may personally have preferred his minister; however, he did not interfere in the matter, and good-naturedly accepted Campos Sales, first publicly nominated by the governor of Bahia, Luís Viana, and seconded by the progovernment parties in São Paulo, Minas, and Pernambuco, as the candidate. The Pernambuco chieftain, Rosa e Silva, was added to the official ticket as the candidate for Vice-President.

The opposition, faithful to the old PRF and led by Castilhos's Rio Grande do Sul Republicans, nominated Lauro Sodré, former governor

---

* One of five small, volcanic islands lying hundreds of miles off northeast Brazil. Long used as a penal colony, it is now a military base and a national territory. JLT

of Pará, and Fernando Lôbo, a Mineiro politician and Floriano's Minister of Foreign Affairs. In a manifesto on February 1, 1898, Júlio de Castilhos justified his party's opposition to Campos Sales's candidacy as a matter of principle, on the grounds that the President had given it an official hue.

As a presidential candidate, Campos Sales was anxious to avoid a situation similar to Prudente de Morais's, and was determined to sever beforehand any ties that might subordinate him to a party. At a political banquet given for him in Rio on October 31, 1897, he concluded an outline of his future administration's program by declaring that he was a candidate of the traditional "Republican party" from the days of the monarchy, and was therefore above factions of the moment. Having maintained his independence from the two large groups who had fought for the political control of Brazil during Prudente de Morais's administration, Campos Sales was free to declare himself thus.

His words had an immediate effect. What was left of both the PRF and the new coalition around Prudente de Morais, neither of which had doctrinal or electoral consistency, quickly began to dissolve. The opposing candidacies of Lauro Sodré and Fernando Lôbo lost all significance from that moment, and were kept alive merely out of courtesy to the two men.

Nine years of political quarrels, plots, military uprisings, and civil war had convulsed the Republic, and reduced the Treasury to extreme penury. To the common difficulties created by an improvised economic and financial policy were added the extraordinary ones resulting from the liquidation of the ventures of the Encilhamento and from the civil war. Though Prudente de Morais's government was well aware of the difficulties presented by the economic, financial, and administrative disorder, it could do little to overcome them. The Finance Minister, Bernardino de Campos, whom Manuel Vitorino had appointed to replace Rodrigues Alves, reported in detail on the Treasury's grievous situation and proposed several measures to meet it, but they were not approved. Among these were: a return to collecting part of the customs duties in gold; an income tax;* the head tax; an increase in excise taxes; and, principally, the transference and lease of some national properties, beginning with the Central Railroad of Brazil.

Prevented by the political agitations that were disturbing the country from carrying out any administrative program, Prudente de Morais

---

* First proposed by Rui Barbosa, which is interesting enough, given his earlier severe criticism of the United States' income tax in his "Letters from England." J M B

limited himself, like his predecessor, to stopgap measures, such as a domestic loan of 60,000 contos and a foreign loan of 1 million pounds in Treasury notes. The high coffee prices that had existed until his presidential term more or less sustained Brazil's economy by producing significant trade balances. In the second half of his administration, coffee prices dropped almost vertically. The average price of a 60-kilo bag, which had been 4 pounds in 1889, plummeted to 10 shillings in 1897, although Brazil's yearly production in this period had increased from 4 to 8 million bags in a world production of 12 million.

The favorable balance of trade of 5 million pounds in 1897 (resulting from £26,750,000 in exports, less imports of £21,500,000), which produced, at the average rate of 7½ pence per milreis, a credit balance of about 160,000 contos, turned into a deficit of more than 100,000 contos after the government's expenses abroad and remittances from Brazil by foreign concerns and persons had been covered in gold. Given such economic debility, the banks' and Treasury's issues of inconvertible paper currency, which totaled more than 700,000 contos by the end of Floriano Peixoto's administration, were a permanent nightmare to the Finance Ministers, who had been trained in the school of liberal economics.

The Union's public revenues made little gain; in fact they actually declined, if the figures are compared in gold at sterling exchange rates. From 170,000 contos in the last fiscal year of the monarchy, during which the milreis was worth 27 pence, the revenues had exceeded 270,000 contos in 1894 and 330,000 in 1897, when the milreis was down to 7 or 8 pence. Because of the depreciation and extraordinary expenses caused by the civil war, the budget deficits proved to be four and five times greater than had been expected. The eight domestic and five foreign banks in Rio had assets of 800,000 and 300,000 contos, respectively, and a combined capital of 317,000 contos, of which only 26,000 contos belonged to the foreign banks.

The budget for 1898 voted by Congress carried with it an estimated deficit of £5,408,000, or 48,606 contos in gold. The sale of warships to the United States, then at war with Spain over the liberation of Cuba, and the conversion into 5 per cent paper bonds of the 4 per cent internal gold loan, reduced the deficit by about 1 million pounds. The government would have to acquire the remaining 4 million pounds in the open exchange market, which was then being juggled by the foreign banks. Congress had calculated the cost of converting paper into gold at the 1897 average rate of 8 pence to the milreis. The rate had since fallen to 5 pence. The paper needed to meet the gold demands, including a Treasury note of 1 million pounds that would fall due that year, therefore amounted to 240,000 contos out of a total gross revenue estimated at 343,000 contos.

Such a situation spelled virtual bankruptcy: the Treasury would not be able to meet its commitments. Prudente de Morais's government, consonant with the old Brazilian tradition, could think of no other solution than another foreign loan. But Brazil's bad credit in Europe's money markets made such a solution impracticable. It was then that there arose the idea, though it was not original, of a funding loan, which would be a kind of moratorium. An example of its application had occurred recently in South America itself.

After the frenzy of paper emissions during the presidency of Juárez Celman in Argentina, the Pellegrini government had signed an agreement with the country's foreign creditors to take out a new loan that would be used to pay the past-due accrued interest. President Sáenz Peña, who had greater confidence in the nation's economic vitality, denounced the agreement, and obtained a reduction in the interest rate for the new loan.

Campos Sales, becoming alarmed at the threat of bankruptcy, which would rob him of the government, planned to go to Europe and reach a direct understanding with the creditors in London. At the same time, Prudente de Morais and his Finance Minister, Bernardino de Campos, had asked Rodrigues Alves to go on such a mission. The cautious statesman applauded the idea, but declined to undertake the task himself and suggested others to take his place. Campos Sales's offer of himself came, therefore, at the opportune moment. His special position as President-elect, the future executor of whatever plan might be agreed upon, lent him singular authority.

In April 1898 Campos Sales sailed for Europe. On arriving in Paris, on his way to London, he found awaiting him the draft of a formal proposal for a funding loan. After his departure from Rio, the manager of the London & River Plate Bank had arrived with a proposal for a moratorium from the London bankers, in the very form for which the outgoing and incoming administrations had been searching. The Rothschilds, closely tied to Brazil's finances ever since her political independence, saw their interests menaced (British capital invested in Brazil amounted to more than 80 million pounds), and hastened to aid a debtor facing bankruptcy by offering a first composition.

They proposed a loan of 10 million pounds, to be guaranteed by all of Brazil's customs duties, and by the revenue of the Central Railroad of Brazil and of the water supply services in Rio de Janeiro. For its part, the government was to withdraw from circulation paper equal to the value of each loan installment, figured at 12 pence per milreis. This paper was to be turned over to the foreign banks, in trust, and burned in public. The government would further agree not to contract any new debts during the period of the moratorium.

In London, Campos Sales obtained from the Rothschilds some changes in their original proposal. The rate of exchange for the paper currency withdrawn from circulation was set at 18 pence instead of 12; the time allowed for interest payments was increased to three years, and for amortization payments to ten years; and the special guarantees for the loan were limited to the customs duties collected in Rio de Janeiro, the other customs houses becoming subsidiary. Although the government planned to burn the paper money, it was to have the option of leaving it on deposit to be used to purchase future bills of exchange.

Certainly such an agreement was a confession of insolvency, and did not greatly honor the Brazilian Treasury's tradition of punctuality. It was, however, in keeping with the logic of the times, when British bankers held sovereign control over the finances of poor or improvident countries, always confident of the diplomatic and, if necessary, military support of the British Empire.

Prudente de Morais's administration, nearing its end and with a successor chosen, closed in peace. On the day he relinquished his powers, Prudente de Morais, who had been received with prejudice, opposed so bitterly during his agitated term of office, and permitted to accomplish very little in the field of public administration, was enthusiastically acclaimed in the capital city. Brazilians were beginning to realize at last the great services the austere republican propagandist had rendered the nation by restoring civil order.

13. Campos Sales
[1898–1902]

*Portrait of Campos Sales — Joaquim Murtinho's financial
Darwinism — The Treasury is filled and the country
emptied — The quantitative theory of money — New party
schisms — Campos Sales's firmness and the unpopularity of
his government.*

The new President, Manuel Ferraz de Campos Sales, was born in Campinas, state of São Paulo, in 1841, the same year as Prudente de Morais, with whom he was a student at the Law Faculty in the state's capital. While still a student he tried his hand at political journalism, writing for the liberal papers of the day, *Razão* and *Província de São Paulo.* On graduation, he began his career as a lawyer in Campinas. Political contests fascinated him. He was elected a provincial deputy from São Paulo in 1867 by longtime Liberals. Opposed to the progressive Liberals, he soon found himself at home among the "advanced" members of the Radical party.

Campos Sales was not one of the signers of the Manifesto of 1870; for that matter, neither was Prudente de Morais. Yet in the following year he was a member of the organizing committee of the Republican Party of São Paulo, and in 1873, after the Itu convention, a member of its executive committee. In their outline of a "Constitution of the State of São Paulo" in the future republic, the Paulista members of the executive committee of the Republican party, Campos Sales among them, set forth the essential features of their federative program. In 1881 Campos Sales returned to the provincial chamber as a Republican deputy, and in 1885 he was elected to the General Assembly along with Prudente de Morais.

Much more than Prudente de Morais, Campos Sales was a doctrinaire; the cast of his mind and his political training placed him on an intellectual par with the French republicans who had been the "loyal opposition" to Napoleon III. Prudente de Morais was noted for his coldness and moral austerity, for being reserved and distant; Campos Sales, on the other hand, was expansive, charming, vain, fond of display, a fluent writer, and an eloquent speaker. His education as a lawyer and journalist had widened his mental horizons and made it easier for him to be more flexible in political action. Sincere, brave, and honest like Prudente de Morais, he also grew in readiness for the highest posts in the approaching republic.

As Minister of Justice in Deodoro's Provisional Government, Campos Sales discharged his administrative duties brilliantly. He initiated innumerable measures directed toward building the judicial structure of the new regime, such as the Penal Code, the civil marriage laws, and the organization of the courts. In the political sphere, he distinguished himself by his liberal attitudes and his solicitude in dealing with the frequent misunderstandings among his fellow republicans.

Thus, he tried to block the nomination of Prudente de Morais as a presidential candidate against Deodoro. In the Constituent Assembly he aligned himself with the radical federalists, and was thus very close in doctrine to Castilhos's Republicans. During Floriano's administration he upheld the legal government, as did almost all the Paulista Republicans, against the rebels in Rio Grande do Sul and in the navy. When the crisis arose between the PRF and Prudente de Morais, Campos Sales did his best to bring about a conciliation. When the break occurred, while he was governor of São Paulo, he sided with the federal government.

The consistency of his previous positions, therefore, gave Campos Sales the prestige that let him place himself above party. When he was presented to the voters, the program that he offered was his own. He said the head of government must never be the head of a party. His functions, therefore, like those of a chief justice, must be apart from partisan politics.

Nor did he disavow his long-standing federalism. Averse to the interventionist policies that Prudente de Morais had tried vainly to establish, Campos Sales reaffirmed his doctrine of a sovereign state within a sovereign union: "The federal authority will not exercise its power within the territory of the states except in matters pertinent to the welfare of the Union, and even then will act through their respective officers, since there should exist no hierarchic or subordinate relationships between the agents of local government and those of the Union."

Scrupulous respect for state autonomy seemed to him basic to the republican system; as he later emphatically declared, Article 6, which somewhat obscurely prescribed the norms for federal intervention in the states, was the "heart of the Republic." His position on parliamentarism was no less radical; the executive and legislative branches should operate in separate fields, harmonizing their functions in the best interests of the nation. The government itself was to be concentrated in the hands of its sole depository, the President, who was also its only agent before other nations. We shall see how Campos Sales's federalism and presidentialism resulted later in the formation of state oligarchies and the crushing of Congress, and rendered it impossible to control republican politics by means of large national parties.

In the meantime, in a country badly weakened and impoverished by partisan dissensions, Campos Sales's political orientation made it possible for him to begin the execution of his financial plan, based on the funding loan negotiated by Prudente de Morais's government, even before his election. For Prudente de Morais's government the funding loan prevented bankruptcy; for Campos Sales's it laid the groundwork for deflation. During the Provisional Government, whether as a member of Deodoro's cabinet or of the Constituent Assembly, Campos Sales had always been hostile to inflationist policy. Without considering himself a specialist in financial matters, he had stood resolutely with those who opposed excessive emissions of inconvertible paper money. The financial disarray of the Republic's governments probably convinced Campos Sales of the urgent need to return to the Empire's traditional policy. As a candidate for the presidency, he declared several times that he put financial reconstruction ahead of all other problems.

Campos Sales's inauguration was attended by representatives of nearly all the great powers; this impressive showing tickled the vanity of Brazilians, who were generally regarded as incorrigible revolutionists. On assuming the presidency, Campos Sales found the nation wearier than ever. The Republic's first civilian government had not succeeded in restoring internal harmony; the strife that had torn the country had prevented the reconstruction of its administration. What hopes could the new President hold out? What would his financial plan mean for the weakened nation?

During the first republican decade, conditions in Brazil were not much different, after all, from those during the twilight years of the Empire. After the Encilhamento's short spell of euphoria had vanished, the Brazilian privileged classes had returned to their former way of life. The rural middle classes, their dreams of easy riches shattered, went back to their abandoned fazendas, where they could enjoy at least a degree of self-sufficiency. Even the great mass of former slaves, who, intoxicated by their unexpected freedom, had deserted the old feudal estates, once more sought the shelter of the "big house."

But the fazendas had lost their former plenty. The downfall of sugar, reduced to serving the modest domestic markets, had ruined the North-eastern sugar barons, and paralyzed their initiative. The crisis in coffee prices was threatening the fazendeiros in the South with a like fate. The extraordinary boom in Amazon rubber bolstered the sick national economy a little, and proved the salvation of the *nortistas* who had been reckless in risking their lives in the malarial swamps of the jungles and in selling their souls to the greedy rubber extractors.

The remarks with which Joaquim Murtinho had begun his report as Minister of Transportation at the beginning of the Prudente de Morais administration were no doubt a guide for Campos Sales. Analyzing Brazil's general economic and financial situation, Joaquim Murtinho did not merely criticize the policies followed until then by the Republic. He also outlined a plan of government based on the formal logic of the nineteenth-century liberal economists. The republican policy, according to Murtinho, embodied two dangerous illusions, a belief in the extraordinary riches of Brazil and confidence in the dynamic capacity of inconvertible paper, which in the final analysis were only different aspects of the same error.

Beginning with the first idea, the republican statesmen had believed it possible to industrialize the country rapidly. An increase in tariffs and steady emissions of inconvertible currency by both the Treasury and the banks were naturally the means by which the government could foment material progress. Since the Brazilians did not possess the initiative and work habits of the North Americans, and Murtinho did not mention the basic elements of heavy industry found in the United States, such as coal and iron, all attempts at industrialization were doomed to failure. The new industries did not get beyond the planning stage. They merely immobilized a part of the capital in circulation, stimulated urbanism, and increased imports, all to the detriment of agriculture, the true source of Brazil's national wealth.

Inflationism spurred speculation and gambling, and, worst of all, depressed the rate of exchange, for to Murtinho, as to all subscribers to the quantitative theory of money, the rate of exchange was tied almost wholly to the volume of paper in circulation. As a logical consequence of the protectionist and industrializing policies, there arose a mania for public jobs and government controls. These in turn were transforming the government into an entrepreneur of works and services, thus [said Murtinho] paving the way for the advent of the greatest plague of modern societies: socialism.

There was nothing new in the doctrine outlined by Murtinho. It could be found in any manual of political economy, and corresponded perfectly to the individualistic conception of the nineteenth-century philosophers. Cold, skeptical, a man of affairs, a Darwinist by instinct and education, Joaquim Murtinho was the most self-consistent of the Republic's ministers. Diagnosing Brazilian life, he also prescribed the remedy, but as a homeopathic physician accustomed to treating symptoms, he applied the same technique to his handling of Brazil's finances.

Brazil's problem was essentially to balance the Treasury's finances. It was therefore absolutely necessary to deflate the currency, cut expenses, increase taxes, abandon public works, return to agriculture, and withdraw the government from industrial activity, which could flourish only under free, individual enterprise. In his rigid understanding of liberal economics, Murtinho dissociated the financial problem from the economic one. Once the government was able to restore the soundness of its money, which would raise exchange rates and balance the budget, the reconstitution of economic forces would come about automatically, without dangerous official interference. The weakest, those least able to adjust, would perish in the competition to survive. Darwin's theory of natural selection was regarded at the time as almost infallible scientific dogma. The state, a mere juridical expression of the social superorganization, should not be influenced by sentimental considerations.

It was easy at first for Campos Sales to adhere strictly to his administrative plans and to carry out the terms of the funding loan. Beginning in January 1899 the government would deposit with the British and German banks in Rio, which would act as trustees, the paper currency withdrawn from circulation according to the terms of the loan. The Chamber, in agreement with the administration, chose to have the paper burned rather than kept on deposit, in order to prevent its possible use in banking transactions that might stimulate speculation in foreign exchange.

A gold reserve fund for the outstanding paper currency was set up; the gold was to be accumulated from customs duties. A fund for the redemption of Treasury bills was also set up. It was to be supported by the revenue from leased federal railroads, budget surpluses, and any other available resources. The government's plan was capped by an increase in taxes.

The percentage of customs duties that had to be paid in gold was raised from 10 to 15 per cent, and in the next year the tariff was thoroughly revised. The government, which had earlier been so averse to a protectionist policy, now went much further in that direction than any of its predecessors, although it announced the tariff increase simply as a revenue measure. Stamp and excise taxes on domestic goods were also created, as well as stamps for direct taxation of income. The Union's fiscal net spread over the entire country; it included all visible sources of revenue and assessed numerous additional tax liabilities. The states copied the federal example, increasing especially the taxes on the exports allotted to them by the Constitution. The already debilitated Brazilian economy, precariously supported by São Paulo's coffee and Amazonia's rubber, had to hand over its meager surpluses to the three overlapping fiscal systems of the Union, the states, and the municípios.

Joaquim Murtinho's deflationist policy was having its full effect on business and banking credit, both inadequately established in the first place. Bankruptcies followed one after another, culminating with that of the Banco da República, which had been created by a merger of the Banco do Brasil and the Banco da República dos Estados Unidos do Brasil. In September 1900 the semiofficial bank suspended payments, which set off a tremendous panic. In keeping with his doctrine of the survival of the fittest, the Minister of Finance let the bank go under.

The reestablishment of credit abroad and the rise in the exchange rates were compensation enough for the domestic hardships. The quantitative theory of money had won a great victory in actual practice. In the four years 1898–1902, while the total of inconvertible paper dropped from 780,000 to 679,000 contos, the rate of exchange rose from 8½ to 12½ pence to the milreis. The national budget showed a surplus, and the government was piling up gold in the London banks.

By the end of these four years, 116,000 contos of Treasury paper had been redeemed. In 1901 it had been possible to resume paying the service on the foreign debt in gold. The government had paid off the Treasury loan of £1,120,000 contracted by Prudente de Morais. The Treasury owed nothing and had a credit balance in its accounts. The market price for the government's foreign and domestic bonds was rising; public revenues had also increased. Campos Sales and Joaquim Murtinho could claim that they had achieved their goal.

But Brazil had grown even poorer. The sugar barons of the Northeast had been ruined; their lands had gone to the money-lenders in the cities. A similar fate menaced the coffeegrowers in the South. The old hopes of urban industrialization had gone glimmering, binding the economy to monoculture and exports. The increased taxes raised the living costs Murtinho had promised to reduce. But the Treasury, saved by the people's increased poverty, had been refilled, and the European bankers had regained their confidence in Brazil as a field for profitable investment.

The Rothschilds were sincere in their praises of Campos Sales at the end of his term of office. The flow of capital from Europe to Brazil, now that the country had been saved from bankruptcy, began once more and continued until after World War I, when American competition appeared on the scene. The Treasury's restored finances would enable Campos Sales's successor, the prudent and clear-sighted Rodrigues Alves, to inaugurate a period of national development.

The execution of the financial plan completely monopolized the attention of Campos Sales's administration. But in order to execute it, Campos Sales first had to tone down party conflicts, diminish Congress's itch for greater independence, and restrain dissension in state politics. The conservative reaction that arose during and persisted after the adoption of the Constitution of 1891 had shown how the chief executive, even without military dictatorship, could run the country with no great hindrance. Using different methods, Campos Sales would arrive at a like position.

The top priority of the financial problem had naturally made Joaquim Murtinho, as Minister of Finance, the cabinet's leading figure. Epitácio Pessoa, who had made a name for himself in the Constituent Assembly while still quite young, and who had been Floriano Peixoto's unrelenting foe, had been named Minister of the Interior and of Justice. Severino Vieira, a politician from Bahia, was Minister of Transportation and Public Works, and Olinto Magalhães, Minister Plenipotentiary in Switzerland, was Minister of Foreign Affairs. General Medeiros Mallet and Admiral Pinto da Luz had taken their posts as War Minister and Navy Minister, respectively. By thus selecting his cabinet from among the various republican factions and freeing himself from any possibility of partisan control, Campos Sales had caused what was left of the PRF and of the Republican party organized by followers of Prudente de Morais to rapidly dissolve, though he did not succeed in eliminating the rancor that divided them.

The approaching elections for a new Chamber and one-third of the Senate in 1900 served to restrain the politicians, who were eager to remain in the government's good graces. Each of the two large, disintegrating groups created by the splintering of the PRF was hoping to win the government's favor, which would make the reelection of its members certain. The state parties presented their own complete tickets, hoping to win at the third and final scrutiny of the mandates, made by Congress and following the one made by the tally boards. There was even some consideration given to electing two chambers in order to force the government to choose between the opposing factions.

To prevent the threatened confusion, the government secured a revision in the rules of the Chamber to provide that the actual mandates would result from the final vote counts signed by a majority of the municipal chambers in each electoral district. It further proposed that the temporary presidency of the newly elected Chamber would be held, not by the oldest member of the previous body, as was then the practice, but by its former president, provided he had been reelected, of course. The new president was to appoint a five-man committee to pass on the validity of the credentials. The committees of inquiry into contested elections would be chosen by lot. Thus, by means of the powerful "Committee of Five," the government could arbitrarily recognize or repudiate the mandates that were presumably from the people.

As an extension of his political plan, Campos Sales secured the support of some large states, principally Minas Gerais, whose governor declared his support to be unconditional. In exchange, the recognition of mandates in the new Chamber and partly reelected Senate would favor the local parties that sided with the government. By serving their interests, Campos Sales won their backing for the execution of his financial policy. Thus any evidence of victory at the polls by the opposition in the states was disregarded in advance; the candidates put up by the local governments were automatically seated. The old comedy of democratic elections in Brazil was being officially sanctioned.

However, the most serious consequence of Campos Sales's political horse-trading with the governors was the immediate consolidation of the state oligarchies. The groups that had gained control of the states were made up mainly of former members of the monarchic parties. They calmly went about setting up powerful machines devoted to graft, bribery, and violence. Although the Congress of 1900 had the same vicious origins as the Congresses, including the imperial Parliaments, that preceded it, it was the one that gave up its last pretense of free political power.

The Union was converted into feuding groups, large and small, concerned much more with their regional interests than with those of the nation as a whole. Their demographic and economic superiority gave São Paulo and Minas the leading positions in political control. Rio Grande do Sul, with Borges de Medeiros at its head, but still under the powerful discipline imposed by Júlio de Castilhos, was another decisive element. It was represented on the federal level by the increasingly prestigious Pinheiro Machado. Pernambuco, Bahia, and the state of Rio de Janeiro were the other "big states" that had numerous representatives in the legislative bodies. The small states gravitated into the orbits of the big ones, as if imitating the international balance-of-power game.

The priority he had given financial problems, and his solution of them, did not exempt Campos Sales from the political difficulties that had plagued his predecessors. His control of politics through the state governors had apparently given him almost unanimous support by Congress, but his hopes were quickly dashed. Partisan feelings were only waiting for an opportunity to explode. Opposition in the newspapers grew from day to day, criticizing the extortionate tax regulations and the scandalous "recognition of mandates." Some former monarchic leaders, unreconciled to the Republic, tried to use the growing discontent as an opportunity for revolution and restoration, but the government, without resorting to a state of siege, easily thwarted their plots.

The opposition political movement headed by Rosa e Silva, the Vice-President, was more serious. It recreated the situation that had arisen between Deodoro and Floriano, and between Prudente de Morais and Manuel Vitorino. Under Rosa e Silva's leadership, the congressional blocs from Pernambuco and Maranhão, allied to the opposition in some of the states, came out against the government's financial policies, especially on the leasing of the railroads [to foreigners].

In September 1901 political dissension led by Prudente de Morais broke out in São Paulo, some of whose brilliant and active deputies threw their support to the opposition in Congress. For some years deep, unspoken grounds for misunderstanding had seemed to exist between Campos Sales and Prudente de Morais. Certain groups were naturally interested in stimulating the dissension, when it had come to light, over the question of choosing a governor for São Paulo. In spite of conciliatory efforts by Governor-elect Rodrigues Alves, Campos Sales's rigid criterion for the recognition of mandates by the Congress had been rejected immediately by some Paulista deputies closely tied to Prudente de Morais. Shortly afterwards, the Paulista faction set forth in a manifesto their reasons for dissent, insisting, as a point of doctrine, on the necessity for a constitutional revision that would moderate the excessive powers held by the President of the Republic.

National public opinion, insofar as such a term applies to Brazil's disjointed immensity, held Campos Sales's severe fiscal administration in low esteem. The public was pleased by the violence of the opposition press campaign, and enjoyed the fiery debates in the Chamber of Deputies, especially during the agitated period when newly elected or re-elected representatives were seated, but its enthusiasms were not aroused by the politicians' campaign, since it was accustomed to doubt their sincerity anyway. The conservative lower-middle classes would not forgive the high taxes, but mostly they wanted the administration's term of office to end peaceably, in the hopes that the new President, Rodrigues Alves, would initiate a less drastic policy. The Republic had already suffered much at the hands of its saviors.

On November 15, 1902, when he stepped down from the presidency, Campos Sales experienced a final outburst of popular antipathy for his government, cleverly fostered by the opposition newspapers. His passage from the presidential palace to the railway station, where he was to embark for São Paulo, was accompanied by prolonged jeering and booing from the crowds that lined the streets. His pride must have suffered greatly from the public hostility, which contrasted so greatly with the acclamations Prudente de Morais had received four years earlier. But Campos Sales's conscience as an administrator must have been clear. After the sacrifice demanded of him by the Brazilian people, he was leaving his successor a house in order, its accounts in balance.

Republican politics had been degraded more than ever by his system of control through the governors. The democratic significance of Congress had been debased. The last hopes of free play between representative institutions were fading. His admitted buying of newspaper influence had officialized journalistic corruption. His extreme monetary deflation had provided a screen behind which bankers and speculators, both foreign and domestic, reaped excellent profits. Nevertheless, Campos Sales had to his credit his perfect personal uprightness, his tolerance, and the firmness with which he met his government's commitments. Without his four years of strong fiscal rule, it would have been very hard for Rodrigues Alves to embark on his large program of public works.

To the further credit of Campos Sales's administration were the first decisive steps taken to develop the Civil Code, submitted to Congress as a draft bill by Clóvis Bevilaqua. In foreign policy he had tried to bring about closer continental relations, which had so greatly concerned the first republican rulers. The arbitration of the old Misiones conflict had not hurt the friendship between Brazil and Argentina. In August 1899 Argentine President Júlio Roca made an official visit to the capital of Brazil, a visit Campos Sales returned in the following year. The Baron of Rio Branco had scored another diplomatic victory in the dispute over Amapá. Joaquim Nabuco, despite his enormous efforts, had not been as successful in the contention with England about British Guiana. But the essential fact in 1902 was that the Republic could look back on its past internal disorders and financial ventures as a closed chapter, and was ready for a new time of order and constructive work.

14. Rodrigues Alves
[1902–6]

The third Paulista administration — The economic import of Rodrigues Alves's candidacy — Economics and state interference — Public works — The social milieu of Rio de Janeiro — The remodeling of Rio de Janeiro — The sanitary campaign — Osvaldo Cruz — The battles against yellow fever and smallpox — Rioting in the streets — Internal agitations — Rio becomes "civilized" — Impetus gained by the nation.

The nomination of Rodrigues Alves to succeed Campos Sales was almost inevitable. The trust he inspired in the politicians and his position as governor of São Paulo made his name almost suggest itself. The politicians led by Vice-President Rosa e Silva, who had opposed Campos Sales, started a movement to oppose Rodrigues Alves also, or rather to oppose the possibly official nature of his candidacy, but it was short-lived. Quintino Bocaiúva, an early Republican and then governor of the state of Rio de Janeiro, which he described as a firm in bankruptcy with himself as receiver, was also nominated, but his was the only state that voted for him. The ruling elements in Pernambuco and Maranhão confined their opposition to nominating the Pará politician Justo Chermont to run for Vice-President against Silviano Brandão of Minas Gerais.

And so, for the third time in a row, a Paulista was elevated to the highest post in the Republic. But unlike Prudente de Morais and Campos Sales, Rodrigues Alves was not one of the early Republicans; rather, he had pursued his public career in the service of the monarchy. Born in 1848 in Guaretinguetá, in the northern part of São Paulo, Francisco de Paula Rodrigues Alves was noted for his industry and intellectual balance even when he was a schoolboy. Joaquim Nabuco mentions the first prizes Rodrigues Alves won every year.* He also distinguished himself at the Academia de Direito [Law School] in São Paulo, where he edited small political journals and, for a while, the Conservative party's news-

---

* They were fellow students at Colégio Pedro II [in Rio]. Nabuco mentions the prizes in his autobiography, *Minha Formação.* J M B

paper. On becoming a member of the party, he gave up his law career to enter politics.

As a provincial deputy in 1872, Rodrigues Alves became known for his views on education, which he argued should be both free and compulsory, a somewhat revolutionary idea at that time. As a general deputy in 1887, he was appointed to the presidency of São Paulo province by the Baron of Cotegipe's Conservative cabinet. The question of abolition was agitating the province and dividing the Conservatives. As the delegate of a cabinet that had tried to hold back the wave of liberation, Rodrigues Alves repressed certain abolitionist manifestations that seemed excessive to him. In doing so he was labeled a slavocrat. In an official document he set forth his belief that the abolitionist cause was just, but that it was necessary to prepare the national economy for free labor, and to step up the attraction of European tenant farmers.

When the Cotegipe cabinet was replaced by that of João Alfredo, Rodrigues Alves resigned the São Paulo presidency and returned to the Parliament. He voted in favor of the May 13th law, and soon after participated in a parliamentary study of the economic problems created by the end of slave labor. Princess Isabel, while acting as Regent, conferred upon him the title of Conselheiro, which would always be attached to his name.

The Conservative chamber of which he had been a member was dissolved when the Liberal Ouro Prêto cabinet came into power. Rodrigues Alves was not reelected. The coming of the Republic thus found him out of office. Like most of the monarchists, he regarded the Republic as a fait accompli against which it would be useless to fight. He decided to give up public life and devote himself entirely to his coffee fazendas, but in the end he agreed, along with other distinguished monarchists, to be a delegate from São Paulo to the Republic's Constituent Assembly, where he displayed the utmost discretion, moderation, and balance.

Under Floriano Peixoto he became Minister of Finance. Responsible for the Republic's finances after the calamity of the Encilhamento, Rodrigues Alves tried to return to traditional cautious policies: retrenchment in public expenses, nationalization of bank emissions, and reduction of the volume of unredeemable paper currency. When he did not receive wholehearted support from Floriano Peixoto, whose succession of Deodoro he had considered unconstitutional, Rodrigues Alves resigned his post. He was then elected to the Senate. Floriano Peixoto, skeptical of all men and little inclined to regard any man highly, seemed nevertheless to esteem Rodrigues Alves. Under Prudente de Morais, Rodrigues Alves was Minister of Finance again, until he was replaced by Bernardino de Campos when Manuel Vitorino temporarily assumed the presidency.

Rodrigues Alves was at that time one of the best types of political ruler: discreet, serene, liberal, and sincere, more concerned with fact than with theory, always placing public interests above partisan or private politics. The radical republicans probably never forgave him his monarchic origins, but most of those who wanted to find the right way to head Brazil once more toward order and peaceful work depended greatly upon his common sense and administrative experience. He had neither Prudente de Morais's extreme detachment nor Campos Sales's fondness for doctrine.

In 1900 he was elected governor of São Paulo. He tried to limit the effects of the dissension between Prudente de Morais and Campos Sales on politics in his state. He remodeled the public services. He revealed a clear-cut understanding of local economic problems. With the governorship of São Paulo the former Conselheiro of the Empire had reached the penultimate rung of the ladder to the presidency of the Republic. The new regime now seemed to feel itself strong enough to accept help from others besides the traditional republicans. However, the importance of Rodrigues Alves's candidacy was essentially economic.

The transmigration of coffee from the valley of the Paraíba in Rio de Janeiro to the São Paulo plateau had been completed. Two-thirds of Brazil's exports, estimated at the beginning of the twentieth century to be 700,000 contos, consisted of coffee, most of it from São Paulo. Brazil's economy was therefore being supported by the rich red soils of that state. Minas Gerais, the other Brazilian state that by reason of its demographic and political importance could compete with São Paulo in running the country, was also connected with the coffee industry.

The policies of the First Reign and of the regency did not have, properly speaking, any economic significance. Brazil was then making her first experiments with liberalism. The Second Reign came into power after the end of the sugar cycle, and thus found its major support among the Fluminense fazendeiros, the slavocratic barons, and the ultraconservatives of the valley of the Paraíba. In its closing phase, when the question of abolition could no longer be ignored, it fell back, as Oliveira Viana rightly notes, on the statesmen in the North, Pernambucanos and Baianos, who were more easily influenced than the Southerners and less bound to an economy of slave labor.

Like the Empire, the Republic had been inaugurated in an atmosphere created by the doctrinal enthusiasms and dreams of grandeur of learned men who lacked experience in public affairs. Deodoro da Fonseca and Floriano Peixoto represented the power of the sword, possibly the only power able to sustain the new regime. The elections of Prudente de Morais and Campos Sales to the presidency did not reflect the desire of the economically strongest state in the federation for political hegemony; it signified merely a natural stage in the careers of two organizers from a region where republican ideals had inspired the best partisan organization.

But the reasons why a third politician from São Paulo became President are different. The Republic was passing from a doctrinal to a building phase, that is, from developing institutions to developing the economy. Prudente de Morais had reestablished civil order. Campos Sales's strong fiscal policy had ended the foolhardy financial ventures of the Encilhamento, put the Treasury in order, and restored public credit. Rodrigues Alves came into the presidency as the symbol of a new policy, although probably neither he nor the other leading men of the period were aware of it. Brazilians, sick of partisan struggles, parliamentary rhetoric, and street riots, and impoverished by tax extortions, were hoping to find in this cautious man a levelheaded executive capable of governing them competently.

Rodrigues Alves filled his cabinet with the best-qualified and most experienced men in public life. J. J. Seabra was appointed Minister of the Interior; Lauro Müller, an Army major with an exclusively nonmilitary career, was made Minister of Transportation and Public Works; and Leopoldo de Bulhões, noted in the Constituent Assembly for his excessive federalism and preoccupation with financial matters, was chosen to head the Ministry of Finance. Marshal Paulo Argolo and Admiral Júlio de Noronha were made War Minister and Navy Minister, respectively. The Ministry of Foreign Affairs was placed under the Baron of Rio Branco, already famous for his great diplomatic victories of Misiones and Amapá.

None of the so-called big states were represented in the cabinet. Putting aside regional politics (later to become almost extinct as a criterion for choosing cabinet members), the new President chose the assistants he considered the most capable, and gave them a free hand within the general framework of his program. "My ministers," he is reported to have said, "do anything they wish, except what I don't want them to."

In an address to the legislature of São Paulo when he became governor, he had outlined what amounted to an administrative program for the whole nation. At the traditional banquet at which the Presidents-elect read their government program, usually more or less vague and innocuous, Rodrigues Alves summarized the ideas that he had previously expounded, and would expound again in his inaugural message to the 1903 legislative session. On the political side, he did not advocate the constitutional revision sought by the dissident politicians in São Paulo, since the framework of the Constitution of 1891 provided ample room for harmony between the federal and state governments and between the executive and legislative branches. He insisted, however, on passage of the Civil Code, and on new laws that would assure greater honesty in elections.

Although he proposed to continue the financial policies of the preceding administration, he observed that the national economy needed to be revived. Brazil needed to equip her ports, develop her internal communications, and improve sanitary conditions in the big cities, beginning with the capital. Despite his long-standing partiality for economic liberalism, he believed that poor, young countries such as Brazil could not dispense with aid to the states. Individual initiative was too uncertain and timid to encourage their development. Cleaning up and modernizing Rio should be the starting point for any constructive policy.

Brazilians were not usually deluded by the promises of politicians about to take office. However, the commitments assumed by Rodrigues Alves struck them as sincere. Without wasting words, he tackled some concrete problems. The politicians wanted only to get closer to the administration. The Congress also, due for reelection under the new President, had no interest in disturbing him.

During Campos Sales's four-year term the federal finances had been put in order. Brazilian credit had been restored in Europe's money markets, which would facilitate recourse to a large foreign loan. In October 1902, therefore, even before Rodrigues Alves's inauguration, a law was passed authorizing an issue of gold or paper bonds for a loan to be used for improvements in the ports of the Republic, the amount for each port to be such that the fees it could expect to collect would cover its portion of the interest and amortization payments. In May 1903 the contract was signed for a loan of £8,500,000, discounted at ten per cent with interest at five per cent, guaranteed by a first claim against a special two per cent tax, to be paid in gold, on all imports and other revenues from ports and docks.

Simultaneously, the government issued bonds for domestic loans to expropriate various port and railroad concessions. The port works of Rio de Janeiro were entrusted to the engineer Bicalho. This marked the beginning of the new building policy. The new works required a wide avenue [today's Avenida Rio Branco] to be cut through the center of the city. A special commission was organized for this purpose, and was placed under the direction of Paulo de Frontin, an engineer whose re-markable ability to get things done had been proved during the last years of the monarchy by the remarkable success of his water system for the city. The Prefecture of the Federal District began a program of ur-ban renewal under the direction of Pereira Passos, another engineer of extraordinary energy.

The capital at the time of the proclamation of the Republic was a vast, provincial town. Set in great natural beauty, between mountains and beaches, it was neglected and run-down. In many ways it resembled a colossal, temporary encampment of human hordes who had renounced life's material comforts. It had narrow streets, tiny squares, few trees or gardens, and decadent architecture of incredibly bad taste, tawdry and ridiculous; the traditional spacious and staid colonial houses had dis-appeared. Its one badly paved central thoroughfare, Rua do Ouvidor, was the daily rendezvous of the local political elite; along it businessmen and bureaucrats rubbed shoulders with adventurers and prostitutes. Rio was not very different from the poor and dirty town that Pedro I had made his imperial capital. The Second Reign, having little interest in comfort and good taste, had resigned itself to the patriarchal physiog-nomy of Rio de Janeiro, which was like that of other large cities in Bra-zil and the rest of the world. It did not see how incongruous its sedate men in frock coats and high hats were among the often indecorous scenes in the main streets.

The old provincial customs still prevailed. The new habits of hygiene, domestic comfort, and open-air living, which the British had started in Europe and which were spreading to other countries, had not yet made themselves felt in Rio. The Cariocas spent their lives in their unattrac-tive houses, indifferent or resigned to fate, concerned mainly with plans for next year's carnival or with the lottery and the *jôgo do bicho** that enthralled the population. The men continued wearing sober, formal attire, while the women dressed almost like Arab women.

The most popular forms of amusement were the little theaters and concert halls. In the winter months the Teátro Lírico was opened for performances by Italian opera companies and French comedy troupes.

---

* A highly popular though illegal gambling game, still in vogue in Brazil. It is based on the winning number of the official lottery. The payoff is similar to that of the numbers game, which originated in Harlem. It is called *jôgo do bicho* (animals game) because the last two digits of the winning number are assigned to one of 25 different animals in alphabetical sequence. Thus, by betting on one animal, one stands four chances in a hundred to win. The winning animal is forecast by dreams, hunches, or association of ideas. JLT

The Encilhamento had put a stop to the importing of fine carriage horses from Argentina. Most of the theatergoers went by mule-drawn streetcars or in the new electric *bondes*,* over whose benches white cloth was spread to protect the passengers' fancy attire. The Cassino Fluminense and some neighborhood clubs held occasional balls. Dance parties in private homes were frequent.

The Bohemian literary set consumed apéritifs in the *delicatessen* and cafés, discussed literature and politics, and made puns, then the most popular form of wit. The *Jornal do Comércio* retained its prestige, and other doctrinaire papers flourished. However, the *Gazeta de Notícias* was livelier, more literary, and more ironic, and provided the best news coverage. The Brazilian Academy of Letters was founded, openly patterned on the French model.

The literary currents remained the same as during the Empire. Sílvio Romero, one of the ardent apologists for Tobias Barreto, founder of the "Recife School" of philosophy, wrote his own *História da Literatura Brasileira*. Machado de Assis, unfettered by any school, wrote the masterpieces of his old age, all tinged with the bitter pessimism of the negative philosophies around him. His last books, however, especially those written after his wife's death, reveal touches of tenderness, of whose existence, after all, he could not have been totally unaware. Introverted, resentful, subtle, he was the perpetual president of the Academy of Letters, and incontestably the great master of Brazilian literature. Olavo Bilac, Raimundo Correia, and Alberto de Oliveira excelled in Parnassian poetry. Aluísio de Azevedo was the most notable of the realistic followers of Zola. Raul Pompéia, a fervent Florianista, wrote his *Ateneu*, in which he revealed his ruthless, almost morbid, personality. The first symbolists made their appearance, without notable success. Eça de Queirós, a model of grace and irony, whose picturesque style and vivacity seemed to lend new forms of expression to the language, was the undisputed literary idol of Portugal.

In attempting to avoid the solecisms of the writers of the Second Reign, the better-known authors and publicists tried to adhere, to the point of exaggeration, to the classic norms of the Portuguese language. They considered the correct use of pronouns, word inflections, Gallicisms, and correct spelling to be matters of capital importance. Rui Barbosa, with his purist predilections, long oratorical periods, and classically rounded phrases, was the leading example of a great writer, and the one who most influenced the new cultivation of good language,

* The name *bondes* given to the new electric cars was derived from the bonds sold by a Canadian company to finance them. JLT

somewhat as Cicero did for the Italian humanists of the Renaissance.

The politicians in Congress were abandoning the British model, to which the statesmen of the Empire had been so susceptible, for that of the French Third Republic. Gambetta was a symbol for the radical republicans. Guizot and Thiers had not yet lost their high reputation. Taine's and Renan's deterministic theories were beginning to outweigh the theories of Comte and Spencer among the new generation of intellectuals. Rui Barbosa had aroused interest in American public law, which was considered indispensable background for interpreters of Brazil's Constitution of 1891, lawmakers, jurists, and government officials. In 1897 Joaquim Nabuco de Araújo published his great work, *A Statesman of the Empire,* dealing with the political evolution of the Second Reign.

Public education had not advanced; the small elite of scholars remained, as always, uprooted from Brazil, unable to emancipate themselves from the European influence on all intellectual activity. Brazilian letters lacked national flavor and identification with national sentiments. In this respect, Euclides da Cunha's *Os Sertões,* born of the tragedy of Canudos, was the first great Brazilian book. Its spectacular success somehow awakened Brazilians to examine things in their own land. Graça Aranha's novel *Canaan,* a drama of the Nordic immigrant in the tropics, may also have been a sign of the approaching esthetic revival, in which Brazil's intellectuals would endeavor to free themselves from subordination to the dogmatic French rules.

Brazil had not had a heroic period in her history such as the one the United States had had. This would explain in part the weak characterizations in even the best Brazilian books, their inability to capture the unrest and uncertainty of the young nation. Brazil's artists and writers lived much more in the atmosphere of Europe than in that of Brazil. Not until the heightening of nationalistic feeling during World War I would Brazilian literature begin its emancipation.

The Republic's first administrations either had not tried or had not been able to do much toward beautifying the capital. In the neglected city with filthy kiosks blocking the streets and squares, yellow fever, bubonic plague, cholera, smallpox, and malaria were common. Brazilians were ashamed of the city's reputation for disease, which was often purposely exaggerated, but they did not know how to improve matters.

Rodrigues Alves's plans opened up prospects of a new life for the capital, but they collided with the old ways, and that was unforgivable. Public opinion rose against him as it does almost universally when large-scale remodeling is undertaken. President Rodrigues Alves was squan-

dering the money collected by his predecessor on sumptuous construc-
tions, and was reviving the illusions of the Encilhamento. Few persons
believed the works could succeed.

The main opposition came from the merchants, nearly all of whom
were coarse and stubborn Portuguese. They were supported by the newspapers, who were anxious for their advertising. But Rodrigues Alves
serenely kept on with his program. Minister Lauro Müller and the engineers Frontin and Passos were turning the city upside down, opening
new streets and widening public squares, indifferent to the clamor of
selfish interests and parliamentary and journalistic demagoguery. Even
more difficult than remodeling the city was sanitizing it: specifically,
ridding it of yellow fever and smallpox. The government had to overcome not only the reluctance and greed of the owners of urban real
estate, many of whom lived abroad on the large incomes from their properties, but also the antiquated ideas, prejudices, superstitions and jeal-
ousies, spitefulness, academic pride, and doctrinal fanaticism of the
people.

Yellow fever probably came to Brazil from Africa. It first appeared in
Rio de Janeiro toward the end of 1849. Science at that time was completely in the dark about how the disease was caused and transmitted,
and only a little less so about how to treat it. Doctors improvised sanitary
defenses out of the methods used against infectious diseases, but it was
all in vain. In the first hot months of 1850, more than 4,000 persons, out
of a population of a little over 200,000, fell victim to the new plague,
which soon became endemic in the dirty, unprotected, tropical city.
Every summer the Fluminenses resignedly awaited the outbreak of the
plague, which especially attacked foreigners and provincials who had
not become immune or were still poorly acclimated.

The Republic had not changed the sanitation methods inherited from
the monarchy. The Americans, however, believed in Finlay's theory that
yellow fever was transmitted by a certain genus of mosquitoes, and were
applying the concept with excellent results in Cuba. Rodrigues Alves,
while governor of São Paulo, had followed with interest experiments
by two Paulista doctors on the "mosquito theory." The idea of wiping
out yellow fever by a systematic extermination of the carrier mosquitoes
was thus known to the President. The previous directors of the public
health department in Rio had already decided to begin such a campaign, but nothing had been done.

The Minister of the Interior, J. J. Seabra, asked Dr. Sales Guerra to
take charge of the public health department. He declined the invitation, but suggested Dr. Osvaldo Cruz, who had been trained at the

Pasteur Institute in Paris. After Cruz returned to Rio in 1899, he worked at the Serotherapeutic Institute of Manguinhos, and gained renown as an eminent bacteriologist. The Director of Public Health of the Federal District, wishing to enlarge the work at Manguinhos, had asked Dr. Roux, the director of the Pasteur Institute, to recommend some specialist for the job. Dr. Roux nominated Osvaldo Cruz.

Raised to the top position at Manguinhos, Osvaldo Cruz enlarged and disciplined the Institute, converting it into an active center for scientific research. The government thus chose to run the federal health services a man whose scientific authority and administrative capacity were already well-established. Convinced that Finlay's theory and the American methods of prophylaxis against yellow fever were correct, he made extermination of mosquitoes the basis of his own program. In a report to the Minister of the Interior, he said: "Among the sanitary problems that should be attacked at once, by far the most important is yellow fever, for which a practical solution already exists. We now need only follow in the footsteps of the Americans who tackled and solved it completely in Havana."

Confident of the President's support, Osvaldo Cruz did not limit himself to revising sanitary regulations. He went directly to the people, explaining the prophylaxis of the plague in a publicity campaign such as the Americans had carried out in Cuba, Central America, and the Philippines. The newspapers, eager for scandal, stirred up popular prejudice against him and his assistants, whom they dubbed "mosquito swatters." Doctors and hygienists denied the Finlay theory, or at least the efficacy of the American methods. Journalists and writers satirized him daily, and were echoed by demagogues in Congress. The courts issued writs of habeas corpus to protect the "inviolability of private domiciles" against the housecleaning efforts of public workers. But Osvaldo Cruz tenaciously and calmly continued the fight, even improving on the Americans' techniques. He was applauded by American and European scientists, and his fame spread internationally.

Deaths from yellow fever were 584 in 1903, when the prophylactic campaign was begun. They declined to 53 in 1904. By 1906 the ancient plague had virtually disappeared, after having claimed about 60,000 victims in 60 years. Victorious in his fight against yellow fever and against frequent outbreaks of bubonic plague, Osvaldo Cruz began a systematic battle against smallpox. Here he was dealing with a disease whose prophylaxis, Jenner's vaccine, had been known since the end of the eighteenth century. In 1811 the Prince Regent, Dom João, ordered vaccination in Rio against smallpox. One of the early decrees of the Pro-

visional Government provided for compulsory vaccination of infants
and for periodic vaccination thereafter, but it had never been complied
with.

Introducing pathogens into the human body to protect it against contagious diseases was always an easy subject for demagogues to exploit.
Even among the most educated classes, prejudice against vaccination
could not be entirely overcome. The positivists, for example, hidebound
by Comte's prejudice against Jenner's vaccine, persisted in denying its
merit. Others admitted its value, but were opposed to making it compulsory. The freedom of the citizen in that period of intransigent individualism was paramount, even over the risk of contagious epidemics.
After a long and heated campaign, a law making vaccination compulsory
was passed by Congress.

A revolutionary campaign was begun by the doctrinaires, some sincere and some fanatic; they included old Jacobins, agitators, street orators, rabble-rousers, and professional brawlers, who set off riots at incendiary meetings. Workmen were incited to strike. From the most
sordid and dangerous parts of the city, from the *favelas* [shantytowns],
the hills, the slums, there emerged the mobs, always ready for disorder,
violence, and crime.

A league against compulsory vaccination, founded to be the center of
the reaction against Osvaldo Cruz, soon spread to take in the government and even the established order. The old dream of a positivist military dictatorship, capable of saving the "purity of Republican principles," reappeared. Senator Lauro Sodré, a military man and politician
who had distinguished himself by his stand against Deodoro da Fonseca's attempted coup, was the head of the revolution. Because of the
depth of his convictions, Osvaldo Cruz could not understand the attack
against him. He wanted to resign to save the government more trouble,
but, strengthened by Rodrigues Alves's trust and support, he withstood
the onslaught.

Street rioting broke out on the afternoon of November 10, 1904, and
again the next day. Disorder, clamor, and direct attacks on the police
increased in the center of the city. Bands of rioters tried to march against
the presidential palace. At nightfall the revolt intensified. Gas lamps
along the streets were destroyed. From barricades, windows, and corners
the police were fired upon. Street traffic became jammed; telephone lines
were cut.

The government decided to act vigorously. The Minister of Justice,
J. J. Seabra, and the Chief of Police, Cardoso de Castro, personally directed the operations. Army and navy forces were called in to help the

police. The rebellion, however, was not confined to civilians in the streets. It spread to the barracks, where a part of the young military had become infected by the revolutionary propaganda. Positivist officers met in the Military Club to organize the insurrection. General Hermes da Fonseca thwarted an attack on the preparatory Military Academy in Realengo, a distant suburb of the capital, but the Military Academy at Praia Vermelha, close to the center of town, rebelled. The military insurrection naturally aggravated the civilian one. Rodrigues Alves was advised to leave the Catete palace and take refuge on a warship, where his authority would be better protected, but he refused, saying, "My place is here and I shall not leave it alive."

Under the command of General Piragibe, the troops loyal to the government marched against the Military Academy on the night of November 14. In a dark street between the presidential palace and Praia Vermelha the first clash occurred. After a few shots, the insurgents retreated. The rebel general was fatally wounded, and the other leaders abandoned the field. At daybreak on November 15, the fifteenth anniversary of the Republic, a mixed brigade of army and navy men took the Military Academy at Praia Vermelha without opposition.

The military insurrection was defeated, but this victory for the government did not end the insurrection in the streets. In some neighborhoods the fighting behind barricades continued. On the waterfront a band of hoodlums defended themselves stubbornly. The famous stronghold of "Port Arthur," named in recollection of the recent Russo-Japanese War, finally gave up when it was threatened with naval bombardment. Rodrigues Alves came through the test and won public acclaim. The Republic had once more survived the disturbances that, except for brief intervals, had plagued its existence. The third civilian President could now peacefully carry on his program of public works.

The remodeling of Rio de Janeiro and the improvements in sanitation were the first victories of the Rodrigues Alves administration, and marked a historic step in the nation's life. It was not only the capital city that was being modernized and beautified, that was ceasing to look like an ugly provincial town. All of Brazil seemed to take on new life, with greater confidence and pride in herself.

The sordidness of the streets and public squares was fast disappearing. The Canadian investment company that had financed the bondes, and would later underwrite the city's light, power, and transit systems, was beginning to replace the inadequate street lighting. The first automobiles were making their appearance in the broad, asphalted, and tree-lined streets. The Cariocas' daily habits were being transformed. Their clothes were less somber and better suited to the tropical climate. Ladies no longer felt ill at ease about walking on Rua do Ouvidor and other downtown streets, which were now cleared of prostitutes. Transatlantic steamers began to anchor at the modern harbor. A fondness for sports, especially water sports, and for open-air living was growing among the young people. "Rio is becoming civilized," the papers said.

New buildings multiplied in the transformed city. Though many remained somewhat scanty, rococo, and garish, and though many were mere hurried imitations of every possible style, on the whole they showed substantial improvement over the houses of the previous generations. The first motion-picture houses began to appear, and with them the first influences of the American way of life.

Other large Brazilian cities were stimulated by Rio's example. The capital of São Paulo was rising rapidly. The principal cities in the North became less satisfied with their own backwardness. Though they were old centers of civilization, as conventional as Rio or even more so, they demanded modern port works, broad streets, and more adequate public utilities. The rich Brazilians in the provinces began spending the tourist season in Rio, now that it was rid of yellow fever, instead of going to Europe. A whole new capital [Belo Horizonte] was built for the state of Minas Gerais.

Rodrigues Alves obviously could not solve all of Brazil's growth problems in just four years. But by carrying out the sanitation and beautification of the capital, he provided the initial push, which his successors could not reverse, and thus provided a new moral climate for Brazilians, one in which other triumphs would take place. Because of the diplomacy of the Baron of Rio Branco, the establisher of the nation's frontiers, a kind of national pride she had not until then known began to grow in Brazil.

15. Rodrigues Alves's Diplomatic and Economic Policies

The Baron of Rio Branco — The Acre question — The Treaty of Petrópolis — Incorporation of the Acre territory — Friction with Argentina — Rebuilding the armed forces — Public works — Federal finances — Exchange and foreign trade — Surplus coffee production — The compact of Taubaté — Presidential succession — Pinheiro Machado and republican politics.

Some of Brazil's disagreements over frontiers with her neighbors remained unsettled. One of Rodrigues Alves's commitments was to settle them. Integrated at last into the republican system of the Americas, and with arbitration of international questions a precept of her political charter, Brazil proposed to define her territory peacefully.

By inviting the Baron of Rio Branco to become his Foreign Minister, Rodrigues Alves was choosing the best man to carry out his new foreign policy. The son of the Viscount of Rio Branco, an eminent statesman of the Empire, the Baron had spent a wild and Bohemian youth. But even as a young man he was known for his works on Brazilian geography and history. During the Paraguayan war he had accompanied his father on a diplomatic mission to the River Plate. He had served in Parliament, taught school, and written political journalism before he entered the consular service. After his victory on the Amapá question, Rio Branco moved into the diplomatic service as Minister Plenipotentiary in Berlin.

Despite his openly monarchic sympathies, Rio Branco adapted himself to the Republic and served it from the start as its general commissioner in Europe for emigration to Brazil. Floriano Peixoto, who had gone to school with him and held him in esteem, appointed him advocate for Brazil in the Misiones dispute, which gave him his first chance to achieve national renown. During his thirty-six years in Europe he had perfected his talent for diplomacy. But in spite of his long stay, as consul in Liverpool, in Victorian England, it seems that the major influence on his character was the Germany of Bismarck and Wilhelm I, then in the full flowering of power and national pride. In close touch with the diplomatic intrigues of Europe that followed the Franco-Prussian War and accompanied the growth of colonial imperialism, the young consul acquired a realistic view of life that would always characterize him.

A sincere patriot and nationalist, Rio Branco was robust in mind and body, disdainful of the merely rhetorical idealism that was always so spontaneous in Latin America, and alert to current developments. He was commanding and authoritative, but was also a polished and shrewd opportunist, skilled in using men's virtues as well as their foibles and defects. In diplomacy even more than in other things, he was convinced that legal forms carry weight only when backed by money or by force.

It was natural that, with his background, Rio Branco should stress Brazil's need to gain international respect. No one was better than he at reconciling a love for Brazil's past with a vision of her future greatness. Although he preserved the substance of the Foreign Ministry's diplomatic traditions, he would never accommodate himself to its bureaucratic old fogies and stuffed-shirt atmosphere.

The confidence and optimism that Rodrigues Alves's public-works policy had created in Brazil was also propitious for the success of the Baron's bold diplomacy. Of Brazil's unsettled disagreements over frontiers, the most serious was with Bolivia, over the vast region of Acre on the upper Amazon. Until the rubber industry began to grow, the disputes about frontiers in the inaccessible rivers, swamps, and forests of Amazonas were not very far-reaching. To Brazil as to Bolivia, both too immense, underpopulated, and unequipped to fully exploit their own regions, the Acre territory was an ill-defined, mysterious, and hostile desert, barely rising above floodwaters, a pretext only for periodic hairsplitting diplomatic discussions. After the discovery of vulcanization [in 1839], industrial use of rubber had grown steadily. This raw material, almost all of which was from the Amazon area, began to assume great importance in Brazil's economy. At the beginning of the Rodrigues Alves administration, rubber accounted for about twenty per cent of the country's exports. Of all the Amazonian regions the most productive in rubber was Acre. Brazilians had occupied the territory and were bravely extracting its natural wealth. The recognition of Brazil's claim to it was therefore essential.

A diplomatic treaty in 1867 had agreed on the boundary between Brazil and Bolivia, but since it had not been implemented, the exact line between Acre and Brazil had never been drawn. From the time the wild rubber industry had begun to flourish, a steady stream of Brazilians had flowed into the nominally Bolivian territory. The Brazilians were mainly sertanejos [backlanders], driven from their drought-stricken homes in the Northeast. The frequent disorders in the area had grown worse since the advent of the Republic, and had in fact become intermittent outbreaks of outright revolt. For example, in 1895 a Spanish adventurer headed a movement to convert the Acre territory into an independent state. The Brazilian and Bolivian governments, trying to settle their differences of the moment, agreed on protocols in 1895 and 1899, one of which drew a protest from Peru. Although Brazil upheld the principle of *uti possidetis,* rooted in the diplomatic traditions derived from Portugal, she sought nevertheless to reconcile it with the treaty of 1867.

Bolivia, finding herself unable to rule a geographic area far from her center of power, signed a contract in 1901 with a syndicate of North American capitalists, the Bolivian Syndicate, who were conceded rights to exploit all of the contested territory. The contract in effect transferred sovereignty over Acre to the Bolivian Syndicate, which assumed the full civil government of the territory and in whose affairs not even the administration at La Paz could interfere. Thus there was instituted in South America a sort of system of capitulations. American businessmen, at that time heavily suspect because of the imperialistic tendencies of their big-stick policy and dollar diplomacy, were installing themselves as the undisputed masters of a vast area in the upper Amazon watershed.

The repercussion in Brazil was intense. The other South American republics, though not inclined to side with Brazil, did not hide their apprehensions either. Campos Sales's administration had not been able to block the signing of the contract or the ratification of it by the Bolivian Congress. It would be left to Rio Branco to resolve the dangerous rift.

In August 1902 a new rebellion, directed by a Brazilian, Plácido de Castro, seized control of the entire Acre region, and forced the Bolivian forces concentrated at the customs port of Puerto Alonso to surrender. Under the command of the President, General Pando, Bolivian troops prepared to march across both highlands and swamps against the Brazilian revolutionists. Rio Branco was not given to useless talk: Brazilian troops in turn started moving toward the upper Amazon. The show of military force enabled him to avoid a war whose future political consequences would have been more dangerous than its immediate ones. The able negotiations that followed resulted in a friendly repeal of the concession to the Bolivian Syndicate. On November 17, 1903, the Treaty of Petrópolis was signed, putting a definitive end to the Acre question.

Prior to the treaty, the American syndicate had been bought out for

£126,000 by the Rodrigues Alves government. Brazil also paid 2 million pounds to Bolivia and committed herself to build the Madeira–Mamoré Railway,* long considered of great political and economic significance to the two countries. In addition to settling an old and irritating squabble, Brazil had peacefully added an area of 180,000 square kilometers [69,500 square miles], the richest in Amazonia rubber, to her national territory, and had foiled the attempt to implant in Latin America the system of chartered companies, which so often in the contemporary history of Africa and Asia had turned into colonial conquests.

In three years the federal revenue from taxes in the Acre territory, though loosely collected, offset the indemnities paid, and covered the cost of the loan for the construction of the Madeira–Mamoré Railway. Ably profiting from the work of his predecessors and his technical advisers, Rio Branco had achieved his greatest diplomatic victory, even in the face of impassioned opposition by a part of the Congress and the press. His popularity grew enormously; perhaps no other man in Brazil had ever won such great prestige.

The dispute with Bolivia having been settled, the Brazilian Foreign Ministry found it easier to negotiate other boundary questions directly with Peru, Ecuador, Colombia, Venezuela, and Dutch Guiana. Another diplomatic victory that greatly affected national pride was the naming of a Brazilian as the first cardinal in Latin America. The United States and Brazil raised their respective legations in Rio and Washington to the status of embassies. Joaquim Nabuco, Brazil's first ambassador to Washington, worked to establish closer relations between the two nations.

Brazil, like other Latin American countries, was beginning to free herself from England's economic and political predominance. In spite of his European education, and in spite of the deep impression made on him by the Second Reich, Rio Branco was a forerunner of the new spirit of continental solidarity and of the transformation in Pan-American doctrine. Rio de Janeiro was the host city for the Third Pan-American Conference [in 1906], at which time it was visited by Elihu Root, the Secretary of State of the United States.

* This short (227 miles) but incredibly difficult line was needed to give landlocked Bolivia access to the navigable portion of the Madeira River in Brazil, which would connect her via the Amazon to the sea. The railroad was built at a very high cost in men and money by an American entrepreneur, Percival Farquhar. But with the collapse of rubber its usefulness was largely destroyed, and it has since been abandoned. For an interesting account of this venture, see *The Last Titan* by Charles A. Gauld, Institute of Hispanic-American and Luso-Brazilian Studies, Stanford University, 1964. JLT

However, Rio Branco's diplomatic victories, or rather distorted interpretations of them, which he could not or did not try to correct, had
created numerous misunderstandings between the Foreign Ministries of
Rio de Janeiro and Buenos Aires. The latter was headed by Estanislaw
Zeballos, who had signed the Treaty of Misiones with Quintino Bocaiúva, and who had been the losing advocate for Argentina when the
question was submitted to the President of Switzerland for arbitration.
In spite of certain similarities of psychology and political training, the
two ministers did not esteem or understand one another. Zeballos was
the embodiment of old anti-Brazilian tendencies that would diminish
only with time. The rivalry between the two men therefore seemed to
reflect a latent animosity between the two nations.

Brazil and Argentina were enacting on the South American stage the
same kind of competition for continental hegemony that marked European diplomacy and led to war in 1914. Everything was a pretext for
the Argentine statesman's animosity, such as Brazil's reorganization of
her army and navy. Many other matters were easily misinterpreted at the
time. Even a false telegram was published, which could have precipitated
a fight between the two countries, as one had the Franco-Prussian War in
1870. The insidious campaign was quelled by the good sense of the
Brazilian and Argentine leaders, and the two largest South American
countries resumed peaceful relations. The Brazilian diplomatic victories
had not been dimmed by Argentine enmity.

The reorganization of the armed services was a great concern during
Rodrigues Alves's term. Brazil needed to build up her material defenses
to match Rio Branco's diplomacy, and to be prepared for any threats
against her security. The settling of internal conflicts and the Treasury's
prosperity permitted the government to begin reforming military training, constructing a modern powder factory, building strategic railroad
lines, etc. For the first time, extensive maneuvers of military divisions
were executed in the countryside near the capital.

It was essential to rebuild the navy, which had been in first place in
Latin America during the Empire, but had been almost wiped out by
the revolt of 1893. In December 1904 the government was authorized to
build a naval squadron of three battleships of 12,000 to 15,000 tons, three
cruisers of 9,200 to 9,700 tons, six destroyers, three submarines, and
other auxiliary craft. At the same time, to complement the navy's rebuilding program, the government built a modern arsenal near Rio.
The training ships, flying the still little-known Republican flag, resumed
plying foreign seas as they had during the monarchy.

The activity of the Ministry of Transportation and Public Works was also intense. Rio's new port works gave it the appearance of a modern capital, and stimulated the country's other maritime cities. Either directly or by concessions, construction was begun on port works at Bahia, Recife, and Belém, and on a mole at Rio Grande do Sul's only harbor. Some of the essential railroad lines were extended, and the first stretches of new ones, notably those that would connect Mato Grosso to the Bolivian frontier and São Paulo to Rio Grande do Sul, were built. For the first time, it seems, the idea took hold that railroads should form a national network, and should not consist merely of separate lines connecting isolated regions to the seaboard as if each were a self-sufficient economic unit.

The handling of public finances was naturally what most interested a former finance minister like Rodrigues Alves. With a broader concept of public finances than Campos Sales, he directed his policy more toward vitalizing the nation's economy. The transformation of Rio, the development of the railroads and of coastal shipping, aroused Brazilians to a more realistic confidence in their country. They were losing a little of their old ingenuous narcissism, which had been satisfied with rhetorical outbursts that cited the riches of the "incomparable land" as one of the reasons "why I am proud of my country." They were beginning to examine the national realities less sentimentally.

The first national census, though inefficient and faulty, had revealed the broad lines of the country's political and economic geography. The population had grown from an estimated ten million in 1872 to seventeen million. From 1890 to 1900 the Federal District had grown from 500,000 to 700,000 inhabitants, and the city of São Paulo from 64,000 to 240,000. The large urban centers in the North, such as Bahia, Recife, and Belém, had not increased, if they had not decreased, in population.

The economic and political axis had moved completely from the North to the South. In 1872 the populations of the two regions were the same; in 1900 the South had three million more people than the North. The states of São Paulo and Rio Grande do Sul had each tripled their populations. The Paulistas' march to the west, extending the coffee plantations, fighting their way through virgin forests and wild Indian territory, was rather like the frontier days of the American West. Immigration intensified during the last years of the Empire—35,000 European colonists had entered São Paulo in 1887—and reached its maximum in 1891, when 216,000 entered the southern states. Though this rate declined in the years immediately following, it rose again to over 100,000 per annum.

Rio de Janeiro, which had always been the center of European immigration, mostly Portuguese, followed by Rio Grande do Sul, mostly Germans and Italians, yielded first place to São Paulo, to whose coffee plantations flowed masses of Italians. In 1900 São Paulo's population of 2,200,000 included 530,000 immigrants. Such an influx naturally modified not only the ethnic characteristics of the southern populations, but the methods of rural work as well. The population of the North, which attracted few immigrants, was subject to undernourishment and poor hygiene, and thus to endemic diseases that produced a high mortality rate, especially among infants. It therefore fell steadily behind that of the South.

São Paulo produced about half of Brazil's coffee, which averaged between sixty and seventy per cent of Brazil's total exports. Amazonian rubber had transformed Manaus into the most isolated urban center in the world, a city of luxury, profligate spending, and speculation. Brazil imported most of her food and almost all manufactured goods. Except in the large cities and the immigrant-swollen South, the extremely low standard of living of the masses, of whose existence the laissez-faire ruling classes were barely aware, had risen very little.

The remodeling of Rio had restored European confidence in Brazil's future, as Rodrigues Alves had believed and promised it would. This in turn had enabled the government to carry out its building policies without hurting its finances or credit.

Faithful to his old liberal ideas, Rodrigues Alves pursued Campos Sales's general policies about paper currency, reserve funds, gradual deflation, gold taxes, etc. The rate of exchange had risen from twelve pence in 1902 to sixteen pence in 1906. The volume of inconvertible paper had diminished. The public debt had been reduced. The yearly budgets showed a surplus. Three million pounds of the loan for the port of Rio were saved for the next administration to use. The Treasury had large funds in London, and its payments were on time. The favorable balance of trade averaged 200,000 contos yearly. Despite the modesty of Brazil's resources, she had entered upon a period of undeniable prosperity.

Economic management would seem to be a tranquil field, but Rodrigues Alves had not always found the going easy. The first big crisis in the overproduction of coffee led the government to oppose the immediate interests of São Paulo's coffeegrowers and businessmen, which aggravated political problems. Maintaining the general lines of Campos Sales's program to raise the value of the currency, which was facilitated by the investment of foreign capital in public works, Rodrigues Alves had succeeded not only in raising the exchange rates, but also in stabilizing them somewhat. But this policy, which served the country's interests in general, did not serve those of the coffee exporters, or those of other groups more or less connected with the nascent manufacturing industries, who were still not satisfied with the already stiff tariff protection they enjoyed. The lower the rate of exchange was, the larger was the number of milreis earned by the sale of coffee in foreign markets. In the same way, the increased price in milreis of imported manufactures would allow a higher margin of profit for goods made in Brazil.

Although the manufacturers were not yet strong enough to impose their point of view on the government, the producers and shippers of coffee felt themselves sufficiently powerful to try to determine economic policies. Coffee prices had been declining steadily, and in 1905 hit bottom, in terms of domestic currency. At the same time, there had been an extraordinary increase in coffee production. Moving away from the worn-out soils in north and central São Paulo, the coffee industry spread westward, reaching out to the new lands in Paraná and Mato Grosso. In the process, virgin forests were razed, railroads built, towns hastily thrown up, and astonishing wealth amassed. The new breed of Paulista bandeirantes acquired, along with a kind of regional pride, habits of luxury, prodigality, and unprecedented daring in business.

Having easily beaten all her competitors, Brazil, especially São Paulo, now almost completely monopolized world coffee production. The 1906 crop reached the unheard-of figure of 22 million bags.* Including the 4 million bags left over from previous crops, the total was 16 million bags in excess of world consumption. This formidable overproduction caused still lower prices, and aroused panic among coffee men and the political interests allied with them. Only direct interference in the markets by the federal government could save them. But they asked not only for immediate help to control the surplus stocks in order to keep up prices, but also for price supports and measures that would have fundamentally changed the government's monetary policy, such as a special rate of 12 pence to the milreis to be set for coffee transactions, in imitation of a price-support scheme practiced in Argentina.

The governors of the three principal coffeegrowing states, São Paulo, Rio de Janeiro, and Minas Gerais, met in Taubaté in the state of São Paulo in March 1906, and signed an agreement to support coffee prices; they did not clear it first with the federal government. The three states obligated themselves to maintain a certain price per bag delivered to the ports of export, and at the same time to hold back those bags in excess

---

* The standard bag of coffee weighs 60 kilos, or 132 pounds. JLT

of world consumption. In order to finance the plan, a tax of 3 francs in gold [per bag] would be levied on the coffee shipped abroad, and would be used to cover the interest and amortization on special loans.

Though he was a large coffee producer himself and a Paulista, President Rodrigues Alves stubbornly refused to endorse the scheme, whose future disaster he foresaw clearly. Even though the government could not prevent the three states from making such an agreement, federalist sentiments still being very much alive at that time, he adamantly refused to allow the changes proposed in monetary policy. In a message to Congress he firmly and calmly criticized the proposed low rate of exchange, pointing out the disruption in the monetary standard it might cause. He was victorious in his fight, but the victory did not last. The politicians of the opposition were able to provoke a crisis over the question of his successor, and thus to pave the way for their interventionist policy, whose failure in 1929 contributed greatly to the success of the revolution of 1930.

Campos Sales's policies had facilitated the establishment of state oligarchies, tight little groups connected more or less by family ties. The persons who could not break into the inner circle formed the opposition, which was already ready to seize whatever opportunities military insurrections and popular rebellions might create. Engrossed in large administrative matters, Rodrigues Alves had not tried to change this situation. Little by little the oligarchies drew together, as Francisco Glicério's PRF had done, into a sort of party federation, led by Pinheiro Machado, a Senator from Rio Grande do Sul who was the spokesman before the administration for the Castilhistas. As President of the Senate, Machado set himself up to oppose the President, and thus became a parallel force that cramped the Executive's freedom of action and threatened to drive him into intransigent positions. There were incidents in some of the states that disturbed public order. Trained in the parliamentary school of the Empire, and believing that the nation would have to learn how to run itself, Rodrigues Alves tried to fulfill his duty as he saw it by staying out of the violent clashes between factions, even though this required sacrificing personal friendships and party interests. In a country in which political traditions and public opinion were so precarious, the President's neutrality seemed to weaken his authority.

In 1904, when he had been in office less than two years, Rodrigues Alves went off on an excursion to Minas Gerais. A political purpose was attributed to his visit: he was laying the ground for Afonso Pena, the Vice-President, to succeed him. The politicians who were in open or concealed opposition to him had found the pretext to stir up public reaction: official candidates. The interference by the head of state in the choice of his successor, though almost necessitated by the lack of any really national parties, was held to be the greatest outrage against the purity of the republican system.

Pinheiro Machado, whose power and prestige in determining federal policies had become well-established during Campos Sales's administration, assumed the leadership of the movement against Rodrigues Alves's alleged purposes. Meanwhile, the party that had gained control in São Paulo and had had three candidates in a row elected President nominated Bernardino de Campos, former Minister of Finance, who eight years before had been considered a possible successor to Prudente de Morais. Rodrigues Alves had no objection to the nomination of his fellow Paulista, who was supported by the same followers as himself.

The politicians who opposed Afonso Pena's official candidacy revived their campaign even more aggressively. They were now fighting against not only official candidates, but also the nominee himself and his ideas. Bernardino de Campos was regarded as a weak man whose attitudes and ideas were fixed. During the civil war in Rio Grande do Sul and the navy revolt, he had been governor of São Paulo, had upheld the legality of Floriano Peixoto's position as President, and had thereby kept his state from becoming involved in the fratricidal contest, which facilitated the nomination of Prudente de Morais for the presidency of the Republic. As Minister of Finance he had championed certain courageous ideas on economic and financial matters. He was not in favor of Campos Sales's unilateral policies, encouraging industry by high protective tariffs, or changing the money standard.

Alcindo Guimarães, a journalist allied with the Pinheiro Machado clique, obtained an interview with Bernardino de Campos in which the presidential candidate outlined his administrative program, which rejected protectionist schemes such as the compact of Taubaté would embody. The groups who felt their interests threatened by Bernardino's attitude opened up a sharp press campaign against him. Pinheiro Machado nominated another Paulista, Campos Sales, whose financial ordering of the nation was beginning to be judged more serenely. After agreeing to the nomination, which seemed to him to make amends for the injustices he had suffered, Campos Sales became convinced he was being used to weaken the prestige of his own state, and withdrew.

After the two Paulista candidates had been sacrificed, Governor José Marcelino of Bahia suggested Rui Barbosa. Barbosa, however, declined the honor on the grounds that the candidacy of a Mineiro would be more viable. The partisans of Pinheiro Machado and Rodrigues Alves therefore agreed on Afonso Pena, whose allegedly official candidacy had been the pretext for the party split. Thus São Paulo lost the chance to contribute a fourth President. The accession of the politician from Minas meant victory for the advocates of industrial protectionism, government intervention in the coffee trade, and financial reform. One of the governors who signed the compact of Taubaté, Nilo Peçanha, was the official [sic] candidate for the vice-presidency of the Republic.

By organizing the party majorities into a single bloc that claimed the right to nominate presidential candidates, Pinheiro Machado seemed to consolidate his own prestige on the national level. Afonso Pena's candidacy, following the collapse of that of Bernardino de Campos, led to an easy victory. Thus there appeared on the Republic's political scene a new Partido Republicano Federal [PRF]. In place of Francisco Glicério's tactful leadership, however, was the forceful command of a man of action, a former caudillo and typical frontiersman, who was at once intelligent, intuitive, brave, rough, tough, and headstrong, which, however, did not keep him from compromising and sidestepping in difficult situations when it seemed like the thing to do.

The lines of his striking face seemed sculptured in bronze; his bearing was military. He loved ostentatious living, sports, gambling, and bold strokes. He was loyal to his friends, and could inspire passionate zeal or implacable hatred in others. He brought distinguished figures and loquacious eggheads under his control as if they had been stolid local political bosses, and had strong ties with businessmen. His residence, "Morro da Graça," a famous mansion on a knoll in one of Rio's middle-class neighborhoods, received visitors indiscriminately, and was a daily Mecca for politicians. Warm and affable, Pinheiro aroused, even among young intellectuals who disapproved of his kind of life and were scornful of his general lack of culture, that kind of enthusiasm that men who easily risk their money and their lives always inspire in others.

Having blocked a new Paulista candidacy, Pinheiro Machado considered himself a sort of informal prime minister to the President-elect. Toward the end of his own term, Rodrigues Alves took care not to exacerbate differences and declined to accept the challenges from Congress that were inspired by Pinheiro. For the first time in the history of the Republic, the administration was not supported by the legislative majority, though this did not disturb its orderly functioning or threaten domestic peace. On November 15, 1906, one former imperial conselheiro handed over to another the powers of government that he had exercised with astuteness, efficiency, and quiet courage, and would assume once again, broken in health and soon to die, twelve years later.

16. Afonso Pena
[1906–9]

Minas Gerais — Afonso Pena's accession — His innovating tendencies — His cabinet — Economic interventionism — The nation's economic structure — New directions of the financial policy — João Pinheiro and Carlos Peixoto — The "Kindergarten" — Davi Campista's candidacy — Marshal Hermes da Fonseca — Pressure on the War Minister — The challenge accepted.

Although Minas Gerais was then the most populous state in the nation, and had a large number of representatives in the Federal Chamber, it had not yet achieved as much political influence as São Paulo or even Rio Grande do Sul. No other part of Brazil maintained so carefully the old, withdrawn, and modest patriarchal traditions and mode of life. The rugged geography of this mountainous hinterland had impressed on its people a psychological make-up that clearly set them apart from the national pattern.

Much more than the sugar baron in the North, the coffeegrower in Rio de Janeiro and São Paulo, or the prodigal and boastful gaúcho in the deep South, the Mineiro was a man of the soil par excellence, a typical peasant. He was parsimonious, narrow, prudent, averse to ventures and to sudden changes, clever at dissembling, and dogged in his efforts, and had a lively political intuition. The Negro slave had not turned him into a feudal master like the sugar barons. The precarious equilibrium of his local consumer economy had made him cautious in business affairs; he lacked the daring of the Paulista, the forest-razing planter of coffee. The absence of a large, overshadowing capital city permitted him a communal life more intense than that in any other Brazilian province.

During the turbulent early years of the Republic, Minas had maintained itself as a neutral zone in which persons persecuted or threatened by revolutions and civil wars could seek shelter. Its rulers tried to live peacefully in the Union and avoid any involvement in the partisan strife outside her borders. The development of coffeegrowing in Minas tied its

economic fate to that of São Paulo. The coupling of the candidacies of a
Paulista, Rodrigues Alves, and a Mineiro, Silviano Brandão (who died
before taking office and was replaced by Afonso Pena), was the first man-
ifestation of coffee's economic hegemony in Republican politics.

The collapse of the candidacy of another Paulista, Bernardino de Campos, opened the way for that of Afonso Pena, the statesman from Minas,
whose election was almost like an expected promotion in his political
career. Afonso Pena was born in 1847, in the old gold-bearing region of
Minas Gerais. After completing the course in humanities at the religious
school in Caraça, renowned for its rigid discipline and humanistic traditions, he graduated in law from the Academia in São Paulo, where he
and Rodrigues Alves were fellow students. From 1874 to 1879 he was a
Liberal deputy in the Minas Assembly and then in the national Chamber
in Rio. In 1882 he was War Minister in the Martinho Campos cabinet;
in 1883 Minister of Agriculture under Lafayette Rodrigues Pereira; and
in 1885 Minister of the Interior and Justice in Saraiva's cabinet.

Like most of the former monarchists, Pena accommodated himself
quietly to the Republic. He was a member of his state's constituent assembly, and in 1892, upon the resignation of Cesário Alvim, was elected
governer, in which office he successfully rode out the stormy era of
Floriano Peixoto and the civil wars. After overcoming local preconcep-
tions and prejudices, he transferred the state government from the old
capital, Ouro Prêto, to the new, planned capital, Belo Horizonte. Like
Rodrigues Alves, Pena was of the high type of imperial politician trained
in parliamentarism under Pedro II's vigilant censorship. For the times,
he was liberal, keenly public-spirited, and meticulous in observing legal
formulas and administrative procedures. During Prudente de Morais's
administration, he was president of the Banco do Brasil. Upon the death
of Silviano Brandão, he became Vice-President of the Republic.

In spite of his placid political career and the traditional conservatism
of the people of his province, Afonso Pena wanted to make innovations
and to assert himself. He tried to surround himself with young men
ready for bold action, almost as if he were in rebellion against the in-
grained cautiousness of Minas's ruling classes. The confidence in Brazil's
future greatness, one of the best results of Rodrigues Alves's presidency
and Rio Branco's diplomacy, stimulated him more, perhaps, than any
other statesman of his day. He dreamed of an industrialized Brazil, rich
and militarily strong.

After becoming President, he traveled over almost the entire country,
and found reasons everywhere for optimism. Although Amazonia was
a green hell, and although the sertanejos from the Northeast who gath-

ered rubber, if they survived the malaria and beriberi, were subjected to
a form of slavery at least as cruel as that formerly inflicted on the Negro
slaves, those who saw only the statistical figures thought Amazonia the
fabled El Dorado. It supplied about 35,000 tons yearly of natural rubber,
at an average price of 400 pounds sterling per ton, which represented
70 per cent of world rubber consumption and 28 per cent of Brazil's total
exports. The compact of Taubaté had forestalled the worst consequences
of the overproduction of coffee. Coffee exports of around twelve million
bags, valued at more than 600,000 contos, accounted for more than 65
per cent of Brazil's sales abroad. New manufacturing industries were
prospering, especially the cotton mills. But such optimism about new
"prosperity" overlooked many unhappy facts: the penury of the wage
earners, underfed and weakened by tropical diseases; the decadence of
the old rural sugar aristocracy; the failure of the romantic idea of education, which had fostered *bacharelismo,** urban parasitism, and fondness for public employment; the corruption of politics by scandalous
election frauds; the stranglehold of the provincial oligarchies; and the
mounting greed of the businessmen, who wanted industrial protectionism, price supports by the state, and public-works contracts.

Afonso Pena retained the Baron of Rio Branco as Foreign Minister.
Marshal Hermes da Fonseca (a nephew of Marshal Deodoro) became
War Minister, and Alexandrino de Alencar became Navy Minister.
Three new men, Tavares de Lira, Miguel Calmon, and Davi Campista,
were made Ministers of Justice, of Transportation and Public Works,
and of Finance, respectively.

In a speech outlining his economic policies the President stressed their
interventionism and protectionism, to which, after all, he had committed himself as a candidate. The old precepts of liberal economics were
forgotten. The theory of the gendarme state, declared the incoming
President, no longer made sense. "The state's high mission," he continued, "also embraces caring for the people's welfare and bettering
their lives; it must act beneficently in social matters whenever individual initiative, in its various forms, shows itself to be incapable or in-
sufficient." The government would stimulate and support the economy
by introducing protective tariffs, increasing immigration, developing internal communications, etc. In brief, Brazil's broad building policy was
to have three main objectives: peopling the land, developing industrial centers, and reforming the monetary system. The famous dictum
of the Argentine statesman Alberdi, "gobernar es poblar," had become

---

* Bacharelismo: a predominance of "doctors," especially lawyers. JLT

one of the administration's mottos. For the second time, Brazil tried to speed up economic development by abandoning her exclusively agricultural position, which had always served the interests of British capitalism so well, and entering an industrial stage.

Pena's government followed through on his predecessor's program of public works. The Department of Transportation and Public Works occupied itself especially with the development of railroads and the introduction of European settlers. The Central Railroad of Brazil pushed its line toward the São Francisco river, with the ultimate purpose (later abandoned, it seems) of reaching Pará through the valley of the Tocantin and thereby connecting the far North to southern Brazil. The São Paulo–Rio Grande do Sul and Rio de Janeiro–Espírito Santo lines were being completed. The building of the Noroeste railroad, intended to tie Mato Grosso to São Paulo and later to eastern Bolivia, was intensified.

Colonel Rondon* was exploring the remote forests of Mato Grosso and Amazonia, catechizing wild Indians, and putting the far hinterland in telegraphic communication with the rest of the country. The coffee planters, abandoning their worn-out lands near the capital of São Paulo as they had those in the Paraíba valley, were migrating toward the Paraná river through the valleys of the Tietê and Ipanema. Creating new wealth everywhere, they were razing virgin forests, driving back the Indians, and throwing up towns typical of the American Far West, as if Brazil too were entering a golden age.

Animated by extreme optimism, the government drew heavily against the future. In order to precipitate the flow of immigrants, it created a special administrative department for "Peopling the Land," and installed special services in Europe that the scandalmongers referred to as "Golden Embassies." The immigration curve, which had dropped from 174,000 entrants in 1897 to 34,000 in 1903, rose to nearly 100,000 in 1908.

The Italian settlers, who had started arriving even before abolition, invaded the newly opened region of São Paulo and took root there, intermarrying with the natives, impressing Brazilians with their hard work, frugality, and sobriety, and doubling their numbers during the Republic's first decade. The Germans settled in Santa Catarina and Rio Grande do Sul; the Poles and Baltic Russians headed for Paraná. In Rio de Ja-

---

* General Cândido Mariano da Silva Rondon, a native of Mato Grosso, was a military engineer of great distinction. He guided Theodore Roosevelt on the famous trip in 1914 when the "River of Doubt" (later renamed Rio Teodoro Roosevelt) was discovered, a trip on which Roosevelt nearly died of fever and starvation. Rondon died in 1958 at the age of 92. JLT

neiro and the large northern seaports, the Portuguese continued to predominate, but were already suffering from the competition in small urban trade offered by Jews, Syrians, Lebanese, and other peoples from Asia Minor, who were refugees from Turkish rule. Brazil seemed to be reproducing on a reduced scale the expansion of the United States during the opening of the West.

But this shifting of internal frontiers did not alter the bases of the nation's economy, then resting solidly on coffee and rubber. Fifteen million pounds were borrowed in 1908 in an effort to come to grips with the crisis in the overproduction of coffee that inspired the compact of Taubaté. A series of short crops brought about a statistical equilibrium between production and consumption, and happily also made it possible to liquidate the loan. Exports averaged 13 million bags a year, valued at more than 400,000 contos. Yearly exports of rubber from Amazonia approached 40,000 tons, worth from three to five hundred pounds sterling per ton, while total world production from other sources was less than half that much. Cacao, tobacco, cotton, mate, and hides, but in much smaller quantities than either coffee or rubber, made up the rest of Brazil's exports.

Domestic trade improved. Home consumption increased for animal products from Minas Gerais and Rio Grande do Sul, as well as cereals from the latter, which cut down on imports and improved the balance of trade. The manufacturing industries that had been the unrealized dream of Mauá and, later, of the men in the Provisional Government, were finally trying to gain a foothold, thanks to the protective tariff. The national exposition of 1908 in Rio de Janeiro was a revelation to the great majority of Brazilians. It had 11,000 exhibitors, and attracted nearly a million visitors. The nation's belief in its own possibilities was increasing.

Rio de Janeiro was gradually losing its old provincial habits and colonial aspect. National pride, which for some years had been boosted by Santos Dumont's aeronautical triumphs abroad, was greatly heightened by Rui Barbosa's success at the Hague Conference [1907], to which Brazil had been the only Latin-American country invited. Modifying Rodrigues Alves's plans for naval rearmament, Afonso Pena's government pressed the English shipyards to deliver the first large warship and the cruisers that would form the basis of Brazil's future modern squadron. Brazilians thrilled at the large vessels anchored in Guanabara Bay. The intense program of the Navy Minister, Alexandrino de Alencar, epitomized in the slogan "Rumo ao mar!" [To the sea!], was vastly popular.

However, what marked President Pena's two-and-one-half years in office most clearly was Finance Minister Campista's monetary reform.

Once in office, Afonso Pena and Davi Campista abandoned the old financial policy, probably more because of their personal convictions than because of their campaign promises. They came out for the monetary reform, proposed by the compact of Taubaté, that Rodrigues Alves had rejected. The plan was simple, and in general imitated the one that had been adopted in Argentina.

The legal standard inherited from the Empire was maintained; that is, exchange parity was held at 27 pence per milreis, or 32 milreis per ounce of 22-carat gold. But the government set up a conversion fund into which proceeds from foreign loans and foreign currencies coming into the country were to be deposited. Against this deposit, limited by law to 20 million pounds, the fund would issue paper at the rate of one milreis per 15 pence. The Treasury's reserves were added to the fund, and whenever the rate of exchange rose to legal parity, the fund's paper would be redeemed at the fixed rate.

The immediate advantage of the new scheme was that it stabilized the rate of exchange and therefore the value of the nation's labor and production. Since the exchange rate tended to rise (the average rate was between 16 and 17 pence) and coffee prices to drop, the idea struck the large Paulista growers as an excellent one. At the same time, the increase in customs duties, and in the percentage of the duties that had to be paid in gold, gave the incipient domestic industries considerable support against foreign competition.

The general prosperity that had marked the Rodrigues Alves administration and the steady influx of European capital, then readily available at low rates, enabled the conversion fund to function with complete success during its first year. Pena's and Campista's reliance on it was thereby justified. After two years, however, the Treasury's inconvertible money attracted a better rate of exchange than the conversion fund's legal-reserve bills. This would lead the next administration to raise the fund's limit from 20 to 60 million pounds and the conversion rate from 15 to 16 pence. The approach of World War I, by shutting off the European money markets, disturbing international trade, and reducing the volume of Brazil's exports, would precipitate the final collapse of the conversion fund. At the moment, however, the outlook for Pena's administration was auspicious; it bequeathed to his unexpected heir [Vice-President Nilo Peçanha] a Treasury in balance and general business conditions that reflected confidence and a desire to excel. The grave political crisis triggered by Hermes da Fonseca's condidacy and the death of President Pena did not upset the existing economic and financial situation, despite the nation's apprehensions.

Pena's economic program had fitted the optimism of the period and the economic interests of the new urban and industrial classes, who were trying to take over control from the old patriarchal sugar barons and coffeegrowers of the Empire. But in order to carry out his ambitious plans, Afonso Pena had first had to try to free himself from the tutelage of Pinheiro Machado and his supporters, who were entrenched in the state oligarchies and administrations and in the Federal Senate. The problem was somewhat like the one that had confronted Prudente de Morais during the heyday of Francisco Glicério and the PRF.

But the men and the tactics of 1906 were altogether different from those of 1894. Prudente de Morais had waited and compromised for a long time before provoking the fight, which he won. Glicério, with the same political background as Prudente, and from the same part of the country, had been peace-loving and tactful, incapable of bold strokes or of violence. Prudente de Morais had been able to gradually undermine him in his own bailiwick, the Federal Congress, which had been left in turmoil by the fierce clashes of the Floriano Peixoto era. Afonso Pena, on the other hand, faced a much more powerful and dangerous adversary: an authentic caudillo who not only had imposed strict discipline on his followers, but also had the unlimited support of his battle-scarred state, which was under Borges de Medeiros's constitutional dictatorship.

Afonso Pena depended heavily, naturally, on the situation in Minas Gerais for his success in the approaching showdown. The governorship of the state had been entrusted to João Pinheiro, a long-time Republican. He was a practical idealist who also surrounded himself with daring young men, and initiated new political and administrative procedures that won him great moral prestige among his fellow citizens.

For president of the Chamber of Deputies, Afonso Pena found another Mineiro politician, Carlos Peixoto Filho, who was young, intelligent, cultured, energetic, and authoritarian. Carlos Peixoto was the first successful politician of the generation born during the twilight of the Empire, whose minds had been shaped by the philosophical ideas of the 1890s. He was a Spencerian, an evolutionist, and an agnostic, immune to both the political and juridical romanticism of the previous generations and the temptations of positivist dogmatism. A certain literary skepticism acquired from Renan counteracted any tendencies he may have had toward Spencer's simple materialism or Taine's rigid determinism. His fondness for economic and financial studies helped him understand the national economy. Despite his wish for power, he was not a fighter; aristocratic by nature, he was disdainful of popularity and vote-seeking. He always believed that government should have

invincible power, and was therefore incapable of inspiring and directing a militant, efficient opposition movement. He gathered around himself a group of young men of like inclinations, picked from the various
state delegations in the Chamber. A young deputy from Rio Grande
do Sul, James Darcy, who had left Júlio de Castilhos's party, was made
leader in the Chamber.

Carlos Peixoto and his general staff of young politicians were ironically referred to as the "Kindergarten." But they were joined by old
politicians who were convinced the Republic's political parties had to
be revitalized, and were either tired of Pinheiro Machado's sway or
anxious to show their support for Afonso Pena's administration. Because ideas about Republican politics, which could not be organized
into national parties, were vague, the contest became more and more
a personal fight: Carlos Peixoto or the "Kindergarten" versus Pinheiro
Machado or the "Morro da Graça," the first personifying the aspirations
of youth, and the second the old-style politics, wily and tough by turns.
The conflict was rather like a clash between two social forces of whose
ultimate purposes no one had become conscious.

With the solid backing of Governor João Pinheiro of Minas Gerais,
naturally a future presidential candidate, the "Kindergarten" won its
early victories easily. Pinheiro Machado gradually began to sense the
isolation that threatened him; even the Senate, his stronghold, could
get out of hand. But when João Pinheiro died [on October 25, 1908],
his successor returned the policies and administration of Minas Gerais
to their usual cautious, temporizing routine. The majority of Mineiro
politicians, who were fundamentally conservative, had little enthusiasm
for an apparently purposeless fight against Pinheiro, and felt little sympathy for Carlos Peixoto.

Pinheiro Machado's faithful partisans, like most of the old Mineiro
leaders, thought the possibility of Davi Campista's becoming a presidential candidate to be even more dangerous than Carlos Peixoto's
rapid rise. After João Pinheiro's death Pena did not conceal his intention of paving the way for Campista's candidacy. The job of organizing
it was handed to Carlos Peixoto, who took it seemingly without much
enthusiasm. The reaction against Davi Campista was promptly extended
to Peixoto also.

Although Pinheiro Machado had accepted Campista's candidacy at
first, he soon turned against it and organized his forces for battle. Rui
Barbosa wrote a long letter to Pena opposing Campista's candidacy,
as much because of its official stamp (remembering that Pena himself
had been selected because of opposition to palace candidates) as because

of the hasty way in which it was put forward, as if purposely to coincide with the elections for the Federal Congress. Pinheiro Machado would have no trouble recruiting the people needed to break up the President's plan from those Mineiro deputies who did not like Campista and Peixoto. Just before he assumed the governorship of Minas Gerais, Venceslau Brás [later President of Brazil] tried unenthusiastically to rally his friends around Campista. The two states most closely tied to the coffee economy, São Paulo and Rio de Janeiro, temporized and sidestepped without openly refusing to support Pena's candidate.

Fully as distant as Carlos Peixoto, if not more, Davi Campista was intellectual, artistic, and somewhat disdainful, and was therefore more or less isolated in the party councils of his state. He made a name for himself in the Chamber as a subtle and ironical orator; and later, when the great debates on the new financial policies took place, he was an ardent apologist for the protectionist and interventionist trends that led to the tariff revision and the compact of Taubaté. Thus, his candidacy would have been another victory for the coffeegrowers and the new manufacturing industries.

But the Paulistas knew perfectly well that the very momentum of the new order inaugurated by Afonso Pena meant it would be carried on by his successor, no matter who he might be. They were not interested, therefore, in tying themselves to Campista's candidacy and sacrificing their alliance with the Mineiro politicians. Bias Fortes, a local chieftain of wide prestige in Minas, offered on his own initiative to run against Campista. The governor, Venceslau Brás, did not wish to compromise his personal situation and the peace of his administration for a candidate to whom he was indifferent; he therefore took a neutral position between his local followers and President Pena. Pinheiro Machado's victory grew more certain day by day; a regular pilgrimage of politicians who had deserted him headed once more to his mansion on Morro da Graça, itself a political barometer. Only a candidate to run against the "official" one was missing.

The name of the War Minister, Marshal Hermes da Fonseca, came to the fore. Initially suggested by some young officers, Marshal Deodoro da Fonseca's nephew seemed to Davi Campista's antagonists an excellent choice. As War Minister, Hermes da Fonseca had acquired great prestige among his comrades-at-arms. He had reorganized the workings of his department and made it more efficient; he had instituted compulsory military service, and had tried to modernize the army by expanding its periodic exercises and maneuvers. His work on national defense was complementary to Rio Branco's foreign policy, and his supporters did not neglect to connect him with the diplomatic successes of the Foreign Office. If Brazil was to have a new and more realistic image, both inside and outside her borders, they said, she had to have a strong and efficacious government, daring enough to free her from the legal hairsplitting that was holding her back. Civilian promotion of the Marshal's candidacy, they declared, would be sufficient to refute any charge that it was being imposed by the military, and thus to gain popular support for it.

The politicians opposed to Afonso Pena began putting pressure on the War Minister to permit himself to be announced as a candidate. Marshal Hermes da Fonseca was essentially a timid man, irresolute, trusting, and good-natured. As a young captain during the Provisional Government, he had remained, according to Rui Barbosa, discreetly in the shadow of his powerful uncle, preoccupied much more with his professional duties than with political intrigues. He rose to higher ranks without bluster. During the uprisings against Rodrigues Alves's government, he had stood on the side of legality and had quelled the revolt in the military academy under his command. As War Minister in Afonso Pena's cabinet he again showed himself completely devoid of ambition, political or otherwise. An official trip to Germany to observe the spectacular maneuvers of Wilhelm II's armies does not seem to have aroused his vanity. One would have said that he would never spontaneously make any move to achieve power.

Meanwhile, his indecisive temperament, his incapacity (like that of his uncle) for suspicion and for putting himself on guard, made him amenable to artful management by the politicians and by some of his fellow officers. Once again around the person of a general sprang up the chronic dreams of a military dictatorship, though one clothed in legal formalities, capable of regenerating by the sword the corrupt society of politicians and businessmen.

In a speech delivered in May 1909, while he was President of the Chamber of Deputies, Carlos Peixoto alluded indirectly to Hermes da Fonseca's candidacy: "The Republic has demonstrated that it can both govern itself and preserve the civil liberties that keep it from falling prey to conscienceless demagoguery, which is the road to anarchy and violence, the main source of Caesarism and tyranny." There followed some anxious days for the politicians and for the nation itself, whose normal life seemed suspended. How would Marshal Hermes and his impassioned partisans react to these words? Either overcoming his inner doubts or yielding to the desperate pressure of his backers, the Marshal finally accepted the challenge and crossed his little Rubicon. In a brief, harsh letter to President Pena, he submitted his resignation as War Minister, saying that although he was not himself a presidential candidate, he nevertheless could not agree with the idea that military men should be denied the chance to achieve the highest post in the Republic. The effect of the letter on the uneasy country was enormous. In political circles the atmosphere was one of panic. The President, badly shaken, tacitly agreed to sacrifice Campista's candidacy, and made no attempt to punish his minister's breach of discipline.

In the Senate an old provincial politician pointedly suggested that the President resign. On May 17th, in another sensational speech, Carlos Peixoto quit as president of the Chamber. In one of his speeches during his campaign for civilian government, Rui Barbosa later compared the stampede of the politicians to a stampede of cattle, set off by the slightest incident. The "Kindergarten" had disappeared, and on its ruins the prestige of "Morro da Graça" and of the audacious gaúcho caudillo seemed permanently reestablished.

Before officially agreeing to become a candidate, however, Marshal Hermes da Fonseca wrote to the Baron of Rio Branco and Rui Barbosa seeking their assent. Fearful of becoming embroiled in the dispute or of being held responsible for the rise of a military candidate, though one to whom he may have been sympathetic, Rio Branco did not reply to the Marshal's appeal. Rui Barbosa was a man of another temper. In a public letter, which his admirers described as "unyielding as bronze," he formally opposed Hermes's nomination and declared his own candidacy. The fight was on. After less than twenty years of its troubled life, the Republic found itself threatened once again with a grave clash between civilian authority and the military forces.

Pinheiro Machado, perhaps to tone down the strong military coloration of Hermes's candidacy, perhaps to establish himself as his sponsor (though Pinheiro may have liked Hermes even less than Rui), hurried things toward a decision by calling a convention of Senators and deputies, similar to the early American caucuses. Rui later related in a Senate speech that Pinheiro had called together four political leaders — Francisco Sales, Francisco Glicério, Antônio Azeredo, and Lauro Müller — to decide between Rui and Hermes. Sales and Müller voted for the military man, and Glicério and Azeredo for the civilian. Not wishing to be the tie breaker, and inwardly hopeful that Rui would be the winner, Pinheiro then consulted the political chieftain of Pernambuco, Rosa e Silva, who chose Hermes. The governments of the states of São Paulo, Bahia, and Rio de Janeiro endorsed Rui Barbosa as a candidate against Hermes. This was the beginning of the contest.

Under pressure from the politicians of São Paulo, Afonso Pena decided to accept Hermes's resignation, and appointed General Mendes de Morais, held to be energetic and strongly in favor of reaction, to be the new War Minister. Public opinion, hostile to Pinheiro Machado's domination, prejudiced against a military candidacy, and worked up by an intense campaign in the press and by public meetings, was surprisingly enthusiastic.

Upon the refusal of former President Rodrigues Alves to run again for office, Rui Barbosa was definitely accepted as a candidate. He was just then emerging from the long unpopularity caused by the part he had played during the Encilhamento, and was heading toward tremendous popular success.

Meanwhile, disillusioned, embittered, and weakened by a spell of grippe, President Pena died on June 14, 1909. Contradicting the doctors, the politicians diagnosed the cause of death as moral traumatism. The death of the old Mineiro statesman, unexpectedly elevating Vice-President Nilo Peçanha to the highest post in government, was the final victory for Pinheiro Machado. From then on, the candidacy of Hermes da Fonseca, backed by the executive machine, continually gained strength.

17. Nilo Peçanha
[1909–10]

*Biographical sketch of Nilo Peçanha — Attempt at concil-
iation — The era of prosperity — Rui Barbosa's position —
Reaction against Hermes's candidacy — The character of the
candidacies — The electoral campaign.*

Nilo Peçanha had first come to notice during the closing years of the
Empire as an abolitionist and propagandist for the Republic. A young
lawyer, he was representative of the new generation of Brazilians: men
with a superficial education and a smattering of law, who, barely keeping
up with the currents of agnostic thought at the century's end, were enthusiastic about the rhetorical forms of liberalism. Accustomed to speaking at popular meetings, when he entered the Constituent Assembly he
became one of a group of romantic orators who seemed to believe sincerely in the power of pompous language and sentimental invocations.

However, Peçanha's public spirit and keen intuition for opportunities and realities checked his demagogic tendencies. He always sided
with Quintino Bocaiúva in the game of politics, and rode out the stormy
era of Floriano Peixoto and the civil wars. Of humble origin and a
Jacobin by nature, he nevertheless took an active part in the electoral
politics of his state [Rio de Janeiro] as a member of its agrarian wing,
left over from the Empire. At the time of the struggle between President
Prudente de Morais and the PRF, Nilo Peçanha had been one of Francisco Glicério's most ardent zealots. When the assassination of Marshal
Bittencourt had given Prudente de Morais the strength to move against
the fanatical Florianistas and Jacobins, Nilo Peçanha had avoided arrest by fleeing.

When Quintino Bocaiúva became governor of Rio de Janeiro, Nilo
worked to consolidate his own position. He succeeded Bocaiúva as governor, and instituted an administration that was rigidly economical

about using public funds. He was one of the endorsers of the compact of Taubaté, whose provisions about paying taxes in gold he did not fulfill. The government of Minas Gerais did not fulfill them either.

His election as the running mate of Afonso Pena, a former Conselheiro of the monarchy, seemed to provide some balance on the ticket and to be a reward for old-time Republicans. His close relations with Pinheiro Machado did not inspire President Pena and the "Kindergarten" with confidence in him as a potential successor to the President. His reputation as an able political maneuverer made him extremely suspect. Opposed by the government of his own state, which the Union supported, Nilo Peçanha could have considered his political career done for, or at least obscured for a long time. The usual seekers after jobs and deals, who throng around rising politicians, fled from him as from the plague.

The death of Afonso Pena placed Nilo in the highest seat in the Republic. On his tact, his authority, and his strength might depend the fate of the candidates then being advanced for the next presidency. Could he prevent the crisis created by Hermes's candidacy from becoming grave? This was probably his first thought on entering the Catete palace. By appeasing the politicians he could control the situation, and could maneuver effectively at the opportune moment.

Nilo's cabinet reflected a similar conciliatory tendency. The Baron of Rio Branco, irreplaceable in the nation's judgment, remained as Foreign Minister. The Ministry of the Interior and Justice was entrusted to Esmeraldino Bandeira, a politician from Pernambuco who had opposed Nilo Peçanha's candidacy for the vice-presidency. The former Finance Minister under Rodrigues Alves, Leopoldo de Bulhões, was returned to the same post. Admiral Alexandrino de Alencar was kept in charge of the navy. Francisco Sá, who had greatly distinguished himself in Congress, was appointed Minister of Transportation and Public Works. The new Department of Agriculture, created under Afonso Pena and now to be inaugurated, was headed by a Paulista member of the government party. Nilo later replaced him (naturally under pressure) by another Paulista who was an ardent supporter of Hermes's candidacy.

Nilo did not neglect administrative matters, being anxious to stabilize his short and agitated term as President of the Republic. The Ministry of Transportation continued to carry out the program of railroad building begun under Afonso Pena. The War and Navy Ministries were equally active. In the Ministry of Finance, Leopoldo de Bulhões was tearing down the bases of Davi Campista's financial policy, even though it had been approved by Nilo himself, since he was one of the signers of the compact of Taubaté.

The influx of European gold was filling the coffers of the conversion fund to the bursting point, greatly exceeding the legal limit for deposits. Faithful to his convictions as a liberal economist, Minister Bulhões had no interest in maintaining the exchange-regulating apparatus; he raised the deposit limit to 60 million pounds and set the new conversion rate at 16 pence, feeling certain, it may be supposed, that at the first sign of crisis in the exchange markets, foreign or domestic, the fund would founder. He also began to pay off the funding loan a year before the time prescribed in the Campos Sales agreement. In passing the government on to his successor, Nilo Peçanha could point to the large Treasury balance as one result of his administration, an achievement that won him a telegram of praise from the Rothschilds, a precious sort of decoration.

According to the main classical indexes the prosperity was continuing. Coffee prices remained high, still enjoying the effects of the first valorization scheme. The gold price for rubber reached about £640 a ton, and the exported volume reached 38,000 tons. That was the high water mark, for during the next year large-scale shipments began from the British plantations in the Far East. Brazil's total exports averaged 60 million pounds sterling yearly, which left a substantial balance of trade in her favor.

Domestic trade developed greater confidence as local markets began consuming foodstuffs grown and goods manufactured in Brazil itself. There was twice as much inconvertible Treasury paper, a little over 600,000 contos, as gold-backed emissions by the conversion fund. Successive loans taken in sterling or gold francs to redeem railroad and port bonds increased the Union's foreign debt. The states and municípios, following the example set by the federal government, mortgaged their best sources of revenue to European bankers; many of them made commitments far beyond their most optimistically viewed ability to fulfill.

The steady influx of European money and the gradual growth of domestic consumption stimulated innumerable small industrial enterprises, which served especially the regions in which they were located and contributed to the stability of the exchange rate. Rio de Janeiro was undergoing constant change; the public utilities provided by the Canadian corporation spurred new growth of its already extensive urban area. A new section [Copacabana] sprang up rapidly on the south side facing the Atlantic, and filled the Cariocas with civic pride. With greater faith in themselves, the Brazilians were feeling more encouraged, more resolute, and less pessimistic.

Nilo did his best to please everybody, and to build prestige and popularity for himself, always taking advantage of any publicity. But the weakness of his political background and his methods, which the opposition classified as dubious, canceled out his good intentions. Indirect methods could no longer stop Hermes's candidacy, which, started by enthusiastic young officers, had become a matter of class pride, and had imposed itself on the politicians headed by Pinheiro Machado. For good or ill, Nilo Peçanha's fortunes were tied to Hermes's, and his authority as head of state was overridden by that of Pinheiro. The civilianist campaign, inspired by Rui Barbosa's vehement oratory and skillfully managed by the government party of São Paulo, the PRP, would be directed as violently against the incumbent President as against the military candidate for the presidency.

The politicians generally admired and feared Rui Barbosa more than they esteemed him. He in turn was indifferent and sometimes scornful toward public opinion. The outcries against his handling of the finances during the Provisional Government, though frequently unjust, had never been forgotten, and cast doubt on his capability as a statesman. His courageous stand during Floriano's government, when he undertook the legal defense of accused politicians, had inspired sincere admiration. Later, after the cycle of fanatic partisan conflicts had ended, Rui Barbosa had discreetly joined the faction in the Senate controlled by Pinheiro Machado. On many occasions he had defended positions that were antipathetic to public opinion, or at least to the opinion worked up by the opposition press, which accused him of being a docile intellectual tool of the powerful caudillo. His conspicuous triumphs at the Hague Peace Conference had deeply touched the vanity of the Brazilians.

The nation was proud of Rui, who was widely regarded as a genius, but the power elite did not really have full confidence in his political sense and executive ability. In fact, there arose at the time the curious theory that great intelligence and vast culture were negative virtues in leaders. In the handling of public affairs a mediocre mind, limited general knowledge, and everyday common sense were more to be desired. An old defense of incompetence was to praise *não preparados* [that is, men who were not specially trained, as officials had been trained during the monarchy, to occupy high posts in government]. Men like Rui Barbosa were fine for oratorical debates in Congress and at international conferences. Medicine was for external use only.

At about the same time a few young Brazilian intellectuals began to criticize the nature of his learning. He lacked an intuitive grasp of the world and of life, of human psychology, and of the country's political realities, and he was overly fond of dialectics and oratorical passion.

Imbued with the liberal culture of the nineteenth century, he had not, they said, tried to enlarge the framework he had chosen. His intellectual outpourings, provoked nearly always by the contingencies of his busy life and highly rhetorical style, seemed to recede in time like images of a vanishing past.

The reaction against Hermes's candidacy was strong enough, however, to rapidly regain for Rui Barbosa the sympathies of the man on the street and even of the Brazilian elites. He became enormously popular everywhere in the country and at all social levels. An intense campaign in the press echoing his speeches in the Senate and in the public squares added still further to his prestige. There erupted even a certain original form of fanaticism: the uncultured masses deliriously applauded an erudite orator, devoid of personal magnetism, who addressed them at great length in a perfectly polished vernacular they surely could not have understood. However, his lack of personal charm was largely offset by the courage of his charges and countercharges, and by the extraordinary force of his sarcasm, in which his bitterness over the injustices and slights he had suffered during his troubled career was frequently revealed.

For these reasons, the tone of Rui's civilianist campaign was distinctly pamphletary. Troubled as he must have been by party commitments, he really did not have any new program to offer, nothing to match the argument he had made as a member of the Provisional Government for juridical reorganization and economic innovation. He frequently preferred to criticize others' mistakes (which he promised not to make) rather than to discuss new issues. At that time there was a general conviction that all the nation's ills were caused by failure to loyally and honestly live up to the Constitution and the existing laws. Republican democracy would fulfill its mission on the day it could rid itself of political bossism and freely choose its representatives.

Tied as Rui was to São Paulo's dominant political faction, his economic and financial orientation was perforce subordinated to the interests of that wealthiest state in the Union. It was, therefore, interventionist and protectionist, which was in many ways in keeping with Rui's own long-held ideas. He was not much concerned with what are today called social problems, but the same could be said of some of the keenest minds of the time, all of whom seemed unaware that beyond the thin urban stratum and its bureaucratic and electoral following, there vegetated an immense and wretched Brazil, poverty-stricken, illiterate, diseased, and forgotten by the government. The grand words picked up from the vocabulary of the European democracies would cure all of

Brazil's ills. Rui Barbosa also avoided any discussion of foreign policy, since it was then in the hands of Rio Branco, whom the nation regarded as infallible. The campaign that so inflamed the country did not, therefore, rise above mere partisanism.

Hermes da Fonseca's candidacy symbolized not only military imposition, but also the irritating dominance of the republican oligarchies and a threat to civil liberties, that is, the petty Latin-American Caesarism, dull and unheroic, of which Carlos Peixoto had warned. On the other hand, Rui Barbosa's candidacy symbolized the upholding of intelligence, culture, and liberal traditions. Stated in these terms, which come close to the truth at that, it would not have been difficult to foresee how successful "civilianism" would be among the nation's more cultured and independent groups. Today, forty years later, Barbosa's campaign can be viewed more objectively: it represented a latent revolt against old abuses, vices, and errors, many of which had persisted after the downfall of the monarchy. Having become collectively more self-aware, Brazilians were beginning to tire of the patriarchal framework that had so well suited Brazil's economy, and had given her, to offset the sham of democracy, an organized judicial system and men of superior moral and intellectual caliber to fill her highest representative posts. It can be said that in 1909 Rui helped blaze the hard trail to free elections, which is still far from being cleared of stumbling blocks and dangers. At the same time, he had found the arena in which his genius would best shine. He received excellent publicity as he traveled all over the country in attention-getting caravans, much like those of the great presidential campaigns in the United States. His talent for oratory was extolled on all sides; throwing off physical fatigue, he spoke for hours with undiminished eloquence, plucking at every emotional string, his magnificent style reaching the heights. His receptions in the capital and in the large cities frequently turned into hero-worship, not infrequently capped by rioting and disorder in the streets as in the ludicrous epilogues to the Roman triumphs.

Marshal Hermes's partisans were a good deal more realistic. Against Rui Barbosa's popular campaign, they could count on support by the military and by the election-controlling political machines in the states. The campaign expenses on both sides were paid for largely by public funds. The generous contributions of the federal government were matched by the state government of São Paulo, and the newly created Ministry of Agriculture was turned into the biggest pork barrel Brazil had ever known. Pinheiro Machado directed his candidate's campaign from his home on Morro da Graça like a supreme commander in his general headquarters. He bravely faced noisy street demonstrations against him, made strategic appointments, and kept the politicians in the Senate in line.

Venceslau Brás, governor of Minas Gerais, was nominated for the vice-presidency on the official ticket. The governor of São Paulo, Albuquerque Lins, was nominated for the same post by the opposition. Thus, after a close political alliance born of identical economic interests, the two powerful states seemed to be drawing apart; but their leaders did not believe that the election of either candidate would affect them much. Once the electoral storm had blown over, Paulistas and Mineiros would come together again, being in agreement on the political economy of coffee and on the incipient industrialization to which they were committed.

In the unrestrainedly partisan atmosphere, Nilo Peçanha tried to be as tolerant as possible. The civilianists freely held their often provocative meetings and parades through the streets. Congress and the opposition papers relentlessly defamed him. The partisans of Marshal Hermes and of Pinheiro Machado, to whom he had refused illegal intervention in the state of Amazonas on a purely party matter, assailed Nilo's equanimity as weakness.

On March 1, 1910, the elections for President and Vice-President were held throughout the nation. For the first time since the beginning of the Republic the voters headed enthusiastically for the polling places. In the Federal District the government obstructed the voting in many parts of town, but even there, as in all the other large cities in the South, where there was greater freedom of expression, Rui Barbosa's victory was enormous. However, the political machines of the state governments, especially in Minas and in the North, were powerful enough to put over the official candidates.

Sitting as an electoral board, the Federal Congress naturally recognized the candidates who had polled the most votes, Hermes da Fonseca and Venceslau Brás. They were shortly proclaimed President and Vice-President for the 1910–1914 term, amid a tumultuous session accompanied by the sound of drums from a large military barracks nearby. The Congress was presided over by the old Republican Quintino Bocaiúva; Francisco Glicério, acting as Pinheiro Machado's lieutenant, kept the majority members in line. As a leader of Marshal Hermes's campaign, perhaps Quintino was doing penance for the opposition he had put up years before to the nomination of Marshal Deodoro.

In a country so long accustomed to fraudulent elections and to the arbitrary recognition by Congress of election results, the official announcement of the winning candidates neither appeased the opposition nor helped them formulate a plan of constructive criticism. For the remainder of President Peçanha's term, there was no end to popular agitation and no lessening of the civilianist virulence in Congress and in the press. The presidential term of Hermes da Fonseca began, therefore, in an atmosphere of general apprehension. Pinheiro tried again, this time more successfully, to merge into one large party—the Conservative Republican Party [PRC]—the several political elements that sided with him and that had supported Hermes's candidacy.

18. Hermes da Fonseca
[1910–14]

Hermes's cabinet — Naval mutinies — Overthrow of state governments — The oligarchies — "Rescues" of Pernambuco and Bahia — Ceará and Padre Cícero — The final "rescues" — Reaction against Pinheiro Machado — João Maria and the Contestado — Pinheiro blocked — Nomination of Venceslau Brás — Financial crisis and World War I.

Lacking political and administrative experience, and being kindly and indecisive, the new President, though he had the military solidly in back of him, let himself become involved in political intrigue. The cabinet with which he began his administration had an obvious party coloration. The portfolio of the Interior and Justice, then a political post, was handed to Rivadávia Correia, a deputy from Rio Grande do Sul and one of Pinheiro Machado's most zealous partisans. The Ministry of Finance went to Francisco Sales of Minas. The Ministry of Transportation was entrusted to J. J. Seabra. To head the Ministry of Agriculture, Hermes appointed one of his Paulista followers, Rodolfo Miranda, who was an adversary, therefore, of the São Paulo government. The Baron of Rio Branco was kept on as Foreign Minister. General Dantas Barreto was made War Minister and Admiral Marques Leão Navy Minister.

The new administration had been scarcely a week in power when the crews mutinied on the navy's largest warships, the *Minas Gerais* and the *São Paulo,* of which Brazilians were so proud and which they could so little afford. The revolt was led by a tough seaman whose first step was to subdue the officers, some of whom sacrificed their lives in the line of duty. With the support of two smaller vessels, the ships began firing on the defenseless city. Panic seized the capital and the politicians. Taken by surprise, the government, having neither the means nor the courage to oppose the mutineers, gave in and agreed to an amnesty, which Congress voted on still under the threat of the powerful guns of the ships. James Bryce, the British historian and former ambassador to the United States, was in Rio de Janeiro at the time, witnessed the humiliating episode, and made some harsh comments about the country.

A new rebellion broke out a few days later on another warship and at a barracks on Cobras Island [out in the bay not far from the center of the city] to enforce demands for the abolition of corporal punishment. The example of rebellion with impunity had borne fruit quickly. This time, however, being more self-confident or less afraid for the safety of the population, the government reacted vigorously, bombing the island and subduing the rebel vessel. The civilianist opposition under the leadership of Rui Barbosa in the Senate had voted amnesty for the crews of the battleships, but now granted the government a state of siege to repress the new rebels. The fear of new outbreaks, or perhaps misgivings over the earlier clemency, resulted in cruel and illegal punishment. The latest insurrectionists, no more witless and guilty than those on the *Minas Gerais* and *São Paulo,* were banished to the outposts of Amazonia to pay for their crime.

Public order restored, the government began to work to overthrow the state parties adverse to it. The state of Rio de Janeiro was the nearest and most urgent target. Alfredo Backer, who had succeeded Nilo Peçanha as governor, had deserted his former chief and tried to nullify his influence in the state with the powerful help of the "Kindergarten." When Nilo Peçanha was unexpectedly elevated to the presidency of the Republic, he had temporized with this new enemy, but had fostered the formation of a duplicate state legislature that could later decide on Backer's successor.

The Hermes da Fonseca government inherited the "Fluminense case" at its height: two assemblies that officially recognized two elected state governors. Under the imprecise and tricky terms of the Constitution of 1891, it would be up to the Federal Congress to settle the matter by federal intervention. The Rio de Janeiro state assembly loyal to Governor Backer, foreseeing federal interference, had had its legitimacy recognized by a writ of habeas corpus from the Supreme Court, a judicial remedy at that time freely applied to political contests. The Minister of Justice, however, found a pretext to use federal troops to "guard" federal offices, the governor's palace, and the state assembly in Niterói, whereupon the candidate favored by the federal government took over the governorship without further ado.

The majority in Congress, as well as the press favorable to the government, justified the coup on the grounds that the Senate had already drafted legislation recognizing the duplicate assembly that had been

formed by Nilo Peçanha. Although this first act of government interference in state partisan fights satisfied the interests of both the large
groups that were battling for hegemony in the Hermes administration, it
was a prologue to other and more violent interventions that would
adversely affect many of Pinheiro Machado's loyal followers.

Marshal Hermes's family, especially his sons, who were young officers, tried to inhibit the influence of Pinheiro Machado and his new
party on the orientation of the government. To this end, they joined
forces with military and political groups that opposed the state governments. The two strongest supporters of the reaction against Pinheiro
Machado were Seabra, from Bahia, and Dantas Barreto, a native of
Pernambuco who until then had avoided partisan activity. The President's oldest son, elected as a deputy from Bahia, was the leader of his
bloc. Later Hermes's brother Fonseca Hermes, a former delegate to the
Republican Constituent Assembly, was made majority leader of the
Chamber. Relying on the unlimited support of Rio Grande do Sul
and its long-time governor, Borges de Medeiros, and sure of the solidarity of the old political chieftains who ruled the states and made up
the great majority of the Senate, Pinheiro Machado compromised and
maneuvered skillfully. He passed the nominal leadership of the PRC to
Quintino Bocaiúva, and was always careful to avoid any encounter that
might weaken him.

Political activities in the former provinces had naturally been thrown
into anarchy by the establishment of the Republic. With the old monarchist politicians standing aside, republican agitators, mainly young
men barely out of the academies, and even nonpolitical independents
who in the general confusion considered themselves fit to manage public affairs, had infiltrated the political life of the states. Floriano had replaced the governors who rejoiced over the November 3rd coup with
military men in whom he had confidence, but under Prudente de Morais
these inexperienced Florianista governors were quietly pushed out of
politics when they failed to fall in line with the state parties in exchange
for legislative mandates.

The politicians left over from the monarchy then began reappearing;
their greater experience in administration and politics assured them of
easy victory in local contests, except in Rio Grande do Sul and São Paulo,
where the original Republicans had been able to establish strong party
organizations. In time they consolidated their positions. In love with
power, and fearing treachery by their supporters, they quietly set up
oligarchies, commonly family oligarchies. These oligarchies were reminiscent of the old patriarchal regimes, with their big houses and their

slave huts. They were especially prevalent in poorer regions and in former slaveholding regions. Their ruling heads were generally peaceable, stable, urbane, methodical, and personally honest men who fundamentally wanted to do the right thing. The more intelligent and flexible, attracted by the advantages of government, were drawn into the oligarchies, which tended to form a privileged ruling class as in the Second Reign. But the system of *do ut des* that had automatically become established between the Presidents of the Republic and the state governors, a system that the exigencies of Campos Sales's financial schemes had forced him to sanction, sealed off public life to men who were not conformists, and thus contributed to economic and administrative stagnation. It also tended to sterilize initiative among the politicians, nearly all of whom were holdovers from the Empire's pacific routine. The petty game of party politics and electioneering monopolized their attention.

The people had long been convinced that without the Union's direct interference, the family groups that had taken possession of political rule in the states would never give it up. Under the serene surface seethed honest revolt, unspoken resentments, and unsatisfied ambitions. If the favor of the federal government should fail or shift, the local opposition would rise up and popular passions would explode. The masses, living in more or less permanent unemployment and misery in the backward northern cities, were always ready to try anything.

The men who wished to remake the state party systems by force were aware of these psychological and social conditions. The successful example of the state of Rio de Janeiro pointed the way. To the more alert public in the large cities, the movement against the oligarchies in the North was explained as needed to purge the republican regime and to defend the purity of democratic institutions. Hence the term "salvation" or "rescue" came to be applied to the violent overthrow of state governments.

The Minister of Transportation, Seabra, set about carefully preparing to capture power in his own state of Bahia. Although he had agreed to the single candidate for the governorship, he knew that only if he himself were seated could he continue to rule politically. He brought the President of the Republic on a visit to Bahia as a show of prestige. However, before the question of succession in Bahia could be settled, the same problem was precipitated in Pernambuco. The "rescue" of this big northern state seemed the one that would be the most difficult to achieve and that would most forcefully impress public opinion.

Since 1894 political control of Pernambuco had been in the hands of

Rosa e Silva, a former Vice-President of the Republic and a Conselheiro of the monarchy. If, because of his habitual reserve and detachment, and his prolonged absences from Pernambuco, he had never been popular there, his correctness and loyalty had nevertheless won him high regard in the upper circles of federal politics. Although he was an adversary of Pinheiro Machado, he was among the first state bosses to agree to Hermes's candidacy. To topple him, therefore, would require both intervention by a prestigious military figure and simultaneous street demonstrations.

The War Minister, General Dantas Barreto, a bold, tough authoritarian of humble origin, who had begun his military career as a volunteer [at age 15] in the war with Paraguay,* agreed to be the candidate of the opposition. Handing his portfolio over to another general who was also involved in the scheme, Dantas Barreto took personal charge of the campaign in Pernambuco. Terrible fighting broke out in the streets of Recife. The young acting governor, Estácio Coimbra, bravely resisted the uprising, which was supported by army units. Betrayed by the regional military commandant and thus without means of defense, Coimbra surrendered the government. Dantas Barreto was thereupon proclaimed governor, the constitutional formality of recognition by the Federal Congress being bypassed.

The conquest of the government of Bahia took place shortly afterwards. When the candidate who had been agreed upon primarily to conciliate the various factions quit, the question of the future government of Bahia boiled up again. The group backing Minister Seabra formed a duplicate legislative assembly. Armed with a writ of habeas corpus issued by the federal district court, they had the commanding general of the military district order two old colonial forts in the Bay of Salvador to shell the city. The public library and the governor's palace were damaged, and the acting governor was forced to resign. The Navy Minister, Marques Leão, resigned in protest against the violence, and that was all. After new writs of habeas corpus, and rioting and shooting in the streets, an interventor took charge of the local government, only to hand it over a few months later to Seabra when he was formally elected at the polls.

The planned reaction against Pinheiro Machado was started with the elections in Ceará. The local opposition put up Colonel Franco Rabelo as its candidate. He had been a secretary of the state government at the

---

* He was also a chronicler, novelist, and playwright, and a member of the Brazilian Academy of Letters. JLT

time of Deodoro's attempted coup, and was now tied to the Dantas Barreto group. Pinheiro Machado's followers put up Colonel Bezerril Fon-
tenelle. The disturbances that had occurred in Pernambuco and Bahia
were reenacted in Fortaleza [the state capital], and the old governor,
Acioli, was thrown out. When the elections were over each side claimed
it had won. Colonel Tomás Cavalcanti, sent from Rio de Janeiro to seek
conciliation, was injured in a bomb explosion. A minority of state
deputies took over the legislative assembly and proclaimed Colonel
Franco Rabelo the governor. Pinheiro Machado and his friends grudgingly accepted the defeat, but when Pinheiro later regained his influence
with President Hermes, he settled the score with Rabelo.

Meanwhile, the majority of the state deputies, armed with a writ of
habeas corpus from the Federal Supreme Court, had transferred their
meeting place to the inland town of Juàzeiro. There they declared Colonel Franco Rabelo to be deposed, and turned the state government
over to the president of the Assembly, Floro Bartolomeu, a physician and
backlands politician who had long been the spokesman for the famous
Padre Cícero.

The history of Padre Cícero Romão Batista was not very different
from that of Antônio Conselheiro, the mystic of Canudos. Though
Antônio Conselheiro was ignorant and half-crazy, he and Padre Cícero,
the sane and semiliterate "saint" of the Cariri backlands, were both
products of the same naïve fanaticism and repressed suffering. In *Os
Sertões* Euclides da Cunha classified them both as socially retarded.

After being unfrocked, Padre Cícero had made himself a prophet of
the parched backlands of the Northeast. The illiterate people of the
vast hinterland of Piauí and Bahia, forgotten by the government and
left to their own instincts, humbly recognized Padre Cícero's authority.
He was the universal godfather. Crime-hardened outlaws as well as
simple souls sought his powerful protection. Battalions of believers
would do anything he asked. Juàzeiro, like Canudos, had become a
monstrous city; toward it the backlands pilgrims streamed. Catering to
the mixture of crude religious sentiment and barbaric fetishism, Padre
Cícero provided both charitable works and "miracles." But, unlike the
primitive Antônio Conselheiro, he was no stranger to political ambition. He made a deal with the old dominant party in Ceará, which
granted him sovereign power in the backlands.

Aligning himself with Pinheiro Machado, Floro Bartolomeu had no
trouble inciting Padre Cícero to order an armed uprising against the
government of Franco Rabelo, who responded by sending a police force
to attack Juàzeiro. Beaten at the fortified town, the police fell back on

Crato, where they were again dispersed. The fanatics of Padre Cícero then took the offensive. Franco Rabelo's resistance was short-lived. The new backlands bandits, avenging the old downfall of Canudos, arrived at the gates of Fortaleza armed with modern carbines, old blunderbusses, and knives. They wore leather hats and crude sandals, and proudly displayed their huge "decorations" of rosaries and amulets. It was a colorful encounter between the medieval hordes of the brutal *sertão* [backlands] and the veneer of contemporary civilization in the coastal areas. The federal government, which had resisted military pressure to come to the aid of Rabelo, intervened at last to prevent fighting inside the city. Colonel Setembrino de Carvalho, who was unconnected with the local strife, was appointed the Union's interventor in the state. Padre Cícero triumphantly returned to his backlands capital of Juàzeiro, his prestige naturally redoubled. Pinheiro Machado had gained a new and resounding victory.

The "rescuing" holocaust spread over all the northern states, from Amazonas to Espírito Santo. The oligarchies that did not go up in flames disappeared prudently in last-minute agreements, which at least spared them the street rioting and bombing. Sweeping across the nation the "rescuers" made no distinction between the followers and the adversaries of Pinheiro Machado and the PRC. Alarmed, Pinheiro Machado tried to contain the "rescue" movement in order to save those oligarchies that were the most devoted to him, among them the Lemos of Pará, the Aciolis of Ceará, and the Maltas of Alagoas. In the Federal District also, duplicate municipal councils were formed that facilitated the victory of the Union government.

In São Paulo, however, the "rescuing" process did not bring down the civilianist government, although Pinheiro Machado's local zealots had done everything they could to topple it. It is possible that the same technique that had worked in other parts of Brazil had been planned for São Paulo also, but the Paulistas forestalled the coup and elected as governor Rodrigues Alves, whose moral authority had remained unassailable, and at the same time attracted Fonseca Hermes, President Hermes's brother and majority leader, to their cause.

Even Rio Grande do Sul was not overlooked: the new War Minister, General Mena Barreto, tried to repeat Dantas Barreto's success in Pernambuco. Scenting the danger in his own bailiwick, Pinheiro Machado forced Hermes to fire the minister and replace him with a military man in whom Pinheiro had complete confidence.

The nation viewed first with amusement, then with alarm, the violent upheavals that convulsed the former provinces. The often grotesque technique of the "rescuers," which threatened to start a new cycle of chronic disturbances, was beginning to appear excessive even to the more serene. Rio Branco, sensing the diplomatic effect of the convulsions, tried in vain to contain them. But in spite of his great national prestige, he was charged by many with having contributed directly to the victory of Hermes's candidacy and therefore with responsibility for what was happening under Hermes's administration. The partisan struggle involved not only the executive and legislative branches of the government, but also the judicial branch; the meetings of the Supreme Court when the political writs of habeas corpus were discussed were as uproarious as the sessions of Congress.

The political confusion became extreme. The "new saviors," installed in the state governments they had overthrown violently though with the support of the masses, set up their own local machines, which were even more intolerant than the old ones. Like all governments born of political convulsions, they were concerned chiefly with stimulating material progress and reacting against the chronic stagnation. Public opinion seemed more wide-awake. In the 1912–14 session, Congress was filled with colorful characters whom the state revolutions had pushed to the surface.

The "rescuers" rapidly lost the good opinion of the more cultured strata of the large cities in the South. However, because the "rescues," being reactions to Pinheiro Machado's hegemony, went so far as to oppose the President of the Republic, the "rescuers" did not lose all public sympathy. The stubborn campaign of the civilianists in Congress and in the press tried to blame the gaúcho caudillo for all the mistakes and crimes of the period. He seemed to be even more thoroughly hated than Hermes.

Wavering between his commitments to the gaúcho chieftain and his own family, Marshal Hermes took no positive stand. He let himself be governed by circumstances, at the cost of public order and administrative achievements. In the end, the family influences proved the stronger. When the President remarried after the death of his wife, Pinheiro Machado contrived to get the President's new father-in-law, a retired admiral, elected to the Senate.

To the federal government, Pinheiro personified the Republican Party of Rio Grande do Sul, built on a foundation of close discipline; whereas to his native state, he was the symbol of the Union's enormous prestige. Dantas Barreto, now governor of Pernambuco, J. J. Seabra in Bahia, and most of the other new state administrations in the North were openly hostile to Pinheiro. The two largest northern states, with many representatives in Congress, thus became focal points of opposition to the gaúcho chieftain, whose candidacy to succeed President Hermes was beginning to make itself evident.

Firmly ensconced in the Senate, sure of the solid backing of his party in Rio Grande do Sul, Pinheiro Machado accepted the challenge from his enemies. The parties that had been thrown out of the state governments, even those opposed to him, such as that of Pernambuco, returned to his leadership. São Paulo quieted down under the governorship of Rodrigues Alves, whose strategy was being discreetly directed by a French military mission. Minas Gerais, once more in the hands of its old cautious and opportunistic politicians, tried, as it had during Floriano's time, to isolate itself from the storm. Venceslau Brás, Vice-President of the Republic and, as such, president of the Senate, betook himself to his home town. The "Kindergarten" had broken up. Davi Campista accepted a diplomatic post in Europe, and Carlos Peixoto, no longer interested in the struggle, also took refuge in Europe. Early in 1912 the Baron of Rio Branco died and was replaced by Lauro Müller.

A third Canudos made its appearance. A primitive illuminato—João Maria the Monk, a member of Antônio Conselheiro's old family—set himself up in the Contestado, a territory claimed by both Paraná and Santa Catarina. The federalist regime had become so debased that the two states, both still sparsely populated, could claim control over the area as if they were two nations separated by traditional enmity. The petty interests of the local parties kept alive the dangerous dispute, which the courts had not managed to settle. The votaries of João Maria the Monk therefore found a propitious field in which to flourish. Like both Antônio Conselheiro and Padre Cícero, João Maria put himself ahead of both the government and the church. At his call the backlanders of the South came running. In spite of the enormous geographic distances that separated them from the Northeast, they closely resembled the caboclos of Bahia and Ceará. They were all symptoms of the same social condition, a condition caused by the hostile coexistence of two stages in the historical evolution of the country.

A contingent of state police sent against the Monk was defeated, and its commander, Colonel João Gualberto, was killed in combat. The public reaction was very similar to the one over Canudos, but this time no one suspected an attempt to restore the monarchy. The same deadly mistakes were made. Small military expeditions followed one another without being able to subdue the fanatics. Finally a division of 6,000 men under Colonel Setembrino de Carvalho cleared the Contestado of the outlaws who had infested it for three years. The border dispute between Paraná and Santa Catarina, however, was not settled peaceably until many years later.

President Hermes's administration suffered, naturally, from the constant disturbances. His adversaries in Congress and in the press gave him no truce. He was forced several times to declare a state of siege, which under the Constitution was intended only as an emergency measure. His ties to Pinheiro had alienated many of his fellow officers. Not having been able to stay clear of political intrigues, Marshal Hermes, like Deodoro, must have tasted bitter disappointment.

Pinheiro Machado was the most logical candidate to succeed Marshal Hermes da Fonseca. Never did a public man enjoy greater prestige. As the undisputed leader of the Senate, Pinheiro wielded as much power as the President. As the boss of all the country's political bosses, he could give orders to most of the state governments, and have them obeyed. Rio Grande do Sul was surrounding him with honors. President Hermes found him a dedicated friend, a man who always supported Hermes's administration during even the gravest crises. The politicians, however, even those who were loyal to him, did not want him to become President of the Republic. They felt about him as they had about Rui Barbosa, although for different reasons; they admired and feared the old caudillo from Rio Grande more than they esteemed him. The ousted politicians in the North and in the small states in the South were willing to support his candidacy, but the Paulistas openly and the Mineiros covertly opposed it. In some of the large northern states, such as Pernambuco and Bahia, political control after the "rescue" movement had been seized by some of Pinheiro's toughest adversaries, which gave added strength to his enemies.

The Brazilian republic, like others, tends not to choose a strong and colorful personality such as Pinheiro to be its supreme leader. It may on occasion select a well-balanced man such as Rodrigues Alves, but it is more inclined to elect men who will act discreetly in office, who will be willing to oblige and compromise. Furthermore, if Pinheiro Machado were to have become a candidate, his widespread unpopularity would certainly have had to be taken into account. Thus, as early as 1913, when he first began to be mentioned as the government's official candidate, the politicians started maneuvering to block him.

The first feelers in Pinheiro Machado's behalf were from Minister Rivadávia Correia to the governor of Rio de Janeiro, who had won his position with government support. On learning about this, Cincinato Braga, leader of the São Paulo bloc, began stirring up the opposition. Although Cincinato was sure Pinheiro's candidacy would be rejected by

Pernambuco, Bahia, Rio de Janeiro, and São Paulo, Minas Gerais remained uncommitted. This led Cincinato Braga to approach the Minister of Finance, Francisco Sales, who was an old political boss from
Minas, and naturally looked upon himself as the rightful successor to
President Hermes. Sales had close ties with the governor of Minas, and
was himself a hill-country politician, given to vague understandings
such as one might have with one's family. He saw at once the danger of
Pinheiro's candidacy: so forceful a figure might spark a new round of
conflicts. Having lined up the Mineiro minister, Cincinato Braga went
to São Paulo to sound the alarm against Pinheiro. Cincinato also happened to meet Bueno Brandão, the governor of Minas Gerais, in the city
of Ouro Prêto, and reached an understanding with him for a solid front
against Pinheiro.

To make their rebuff to Pinheiro seem less pointed, the governors of
São Paulo and Minas also agreed to rule out other politicians, such as
Nilo Peçanha and Dantas Barreto, and not to endorse any of their own
partisans as candidates. Thus the two largest states returned to joint
political action after having been split apart during the civilianist campaign. Thereafter, a group in the Federal Chamber composed of the
deputies from Minas, São Paulo, Rio de Janeiro, Pernambuco, and
Ceará was referred to as the "coalition," as opposed to the "conservatives" of Pinheiro Machado. Bahia, standing alone, insisted on Rui Barbosa [a favorite son] as a candidate. Foreseeing possible disaster for his
own candidacy, Pinheiro nominated former President Campos Sales,
who only agreed to become a candidate as a measure of conciliation.

But Campos Sales died that year, and new problems arose. A new effort to nominate Rui Barbosa, which was supported not only by Pinheiro
Machado but also, according to Antônio Azeredo and Rivadávia Correia, by President Hermes, was premised on an agreement by Rui to
abandon his civilianist objectives. This Rui absolutely refused to do, as
he had when a ministerial appointment in the Ouro Prêto cabinet was
offered to him on similar terms.

Meanwhile, the governments of Minas Gerais and São Paulo had
agreed to nominate Venceslau Brás, and thus reward him for his discreet
behavior as Vice-President. Pinheiro Machado also gave him the nod.
Meeting together in August 1913, Pinheiro Machado's "conservatives"
and the "coalition" announced their nomination of Venceslau Brás and
Urbano Santos as candidates for the presidency and vice-presidency of
the Republic for the 1914–18 term.

Rui Barbosa, having the official support of Bahia, maintained his own
campaign with Alfredo Ellis, a Paulista senator, as running mate. A new

party, the Liberal party, was organized to promote the former civilianist platform. But Brazil's attention was absorbed by the war clouds in Europe, and she was not in the mood for a campaign such as had agitated the country four years before. Venceslau Brás was not temperamentally inclined to a contest of the style promised by Rui Barbosa's eloquence. Moreover, Venceslau's victory was assured by the powerful political machines of the states. The Liberal party quickly faded away as so many similar republican endeavors had. Rui Barbosa, again bitterly disappointed and filled with apprehension by the dangers of war in Europe, dropped out of the race.

The short period of prosperity begun during the Rodrigues Alves administration had begun to falter. The first war clouds appeared over Europe. European capital, which had sought outlets in Latin America, began to withdraw. The term of the funding loan contracted for by Campos Sales came to an end.

The native rubber of Amazonia was beginning its decline. Rubber-growing in the Far East had begun experimentally in Ceylon in 1876 with seeds from Amazonia. In 1905 plantations were started in other British possessions in Asia. Under rational cultivation, Oriental rubber could offer a return many times greater than was possible from rubber grown in the virgin forests of Amazonia. In 1911 exports from the Orient equaled those from Brazil. In 1913 the Orient produced 48,000 tons, Brazil only 39,000. In 1914, the last year of Marshal Hermes's term of office, the Amazonian production remained the same, but that of the Orient rose to around 100,000 tons. With the rubber crisis, the precarious edifice in Brazil's far North crashed. Discouragement and poverty replaced the former opulence and prodigality of a land of adventure, exploitation, and easy riches.*

The success of the first government interference in the coffee market, which began with the compact of Taubaté, stimulated a new policy to support that commodity. In 1913 and 1914 new loans of 7.5 and 4.2 million pounds, respectively, were negotiated for that purpose. During Hermes's four-year term, emissions by the Treasury and the conversion fund averaged between 800,000 and 900,000 contos. The natural growth of the country, with the now slow, now accelerated, expansion of its internal economy, made it possible to absorb the increasing volume of currency without catastrophic effects on the rate of exchange. In 1911

* Still standing in Manaus, capital of Amazonas and over 900 miles inland, is the million-dollar opera house built during the rubber boom. It is a relic of a period when not only opera companies but ladies' fineries and other luxuries were brought over from Europe. JLT

and 1912 exports exceeded one million contos, but in 1913 and 1914 they were only 750,000 contos, which was less than total imports. In that same period, the average rate of exchange dropped from 15 to 10 pence to the milreis. The Union's yearly revenues barely reached 600,000 contos, which was not enough to prevent a series of budget deficits.

Faced with diminished revenues, no foreign resources, exports declining in both volume and value, and a permanent state of political and social crisis, the government could have no plan of action, no program to follow. In 1913 it obtained a loan of 11 million pounds. When feelers for more were unsuccessful the next year, the government blocked the conversion fund and suspended redemption of its notes, and the Treasury again started printing money to cover the budget deficits and to provide funds for bank loans to business and industry. By the end of 1914 the inconvertible Treasury bills amounted to almost one million contos, and the conversion fund notes to only 150,000 contos. However, none of these expedients could prevent the ultimate crisis in the federal finances. During his last year in office, the President negotiated a new funding loan of 14 million pounds, interest payments on which were postponed for three years and amortization payments for thirteen years. The public's indifference to this second moratorium was greater even than to the first, but it provoked noisy opposition in Congress and in the press.

In the Department of the Interior and Justice, which at that time took in public education, Minister Rivadávia Correia decreed a general educational reform based on the Comtist philosophy. The secondary schools were given complete didactic and administrative autonomy, and the humanities ceased to be simply preparatory courses. In a country accustomed for centuries to state interference in education, the Rivadávia Correia reform was doomed to failure. Secondary schools sprang up everywhere, aggravating the old problem of a superabundance of degree-holders who were wretchedly educated and inevitably wanted public jobs. Thus whatever benefits might have accrued from a policy that freed education from bureaucratic officiousness were lost in the unsuitable environment.

In the Ministry of Foreign Affairs, Lauro Müller maintained the Rio Branco tradition. Former President Campos Sales was appointed minister to Argentina, which, in turn, sent Brazil her former President, Júlio Roca. Thus the last of the misunderstandings that had envenomed the relations between the continent's two biggest countries were dispelled. The Department of Transportation and Public Works continued constructing railroads and extending telegraph lines. Continuing the program he began as Afonso Pena's War Minister, Marshal Hermes regularized the military draft and strengthened Rio de Janeiro's defenses by constructing the Copacabana forts. In the large maritime cities in the North, such as Bahia and Recife, modern port construction was started at last.

In August 1914, just three months before Hermes's term expired, World War I erupted, and a new stage began in Brazil's economic and social evolution, as in all the American nations that were more or less restricted to a system of monoculture and an economy of exports. Absorbed in the war, Brazilians accepted with indifference the inauguration of President Venceslau Brás, whose four-year term would be spent in the shadow of the war.

19. Venceslau Brás
[1914–18]

Outbreak of the war — Decline of Pinheiro Machado — The
1915–17 legislature — Immediate consequences of the war —
Rui Barbosa's speech in Buenos Aires — Brazil's share in the
war — Effects of the war on economy and literature.

The world was incredibly shocked by the war, even though many felt that the destructive power of modern weapons would make it short and decisive. The Brazilian elites, brought up to worship France and admire England, suffered agonies at the start, when German victory seemed certain. Then the war settled down to the monotony of the trenches, and everyone tried to find consolation by hoping for an ultimate Allied victory, a victory for "justice and freedom."

Venceslau Brás's administration, inaugurated in the early months of the war, dropped to second place in the nation's interest. Venceslau had arrived at the presidency at forty-five years of age, after a rapid, honorable, and lackluster career. He was patient, temporizing, flexible, and tolerant, and was never inclined to force matters. His tactic was always to sidestep the issue and hope it would be resolved by time. The rapidly spreading war served him in two ways: it diverted the people's attention from domestic problems and gave him a chance to call them to national unity.

After the failure of his campaign to become President, Pinheiro Machado's star began to set. Though the majority in Congress still obeyed him, the respect and fear he had always inspired began little by little to be diluted. The Catete, at the same time, was cautiously fortifying its political autonomy. When the President's cabinet was formed,* Pi-

---

* The cabinet was composed of Carlos Maximiliano from Rio Grande do Sul, Minister of the Interior and Justice; Lauro Müller from Santa Catarina, Minister of Foreign Affairs; Sabino Barroso from Minas Gerais, Finance Minister; Tavares de Lira from Rio Grande do Norte, Minister of Transportation; and João Pandía Calógeras, born in Rio, Minister of Agriculture. JMB

nheiro Machado's prestige suffered a heavy blow, for he proved unable to get his nominees appointed to it. Confident of the support of Minas Gerais and São Paulo, of numerous blocs in the Congress, and of the "rescuers" in the North, such as General Dantas Barreto, who had always been hostile toward Pinheiro, the President was able to act with greater independence.

Another setback for Pinheiro was administered in the state of Rio de Janeiro. Two candidates had run for the governorship: Feliciano Sodré, backed by Oliveira Botelho and Pinheiro Machado, and Nilo Peçanha. Duplicate legislative assemblies were elected, and each proclaimed its candidate the winner. The Federal Supreme Court, as it did frequently at the time, recognized by habeas corpus the legitimacy of the assembly controlled by Nilo Peçanha's supporters. The dispute remained unsettled when President Hermes's term ended. President Venceslau ordered the federal forces in Niterói [the state capital] to enforce the court's ruling, which put Nilo in the governor's chair.

Still another instance of President Venceslau's independence occurred during the seating of the 1915–17 legislature. Pinheiro Machado had forced Congress not to recognize General Dantas Barreto's newly elected senatorial candidate, and in his place had put Rosa e Silva, a member of the opposition to Barreto and a former foe of Pinheiro's. President Venceslau at once reshuffled his cabinet; he appointed the spurned legislator, José Bezerra, as Minister of Agriculture, replacing Calógeras, who moved over to the Finance Ministry when Sabino Barroso resigned.

The dissidence between the Catete and the Morro da Graça was no longer disguised. The former civilianist opposition, forgetting that when Venceslau Brás was Vice-President he had been their constant target, redoubled their campaign against Pinheiro Machado, insisting that he be eliminated from public life at all costs. In the Federal Chamber a deputy from Pernambuco submitted a mock bill that had a single provision: "Let General Pinheiro Machado be eliminated."

On the afternoon of September 8, 1915, in the lobby of the Hotel dos Estrangeiros in Rio, a paranoiac, apparently a classic regicide, stabbed Pinheiro in the back. He died from the treacherous blow, as he had predicted many times he would. The extraordinary emotion the crime aroused in the nation passed quickly, as is usual after all stirring events in Brazilian life.

Free of Pinheiro's competition, the President concentrated political rule in his own hands. But his authority was always mild and compromising. He guaranteed agreements made between the states. He resolved the conflict for control of Mato Grosso by proposing the local bishop, Dom Aquino Correia, for governor. He successfully ended the

fight between Paraná and Santa Catarina over the Contestado by bringing the two governors together in an agreement. He pushed the Civil
Code on to completion, a project that had been held up in Congress for
years by arguments among legal experts and philologists.

When the war in Europe began, it panicked the business world. International trade was disrupted and the exchange market disorganized.
The volume of exports and imports dropped steeply. Venceslau Brás,
having inherited a burdensome legacy from his predecessor, now saw the
problems of his own administration aggravated. Since the war was generally expected to be settled quickly, the government hesitated to issue
more inconvertible Treasury bills, preferring short-term notes instead.
Public revenues dropped, and payments for the ordinary expenses of
administration fell behind. For a while, these payments were made in
silver and nickel coins. The government raised the percentage of customs
duties that had to be paid in gold, and increased excise taxes.

When the war became stalemated, the Allied powers turned to the
countries that could supply raw materials and foodstuffs, including Brazil. The prices of goods for export went up. Shipping space in the vessels
that made the dangerous Atlantic crossing was fought for. The prospect
of an extraordinary volume of business put new life into the nation's
economy. New industries were born, and the old ones were reorganized.
All the raw materials and foodstuffs Brazil could produce, and even
some manufactured goods, found immediate and profitable sale in Europe. At the same time, the difficulty of importing manufactured goods
forced the Brazilian consumer to buy goods made in Brazil, even though
they were of poorer quality. The production of field and factory multiplied.

But all of this was improvised from day to day, without plan and
without government coordination. The difficulties of obtaining banking
credit and, principally, the chaos in transportation caused great losses, as
still happens. Commodities intended for shipment piled up and spoiled
at railroad stations in the interior for want of transportation. Everyone
believed that on the day the war ended the extraordinary volume of
business would also cease, and that profits had to be made in any way
possible from the opportunities of the moment. Eager for such profits,
but also worried about the future of their country, the Brazilians left the
government alone and let it forget the permanent revolutionary unrest
for a while. Some discontent was provoked by the increasing cost of living and by agitators, but it passed almost unnoticed in the formidable
noise of war. Brazilian intellectuals kept up intense propaganda in favor
of the Allies, especially their old favorite, France.

England's economic hegemony had at times inflicted painful hardships and humiliations on Brazil, as well as on other impecunious and politically fragmented Latin-American countries. The interests of foreign bankers often seemed to have the highest priority in their governments' financial policies. But any reservations Brazilians had about England's bankers did not affect the admiration that country inspired in Brazil's public men. Germany had won no Brazilian sympathies, except in certain military and scientific circles. One would have said that the Brazilian intellectuals had never forgiven Germany for defeating France in 1870, though it was the France of the detested Napoleon III.

In spite of the relative insignificance of her contacts with the United States, which had been almost worshiped during the days of the founding fathers, and the resentment aroused by the American imperialist policies in Mexico, Central America, and the West Indies, Brazil felt that her own diplomatic policy had to be tied more closely to that of the United States. The facts of life, especially during a war that threatened to involve the whole world, gave Pan-Americanism a new and more concrete significance. On a special mission to Argentina, Rui Barbosa spoke at the Law Faculty in Buenos Aires, criticizing the long-held concept of neutrality. This courageous discourse intensified the already strong Brazilian sentiment in favor of the Allies. When the United States declared war on Germany in 1917, Brazil could no longer maintain neutrality. When Brazilian ships were torpedoed in the Atlantic, Brazil immediately broke off diplomatic relations with Germany.

President Venceslau, apparently the most peaceable of men and the most desirous of governing without conflicts and hatreds, was forced by public opinion to involve Brazil in the foreign war, which did not really affect Brazil militarily. The step she took was mostly a demonstration of political solidarity with the United States. Brazil continued sending Europe all the supplies she could spare. A few commissioned officers and doctors were all the men she contributed to the war. With the official declaration of war, the government decreed a state of siege in the entire country, but did not use it for political ends or personal persecutions. The small crisis brought on by the resignation of Foreign Minister Lauro Müller, suspected of German sympathies because of his German ancestry and some of his attitudes, was easily settled when Nilo Peçanha replaced him.

The war's indirect effects on Brazilian economic and literary life may be of greater interest. The economic system prevailing in the world before the war seemed to divide the nations into two large groups: the supercapitalized, superindustrialized ones that loaned money and exported manufactured goods, and the agricultural countries that supplied raw materials and colonial products. The first had no interest, therefore, in aiding the industrial development of the second. Free trade, which had served the British empire so well, was the economic ideal of the nineteenth century. Gradually, however, in the United States and continental Europe a protectionist reaction had set in, which amounted to government interference in the free play of economic forces. The idea grew that the strongest nation was the one that could best supply itself; the permanent threat of wars counseled maximum self-sufficiency.

This line of thought was naturally reflected in Brazil. In spite of the difficulty of founding basic industries, either because of the poor quality of Brazilian coal or because of its distance from the iron ore reserves in Minas Gerais, there were many things Brazil could make for herself. A manufacturing industry would use native raw materials and free Brazil from her dependence on foreign markets. But despite the dreams of Ouro Prêto and Rui Barbosa, attempts to start industries soon failed, and Brazil returned to the traditional agricultural policies of the monarchy. The successes of coffeegrowing and rubber extraction were enough to support the economy. The crises brought on by the overproduction of coffee and the collapse of rubber revealed clearly how dangerous it was to rest Brazil's economy on a few agricultural and extractive products that were subject to the sudden ups and downs of foreign markets. The program instituted under President Afonso Pena was geared to this new outlook.

The war in 1914 confirmed the subordinate status of countries that depended on others for the necessities of life. It also proved that Brazil could improvise various industries or, at least, semi-industries. Economic nationalism sprang up during the war, and opened up new vistas for Brazilians.

A desire for economic self-sufficiency is always accompanied by a desire for intellectual emancipation. If there is a market for manufactured goods, there must be one also for the products of the spirit. At the beginning of the twentieth century, the old materialistic philosophies were in decline. William James's pragmatism, Bergson's intuitionism, and Neo-Thomism represented the best of the new *Zeitgeist*. But the response to it in Brazil's sparse intellectual circles was anything but lively. The desire for a literary renaissance, inspired by nationalistic considerations in almost all countries like Brazil, was much more active. By destroying so many nineteenth-century illusions, the war of 1914 stimulated the desire for autonomy in all fields, and made the new generation of Brazilian intellectuals more curious about everything to do with their own country. This awakening of a new kind of nationalism, which certain politicians described as an ominous xenophobia, proved to be the prelude to a new literary movement that began a few years later.

President Venceslau's administration, inaugurated at the start of the war, ended during the trying days of the Spanish flu, which in its round of the world struck Brazil at the time of the armistice in 1918. The world holocaust had allowed peace within Brazil's borders. The Brazilian people, who had accepted Venceslau without enthusiasm, now bade him farewell without regrets, but with evidences of their esteem. For all his provincial placidity, he had given them four years of public order, during which he had not tried to oppress them by curtailment of their civil liberties. The final victory of the Allies satisfied the most ardent hopes of the national elites. The extraordinary increase in business caused by the war gave rise to a general belief in the country's growing prosperity. Even the choice of Venceslau's successor, former President Rodrigues Alves, was made without bitterness or difficulty; and was popular with the public.

20. Epitácio Pessoa
[1918–22]

Brazil after the war — Interim administration of Vice-President Delfim Moreira — Biographical sketch of Epitácio Pessoa — False prosperity — Political conflicts — Revolutionary ferment — The "Republican Reaction" — Change of administration in Pernambuco — Government victory — Revolt in Copacabana — Centennial exposition — Great undertakings of President Epitácio Pessoa.

During the war Brazil's exports rose from £26,470,000 in 1914 to £78,-177,000 in 1919, producing trade balances in her favor that reached £52,000,000 in 1919, when the sterling rate of exchange reached 18 pence to the milreis. This economic prosperity influenced the general climate of the country. Various manufacturing industries that had started during the war were trying to take firm root and grow. The participation of Brazil in the Versailles Peace Conference caused intense public pride. President Wilson's exhortations aroused the Brazilian intellectual elites to hope that under the League of Nations the world would enter a new phase of history, and that the war that for four years had laid the world waste would be the last among civilized peoples.

In this optimistic atmosphere, the domestic political situation lost much of its importance. President Venceslau's succession was carried out in perfect order. He had ably managed the election of Rodrigues Alves, who thus became President for the second time. Delfim Moreira, governor of Minas Gerais, was elected Vice-President.

President-elect Rodrigues Alves was not able, however, to take office on November 15, 1918, because of an illness that kept him in Guaratinguetá, São Paulo, and then in his home in Rio, where he died on January 18, 1919. During the President's disability, the reins of government were held by the Vice-President, Delfim Moreira. This Mineiro politician had certainly never dreamed he might become President. He was modest, honorable, cautious, and undistinguished, had no political or social background, and was also a victim of a serious disease that was gradually undermining him. However, some of his shortcomings were offset by the common sense and natural political shrewdness of his mountain-folk inheritance. As long as President Rodrigues Alves remained alive, the Vice-President had to move with great discretion. His authority was impaired; the ministers with whom he governed were not of his own choosing. When Rodrigues Alves died, Delfim Moreira assumed all the presidential functions in his own right. He tried, however, to interfere as little as possible in national politics and in those of his own state. In administrative matters he deferred entirely to the judgment of his ministers, especially of Afrânio de Melo Franco, Minister of Transportation, who became a sort of chief executive aide, and of the Minister of Finance, the Mineiro banker João Ribeiro. Paulo de Frontin, prefect of the Federal District, took up again Pereira Passos's work of remodeling Rio de Janeiro.

Having been one of the belligerent nations, Brazil was invited to send representatives to the Peace Conference at Versailles. Rui Barbosa seemed the natural choice to lead the mission, not only because of his extraordinary intellectual eminence, but also because of the singular prestige with the Allied powers his famous speech in Buenos Aires had brought him. President Rodrigues Alves explicitly repeated the invitation to head the Brazilian delegation that had been made in his behalf by the Vice-President. But the attitude of the Foreign Minister, who seemed to want the honor for himself, caused Rui to question the sincerity of the invitation, though not President Alves's good faith in the matter; furthermore, the other members of the delegation had been named without prior consultation with him. Upon Rui Barbosa's refusal to accept, Epitácio Pessoa was named instead. Epitácio had been a minister under Campos Sales, a Supreme Court justice, and a senator from Paraíba, and was justly renowned for his intelligence, juridical learning, and energy.

The death of Rodrigues Alves again raised the problem of presidential succession, which was always ticklish to handle and pregnant with violence. During Pinheiro Machado's time, the candidacies were influenced largely by his exceptional personal prestige. Whether he won or lost, declared his preferences or not, no one denied his authority. After Pinheiro's death, Brazilian politics were left without a mentor who could command obedience, except for the man who happened to be President at the moment. Vice-President Delfim Moreira, ill and tired, was not interested in the presidential succession. It was therefore left up to a group of politicians, principally from São Paulo, Minas, and Rio Grande do Sul, to nominate a successor to Rodrigues Alves. The governors of São Paulo and Minas at the time were two relatively young men: Altino Arantes and Artur Bernardes. The former could not be nominated because of opposition from Minas and Rio Grande. This implied indirectly the choice of Bernardes. Among the other representative figures at the time remained Rui Barbosa and Borges de Medeiros, the perennial governor of Rio Grande and undisputed head of the strong party founded by Júlio de Castilhos.

Nilo Peçanha hastened to take the initiative in promoting the candidacy of Rui Barbosa, in which he was seconded by the governing politicians of Pará. The leaders of São Paulo, Minas, and Rio Grande, and of other states whose attitudes on the presidential succession were less decisive, agreed to Rui's candidacy, at least tacitly. But the truth was that no politician had ever honestly wanted Rui to be President; his intellectual independence, his strong will, his doctrinaire tendencies, his uncompromising positions, his disdain for petty politicking, his rejection of any party discipline, made him very much feared by the republican oligarchy. Because of this, when the Mineiro politician Raul Soares supported the nomination of Epitácio Pessoa, support for Rui Barbosa quickly disappeared. It was unheard of for the representative of a small state to aspire to the presidency. It was only Rio Grande's opposition to any candidate from either São Paulo or Minas, and the fear of Rui Barbosa's candidacy, that led the politicians to nominate Epitácio, and even then only because he was at the moment on a diplomatic mission abroad.

Betrayed again by politicians who pretended to back him, Rui found himself once more in opposition to the little group that dominated the country. Agreeing afterwards to run as an opposition candidate, though he was already in his seventies and sure of defeat, he repeated his civilianist campaign, going on long, uncomfortable trips to various parts of the country, including his native state [Bahia], from whose government had come the first and strongest plea against his candidacy. In spite of the large vote in his favor—he won in nearly all the large cities—he decided not to contest the election results, but instead to publish a manifesto to the nation.

Epitácio Pessoa was born in Paraíba in 1865. After a good grounding in the humanities, he made a brilliant record at the Law Faculty in Recife, whose environment of agnosticism and veneration for law left a permanent mark on him. Arriving in Rio on the eve of the proclamation of the Republic, he made contact with Deodoro da Fonseca through his uncle, the Baron of Lucena. Appointed Secretary-General of Paraíba by its first republican governor, Venâncio Neiva, he was elected the following year to the Constituent Assembly. He later distinguished himself by opposing Floriano Peixoto in Congress with impunity. When Campos Sales was making up his cabinet in 1898, he surprised Pessoa by offering him the Ministry of Justice and the Interior. (According to his own testimony, Epitácio was always surprised by nominations for the highest offices, including the presidency. His avowal on this point, entitled *Pela Verdade,* is an interesting document of republican politics in Brazil's strange federation.) He proved to be a hard-working and energetic minister. Leaving the cabinet after a disagreement with Campos Sales over a reform in education that would later bear Epitácio's name, he was shortly afterwards appointed by Campos Sales to be Chief Justice of the Federal Supreme Court and then to be Attorney General of the Republic; in both positions he exercised his duties with his usual brilliance and courage. After resigning for reasons of health, he reentered politics in his native state and was elected to the Federal Senate. He also carried out some technical missions both at home and abroad. He was always grave, ceremonious, polished, well-groomed, sociable, and very careful about his public and private attitudes.

Chosen to head the Brazilian delegation to the Peace Conference, he endeavored to repay the confidence of his government and countrymen. Whenever he could act he proved himself outstanding. Two big questions were of prime interest to Brazil: the status of certain Brazilian funds frozen by Germany during the war, and the use Brazil had made of some German war vessels.

In 1914 São Paulo had 1,835,361 bags of coffee warehoused in Hamburg, Bremen, Trieste, and Antwerp as security for two loans from European bankers. Fearing it might be confiscated by the German government when the war started, the government of São Paulo ordered the coffee to be sold and the proceeds (125 million prewar marks) deposited in a German bank. Germany then embargoed the money, promising to restore it after the war. Brazil sought restitution of the full amount, plus interest, at the original rate of exchange, whereas the committee on finances at the Versailles Conference would only agree to include the German debt in the peace treaty at the current rate, in marks worth ten per cent of their value in 1914. The Brazilian position, thanks to the efforts of Epitácio Pessoa, which were supported by President Wilson, won out in the end.

But the question of the German vessels was more difficult. In January 1917 Brazil had seized the German vessels in her ports, but, with her extreme regard for private property, had refrained from confiscating them, unlike other nations, even after she declared war on Germany. Brazil now wanted to buy the vessels for a suitable indemnity. England, France, and the United States, who dominated the Conference completely and were in great need of ships, opposed the Brazilian claim, which finally triumphed only after President Wilson again gave Brazil his direct support. This question was complicated by the fact that the ships had been under charter to France, which resulted in a lengthy and irritating diplomatic discussion that was settled eventually during Epitácio Pessoa's administration in Brazil's favor.

In the atmosphere of Versailles in 1919, neither Brazil, nor the other belligerent Latin-American countries, nor the small European nations that were brutally sacrificed could long retain their illusions. The committee of the five great victorious powers, France, England, the United States, Italy, and Japan, was the supreme arbiter of the fate of the vanquished nations, of Europe, and of the world itself. In the committee, three men, Clemenceau, Lloyd George, and Wilson, overshadowed all the others. The presence of other nations in the palace of Versailles was mainly ornamental. Neither President Wilson's great dream of the League of Nations nor his famous Fourteen Points could conceal the disillusionments and dissensions inside the Conference. The Americans' increased disenchantment with the spectacle in Europe, and the selfish attitudes of isolationists, kept the United States out of the League, thereby foredooming it to failure. But Brazil was given another demonstration of the United States' solidarity with her in foreign policy. Epitácio Pessoa, who had already been the official guest of the Kings of Italy and of Belgium, and was by then President-elect of Brazil, was invited to visit the United States before returning to Brazil.

On arriving in Brazil from the United States [July 21, 1919], he took steps to assert his independence from the narrow politics of the parties. In forming his cabinet he went against usual practice by appointing men for practical rather than political reasons. His ministers were: Alfredo Pinto, a jurist and former politician, Interior and Justice; Azevedo Marques, a law professor from São Paulo, Foreign Affairs; Piros do Rio, a Paulista engineer, Transportation; Homero Batista and Simões Lopes, both gaúcho politicians, Finance and Agriculture, respectively; Calógeras, and Raul Soares, both Mineiro politicians, War and Navy, respectively.

In offering the military portfolios to two civilians, Epitácio Pessoa resisted not only impertinent pressures but even threats from certain groups of military men, especially from the navy. The admiral who was Navy Minister under Delfim Moreira called on Pessoa and advised him to change his plan. The President-elect replied that the civilians would be appointed to the military portfolios on the following day, and that the navy could, if it wished, take the responsibility for disturbing constitutional order. The Brazilian people applauded the new administration sincerely. For the first time, the presidency was occupied by a notable civilian politician who had had experience not only in Congress and the Ministry of Justice but in the Supreme Court as well, and, being from a small northern state, had no commitments to either a large bloc in Congress or large vested interests in industry and agriculture.

In spite of the penury of the Treasury, the business climate was optimistic, but President Epitácio, who in a speech the year before, at a banquet honoring President-elect Rodrigues Alves, had discussed Brazil's political and administrative problems at length, was not deceived by surface appearances. In a message to Congress he criticized the excessive tariff protectionism and the discounting of the future by undue recourse to credit and paper money. The country should not count on an indefinite increase of its sales abroad. As soon as the worst effects of the war had been cleared up, Europe would try to rebuild her industries and reestablish foreign trade. A policy of prudence and economy was therefore essential. Clearly, such ideas did not sit well with the powerful political groups and the manufacturing industries who favored tariff walls. Other positions taken by the President stirred up lively opposition against him in Congress and in the press. Never had the nation's chief executive vetoed so many bills, including one for an increase in military pay, and, for the first time in the history of the Republic, one for budget appropriations.

The President's logical estimate that the war-created prosperity was precarious soon proved correct. Exports fell off drastically, and in 1920 were even less than imports. Economic instability, reflected in the adverse rate of exchange, alarmed industrialists, coffeegrowers, and merchants alike. São Paulo became intensely eager for more federal subsidies for coffee. President Epitácio could not long resist the strong pressure of the coffee interests, which were, after all, the interests of the entire national economy. The steadily falling price of coffee, accompanied by a declining rate of exchange, created near panic. The federal government decided to borrow nine million pounds, with which it bought up some surplus coffee and stored it in warehouses in Brazilian ports. This succeeded in preventing a further drop in prices. Later on, to round it out, the Treasury discounted a note for four million pounds at the Banco do Brasil. Two other large foreign loans continued the change in Epitácio's financial policy. Fifty million U.S. dollars was borrowed expressly for public works to protect the Northeast against its perennial droughts, and another 25 million U.S. dollars was borrowed to electrify the Central Railroad of Brazil and make other railroad improvements. Influenced by the new banking theories in Germany, the Finance Minister, Homero Batista, created a rediscount department in the Banco do Brasil to issue Treasury bills against trade acceptances.

Meanwhile, opposition to the Pessoa government was mounting steadily, both in Congress and in the press. The administration's political activity, as well as its economic and financial operations, were vehemently criticized. The most bitter accusations were leveled against the President, who only a short time before had been so greatly praised. Of a fighting temperament, loving conflict and danger, Epitácio Pessoa defended himself against the attacks. Thus there was created an atmosphere of controversy and antagonism that was conducive to revolutionary changes. The administration's normal functioning was being obstructed, as it had been during the civilianist opposition to Hermes da Fonseca.

An election in Bahia contributed to greater turmoil. Two candidates were claiming victory: J. J. Seabra, backed by the local government, and another politician backed by Rui Barbosa. Claiming that Seabra's victory was fraudulent, some backlands chieftains initiated an armed movement, threatening to march on the state capital to keep him from taking office. After the commanding general of the federal forces in Bahia failed to settle the matter peaceably, President Epitácio acceded to the request of the governor of Bahia for federal intervention, but not until after he had tried to resolve the dispute by suggesting a third candidate. The President's intervention in Bahia in behalf of Seabra, which he justified according to the controversial Article Six of the Constitution, added fuel to the opposition flames.

In the early months of 1921, or nearly two years before President Epitácio's term would expire, the politicians—as was their old habit—began selecting his successor. The nomination of Artur Bernardes, then governor of Minas Gerais, was agreed upon at once by all except Borges de Medeiros, who believed a candidate's platform had to be heard before he was nominated. Convinced that the President should not interfere in the choice of his successor, Epitácio Pessoa also agreed to Bernardes's nomination, though it was being made midway through his own term of office. As a reward, the politicians of Minas and São Paulo offered to let him nominate Bernardes's running mate, an opportunity the President declined. He did stress, however, that a man from one of the northern states should be nominated. Soon the governor of Bahia, J. J. Seabra, and the governor of Pernambuco, José Bezerra, both announced their candidacies for the vice-presidency. The ensuing dispute between their respective backers in the two states, who were nonetheless united in supporting Bernardes for President, threatened to upset the working agreement between the Minas and São Paulo factions. To keep the split from widening, President Epitácio appealed directly to both northern governors. But when his efforts proved useless, he proposed a third candidate, Senator Urbano Santos of Maranhão, who had been Vice-President during the administration of Venceslau Brás.

Political peace, however, had been shattered. The dissident politicians, including the two frustrated vice-presidential candidates, now formed a coalition called "Republican Reaction" and nominated their own candidates: Nilo Peçanha, who had backed Bernardes, for President, and J. J. Seabra for Vice-President. Once more the small group of men who ruled Brazil by controlling the large states was split, not because of different ideas or platforms but because of large and small vanities, injured feelings, and the desire to keep their political machines in power. All the revolutionary hankerings that had barely been held in check because of the war during Venceslau's administration no longer had to be restrained. Exploited by clever demagogues, the partisan campaign soon agitated even the military. Everything indicated that the internal peace that had begun under Prudente de Morais and flourished under Rodrigues Alves was over. We can see today that the close of Epitácio Pessoa's administration marked the beginning of the revolutionary campaign that would culminate in the victorious movement of 1930 and in the authoritarian state of 1937. In spite of the outward differences, the upheaval had its genesis in the civilianist reaction of 1909, when Rui Barbosa, rebelling against the oligarchy that controlled Brazil, and that he had been part of for a time, had demonstrated that even though the middle classes habitually failed to vote and the masses were indifferent, they could be appealed to directly, for both good and bad purposes. The more rapid growth of the economy, the movement away from the farms to the cities, and the unrest in the aftermath of the war gave birth to a new state of mind in the people that was not perceived by the politicians, even the most clear-headed ones, whether they had shared the spoils of government or not. Today we can easily trace the subversive movements that shook Brazil between 1921 and 1930, and that probably would have begun in 1914 or 1915 but for the war, to old disillusionments, honest grievances, reactions to world crises, ambitions, common demagoguery, and love of adventure and disorder.

Though hit full-force by the revolutionary wave, President Epitácio, courageous as usual, guaranteed his office would be transmitted in the time-honored fashion to his duly elected successor. The people, aroused by the contest over the next presidency, cared little for any other matters that might affect the nation. The opposition to Artur Bernardes reached a virulence unprecedented in previous campaigns. He was reviled mercilessly by his antagonists in Congress and in the press. One large Rio newspaper published a letter containing insulting remarks about the army that he had allegedly written to Raul Soares. The document had all the earmarks of a forgery, but it was an excellent pretext to stir up the prejudices of the military. Bernardes and Soares accepted the unfortunate suggestion of some friends to submit the document to be appraised by a committee of the Military Club, since they were certain its members would unanimously pronounce it a forgery. But the committee instead unanimously declared it to be authentic, as President Epitácio had foreseen they would. The fight grew more bitter. The candidates of the "Republican Reaction" went about the country rousing street mobs.

An election in Pernambuco necessitated by the death of its governor, José Bezerra, provided a new reason for demagogic excitement against Epitácio Pessoa. Two large political groups were contesting control, and both offered candidates for the vacant governor's chair. One group was headed by Senators Manuel Borba and Rosa e Silva. The other, headed by Estácio Coimbra, majority leader in the Federal Chamber, and General Dantas Barreto, included some relatives of President Epitácio. The opposition charged that the President of the Republic was trying to deliver political control of Pernambuco to his own family. The fight between the two groups broke out in Recife, accompanied by the usual imported bandits from the backlands, street riots, shootings, ambushes, telegrams, and biased articles in the newspapers. The opposition accused Epitácio of placing army troops at the disposal of one of the candidates of the group that included his relatives. The President denied this charge, and published his correspondence with the military commander of Pernambuco.*

The Military Club, already fired up against Bernardes, appealed to the garrison in Pernambuco to resist the imagined orders from the fed-

---

* In her excellent biography of Epitácio Pessoa, Laurita Pessoa Raja Gabaglia reveals that members of Epitácio's family had taken advantage of his trust, and had made unauthorized use of his name to approach the commander of the federal troops in Pernambuco. J M B

eral government. This extraordinary telegram was signed by the president of the Military Club, Marshal Hermes da Fonseca, who, as when he was head of state, permitted himself to be maneuvered by intriguers, ingenuously believing he might be able to return to the Catete. When he was questioned by the War Minister about the telegram, the Marshal confirmed he had written it, and when the government ordered him reprimanded, he rejected the reprimand and was arrested. The government also closed the Military Club, as Prudente de Morais had once done. The electoral dispute in Pernambuco was settled shortly afterward by the withdrawal of the two candidates and the nomination of a third: Sérgio Loreto, a federal judge.

In March, on the date set by the Constitution, the presidential elections were carried out peacefully throughout the entire country. Artur Bernardes won by about 150,000 votes over Nilo Peçanha. But as often happened during that era of debased representative government, the election did not put an end to the strife. Bernardes was booed as he rode up the main avenue in Rio. The "Republican Reaction" announced that it did not accept the victory of the government's candidate. Mutinies erupted in various states; the government declared that they followed a plan for general revolution. Marshal Hermes, president of the Military Club, and therefore, he thought, spokesman for the army, proposed in a letter to the Vice-President of the Senate, Antônio Azeredo, that a "court of honor" be appointed to confirm the results of the election, since the verification by Congress required by the Constitution did not inspire confidence in the military. Nilo Peçanha, J. J. Seabra, and Borges de Medeiros, a little less radical than the Marshal, suggested an alternative: that a court or commission of arbitration be made up of an equal number of delegates from the two parties to look into and pass on the election, but without prejudice to the subsequent decisions of Congress. Nilo Peçanha pointed out in a letter also addressed to Azeredo that this was similar to what had previously been done in the United States and Chile.

Epitácio Pessoa called a meeting in the Presidential palace, the "meeting at the Catete" as it came to be known, of some Mineiro and Paulista leaders, the Vice-President of the Senate, and the War and Navy Ministers; the meeting was to expose the gravity of the situation, which seemed to him extreme, and to decide what to do about the proposed court of arbitration. The proposal was voted down, but the President's attitude and words lent themselves to varying interpretations afterwards. He is supposed to have suggested that President-elect Bernardes withdraw in favor of a third candidate who would have sufficient prestige to pacify the nation. For his part, he could assure the orderly inauguration of his successor, but he did not know what might happen after the new administration was installed. Later, in a speech in the Senate and in a book, Epitácio denied that he had made such a suggestion. However. in a letter* to Bernardes reporting on the meeting, Raul Soares stated that, in view of the President's exposition of the dangers facing the nation, he had asked him whether, since it was impossible to dissolve the army, the only solution lay in the withdrawal of the President-elect, and that Epitácio had replied: "Exactly, Bernardes's withdrawal would be the answer."

This latest scheme, having been put forward tardily at that, was killed by Raul Soares's immediate rejection of it, and Congress proceeded to recognize the majority candidates as the winners of the two highest government offices. When Vice-President-elect Urbano Santos died before he could take office, J. J. Seabra petitioned the Federal Supreme Court for a writ of habeas corpus that would make him Vice-President. The Court naturally denied such an extravagant request, but the fact it had been made at all revealed once again how bad things were. Estácio Coimbra, the government's leader in the Chamber and a former governor of Pernambuco, was nominated for and elected to the vice-presidency.

On July 5, 1922, the Igrejinha fort in Copacabana revolted, and the Military Academy mutinied, expecting naturally that other army units would do the same. The rebel fort fired a few shots against strategic points in the city. The government struck back with most of the troops that had remained loyal, and with war vessels. The uprising at the Military Academy and at some barracks was easily put down. When the fort was bombed, all but a small group of young officers and men surrendered. The "Eighteen of Copacabana," as they came to be known, came out to fight on the beach, where most of them sacrificed their lives against the powerful government forces.† President Epitácio's dramatic victory fulfilled his promise and his duty to maintain civil order, and enhanced his personal prestige. But there was no letup in the political and military agitation, nor any lessening of the hatred against the President-elect.

Epitácio Pessoa's administration ended with an international exposition commemorating Brazil's first century of independence from Portugal. The prefect of Rio, the engineer Carlos Sampaio, had begun by demolishing a historic hill‡ in the city to make a strip of new land along

---

* Published, with Bernardes's reply, in Virgílio de Melo Franco's book, in October 1930. JMB

† Among the few survivors was Eduardo Gomes, who became a high-ranking officer in the Air Force, and a presidential candidate in 1945. JLT

‡ This was the Morro do Castelo (Hill of the Castle), whose former site is now the heart of Rio's downtown business district. JLT

the bay, and here the pavilions of the exposition were built. The centennial exposition let the Republic take stock of its economic activities. In attempting to abandon its exclusively agricultural tradition, it had tried to develop manufacturing industries. The disruption of European production and commerce by World War I had given Brazil, and other nations like her, the best possible opportunity to begin using indigenous sources of wealth. The great industrial nations of Europe, working to recover from the ravages of war, were eager to regain their Brazilian markets. The centennial exposition was the first opening offered them. The President of Portugal, Antônio José de Almeida, paid Brazil an official visit. (A similar honor had been paid the nation in 1920 by Albert, King of the Belgians, whose heroic stand during the invasion of his country by Germany had made him one of the great contemporary figures.) Another event that made a good impression at home and abroad was the repeal of the law that banished the imperial family from Brazil, and the removal of the remains of Pedro II and the Empress Teresa Cristina from European to Brazilian soil.

In a summation of Epitácio Pessoa's major undertakings, the public works to combat droughts in the Northeast would rank among the most noteworthy. For a long time periodic droughts had scourged the northeastern backlands; the central governments of both the monarchy and the Republic had limited themselves to rendering emergency aid. The Republic's administrations had tried to build some dams, and in 1909 a special department had been set up to centralize and systematize the work. President Epitácio, a Northeasterner himself, and therefore deeply aware of the extent of the recurring calamity, had initiated a much broader plan. He obtained authority from Congress to borrow up to 200,000 contos for building dams, roads, and harbors to make the drought area permanently habitable and prevent the periodic exodus of its population. Contracts were awarded to American firms, and work was begun immediately. Like all the undertakings and accomplishments of the Pessoa administration, this one, generously intended to rehabilitate a vast region economically, gave rise to both enthusiastic plaudits and bitter criticisms. Another controversial contract was made with a foreign corporation to develop a steel industry and export iron ore.*

On the date prescribed by the Constitution, November 15, 1922, Epitácio Pessoa handed over the reins of administration to Artur Bernar-

---

* The corporation was the Itabira Iron Ore Co., the greatest dream of Percival Farquhar, the American capitalist and entrepreneur who had built the Madeira-Mamoré Railroad and other large-scale projects in Brazil. Although his Itabira project was backed by President Pessoa, Bernardes blocked it, and it finally died a slow death during the Vargas regime. JLT

des, as he had sworn he would at the "Catete meeting." But the atmosphere of the country, especially in the capital, was one of general anxiety. The new President would find it hard to prevent the outbreak of new revolutionary movements.

It was impossible at the time to form sound judgments on President Pessoa's actions during the three-and-a-half years of his administration. His temperament was much more that of a man of law and justice than that of a politician and executive. Almost all his policies and important administrative acts had been harshly criticized, if not denounced. Implacable enemies did not spare even his private life. For all his virtues and faults as a public man, his successes and failures as an executive, it can be said nevertheless that the Republic has never had a more distinguished, a more vigorous, or a more brilliant President. It can be said also that Epitácio Pessoa's administration was a turning point in the history of Brazil, for during it greater powers came to be concentrated in the hands of the President, thanks in part to Pinheiro Machado's exit years before.

21. Artur Bernardes
[1922–26]

Biographical sketch of Artur Bernardes — Financial crisis — Political crises in state governments — Increases in Executive power — Revolution in São Paulo — The Prestes column — Financial policy — Literary modernism — Bernardes's accomplishments — Disintegration of the Republic.

Artur Bernardes was installed as President of the Republic on November 15, 1922. His Vice-President was Estácio Coimbra, governor of Pernambuco under Hermes da Fonseca, and majority leader in the Federal Chamber under Epitácio Pessoa. The new President's cabinet was made up of militant politicians.* Neither the election of Bernardes nor his confirmation by Congress had diminished the opposition. There were open plots against him in both political and military circles.

Only forty-seven years old, Artur da Silva Bernardes had risen very rapidly in politics. During his several terms as a federal deputy he had always been judicious and discreet, never outstanding in any way as a member of the large bloc from his state. As secretary of finance in Minas, he showed his ability as an administrator. On becoming governor of the state, he instituted new policies opposed to the old provincial partisan habits. Like João Pinheiro, Carlos Peixoto, and Raul Soares, Bernardes was an example of the successful younger politicians of his conservative mountain state. When President Rodrigues Alves died, Bernardes was one of those mentioned as a possible replacement. He was later chosen by the political chiefs of Minas and São Paulo to succeed Epitácio Pessoa.

The legacy inherited by Bernardes was very burdensome: political tur-

* Minister of Justice: João Luís Alves, who was followed by the Mineiro Afonso Pena Júnior. Finance: Sampaio Vidal from São Paulo, followed by Aníbal Freire from Pernambuco. Transportation: Francisco Sá from Ceará. Agriculture: Miguel Calmon from Bahia. General Setembrino de Carvalho was returned as War Minister, and Admiral Alexandrino de Alencar as Navy Minister; upon the latter's death Admiral Pinto da Luz was appointed to the post. The prefecture of the Federal District was given to a politician from Minas, Alaor Prata. JMB

moil, threats of revolution, and a serious economic crisis. A few days after his inauguration, his Finance Minister, Sampaio Vidal, reported publicly on the nation's financial situation, which included oppressive debts, budget deficits, declining exports, and the lowest rates of exchange since 1894. Epitácio Pessoa replied to the Finance Minister's severe criticisms; the lively exchange that followed revived the debates in Congress and in the press over the uses made of various foreign loans. But the crisis that afflicted the country was not caused just by errors in the handling of finances, but essentially by the situation created by the European war, for, as President Pessoa had predicted, once Europe had recovered from the worst effects of the war, Brazil's favorable trade balance was radically reversed. In 1920 she suffered a trade deficit of £17,484,000, and the milreis dropped to seven pence. The volume of inconvertible currency rose from 900,000 contos in 1913 to 1,700,000 in 1920, and gold prices for Brazil's principal exports took a nose dive. The exacerbation of partisan conflicts at the start of Bernardes's administration only worsened the Treasury's predicament.

Like his predecessor, Bernardes spent most of his time and attention trying to safeguard public order. Instead of a policy of moderation that might have tempered the hatreds built up during the recent campaign, instead of "the President forgetting the insults to the candidate," to use his own expression, he adopted a policy of reaction, including laws that curtailed freedom of the press, prolonged the state of siege, and disbanded state political machines that had been adverse to him. A new policy that increased credit to support coffee prices was implemented by an agreement with the Banco do Brasil that in effect enlarged the rediscount department created during Pessoa's administration.

The so-called political cases kept increasing in number and severity. At the very start of Bernardes's term there arose a fight over the governorship of Rio de Janeiro. As usual, duplicate legislative assemblies had been formed, each backing its own candidate. Nilo Peçanha's party, which was opposed to President Bernardes, had obtained a restraining order from the Federal Supreme Court that would permit the current governor, Raul Fernandes, to continue in office. The President at first seemed disposed to obey the court order and, if need be, to use army troops to enforce it. But continuing disorders in Niterói and other parts of the state, and the weakened discipline of his own local police, kept Governor Fernandes confined to his palace, since formal recognition of his status by the federal authorities had not been forthcoming. The dispute between the parties, as in similar situations in the past, had to be settled by Congress, which was in recess, but the state of siege was still in effect; President Bernardes therefore decreed federal intervention and appointed an interventor. Unable to resist, and with his capital occupied by the army, Fernandes gave up. When Congress reconvened in May, the state of siege having been kept continuously in effect, it approved the presidential decree, ratified the interventor's acts, and dissolved the state's legislative assembly, annulling at the same time the laws it had enacted. Shortly afterward, Bernardes's candidate was peacefully elected and seated in the governor's chair.

At the same time the gubernatorial election in Rio Grande do Sul was being fought out. Borges de Medeiros, who had been governor continuously since the death of Júlio de Castilhos, was running for another term. The strong and stubborn local opposition, which dated back to the early days of the Republic, nominated Assis Brasil. When Borges de Medeiros was declared winner of the election, and after an attempt at conciliation failed, the opposition took up arms, naturally hoping to be supported by President Bernardes, whose candidacy for President had been fought by Medeiros's Republican party.

But President Bernardes made new attempts to reconcile the parties. He first sent down Comptroller General (and former Minister of Justice) Tavares de Lira. When Lira failed he was replaced by the War Minister, General Setembrino de Carvalho, who successfully promoted the "Pedras Altas agreement," named after Assis Brasil's cattle ranch, where it was signed. Under this agreement Borges de Medeiros would remain governor, but the state constitution, so clearly informed by positivist doctrines, would be revised, reelections would be forbidden, and the office of vice-governor, until then appointive, would become elective.

The party into which all the elements of the opposition were merged nationally took the name of Alliance for Liberation. In São Paulo the nomination of Washington Luís to succeed Governor Carlos de Campos provoked a new partisan crisis, but it was soon quelled. In Bahia and other states, President Bernardes tried to lend strength to his fellow party members and thus to his own organization. During his long and stubborn resistance, the President revealed a cool and calculating courage, which, if it did not arouse enthusiasm, did inspire awe. The other political authorities of the nation seemed to resign themselves to the Executive's supreme sovereignty.

When President Bernardes felt sufficiently sure of support by the Congressional majority and the state political machines, he obtained changes in the Constitution of 1891, something President Pessoa had not been able to do. These consisted mainly of a prohibition of the *cauda orçamentária* [literally, budgetary tail], a special-interest rider tacked onto the budget bill by way of disguise, for years a source of great abuses; a curtailment of the reach of the habeas corpus, which had degenerated into a political device; a grant to the President of some rights to veto legislation; and regulations allowing dangerous foreigners or "undesirables" to be expelled. In general, the constitutional changes were intended to strengthen the authority of the federal government, especially the powers of the Executive. But the President's repressive policies did not extinguish, and may have stimulated, the revolutionary ferment, in which were merged demagogic incitements, common lusts for power, and honest hopes for a more democratic way of life, or at least one less bound by the patriarchal legacy of the Empire. No sooner was one civilian or military plot disposed of than another rose in its place.

On July 5, 1924, two years to the day after the uprising of the fort at Copacabana, a revolution erupted in São Paulo under the leadership of Isidoro Lopes, a retired general who had taken part in the civil war in Rio Grande do Sul. He was supported by a group of young officers who had been openly conspiring from the time of President Pessoa's government. Most of the federal garrison stationed in São Paulo went over to the general. Public sentiment in São Paulo was also favorable to him. Governor Carlos de Campos abandoned his palace, and took refuge in one of the city's suburbs, protected by troops sent from Rio and other nearby points. With the full support of the state governments and Congress, President Bernardes reacted vigorously, after rejecting offers of conciliation. Army and navy personnel, and police forces from the states, besieged the Paulista capital and threatened to bomb it. Unable to resist, the rebels retired from the city in good order, twenty-two days after the start of the insurrection, and moved west and south. A part of them concentrated in Paraná, across the river from Paraguay in the area formed by the angle of the Iguaçu and Paraná rivers, where, under constant pressure from government forces, they finally surrendered Catanduva, their jungle stronghold. The federal government had once more defeated a poorly organized revolution, one whose objectives were ill-defined and whose sudden outbreak was like the rupture of an abscess that had been festering a long time. In Amazonas, Pará, Pernambuco, Sergipe, and other parts of the country, the São Paulo revolution inspired more disorders, which the local governments subdued by themselves or with federal help.

In October the revolutionary movement in Rio Grande do Sul broke into violence in the former Misiones territory, in the old flying columns and guerrilla warfare that had so often devastated the state. A column of rebels led by young Luís Carlos Prestes*—the "Coluna Prestes," as it came to be called—headed north out of Alegrete, near Uruguaiana and the Uruguay border, intending to link up with General Isidoro Lopes's forces from São Paulo. The column, more than a thousand men, was a motley crowd of exiled former officers, veterans of the old civil wars and more recent insurrections, caudillos, common foot soldiers, and assorted adventurers. Their extraordinary march would take them more than 6,000 miles up into Maranhão [thence west to the border], battling their way against regular army troops, local police forces, provisional battalions from Rio Grande do Sul, and even bandit mercenaries. They forded rivers, climbed mountains, and slashed their way through jungles, ravaging the countryside as they went, in a desperate effort to keep alive the flame of revolt, until finally, after two and a half years, with 800 ill-equipped, exhausted men left, Prestes sought asylum in Bolivian territory.

On November 6, 1924, the warship *São Paulo* rebelled [inside Guanabara Bay] and threatened to blow up the Catete palace. But feeling cut off from the rest of the navy, or reluctant to damage the city, the mutineers on the old vessel changed their minds, and steamed out of the harbor under fire from the forts and other ships. They later put in at Montevideo and surrendered to the Uruguayan authorities.

Such permanent public disorder showed there was an inherent flaw in the Executive's political program, in spite of his many dictatorial powers. The lack of real national parties, the want of political education among both the ruling classes and the masses, and the country's low economic level, all contributed to a continuing debasement of public life. What with chronic states of siege, pronunciamentos, and successive revolutions, Brazil's republican institutions were showing signs of breaking down.

A gradual improvement in the economic situation was reflected in the public finances. In January 1923 Congress approved a contract, which it ratified in April of the same year, between the government and the Banco do Brasil creating a Department of Emissions. It was a new attempt to clean up the monetary muddle. The bank undertook to redeem the outstanding paper currency—about 1,900,000 contos—whenever the reserve fund reached 100,000 contos, which would then be converted into gold whenever gold could be bought at twelve pence per milreis. The Treasury transferred ten million pounds of its gold reserves, worth 300,000

---

* Prestes later became Brazil's top Communist leader, and has remained so until now (1965). Many years of his turbulent career have been spent in jail and in exile. JLT

contos, to the bank, against which the latter was authorized to issue paper money based on one-third in gold (at twelve pence) and two-thirds in trade acceptances. The bank's notes were to be redeemed in gold at twelve pence to the milreis whenever the gold reserves equaled 60 per cent of the emissions. The Minister of Finance, Sampaio Vidal, and the president of the bank, Cincinato Braga, both Paulistas, quickly went beyond the emission limits set by law. Probably fearing inflation, the government provoked a political crisis and forced them to resign. In replacing Vidal by Aníbal Freire, a deputy from Pernambuco, President Bernardes converted the policy of easier credit initiated by the bank to a positively deflationary one. Exchange rates and the Treasury's situation both improved, in spite of the heavy expenses incurred in quelling the revolutionary movements.

In complete control of federal politics, President Bernardes set in motion the candidacy of Washington Luís, governor of São Paulo, to succeed him in the presidency. The choice for the vice-presidency was a little more difficult. The first person suggested, it seems, was Miguel Calmon, a politician from the North, then Minister of Agriculture. But when the governor of Minas, Melo Viana, began to voice his dissatisfaction publicly, he was quieted down by being selected as Washington Luís's running mate. In 1923 both Rui Barbosa and Raul Soares, the political leader of Minas Gerais, died.

In São Paulo, a new artistic and literary movement was launched by a group of young intellectuals. Their chief figure was Mario de Andrade, who, with the customary exaggerations of the innovator, proclaimed his scorn for old, sterile forms and European imitations. The group was joined by the highly successful author and member of the Academy, Graça Aranha. The "Semana de Arte Moderna" [Modern Art Week] held in São Paulo captured attention in Rio also, and stirred up an inoffensive and amusing battle between the old and new literati.* If on the purely literary level the "modernism" promulgated in São Paulo was part of the search for new artistic values also going on in music and the plastic arts, on the sociological level it was part of the awakening of nationalistic sentiments that was one of the aftereffects, in Brazil as elsewhere, of World War I.

President Bernardes's administration ended in relative peace. The condition of the Treasury had improved under Minister Aníbal Freire's sound financial policies, and service payments on the foreign debt, sus-

---

* From this movement there developed, among other things, the now world-famous São Paulo Biennial Art Exposition. JLT

pended since the funding loan of 1914, were resumed. The two Ministers of Justice, João Luís Alves and Afonso Pena Júnior, had worked hard to remodel the judiciary and public education. The Ministers of Transportation and of Agriculture, Francisco Sá and Miguel Calmon, had also been active. However, the conduct of foreign affairs under Félix Pacheco, a journalist, had been tumultuous and blundering. Brazil had abandoned the League of Nations, and had become involved in noisy incidents at the Pan-American Conference in Santiago in 1924.

But what the impartial observer could see behind the revolutions and reactions was the rapid dismantling of the republican state of 1891. After nearly forty years of tormented existence, presidentialism and federalism had proved they could not honestly be applied in Brazil. All their fine concepts had been corrupted in practice. The representative system was a vast hoax, as it had been during the Empire; there were not even national parties, as there had been in the Empire. Government-controlled elections in a patriarchal regime made it possible to select men for their individual worth, but became dangerous in the Republic when they reflected popular passions whipped up by oppositionist demagoguery.

In order to survive, the governments, powerful in many ways and not averse to despotism, were forced constantly to resort to states of siege or to what amounted to the same thing, suspension of constitutional guarantees of civil liberties. Federalism had been converted into narrow and intransigent regionalism. Every big state looked upon itself as an independent power, with smaller states in its sphere of influence. Alliances between states were formed as in the game of international politics. Through their large congressional blocs, they controlled the President, frequently obliging him to come to terms or negotiate with them. The different regions, such as the North and the South, opposed one another. It was difficult to build a nationally oriented economy; regional interests were put ahead of all others. The states fought among themselves by means of border taxes, disguised by various names, in open defiance of the Constitution. The states had their own armed police forces, which sometimes resembled small armies; some were even trained by foreign military missions as in São Paulo. Senators and deputies in Congress were not divided by party lines but by the states to which they belonged. It was impertinent, for instance, for a deputy from any state to touch on political or even administrative matters of greater direct concern to another state. The airtight nature of the federal and state governments provoked violent opposition and constant resorts to disorder. Politicians wanting to hold on to power or to regain it did not hesitate to involve the military in bitter partisan disputes. In the prevailing general unrest it was almost impossible to establish any continuity of administration. Each President and each state governor had to improvise his own methods, which were nearly always contrary to those of his predecessor. A typical change of policy was Bernardes's abandonment of the public works for drought control in the Northeast that had formed the basis of President Pessoa's administrative program. Whether the planning or execution of the project was faulty or not, the conditions to which the enormous area was condemned by its abandonment, or the losses to the Treasury, mattered little. The ease with which Brazil's financial policy was radically altered during Bernardes's term was another clear illustration of the lack of administrative continuity.

Bernardes's constant struggle to maintain public order understandably influenced much of his administrative program. He neither forgot nor forgave affronts, and his strong authoritarian tendencies and rigid, Jacobinic nationalism did not inspire public sympathies. And yet, by enforcing the law and instilling in the nation a certain boredom with riots and revolutions, President Bernardes left his successor a better situation than he himself had inherited. The incoming President would have to extinguish the last incitements to strife, and thereby bring about that "moral order" Thiers regarded as the indispensable concomitant of "physical order" in the streets. Brazil, outwardly weary of the partisan contests and constant insurrections, hoped the new administration would inaugurate domestic peace, during which economic recovery could continue undisturbed.

22. Washington Luís
[1926-30]

Washington Luís's cabinet — Road building — Monetary stability — Coffee policy — First signs of the depression — Júlio Prestes, governor of São Paulo — Borges de Medeiros — Antônio Carlos and the government of Minas Gerais — The struggle to succeed Washington Luís — Rio Grande do Sul's importance — Rebellion in Paraíba — The election and the revolution — The reasons for the revolution.

Although he had never held any federal office, Washington Luís, a Fluminense who had moved to São Paulo as a young man, had gained national fame for the energy and administrative ability he displayed as governor of São Paulo. Unlike the grave, formal, and remote Artur Bernardes, the new President appeared frequently in public, looking full of health and vigor, handsome, cheerful, and satisfied, and because of this he attracted sincere public sympathies. His suspension of the chronic state of siege and his restoration of freedom of the press gave the nation a sense of relief. Having ascended to the presidency uncontested, and therefore without leaving smoldering animosities behind him, he could easily have increased his popularity by agreeing to a general amnesty for the rebels who had fought Bernardes. He refused to do so, however, either for party solidarity or for some other reason, though he ran the risk of stirring up the old political wrangles.

His cabinet was distinctly political in character, made up of party leaders in the Chamber who were chosen without regard for whether they had any aptitude for the duties of the ministries to which they were appointed. Thus, Viana do Castelo from Minas Gerais received the Ministry of Justice; Otávio Mangabeira from Bahia, the Ministry of Foreign Affairs; Getúlio Vargas from Rio Grande do Sul, the Ministry of Finance (later replaced by Oliveira Botelho, leader of the Rio de Janeiro bloc); Vítor Konder from Santa Catarina, the Ministry of Transportation; and Lira Castro from Pará, the Ministry of Agriculture. General Sezefredo Passos was appointed War Minister, and President Bernardes's Navy Minister, Admiral Pinto da Luz, was returned to that post.

A nonpolitical appointment was of Antônio Prado Júnior, to the prefecture of the Federal District.

Two of Washington Luís's major objectives were to build roads, which were badly needed to handle increasing traffic, and to reform the finances. The Rio–São Paulo and Rio–Petrópolis highways were started at once, the latter as a first step toward Belo Horizonte. The example set by the federal government stimulated the state administrations. President Afonso Pena's old slogan, "To govern is to populate," was replaced by a new one: "To govern is to build roads." But most important of all was financial reform.

The classic theory and practice of public finance held that monetary stability was always the result of balanced budgets, equilibrium in the international balance of payments, containment of credit, orderly management of the national debt, etc. In economically underdeveloped countries like Brazil, there had grown up two doctrines about foreign exchange. The papelistas put the principal blame for fluctuating exchange rates on unfavorable trade balances, and favored protective tariffs and speeding up industrial development. Their opponents held a somewhat physiocratic or laissez-faire attitude, believed in the quantitative theory of money, blamed the depreciation of currency on the superabundance of printing-press money and inflation of credit, and opposed city planning, industrialism, and interference by the state. The first was exemplified by the emissionist policy of Rui Barbosa in the Provisional Government; the second by the rigid deflationary policies of Campos Sales and Murtinho.

The economies of the nations that engaged in World War I were profoundly disturbed by the war's aftereffects. There was a period of violent monetary fluctuation, from which only a few (England, for example) managed to escape by resorting to such desperate measures as greatly increased taxes, balanced budgets, and debt reduction. The countries of continental Europe most devastated by the tragedy attempted other solutions. Although they did not spurn the old ways altogether, they thought it possible to achieve a quick, partial stabilization as the starting point for a return to financial equilibrium. This was the policy followed by France, with her widely discussed Poincaré experiment, which Washington Luís had observed at first hand before taking office in 1926, and with whose spectacular success he was naturally deeply impressed. But the very great differences between Brazil and France, with her old capitalistic economy and financial machinery, including the Bank of France, called for different techniques in Brazil. There was no need to stimulate a rise in the milreis, since it was already increasing in value.

In 1926 the average rate got down to about seven pence to the milreis. However, even this low rate did not seem safe to Washington Luís, and he forced it down to five pence to decrease the possible risks. This was directly contrary to the generally accepted policy of stabilization, which was to seek a rate higher than the current average, as Brazil had tried with her devaluation schemes in 1833 and 1846, when par was 43½ and 27 pence, respectively. The Campista conversion fund reform had maintained this latter rate, even though the rate for conversion of gold notes was fixed at 15 pence. The five-pence rate was termed "dirt cheap" by its opponents.

The new President, in office less than a month, submitted a money reform bill to Congress that was passed into law two weeks later. Briefly, it consisted of three sequential phases: stabilization proper, convertibility, and coinage of the gold cruzeiro to replace the milreis. The new standard for the milreis was fixed at 200 milligrams gold, .900 fine, which corresponded almost exactly to 40 milreis to the pound sterling. A special agency, the stabilization fund, was created and granted authority, like the former conversion fund, to issue paper currency against Brazil's gold credits in London and New York. Similar authority would be granted to the Banco do Brasil if the stabilization fund were extinguished. The bank was charged to keep the exchange at the new parity, at rates that should correspond exactly to the national monetary situation. To the new stabilization fund would be transferred all present and future gold in the country. To get its new plan started, the government obtained a foreign loan to liquidate the floating debt left by the Bernardes administration. Thus, there coexisted in Brazil for some time three kinds of money: the Treasury's inconvertible bills, the old notes of the Banco do Brasil, and the gold certificates of the stabilization fund.

Washington Luís's plan was just one more Brazilian monetary experiment. Bernardes's German-inspired doctrine of bank emissions backed by a two-thirds reserve of convertible bills of exchange was abandoned for one that was more radical, and French-inspired, but just as faulty as the conversion fund of Afonso Pena, since the credit structure had not been underpinned by a central bank that could issue currency and rediscount bills. The gold from foreign loans was wrongly supposed to give metallic backing to the outstanding volume of fiduciary currency, which was about 2,600,000 contos.

In any case, the immediate effects of President Luís's policy were salutary. There was order in the public finances, and budgets were kept in balance. With the prevailing peace and high prices for coffee, the nation seemed to breathe easier and gather its strength for a surge of progress. The President's confidence in his stabilization plan did not then seem too optimistic.

The federal and São Paulo governments had consolidated their policies on coffee. The first emergency intervention by the government to support coffee, set off by the compact of Taubaté during the Rodrigues Alves administration, had turned into a permanent system of support by loans from foreign sources and from the Banco do Brasil during the administrations of Epitácio Pessoa and Artur Bernardes. Toward the end of Bernardes's term, the federal government withdrew its support of coffee, leaving the task entirely up to the state of São Paulo. Having no right to issue money, São Paulo created the Coffee Institute to be able to resort to foreign bankers. Special taxes in gold were collected to guarantee the service on the foreign loans, and the Banco de São Paulo, which handled the Institute's funds, also handled the financing of the coffee industry. The coffeegrowing states met yearly to set export quotas. Having absolute control of the market, the Institute was free to fix prices by withholding shipments and accumulating enormous stocks. Carried away with itself, the Institute forced prices up to extraordinary heights and precipitated intense speculation.

In the meantime, there appeared the first signs of the depression that, starting with the New York stock-market crash in 1929, would spread throughout the world and strike Brazil full force. Diagnosed at first as a simple case of overproduction, like so many others that periodically upset the rhythm of capitalist countries, this depression, it was soon realized, had causes that were much more profound; its effects would be not just more severe than usual but catastrophic. The grave coffee situation, with a record harvest of 29 million bags and a steep drop in prices, became alarming in view of the President's unyielding refusal of São Paulo's appeal to aid it by a new issue of currency. Washington Luís had always been against any form of artificial price support. Having no other credit to turn to, the São Paulo government had allowed about 20 million bags to pile up in storage warehouses. In spite of so many adverse factors—the flight of gold, diminished exports, reduced public revenues, etc.—the drop in currency value and the resulting increase in prices had been relatively small.

From the end of 1929, the inconvertible or "bad" money suffered noticeable depreciation, and as always happens, in keeping with Gresham's law, began to drive the redeemable or "good" money into hiding. The demand for stabilization-fund notes was intensified, which reduced the gold reserves from foreign loans. From about 800,000 contos on hand in January 1930, the reserves dropped to 125,000 by September 1930, while the pound sterling was quoted at six milreis above par. The mirage of stabilization was fading.

Not only in Brazil but also in other countries that had tried monetary reform catastrophe followed the New York stock-market crash. The Poincaré plan itself proved ephemeral, and later even the strongest coins, the dollar and the pound, had to be devaluated. However, it would be unjust to deny the immediate beneficial results of Washington Luís's reform. It was justified by the nation's general prosperity during the early part of his administration; and for three years it fulfilled its overall objective of developing the nation's economy more rapidly. The figures for São Paulo, for instance, were most auspicious. Between 1921 and 1929, when the population increased 52 per cent, gross production rose 324 per cent, exports through Santos 165 per cent, imports 180 per cent, state revenues 820 per cent, federal revenues 227 per cent, revenues of the municípios 271 per cent, and banking transactions 224 per cent. In 1929 the per capita production reached 670 milreis and per capita exports 400 milreis, equivalent to that of the United States and France, compared with per capita exports of 120 milreis for the entire country. São Paulo's favorable balance of trade made up for the unfavorable ones of the other states, and provided the Union with the credits needed for the international balance of payments. Of nearly five million contos total production, almost half was industrial.

In keeping with the Republic's old habit, Washington Luís had barely begun the third year of his term when the politicians started discussing possible candidates to succeed him. Júlio Prestes, the Paulista politician who had been majority leader in the Chamber from the start of Washington Luís's term, seemed to be the man who the President was most confident would follow through on the financial reform he had started. There was no lack, therefore, of prophecies of his eventual rise to power. However, the politicians, who were more accustomed to viewing such matters realistically, believed that the President would be more inclined to favor Getúlio Vargas, in order not to be relegated to a secondary position in his own state.

The unexpected death of the governor of São Paulo, Carlos Campos, strengthened Júlio Prestes's candidacy. His father, Fernando Prestes, was the deceased governor's lawful successor, but did not assume the post, in order to let his son win it for himself in the election that was then held to fill the vacancy. Júlio Prestes, still a young man, whose political experience had been almost entirely at the state level, was considered to be both intelligent and courageous. As governor of the state whose high coffee prices and surge of urban industries were creating much prosperity for it, he would prove himself a diligent administrator as well. In these circumstances, his nomination to succeed Washington Luís was taken for granted. The most prominent national politicians, however, were members of an older generation, and did not willingly and sincerely endorse the candidacy of the young Paulista governor, for it not only had an undisguised official origin, but also meant passing over one of their number. But in a regime of highly concentrated Executive powers it was not easy for them to oppose it openly.

Among the other public men who at the time seemed qualified for the presidency of the Republic, three stood out: Estácio Coimbra, Antônio Carlos, and Borges de Medeiros.* But although Estácio was governor of Pernambuco, had been Vice-President of the Republic, and was recognized for his personal qualifications, he had no large following of voters.

Antônio Carlos [Ribeiro de Andrada], then governor of Minas Gerais, was one of the most unusual personalities ever to figure in Brazilian politics. Bearing the tradition of a great name,† he was aristocratic, elegant, and distinguished. His disdain for cheap popularity did not keep him from being affable. He was essentially a skeptic, an eclectic, in short, a virtuoso at whatever he turned his hand to. His mind was keen, subtle, and quick. He was exceedingly shrewd, a powerful debater, and a proven parliamentary leader. Yet he was insensitive to art and to general ideas, and not given to introspective thought; he made up for his cultural lacks by mental acuteness, intuition, and experience. He was ironic, played with words like a juggler, and was famous for his sallies and witticisms. He was prodigal with promises. Although he inspired lively sympathies, he also aroused undisguised distrust. He was a bit reminiscent of Briand, and one could have applied to him Joaquim Nabuco's summing up of the Baron of Cotegipe: "He was all brains." A student of finance, he wrote a few books on the subject, and was a long-time expert on revenues in the Federal Chamber. He was a radical antipapelista, but resorted frequently to the printing press when he was Finance Minister under President Venceslau Brás, just as later he would not balk at accepting, in broad outline, President Washington Luís's monetary reform, which was so contrary to his own ideas.

* Antônio Augusto Borges de Medeiros, to give him his full name, remained a powerful influence in his state until just before he died in 1961 at 97 years of age. Before he died, the federal government, which he had fought so hard and so often, awarded him its highest decoration. JLT

† His grandfather was one of the three Andrada brothers, who were powerful figures in bringing about Brazil's independence from Portugal. The best-remembered of the three today is José Bonifácio de Andrada e Silva, the Patriarch. JLT

On being placed in the governor's chair in Minas Gerais almost single-handedly by Bernardes, he acted quite unexpectedly. Instead of the usual discreet Mineiro policies and cautious administration, he engaged in vast publicity and spectacular, though often worthwhile, initiatives. It required no great insight to see that the real purpose behind Antônio Carlos's performance was to build up his own candidacy to succeed Washington Luís. Though he could have had no doubts about the latter's disapproval of him, or about that of the straitlaced and guileless Bernardes, he imagined, perhaps, that they would be compelled by circumstances to accept his nomination in the end. It was therefore politic not to precipitate an irreparable break, but rather to support Washington Luís through the large Mineiro bloc in Congress. When he became convinced, however, that he was not going to receive Washington Luís's endorsement or cause him to give up Júlio Prestes for a third candidate, his opposition become overt.*

It is an old truism that advancing age implies a cooling of the passions, more tolerance and understanding of men and events, greater capacity for detachment, and renunciation if not final disenchantment. However, one sees the reverse occasionally in philosophical speculation, literary and artistic production, and political activity. Hesitant, reticent, ambivalent young men become self-assertive and radical on the threshold of old age, as if they have tapped a new source of energy, obstinacy, and pugnacity in the depths of their own personalities. This, in a way, was the case with Antônio Carlos. Approaching sixty years of age and having a great state's machinery at his disposal, he knew his last chance to become President was slipping through his fingers; but, as he declared, he could still prevent the success of the official candidate.

Naturally, Antônio Carlos would not take such a final step, that is, carry party dissension to the limit regardless of consequences, without inner struggles with his own temperament, his conservative training, and his fear of launching Brazil on a venture that would trample on the Constitution and that he would soon bitterly regret. As an old schemer, he tried to split the majority that had gathered, without great enthusiasm, around Washington Luís and Júlio Prestes. This explains his attempts to promote several other candidacies, of some Paulista chieftains and of Estácio Coimbra. It seems, from all indications, that he would have considered a Rio-Grandense only as a last resort, not, certainly, be-

* On returning from Pernambuco in the summer of 1929, I ran across Antônio Carlos in Minas Gerais, who said to me in an incisive tone of voice, which was not habitual, that though he knew he could not force the Catete to support his candidacy, he had enough strength to prevent the victory of Júlio Prestes. I related these words to Estácio Coimbra, and later to some of my fellow party members in the Chamber. No one believed that Antônio Carlos would carry out his threat. JMB

cause he thought gaúchos were less entitled to the presidency than anyone else, but because the campaign might acquire an irrevocably revolutionary character if that battle-scarred, politically united state were
brought into it.

Given political calm and economic prosperity, Antônio Carlos's dissidence would have had only limited influence. Several times during the
life of the Republic there had been majority splits over presidential candidates, as during the civilianist campaign, without wrecking public order. On other occasions, Rui Barbosa had run against candidates supported by the government majority. As the leader of the "Republican
Reaction," Nilo Peçanha had drawn Rio Grande do Sul into his fight
against Bernardes. But now, for the first time, Minas Gerais was opposing the candidacy of a Paulista that was supported by the federal government.

Coming during economic depression and political ferment, Antônio
Carlos's rejection of Júlio Prestes's candidacy created a singular situation in republican politics. Accustomed or resigned to victories by the
entrenched administrations, and doubting Carlos's disposition to fight,
the majority politicians did not get very excited, and left handling the
campaign to the President. The latter, imperious, proud, and obstinate,
was not given to compromise, and seems to have spurned any suggestion
of it.* Dropping Prestes's candidacy seemed to him, if not disloyalty, at
least a weakness that could permanently harm his own prestige. Neither
could Prestes, according to the prevailing political morality and out of
simple aversion to quitting, withdraw from the contest without loss of
political and personal face.

Borges de Medeiros, chieftain of the battle-hardened Republican Party of Rio Grande do Sul, and a sort of perpetual governor until the pact
of Pedras Altas put a stop to his reelection, was held in high regard
throughout Brazil because of his austere integrity. But his dogmatism,
his provincialism, and his authoritarianism put off the politicians from
other parts of the country. As the successor to Júlio de Castilhos he had
the young republican leader's capacity for discipline and command, but
not his warm, outgoing personality. As long as Pinheiro Machado was
alive, Borges de Medeiros gave him complete control of the state's blocs

---

* In her biography of Epitácio Pessoa, Dona Laurita Pessoa Raja Gabaglia mentions
that when Epitácio returned from Europe he made a special call on President Washington Luís to propose dropping Júlio Prestes and Getúlio Vargas, and selecting any
other qualified third party. This approach had been suggested to Pessoa by Afrânio
de Melo Franco in a letter, and was approved by the heads of the Liberal Alliance,
Antônio Carlos, Getúlio Vargas, and João Pessoa. But the President, convinced his
man would win, refused attempts at conciliation. JMB

in Congress. After the valorous caudillo's death, he appointed other worthy men to these posts, but their authority was limited, since they were always subject to Medeiros's final decision. He often gave the impression that he would have ruled his state, if he could have, not from the governor's palace in Pôrto Alegre, but from his small ranch in the interior. Such isolationism would have made it very difficult to integrate that border state, already so distant geographically and historically, with the mainstream of Brazilian life.

After doing penance as prescribed by Bernardes in the Pedras Altas agreement, Medeiros had returned to the good graces of the Union government. After being debarred from the governorship, though not from the leadership of his party, Borges de Medeiros had naturally lost some of his former authority. Beside him, the young governor, Getúlio Vargas, was rising in prestige. A group of young politicians seemed less inhibited by the old discipline and more anxious for a direct voice in federal affairs. Antônio Carlos's dissidence had given Rio Grande do Sul her best chance yet. From the beginning of the Republic, her singular legal organization, influenced by Comtist philosophy, had been under the control of her powerful leaders, Júlio de Castilhos and Borges de Medeiros. The intensity of the battles in Rio Grande do Sul had kept her sons out of the Catete. Possibly the rulers of the Empire and of the Republic preferred keeping it that way to stimulating the local dissensions. In spite of his extraordinary national prominence, Pinheiro Machado was vetoed by São Paulo and Minas as a candidate to succeed Marshal Hermes. After Pinheiro's death, even the possibility of a gaúcho presidential candidate, except Borges de Medeiros, could not be imagined. The other states would always remain hostile, though not always openly, to that possibility. But now things had changed: the state was politically united, and a Rio-Grandense was a candidate for President.

The dominant position of Rio Grande do Sul had often upset majority candidates, not so much because of differences over platforms or personalities, as on grounds of form, official protocol, methods of nomination, etc. Júlio de Castilhos, for example, had opposed the nomination of Campos Sales, and Borges de Medeiros those of Davi Campista and Artur Bernardes. The Campista candidacy had died at birth; and when Nilo Peçanha was beaten at the polls, the gaúcho chieftain called it quits, thus killing any notion of turning the political contest into a revolution. However, within the Rio-Grandense Republican party itself there was still a strong current favoring conciliation with Washington Luís and Júlio Prestes, whereas the Liberation party [the Alliance for Liberation] had drawn together the local opposition, in an understanding with the opposition in São Paulo (the Democratic party), and the young military men left over from the unsuccessful revolts against Epitácio Pessoa and Artur Bernardes.

The misgivings that assailed Antônio Carlos up to the last minute were shared by Borges de Medeiros and Getúlio Vargas. In letters to Washington Luís, some of which were published, Getúlio Vargas explicitly reiterated his solidarity with him. In May 1929, when João Neves, leader of the gaúcho bloc in the Chamber, had already started a movement in favor of a gaúcho candidate, Getúlio Vargas, as if to discredit Neves, wrote the President, saying that he had decided

not to express myself in any way on the succession to the presidency, in order to avoid any disturbance of the atmosphere, to leave Your Excellency completely free to deal with the subject whenever you think it opportune, and to prevent the meddling of busybodies, promoters of candidacies, or self-appointed advance men, who would gamble with the name and prestige of Rio Grande do Sul in order to lay claim later to personal rewards.

At another time he wrote: "Your Excellency may be certain that the Republican Party of Rio Grande do Sul will not fail to support you at the right time." Washington Luís had set September 1929 for the beginning of talks about Presidential candidates. Besides direct correspondence with the President, Vargas had authorized an old friend and fellow party member, Paim Filho, to take a position exactly opposite that of João Neves, that is, one of support and solidarity with the President and the governor of São Paulo, which position Paim Filho apparently maintained until the outbreak of the revolution.

In June 1929, Antônio Carlos, Getúlio Vargas, and Borges de Medeiros ended their vague conversations and entered a pact through their representatives, Francisco Sales, secretary of the interior of Minas Gerais, and the deputies José Bonifácio and João Neves. This agreement was typical of republican politics. Under it the two states agreed irrevocably to nominate a gaúcho (either Borges de Medeiros or Getúlio Vargas) for President. In case President Washington Luís were to counter by agreeing to a Mineiro candidate [i.e., Antônio Carlos], the vice-presidency would go to Rio Grande do Sul. The agreement was contingent on Borges de Medeiros's ratification. With this basis in the official apparatus of two big states, all the small parties of opposition throughout the nation, and all the malcontents, both civilian and military, were now joined together to fight Júlio Prestes's candidacy. This coalition, which closely resembled the "Republican Reaction," was called the Liberal Alliance.

Of course, it is not possible to reconstruct all of the plot that preceded the 1930 revolution, nor are all of its details of interest to those who try to see events in terms of historical synthesis, that is, see which events, perhaps seemingly of secondary importance, are landmarks in the final interpretation of a period. The bibliography about 1930 is lengthy: books, monographs, pamphlets, depositions, reports, etc., nearly all of them are contaminated by the passions of the moment. But some, such as Barbosa Lima Sobrinho's *A Verdade sôbre a Revolução de 1930*, give a more orderly exposition of the facts and judge them more impartially. Such more reliable documents, and personal acquaintance with the men who helped prepare the revolution, can bring us to safer conclusions.

Vargas was afterward accused of cold duplicity in the style of Floriano Peixoto. He had tried to cultivate the confidence of Washington Luís, who esteemed him and had made him a minister, and had thereby contributed to his rapid rise in politics. Perhaps it had not been calculated duplicity but the uncertainty of a cautious nature, whose restrained enthusiasm was mixed with selfishness and self-seeking, the nature of one who did not like to commit himself fully. These same temporizing tendencies were to reveal themselves during Vargas's long rule of the Union. A revolutionary solution frightened him, less because of Borges de Medeiros's doctrinaire abhorrence of it than because of its possible personal political consequences. The ideal would be to reach the presidency by means of the friendly backing of Washington Luís. Even after he had been officially nominated by the Liberal Alliance, he wrote again to the President, as did Antônio Carlos, still hoping for a political settlement in his favor. Surprised, even astounded, Washington Luís replied to both of them, perhaps with a grain of malicious humor, that the governors of all the states except Paraíba, which had not yet been heard from, had declared themselves in favor of Júlio Prestes.

The failure of this last move began the presidential campaign. The general atmosphere in Brazil was most propitious for the opposition. If the enthusiasm of the masses that filled the public squares was mainly superficial, and always easily moved by demagogic words, the support of what might be termed the lower, middle, and even upper bourgeois classes seemed more sincere. The oligarchic regime inherited from the Empire had never fostered governments actually elected by the people, though under the impact of extraordinary circumstances, some of them, Floriano Peixoto's, for example, seemed to represent the wishes of the overwhelming majority. After Rui Barbosa's civilianist campaign, the isolation and unpopularity of the government had grown apace, and they increased further with the fight over the succession to Epitácio Pessoa. The executive heads of the federal and state governments embodied both the means to restrict civil liberties and political and administrative corruption, which are alone enough to justify all revolutions. The situation was like that of the other underdeveloped, politically immature Latin-American countries, about which Keyserling observed: "All the South American revolutions, motivated by the corruption of the government in power, end like the preceding ones, with the difference that the ruling cliques and persons are no longer the same."*

Almost all government leaders are eventually deluded by their tendency to believe the plaudits of friends, partisans, or self-seeking flatterers. Washington Luís did not perceive or did not want to perceive how much the general esteem he had at first been held in had dropped. This was a form of disapproval directed less against him than against the order of things he stood for. His adversaries, whose critical attitudes made them more aware of the true situation, took advantage of it by filling the campaign in the Congress, in the papers, and in the streets with vehemence, and even open threats of armed violence. They did this not only in the capital, but also in such other parts of the country as the North and Northeast, regions in which chronic poverty and oppressive local governments had long brewed revolutionary ideas. They also used this opportunity to recruit the young military rebels, many of whom were in exile in the Platine republics under the command of Luís Carlos Prestes, who, on becoming an orthodox Communist, would lose interest in rivalries among bourgeois politicians.

Meanwhile there was no cessation of political maneuvers, ups and downs, advances and retreats, periods of euphoria and of discouragement. When Estácio Coimbra turned down the candidacy for Vice-President on the ticket of the Liberal Alliance, it was given to the governor of Paraíba, João Pessoa, who had refused to support Júlio Prestes. In Minas the Vice-President of the Republic, Melo Viana, balked in his ambitions to return to the governorship of his state, withdrew from the party in power, and was followed by the vice-governor, and by numerous federal and state deputies, municipal chambers, and local political bosses. This split was singularly significant, since political cohesion in Minas was one of the conditions of Antônio Carlos's pact with Rio Grande do Sul. Getúlio Vargas thus had a new opportunity to try to reconciliate with Washington Luís, from which a curious gentleman's agreement developed: Getúlio Vargas was not to go campaigning outside his own state and would accept the results of the national balloting, and Washington Luís and Júlio Prestes would not support the opposition to Vargas in Rio Grande do Sul, would urge Congress to recog-

* Keyserling: *Meditaciones Sudamericanas.* J M B

nize deputies elected from that state, and would resume friendly relations with the powers in office there. If elected President, Getúlio Vargas would assume identical commitments toward São Paulo; Minas Gerais and Paraíba were ignored in the deal. Nevertheless, no doubt under pressure from his local partisans, Vargas did go to São Paulo and to Rio to read his administrative platform before large public gatherings. As such documents usually are, it was a more or less innocuous statement into whose rhetorical clichés whatever contradictory promises one pleased could be fitted.

The general state of mind was complete tranquility; Washington Luís and Júlio Prestes were perfectly confident and unshakeably optimistic. The solid support of the governors of seventeen states and of the chief political bosses in the Federal District assured them a spectacular victory. The politicians of the period, nearly all survivors from the 1880s and 1890s, looked upon revolutions in their country, as upon all others in Latin America, with scorn, provided, of course, they themselves were not the revolutionists' target; they sought to avoid trouble by agreements between the ruling oligarchies, though they were repelled by any thought of yielding to threats. It was therefore hard for them to perceive how serious the movement taking place before their eyes actually was, even though they sensed people's uneasiness and indefinable weariness, and the confused desire for a new start, a new kind of government. Later, when the opposition became more aggressive, the confidence of the politicians was naturally shaken. The more perceptive or experienced ones began to be apprehensive. Lack of understanding, inability to back down, or even personal whims could plunge the country, already suffering economically, into revolutionary turmoil. The private thoughts of the governor of Pernambuco, Estácio Coimbra, who had succeeded in reuniting his party after both its wings had fought to win his allegiance, were typical. Unenthusiastic, but still bound to his constituents, he did not dare reopen on his own a discussion of the candidates for the presidency.*

Bahia's political situation was less solid than that of Pernambuco; in the government party itself, two groups were fighting each other. It was even more deeply committed, since its governor, Vital Soares, was Júlio Prestes's running mate.

---

* When I, then active in politics and soon afterward elected to succeed Estácio Coimbra, stopped off in Recife on my way back from Europe in 1929, Coimbra confided to me his great regret that he had failed to grasp the seriousness of the situation and had not seized the opportunity to put out the fire by forcing a third candidate [himself] to be chosen. J M B

Debates in Congress, especially in the Chamber of Deputies, became more angry. At the close of the sessions, a majority deputy from Pernambuco, Sousa Filho, was assassinated in the lobby of the building by a minority deputy from Rio Grande do Sul because of a violent quarrel between Sousa and the Rio-Grandense's son.

At the start of 1930, a subversive movement broke out in the backlands of Paraíba. The causes of the Revolution of Princesa (the town where it started) were both political and economic. The state governor, João Pessoa, had two principal aims: to clip the wings of the backlands bosses, modern-day feudal masters who were often recruiters and protectors of *cangaceiros* [mercenary bandits], and to divert Paraíba's commerce away from Recife to Paraíba's own capital and its seaport [Cabedelo]. Among the backlands chieftains none was more powerful than José Pereira of Princesa, an old friend of the Pessoas. A threat by Pessoa to exclude a former governor and old friend of Pereira's from the ticket of federal deputies resulted in a violent break, which the local opposition soon took advantage of, between the two men.

Its economic objectives led the state government to impose a large variety of taxes on goods brought in through the port of Cabedelo and across the borders of neighboring states, which made the traditional trading between the backlands and Recife practically prohibitive. Such a policy, besides being clearly unconstitutional, hurt the backlands traders as much as the business houses in Recife with whom they dealt. Furthermore, the leading business houses in Recife were owned by relatives of João Pessoa. Thus the partisan dispute between Pessoa and José Pereira, aggravated by family rivalries, threatened to turn into rebellion. Barbosa Lima Sobrinho described the dispute as an unpredictable duel between the impetuous governor and the backlands bosses, jealous of their old privileges. Although the Union government took no official position on the dispute, it did permit some of its partisans to egg on and assist Pereira, since the opposition to Washington Luís and Júlio Prestes was trying to help João Pessoa. Paraíba was being made a testing ground for civil war, like Spain on the eve of World War II.

Minor disturbances occurred in other parts of the country. There were incidents with the opposition's caravans campaigning in the northern states, and an eruption of violence in a Mineiro town during which Vice-President Melo Viana was wounded, but in spite of everything, the national elections on March 1st, 1930, went off quietly. As had been expected, Júlio Prestes and Vital Soares won more than 950,000 of the 1,500,000 votes cast. Except in large urban centers, where voters had always been more free and more observant of the law, the elections were polluted by the usual corruption. On both sides the powerful pressure of the state machines was felt. The most judicious politicians of the Liberal Alliance tended to accept the verdict of the voting; Borges de Medeiros gave a statement to this effect to a Rio newspaper. But the more inflamed gaúchos disagreed with their old chieftain, who was obliged to amend his original remarks. With the direct intervention of Getúlio Vargas, a new modus vivendi with the federal government, which might forestall a revolution, was agreed upon.

On May 3rd, the day prescribed by the Constitution, the Federal Congress began its preliminary sessions. One of its first tasks was to study the results of the voting for President and for the election of its own membership. The nation was accustomed to Congress's abuses and scandals in fulfilling that function; the "recognition of mandates" often appeared to be merely new elections. But when national politics were divided over the presidency, the labors of recognition became extremely important, for they indicated Congressional leanings. Not foreseeing the possible consequences, the majority that had supported Washington Luís and Júlio Prestes, and that was always very conciliatory toward the gaúcho politicians in power, refused to recognize candidates, presumably duly elected, who had been backed by the governments of Minas or Paraíba, whose entire delegation was barred. As a result, the proclamation of Prestes's victory, and Borges de Medeiros's statement that he would accept it, failed to quiet partisan dissensions.

The arbitrary recognition of mandates gave new life to the radicals. Revolution was openly plotted. Borges de Medeiros's pacifism seemed shaken. In a manifesto to the nation, Governor Vargas condemned the purging of the Minas and Paraíba delegations in enigmatic language that combined subversive threats with appeals for harmony:

There are today no differences of opinion about the need to reestablish tranquility, which depends entirely on a policy of tolerance, respect, and guarantee of rights by the ruling powers, a policy that will be the more laudable the stronger the ruling powers believe themselves to be.... [The need], however, is greater than they imagine, and I do not believe that the necessary rectification will be long delayed before we shall see Brazilian democracy under a regime committed to the nation's happiness.

Naturally, the articulation of a revolutionary movement can never be easy, even in countries where respect for constitutional authority has always been precarious. Circumstances change radically; solemn promises are broken; treachery appears; discouragement sets in. If there was a general weariness and longing for a new political order, there was not the violent popular enthusiasm on which great revolutionary aims must depend. The sincerity of the opposition leaders was also dubious, since they were divided by ambitions, personal vanities, false pride, and regional rivalries. They all had the same corrupt origins, and were more or less guilty of the same delinquency and despotism they ascribed to Washington Luís. The armed forces, which in the end must decide the success or failure of revolutions, were largely indifferent to the temptations of subversion.

Only the spark that starts the blaze was lacking, and it was provided in July by the assassination of João Pessoa in a confectioner's shop in Recife. The crime, which the Pernambuco police could not have prevented, was caused by local disputes and personal enmities. But as always happens when a man is sacrificed during a political campaign, the opposition soon gave it a partisan twist. The repercussion in the nation was unprecedented, especially in Rio Grande do Sul, where the most inflamed politicians wanted to launch the revolution at once. Borges de Medeiros and Getúlio Vargas would be powerless to forestall it. From then on, no one could doubt it was coming, notwithstanding brief periods of respite.

Meanwhile, revolutions set off by the economic depression were making the rounds of the South American republics, finally hitting Argentina. The shock in Brazil was as great as it was in the nearby countries. Everyone believed that Argentina's political culture had exempted her from that sort of political upheaval. The violent overthrow of the Irigoyen government revealed how profound the revolutionary ferment was in all the Hispanic-American continent. This is not the place for a special study of the subversive movement in Argentina, or of the Irigoyen government, but, whatever the peculiar character of the revolution, it was an expression of the nagging discontent in nearly all the Latin-American republics brought on by both internal causes and general world conditions in the interval between the two great wars. Its immediate impact on already disturbed Brazilian circles was unmistakable.

It would be monotonous and of merely chronological interest to follow step by step the later movements that preceded the eruption of the revolution in Brazil on October 3, 1930. (The date had been set and postponed several times.) The important thing is that it broke out in the same three states that had backed the Liberal Alliance: Rio Grande do Sul, Minas Gerais, and Paraíba, which were already acting like belligerents in an international war, what with their police armies and their legal conflicts with the Union.

Although it had been repeatedly announced, the revolution caught the central and state governments unprepared to defend themselves. There was no overall government plan, no coordination of objectives, only scattered, if intrepid, delaying actions that took the lives of many men loyal to the Union. More and more military units went over to the rebels, or remained neutral, which amounted to the same thing. President Washington Luís did not lose confidence in his victory until the last moment; the state governors were less optimistic. The governments in the North, undermined by their opponents' old and stubborn campaign, or too strictly bound by legalistic formulas, fell with little or no struggle. Thus, the rebel column that left Paraíba under the command of Captain Juarez Távora to assault Recife again had no trouble getting to Bahia; the first attack on Recife had been called off when expected reinforcements failed to join up. The other northern states, except Pará, fell in the first skirmishes.

The rebel troops of Rio Grande do Sul, consisting of army, police, and civilian battalions under the military command of Lt. Col. Góis Monteiro, with Getúlio Vargas as supreme leader of the revolution, had little difficulty reaching the border between Paraná and São Paulo; the small core of resistance offered by the government of Santa Catarina was isolated on its island capital. In Minas (where Antônio Carlos had been succeeded by the duly elected Olegário Maciel) as in Rio Grande do Sul, the focal points of federal resistance were surprised and quickly overcome. The rebel columns, poorly trained and equipped, moved against the states of Rio de Janeiro and Espírito Santo; the weak federal defenses crumbled everywhere, often by the treason of trusted military chiefs. The region around Itararé, on the Paraná–São Paulo border, was expected to be the center of hostilities. The expected battle ("the greatest in Latin-American history, except that it didn't take place," was a famous quip of the period) would decide the success or failure of the revolution. According to the undoubtedly exaggerated statement of the revolutionists' high command, 30,000 men, who were perhaps quite unsure of victory, had moved up from the South. The governments of the Union and São Paulo held the appreciable advantages of being closer to their supply centers and having better communications.

At this stage, a group of high-ranking officers in the Rio garrison, who had already sent two unanswered ultimatums to the President, stepped into the fight, presumably by prior agreement with the rebel chiefs, and delivered the death blow to the constitutional legality so bravely defended by Washington Luís. Without further military means, opposed by the shabby emotions in the streets (which had been aggravated by the calling up of reservists to defend the government), ill-served by high military assistants, and almost alone in his willingness to fight on, the President was arrested and imprisoned in one of the Copacabana forts, from which he later embarked for a long exile in Europe and the United States.* The Archbishop of Rio, Cardinal D. Sebastião Leme, accompanied him to prison, rendering a last tribute to him as a citizen and the head of state.

The action taken by the Junta Pacificadora, which consisted of Generals Tasso Fragoso and Mena Barreto and Admiral Isaías de Noronha (the navy was neutral), made further armed conflict useless. The harshness of the telegrams sent by Getúlio Vargas, Góis Monteiro, and Olegário Maciel seem to show that understandings between them and the junta did not run smoothly. The junta, to justify its peacemaking purpose, was willing to hand over the government to Vargas only as the chief of a victorious rebellion and therefore only until new elections were held, not, as Vargas and his companions demanded, as a replacement for the deposed President. Wanting in boldness or authority, however, the junta delivered the government to Getúlio Vargas without reservations of any kind on October 24, 1930, just twenty-one days after the insurrection had started. During that time, the junta had published numerous edicts appointing ministers of state, dismissing functionaries, revoking decrees of the defunct government, and regulating the administrative services.

Thus ended the brief adventure which had mixed together persons of every origin and character: three former Presidents, Venceslau Brás, Epitácio Pessoa, and Artur Bernardes; old conservative politicians such as Antônio Carlos and Borges de Medeiros; oppositionists in São Paulo; young politicians, including João Neves, Osvaldo Aranha, Flores da Cunha, Lindolfo Collor, Maurício Cardoso, and Batista Lazardo from Rio Grande do Sul, Virgílio de Melo Franco, Francisco Campos, Cristiano Machado, and Mário Brant from Minas, Pedro Ernesto and Adolfo Bergamini from Rio de Janeiro, and José Américo from the North; and young military men, such as Juarez Távora, João Alberto, Eduardo Gomes, and Juraci Margalhães. Some, especially the young military men, were sincere idealists; others were simply ambitious, resentful, or spiteful, men who had nothing to lose.

Frenzied demonstrations broke out in the streets of Rio when Vargas took over. The city, a no-man's-land in semianarchy, was occupied by gaúchos and by johnny-come-lately revolutionists. Red handkerchiefs, dark rumors, abrogation of political rights, banishments, arbitrary dismissals, a desperate scramble for offices and other sources of profit, fear-

---

* Washington Luís did not return to Brazil until 1946, after Vargas had been ousted the first time, though he probably could have returned sooner if he had wanted to. JLT

ful threats not carried out, dazzling promises—the spectacle, in short, was typical, but without the executions, of the victorious revolutions of Europe. The events in the capital were repeated in São Paulo and, less spectacularly, in other parts of the country.

The democratizing revolution had not matured any constructive plans beyond the old aspirations for "justice and representation." In an atmosphere of general disorder and panic, actively stimulated by the right and left and by anxious forebodings of a new world war, it moved toward the inevitable sequel of every such revolution, toward the "saving" dictatorship, which in turn would breed new revolutions based on the direct emotional support of the masses, something quite new to Brazil. The beaten politicians, victims of the accumulated errors of past eras that they had perpetuated, of circumstances, and of misunderstandings and blunders, resigned themselves to their misfortune, waiting patiently, amid the tumult rocking the nation, for dissension and disenchantment to grow among the winners and make possible a reparation of the injustices they had suffered in the hour of their opponents' triumph.

We have often referred to the causes of the 1930 revolution. We think it possible now to attempt a synthesis of them, but without getting involved in academic debate over the complex problem of historical causality. Preexisting general conditions, combining at a given moment with other, fortuitous ones, give rise to a series of events that may bring about a sudden change in the order of things, but not, of course, because of a rigid, deterministic relationship between cause and effect, from which one might by induction arrive at laws as in the positive sciences. The supervention of human motives, which are reflected in the acts of an individual or group of individuals, can change, precipitate, or delay what appears to be an irresistible course of events.

Such was the case with the 1930 movement. Many observers and interpreters of Brazilian life, including some foreign ones, have seen as the revolution's chief general cause the conflict between the two stages of Brazil's economic and social evolution: the stagnation and archaism of the rural regions, and the progressive dynamism of the big cities, mainly Rio and São Paulo, accelerating toward industrialization. But in 1930 the contrast between the two forms of civilization was still very weak. The political revolutions of the time occurred in the more backward of the Latin-American republics, where there was no antagonism between the sleepy countryside and the awakened city. Even the rebellion against Irigoyen was explainable in other terms.

Yesterday, as today, the prime factors in the building up and eruption of revolutions were the economic weakness and political unenlighten-ment not only of the masses but of the middle classes. Economic weak-ness, chronic in most of Brazil, tends to create a vague state of discontent, silent resentment, and unsuspected repressions that will explode in any serious political crisis. A deep and prolonged business depression—such as occurred in São Paulo—produces like effects among the richest and most self-assured social strata. Governments are then held to blame for hardships and evils. On the other hand, whenever private enterprises falter or their chances of success appear uncertain, governments become the supreme and only distributors of advantages and benefits. Winning and holding onto control of the government by any means becomes, therefore, justified.

The apathy of the masses, crippled by long patronage and passive obedience, places them all but outside public life, but it also lends them an almost messianic receptivity to demagogic and radical solutions. The latest grievances of the so-called conservative classes and the emo-tionality of the masses join to prepare a climate favorable to revolution. This occurs principally in countries like Brazil, where even now, pre-cisely because of the scantiness of political training, respect for demo-cratic institutions has not been consolidated and common obedience to the law cannot be counted on.

As we have stressed, the situation created by the New York stock-market crash in October 1929, which badly hurt Brazil's coffee economy and in time provoked the violent overthrow of nearly all the Latin-American governments, was a causative, fortuitous factor of Brazil's 1930 revolution. The political factors were many. One, for example, was the often sincere yearning for a less degraded representative regime, an irksomeness induced by the oligarchic, semipatriarchal system inher-ited from the Empire; there was a generalized conviction that it could not be destroyed peacefully or within the framework of the Constitu-tion. The idea grew that the principle of pure elections by the secret ballot could not be realized within the existing system.

The intangible dominance of the two big states, São Paulo and Minas, with their virtual monopoly of the presidency, was another source of irritation, especially to Rio Grande do Sul and other states in the sec-ond rank. In fact, of the eight civilian Presidents, four had been Paul-istas and three Mineiros. The election of Epitácio Pessoa of Paraíba, as he himself recognized, had been due to political circumstances of the moment. Obviously, in a federation as unbalanced as Brazil's, the hege-mony of the richest and most populous states was inevitable.

In poor, disjointed Brazil, in which a strong domestic market has not yet developed, whose economy is dependent on exports and short of capital, and which is incapable of channeling her political activities into large national parties, the economic contrasts between the various regions and states are much sharper than in, say, the United States. The relative economic segregation exacerbates the political rivalries, which, however, does not keep local partisan passions from occasionally overshadowing the contest for dominance in national politics. An instance of this occurred in São Paulo, where the opponents of the Republican party, which had long received government favors with impunity, were among the most ardent apologists for the 1930 revolution.

Another condition propitious to the revolution was the perennial unrest of the military groups, who looked upon themselves, often sincerely and ingenuously, as destined to "save" the nation from the thralldom of "highbrows" and "professional politicians." Actually, only a minority of the military were attracted by the political disputes. The navy, dismantled after its revolt against Floriano, recovered its former prestige under the rearmament program of Rodrigues Alves and Afonso Pena, and was always less tempted than the land forces by partisan activities and plots against legal order. The mentality, behavior, and standard of living of the army had been greatly changed under the influence of better training and discipline, the French military mission, and better pay. The rough old trooper of the war with Paraguay and of the closing years of the Empire, like the military positivists and fanatic Florianistas, was fading into the past. Trips and training periods abroad, and more eclectic courses in the military academies, opened the minds of the young officers, giving them a less dogmatic understanding of things and a keener sense of their professional duties and social importance. The "Republican dictatorship," puritanical at bottom, was no longer an ideal to them. Nevertheless, even among those who were least in sympathy with it, the belief had never disappeared that in crisis the nation had only to turn to the heroic remedy of force, at least for the time being, to restore both physical and moral order. Among civilians such an idea was not considered grotesque, nor is it in other countries like Brazil, countries doubtful of their political superstructure and unsure of their course.

But the immediate cause of the revolutionary movement, to the extent that it can be attributed to the actions of a few men, may be found in the clash of temperaments and methods between Washington Luís, Antônio Carlos, and Getúlio Vargas. We have already highlighted the integrity and inflexibility of the first, and the subtlety and pliancy of the second, employed to further their unyielding desires and ambitions.

The advent of the third player, crafty and two-faced, would make the game more dangerous. Had Washington Luís yielded to the various suggestions for a friendly settlement of his succession, and dissociated himself from Júlio Prestes while there was still time, as Rodrigues Alves had from Bernardino de Campos, the revolution would have been averted.* The same would have been true if Getúlio Vargas had acted openly and decisively from the start, either by going along with Washington Luís and Júlio Prestes or by opposing them overtly. However, there is nothing more arbitrary and gratuitous than making assumptions to reconstitute history; what we want is to arrive at facts. And the fact is this: the revolution came, and triumphed, and brought as its supreme chief one of the men who had least wanted and most feared it.

* In addition to the letter Afrânio de Melo Franco had addressed to Epitácio Pessoa asking him to intercede with Washington Luís in behalf of partisan peace, there is another, lesser-known piece of testimony by Afrânio. In an article in *Estácio Coimbra —In Memoriam,* Afrânio de Melo Franco states that at one point the leaders of the Liberal Alliance, including Getúlio Vargas, were willing to accept the compromise candidacy of the then governor of Pernambuco [Estácio Coimbra]. J M B

23. The Era of Getúlio Vargas
[1930–45]

Profile of Getúlio Vargas — The October Third Club — Program of the Provisional Government — Social legislation — Financial reorganization — São Paulo and the Constitutionalist revolution of 1932 — The Constitution of 1934 — Integralismo — Political struggles — The November 10th coup — The Estado Novo — The Constitution of 1937 — Social changes — Economics, foreign policy, and World War II — The end of the Estado Novo — Overthrow of Getúlio Vargas.

Without clearly defined directions, with no deep understanding of the great problems involved in trying to build the nation, and with a traditional political climate of electoral clans and family oligarchies that had always tended to convert the parties into syndicates dedicated to win at any price and enjoy the immediate advantages of government, it had always been very difficult to have any spirit of administrative continuity. It was a rare President who had not tried to undermine the work of his predecessor by exaggerating the problems he encountered and by improvising new directions. His program as a candidate never bound him to any precise commitments, nor was high performance demanded by his partisans or by public opinion. For the four years of his term of office, or at least until the nomination of his successor cut down his prestige, he would represent omniscience incarnate, if not infallibility, in managing national affairs. If this could happen among Presidents who had the same origins and represented the same dominant groups, then the habitual fault-finding and repudiation would naturally be exaggerated by one brought to power by a revolutionary movement that was destructive both by definition and by proclamation.

No one in Brazil has been discussed more than Getúlio Vargas; judgments of him range all the way from unlimited eulogy and deification to the harshest criticism and absolute damnation. At the same time, no one—neither Dom Pedro II, during his long and peaceful reign, nor Floriano Peixoto, during his brief dictatorship—ever held greater power. As the unrestricted chief of the Provisional Government, as a constitutional President elected by Congress, as a dictator under a Nazi-like charter that he autocratically granted the nation, finally as a constitutional President duly elected by the people, Vargas 'ruled Brazil for nearly twenty years like one of the old grantees of the Portuguese Crown, who received vast provinces; even during the two terms when his powers were constitutionally delimited, the economic power he wielded through the government banks and the various *autarquias* [semiautonomous government agencies] offset the political restraints on him.

Thus the good or evil that Vargas brought Brazil can be attributed more to him personally than to the structure of the state, or to the good or bad functioning of its political and administrative machinery. Because of this, naturally, few Brazilian journalists could resist the temptation to try to unravel his enigma. His administration did not resemble that of any of his republican predecessors. He did not fulfill, either usefully or disastrously, any constitutionally fixed term of office. But the many years he was in office, and their coincidence with notable changes in Brazil's economic and social structure, stamped the era with his name (whether it was good or bad is beside the point at the moment), as their eras were stamped by Pedro II, Franklin Roosevelt, and, a closer neighbor, Irigoyen of Argentina. Historically, his era was in some ways like Napoleon III's; in other ways, like that of some caudillos in the more retarded countries of Hispanic America.

The psychological interest Getúlio Vargas arouses is by itself enough to show that he was no ordinary figure. The resources of his opportunism and political shrewdness must have been much more varied and effective than his enemies give him credit for; otherwise there would be no way to explain his constant success in dealing with politicians for almost a quarter of a century, unless we accept without question that they were totally incapable of defending themselves. In the same way, his success with the proletarian masses could not be understood either, since his origin, training, and appearance were all so markedly bourgeois.

Until his accession to the supreme post in the Republic, Vargas barely stood out among the career politicians of his state. He was born April 19, 1883, in São Borja, in the former region of the Jesuit missions, on the east bank of the Uruguay River across from Argentina. His family were well-to-do cattlemen, traditionally involved in partisan conflicts that sometimes degenerated into violent and bloody feuds. His father, Manuel Vargas, fought in the war against Paraguay. In the Federalist revolution of 1892, he was one of the guerrilla chieftains, and afterwards an honorary general of the Castilhistas. These, then, were the early impressions—foreign wars, frontier caudillism, and fierce partisan conflicts—that stamped themselves on Getúlio Vargas for life and partly explain his Jacobinism.

After a time spent in Ouro Prêto (Minas) in preparatory school, Vargas decided on a military career, and returned to Rio Grande do Sul to enter [at 17 years of age] the cadet training school at Rio Pardo. He served for a time as a sergeant in the garrison at Pôrto Alegre and in Mato Grosso, where the Baron of Rio Branco had concentrated some army troops as a show of force during negotiations with Bolivia over the Acre territory. Disillusioned, perhaps, about the glories of a soldier's life, he abandoned the career he had begun, and entered the Faculdade de Direito [law school] in Pôrto Alegre [1903–7]. He went through a phase of being absorbed in literature, in which he never entirely lost interest. Much later, in a newspaper interview, he recalled his eclectic preferences for Zola, Nietzsche, Baudelaire, Euclides da Cunha, and Gonçalves Dias. Philosophic speculation probably did not interest him, except for Comte's positivism, his party's official doctrine, whose schematic and reactionary treatment of political organization may have both satisfied his interest in general ideas and appealed to his innate and undefined attraction to the authoritarian state.

Following a short period in public service and as a lawyer, Vargas finally entered the active political cadres of Castilhos's old party under the rigid discipline of Borges de Medeiros. Although he had no particularly brilliant personal qualities, he had already impressed his colleagues and the higher-ranking figures in the party with his poise, discretion, and self-control. While a state deputy, he was made leader of the state assembly, whose function, however, had been reduced merely to budget-making. As a federal deputy in 1924–26, and leader of his bloc, he appeared the very model of a modest and prudent legislator. When he was appointed to the Finance Committee he was not ashamed to admit that he knew nothing of the subject. However, this lack of interest in economic and financial matters did not keep him from accepting the post of Finance Minister that President-elect Washington Luís had reserved for him. His stay in the government's most important ministry [1926–28], which required him to put a new financial plan into operation, aroused him to no great interest. He was very attentive to all aspects of the game that were related to the players themselves, but things in general, and more especially in detail, held no interest for him. Contrary to the tendency toward permanent mistrust typical of the average caudillo, he was overly trusting about routine administrative matters and the persons who handled them in his name.

Vargas's position as a minister in the federal government led to his being chosen governor of Rio Grande do Sul [1928–30], although that choice meant passing over others who had served the party longer and who might have had greater claims to the office. Borges de Medeiros was nominally still the all-powerful head of the official party, but the Pedras Altas pact [forbidding his reelection as governor] had somewhat curbed his authority. The new governor felt himself freer to act on his own initiative in both administrative and political matters. His first step was to unite the local parties in a *Frente Unica* [single front], to function on the federal level, at least, as a catalyst.

Political victory seems to give premeditated purpose to a man's previous attitudes or casual acts. And so, after Vargas's elevation to the chief executive position in the nation, it was easy to assign ulterior motives to his earlier peacemaking within his own state: an instinctive strategist, he was aiming at new triumphs. It is more likely, however, that he had merely obeyed his natural inclinations. Tenacious, brave in the face of danger, obsessed with power, he did not like to provoke or live in an atmosphere of strife, although later, during his administration of the Union, his fighting spirit became somewhat keener. What always interested him was to win, whatever his objectives, by means of patience, temporizing, and adjusting to new circumstances, by not making unnecessary enemies and being always ready to make friends, moti · vated more perhaps by inner tolerance than by design, by handing out government favors, jobs, gratuities, and bounties, and without taking into account even the elementary personal qualities of the beneficiaries. He revealed himself in this light during the presidential campaign, and almost always appeared in it during his stay in power. A certain phrase ascribed to him defined his methods: never to make enemies who could not be changed into friends.

The origins of the 1930 revolution were political or civil, but its final outcome had depended on the attitude of the armed forces, that is, on direct interference by a small part of them, or on inaction or lack of interest in the struggle by the majority who remained loyal to the legal government. Among the military in the vanguard of the revolution there stood out a group of young officers, survivors of earlier uprisings and pronunciamentos, nearly all of whom had been in exile in neighboring republics or in hiding in Brazil. On assuming control of the government on October 24, 1930, Getúlio Vargas could not or did not want to curb the exuberance of these young followers, who had no political or administrative experience. Some were inspired by a sincere though confused desire to correct and innovate; others were moved simply by political or career ambitions. This was the triumphal era of the

Tenentes [Lieutenants], of whom a Jacobin Club in the style of 1789, the October Third Club, had become the symbol. The club, and later the October Legion, were born of the pact made in Poços de Caldas [a spa in Minas; probably in early 1931] between the Minister of Justice Osvaldo Aranha, Captain João Alberto, the interventor in São Paulo, and Captain Juarez Távora, who had been handed the power of a Roman proconsul over the entire North, from Amazonas to Espírito Santo. He was dubbed the "Viceroy of the North." Getúlio Vargas—handsome, rather imperious (even though he was short and tended to be fat), affable, smiling, cordial, and enigmatic—resigned himself to this dispersion of power, and patiently waited for the right moment, after his companions had begun to fade out, to assert the absoluteness of his dictatorial mandate.

The October Club and the October Legion symbolized the radical wing of an ideologically confused revolution that proposed, by indefinitely prolonging arbitrary government (according to João Neves, in his book *Por São Paulo e pelo Brasil*), "to guarantee the continuation of the present dictatorship until it has completely fulfilled its purpose, that is, the radical transformation of the politico-administrative environment bequeathed it by the recently extinguished regime," and to wipe clean the slate of the past by eliminating political parties, suppressing state police forces, controlling the army, etc. If the movement was distinguished by any doctrine beyond the general inspiration of authoritarian governments, it was one of antifederalist reaction coupled with strong nationalistic tendencies, under the influence perhaps of Alberto Tôrres's confused ideas, refurbished and better systematized in the "centralizing" of Oliveira Viana's sociology, but corresponding, in the end, to Getúlio Vargas's own inclinations.

On assuming unrestricted control of the government on November 3rd, just one month after the outbreak of the revolution, Getúlio Vargas retained as Ministers of Finance, War, and Navy, Afrânio de Melo Franco, General Leite de Castro, and Rear Admiral Isaías de Noronha, respectively; they had been appointed by the junta. Osvaldo Aranha, who had been coordinator of the revolution in Rio Grande do Sul,* was named Minister of Justice and Domestic Affairs; José Maria Whitaker, a banker who had been a member of the São Paulo secretariat, became Finance Minister; Assis Brasil of Rio Grande do Sul became Minister of Agriculture; and Juarez Távora became Minister of Transpor-

---

* He later became Brazil's popular and effective ambassador in Washington (1934–38), Minister of Foreign Affairs (1938–44), Brazilian Representative in the United Nations (1946–47), and President of the General Assembly of the UN in 1947. JLT

tation, but was soon replaced by José Américo de Almeida, who had been João Pessoa's secretary and had become the most important figure in the North after Távora.

The first decree of the Provisional Government drafted into the standing army all the "patriotic and state units that had served the revolution." The emergency administrative measures taken by President Washington Luís during the hostilities were revoked, and full amnesty granted to "all civilians and military men involved in the revolutionary movements that had taken place in the country." On November 11, the government published the organic law that defined it. It ratified the dissolution of the Federal Congress and of the legislative bodies in the states and municípios, but prescribed that the constitution to be drawn up would preserve the federative republican system, and would not restrict the rights of municípios, of Brazilian cities, or of individuals contained in the Constitution of 1891. The dictator was to exercise all functions of the executive and legislative branches; the judiciary would continue under the existing laws, but would be subject to whatever modifications and restrictions might be imposed on it. The powers of the interventors in the states were identical to those of the national dictator, to whom their acts could be appealed. Contractual obligations of the federal, state, and municipal governments for loans or any public credit operations were maintained in status quo, but other contracts, concessions, and agreements were made subject to review. Rights acquired by active or inactive functionaries and public servants, including magistrates, were not guaranteed by the new law. The Provisional Government went much farther, therefore, than the one that followed the overthrow of the monarchy in 1889. Wholesale dismissals from public employment, made under broad interpretations of the new law, resulted in a regular spoils system and a wild scramble for notary offices, jobs, and profitable appointments.

There was no letup in the task of legislation. One of the more important decrees of the period established the Ministry of Education and Public Health, which the Mineiro politician Francisco Campos was appointed to head. The Revolutionary Tribunal, an instrument to persecute and humiliate defeated adversaries, became nearly functionless after it was condemned by the cooler heads among the revolutionists, who were more interested in rebuilding than in persecuting defenseless men, who, though they had once occupied high political and administrative posts, were now mostly poverty-stricken.

The revolutionary government had easily won recognition by foreign powers. The Ministry of Foreign Affairs, under the able direction of

Afrânio de Melo Franco, sought to steer clear of the revolutionary storm and to keep alive Brazil's strong diplomatic traditions, particularly her policy of closer ties with the rest of the continent, which was maintained by Melo Franco's successors, who included Osvaldo Aranha, José Carlos de Macedo Soares, João Neves da Fontoura, and Raul Fernandes. Through Melo Franco's good offices, after the League of Nations intervened without success, the border conflict between Peru and Colombia over Letícia on Brazil's Amazonian frontier was settled. Attempts by the South American republics, again after failure by the League, to stop the prolonged Chaco War [1932–35] between Bolivia and Paraguay were more difficult. The Itamaraty obtained several bilateral trade agreements with a "most favored nation" clause in them.

In the Ministry of Transportation José Américo de Almeida resumed the work on drought control in the Northeast first undertaken during Epitácio Pessoa's administration. The Ministry of Education formulated a big plan for national reform of public instruction, but it did not get off the ground. In the other ministries, there was no letup in the drive to reform and reorganize, whether beneficially or harmfully, the public services.

The ideological clashes of Europe had always echoed very weakly in Brazil. The laws abolishing slavery were the only social legislation during the monarchy, and the idea of such legislation continued to grow only slowly during the "Old Republic." It was studied by Congressional committeees, and a few laws, temporizing as usual, were passed. Relations between employers and employees were regulated by civil laws codified in 1917 and by the Commercial Code, but no specific body of law, such as was being enlarged and coordinated in the industrialized nations of Europe, was established. After World War I, Brazil's own progress toward industrialization, as well as the commitments she assumed at the periodic Geneva conferences, led to the first laws that benefited the workers directly; these laws covered hours of work, industrial accidents, paid vacations, pensions and retirement funds, etc.

After the 1930 revolution, the Ministry of Labor was established. Later the departments of Industry and Commerce were added to it, probably more for economy than out of a desire to tie the three state-supervised activities more closely together. Under its first director, Lindolfo Collor of Rio Grande do Sul, the ministry promoted a great deal of legislation, and established judicial standards for nationalization of labor, minimum wages, identification and employment passbooks, unionization, etc. During the [Vargas] Provisional Government, labor policy was characterized by nationalistic inspiration, by a spirit of conciliation and arbitration between employers and employees, and by a single labor union under government control. Even though the program begun by Collor suffered from uncertainty and improvisation, and was finally abused and debased by official demagoguery, it was the greatest and most daring accomplishment of Vargas's administration.

The Labor Court was created with the same guarantees as the common courts, but since it was restricted entirely to urban workers, it left the immense mass of the unorganized rural proletariat in conditions that in many ways were no different from those prevailing before the labor movement. Social welfare activities were developed enormously, and often preposterously, by means of numerous semiautonomous agencies [*autarquias*] for specific classes of workers, which became instruments of political maneuvering for the government itself.

The legacy left by President Washington Luís was not as promising as one might infer from his manifesto of October 10, 1930, in which he denounced the revolutionary movement. The cycle of economic prosperity and of good order in the Treasury to which he pointed, citing the nation's credit abroad, the stabilization of currency, increases in the volume and value of national production, budget surpluses, etc., had ended a year before with the New York stock-market crash. According to repeated statements by the Washington Luís administration, which gave rise to passionate controversy that continued even after the victory of the revolution, each of the fiscal periods of his four-year term had closed with a surplus. The volume of paper money in circulation, even after the expropriation of the Banco do Brasil, was only a little more than three million contos, an amount equal to the federal income.

To judge by the revelations of the revolutionary government, which made no allowance for the world depression, the situation was exactly opposite to that pictured by Washington Luís, in fact, was one of complete fiscal ruin. The surpluses for 1927–29 had turned into a deficit of 1,300,000 contos. The outbreak of the revolution had forced the government to take emergency measures, such as declaring a state of siege, intervening in the states, calling up reservists, stockpiling, declaring a business moratorium, etc. To meet the extra expenses caused by the revolution, the Banco do Brasil had been authorized to issue 300,000 contos, guaranteed by one million pounds of the gold reserve and by bills of exchange. The Treasury had afterward (as permitted by the 1926 law) appropriated for other purposes the entire gold reserve of ten million pounds, and at the same time assumed responsibility for the 592,000 contos previously issued by the bank. Since the volume of paper currency had meanwhile been increased by an issue of 170,000 contos (out of the 300,000 authorized), the Treasury's burden of responsibility had been further increased by that much. The various expedients to which the bank and Treasury had resorted to support the rate of exchange had taken most of the nation's gold reserves, whether in coin or bullion, including those obtained from foreign loans to the Union, the states, and the municípios. The credit balances of the Banco do Brasil abroad had also turned into debits. The transfer of the gold reserve of the bank to the Treasury, which amounted to a new emission, was harshly condemned. The revolutionary government proposed to correct the errors and abuses of the preceding administration, to punish its crimes, to restore order, integrity, and competence, and thus to "open up to the nation the wide horizons of a radiant future."

Under José Maria Whitaker the financial management of the Vargas government stuck to the classic methods of Joaquim Murtinho: curtailing expenses and increasing taxes, to make possible a balanced budget in spite of the decrease in public revenues. To meet service requirements on the foreign debt, the government used the remainder of the gold in the Banco do Brasil and the stabilization fund, as the previous government had done to support the exchange rate. Abandoning Washington Luís's intransigent policy, the government intervened directly in the coffee business in order to achieve a "statistical equilibrium" for it. A special tax of 10 shillings, later raised to 15, was created to purchase stored coffee, which was then burned. Some of the coffee was bartered for American wheat.

At the end of 1931, José Maria Whitaker was replaced as Finance Minister by Osvaldo Aranha, who did not adhere to his predecessor's policies. He brought to his new job the same nervous restlessness that had marked his passage through the Ministry of Justice. Influenced probably by the idea of pioneering methods, like the New Deal soon to be tried in the United States, he may have felt that a psychological reaction against the depression could be started by means of a public-works building program and an increase in wages. But since he could not resort, as Roosevelt could, to domestic credit by means of various compulsory or voluntary loans, he had to content himself with the old expedient of Treasury emissions. The system of direct purchase of coffee was replaced by one of "sacrifice" [controlled production quotas], and the National Coffee Council was changed into a department attached to the Finance Ministry. This new and expensive apparatus, as Daniel de Carvalho remarks in his *Estudos de Economia e Finanças*, did not devote itself to improving and cheapening the product, but insisted, as it still does, on artificially maintaining high prices that resulted in stimulating competitors in the world markets.

In keeping with the suggestion of British experts, the Otto Niemayer

Mission sent out by Brazil's old correspondents, the Rothschilds, a new funding scheme to consolidate the service on the foreign debt was arrived at, in the form, even more undisguised than the previous ones, of a composition by debtors on the verge of bankruptcy. The Osvaldo Aranha scheme assumed a service requirement on the foreign debt of twenty million pounds, or, again according to Daniel de Carvalho, an amount that equaled the country's total available bills of exchange or trade acceptances. The foreign debts of the states and municípios, which had resulted from onerous and frequently scandalous loans, were also set in order. A special committee on economic and financial studies rendered useful services in this matter. The readjustment of agricultural loans—the Readjustmento Econômico—was another move initiated by Osvaldo Aranha. Although political in character, it could have proven of great economic value if it had not been overdone, and especially if it had not opened the door to other "readjustments" that were mere transparent favoritism.

The nation, meanwhile, had been disturbed by incidents that seemed to forebode general anarchy. The enthusiasms of the first triumphant days cooled down quickly, especially among the civilian politicians and conservative middle classes who had applauded Vargas so vigorously. In the states, military and occasionally civil disturbances followed one after another rather as they had during the era of Floriano Peixoto. In São Paulo, the dangerous confusion mounted. On the day it took over the government, the Junta Pacificadora had ordered the general commanding the military region of the state to assume the government of São Paulo and to suspend further hostilities. The governor then in office could no longer rely on the commandant of the local police, and gave up without resistance. Júlio Prestes, who had resigned the governorship in order to qualify for election to the presidency, had taken refuge in the British Consulate. By public acclamation, there came into being a secretariat, headed by General Hastínfilo de Moura, that included some outstanding personalities, politicians of the Democratic party and businessmen; it came to be called the "Forty-Day Government." This eliminated the possibility of any armed resistance to the invading forces then encamped along the Paraná border. However, neither Getúlio Vargas nor his general staff of politicians and officers was pleased with the solution offered by the junta. Five days later, Lieutenant João Alberto took over in São Paulo as military deputy of the revolutionary government; in reality he held veto power over the secretariat, then presided over, following the removal of General Moura, by Plínio Barreto. Thus began the confused state of affairs that the revolutionaries classified as

São Paulo's "mistakes" and that would explode into the constitutionalist revolution of 1932. Similar "mistakes" occurred in Minas Gerais, where Governor Olegário Maciel, the only one who had retained his lawful title, came close to being deposed.

In March 1932, speaking in Petrópolis to representatives of the October Third Club, Vargas insisted, as he had on other occasions, on the need to "clear the ground of the weeds that are choking it" before establishing a constitution, to "rebuild the nation morally and materially, clean up politics and reform the administration, in order to secure her economic and financial restoration." The "peaceful preaching of their ideas" by the young revolutionaries therefore deserved his applause. Those who wished to speed up the return to a constitutional regime were "wailers, yearning for the easy delights of power . . . incorrigible doctrinaires, out of touch with the national realities."

Naturally, within the ranks of the revolution itself, the radicals were opposed by the moderates, "the liberalizers," those who had remained faithful to the political structure of 1891, and the career politicians for whom the revolution had ended with the ousting of Washington Luís, a symbol of the mistakes, abuses, and corruption that had so long perverted democratic institutions. The split widened, especially in São Paulo and Rio Grande do Sul. The common people, already half-disillusioned about the revolutionary promises, feared new armed clashes most of all. Cabinet ministers and federal interventors followed one another in rapid succession; incidents and public disorder increased.

A raid on a Rio newspaper by a group of fanatics precipitated the crisis, which had already been foreshadowed by the departures of the first War Minister [General Leite de Castro], and of the Minister of Justice and the Rio Chief of Police, both from Rio Grande do Sul. The center of greatest unrest was São Paulo, where the politicians of the Democratic party had not got over their original disappointment at Getúlio Vargas's failure to keep his alleged promise to appoint a Paulista interventor; he had named João Alberto instead. Partisan agitation and the economic downfall of coffee had so troubled Alberto's administration that after a few months he passed the job on to Laudo de Camargo, a judge of good reputation, but Laudo was soon dismissed from office with a brief note. The judge was followed by the commandant of the military region, an honest, positivist general, whose conduct of affairs was marked by some preposterous and fanciful attitudes. The irritation of the Paulistas increased day by day. Being ruled by military men from other states who did not share their local interests and aspirations seemed to them humiliating and intolerable. A "civilian and Paulista interventor" became the burden of their demands, to which Vargas, under pressure from his Rio-Grandense followers, was forced to accede.

But the appointment of the widely acclaimed Pedro de Toledo, former Minister of Agriculture in the Hermes da Fonseca cabinet and former ambassador to Argentina, was no longer enough to relieve the tension. And in spite of Vargas's measures to "reconstitutionalize" the nation—such as appointing commissions to elaborate an electoral code and to draft a constitution, choosing judges for the electoral boards, and setting May 1933 as the date for elections—the Paulistas and other liberal elites were not sure of his sincerity. An armed plot against Vargas began in São Paulo. The two large parties—the Paulista Republican party (PRP) and the Democratic party—joined in a united front, around which the great majority of the state's citizens and social classes rallied with great enthusiasm, and which had close ties with the Liberation party in Rio Grande do Sul.

The revolution exploded on July 9, 1932, under General Bertoldo Klinger, commandant of the Mato Grosso military region, whose rebel forces were made up of the state military police, the greater part of the federal garrison, and volunteer civilian battalions. It is still very difficult to reconstruct the political moves that preceded the uprising and its complex immediate causes, which included some connections outside Brazil and some vague hankerings for separation from the Union; these were intensified afterwards by natural resentment at defeat. It is equally difficult to follow the various actions of the military campaign waged on Paulista soil for more than two months. It seems to have been poorly articulated and hurriedly put together. In a manifesto to the nation on July 12th, Vargas admitted that the federal government had been surprised by "the news of a seditious movement, clearly reactionary in character, that has broken out in São Paulo."

The rebels had felt sure of the nation's moral support, but most of all of military support from Minas Gerais and Rio Grande do Sul. Both states failed them. The governor of Minas, Olegário Maciel, and the interventor in Rio Grande do Sul, Flôres da Cunha, sided with the federal government and joined their police forces and civilian battalions with the local federal garrisons to move against the Paulista revolutionists. They easily subdued local insurgent strongholds and arrested some of the leaders, such as Artur Bernardes (the former President) in Minas and Borges de Medeiros in Rio Grande do Sul. Without support from the navy, which had blockaded the state's coast line, denied international recognition of a state of war, which Governor Toledo had requested of the foreign consuls in São Paulo, theatened with bombing from the air, with public opinion in Rio suffocated by the state of siege, and with Vargas easily able to raise troops in all the northern states, the Paulista revolutionists soon found themselves surrounded by Union forces commanded by General Góis Monteiro.

Having lost the advantage of a quick offensive march on the Federal District, the Paulistas were reduced to small trench warfare. Thus their surrender [Sept. 29, 1932] was not long in coming, and with it the sacrifice of their extraordinary efforts and civic fervor, including that of their factories, which had been converted to war production. The Vargas government did not indulge in new forms of reprisal against the beaten foe, but repeated those of 1930, notably imprisonment, banishment, and abrogation of political rights. Although militarily defeated, the Paulista revolution did nevertheless attain its principal, or at least most clearly stated, objective: forcing the government to stop quibbling and convoke a constituent congress.

One of the major promises of the 1930 revolution was fulfilled: the radical reform of the electoral system by institution of the secret and compulsory vote, including votes for women, and the creation of a body of special electoral laws, and of a special electoral judiciary with regional courts in the states and a superior court in Rio. The first experience with the new system would reveal, however, the inherent defects that still pollute it, such as the slowness in counting the votes and, above all, the opportunities still open for fraud and bribery. In any case, the elections for the constituent congress that convened in November were held quietly, and in the following year [1934] Brazil received her second political charter. Its great innovation was the provision for class representation, a social concept that gave labor unions and professional and trade associations a direct hand in the conduct of government.

In a formal democracy the state is a purely political structure, and so therefore are its representative bodies. The persons elected to them personify the state's sovereignty. This fundamental principle of representative government seemed established until the profound changes brought about by World War I, the appearance of Russian Communism and Italian fascism, forced a reappraisal of the theoretical values of liberal and essentially individualistic democracy. By destroying its social classes, Communism eliminated the problem of their representation. Fascism, slightly reminiscent of Roman Caesarism or of Napoleon III's authoritarian empire, claimed the corporative state as its original creation. Political representation alone, it said, even when legitimate, was incomplete. The individual belongs to a class, to a trade or profession with specific economic interests. Class representation would there-

fore join the economic to the political. This is not the place to repeat
the abundant arguments against such a concept. The Brazilian Constitution of 1934, not daring to go as far as Italian fascism or to repeat the
disastrous experiment of the German Weimar Republic, which had two
separate chambers, political and economic, combined both elements in
the same branch of Congress.

Under this system, fifty class representatives elected directly by their
unions or associations were added to the 250 political representatives.
From the very start they failed to be effective. Having been chosen indirectly by the government through the unions, they promptly merged
with the political representatives, were contaminated with the same
evils, and became a mere tool for parliamentary maneuvers. They contributed therefore to an early loss of prestige by Congress.

But even without the debased class representation, the Constitution of
1934 seemed doomed to a short existence. Lacking the ideological unity
of the Constitution of 1891, it reflected the confusion of the times and
the political inexperience of most of its authors, and it was burdened
with as much detail as a set of regulations. It kept the federalist and
presidentialist structure of 1891, but provided for tighter control of the
President's authority and for indirect safeguards against the excesses of
federalism. The direct responsibility of the ministers of state for their
acts, and their privilege to appear before Congress and engage in debate, but not to vote, tempered the early rigorousness of presidentialism.
If the ministers were members of Congress, they did not lose their mandates but were substituted for by their alternates. The President and the
state governors, whose reelection was forbidden, would continue to be
elected directly by the people, except that the choice for the first term
under the new Constitution would be made by Congress. The office of
Vice-President was abolished; an unexpired presidential term was to be
filled by the presidents of the Chamber, the Senate, and the Supreme
Court, in that order.

The composition and functions of the Senate were severely curtailed.
The number of Senators was reduced to two for each state, their mandates to run for eight years and be renewable for four years. Since its
functions were not clearly defined, the Senate's nature became somewhat
vague. It was not mentioned in the chapter on legislative powers, and
was assigned the special duty to promote "coordination of public authority, maintenance of administrative continuity, safeguarding of the
Constitution," etc. In the period between congressional sessions, one-
half the Senate would be converted into a standing legislative body. The
Senate could not take part in budget legislation, but could propose the

revocation of administrative acts it considered illegal, and could suspend execution of laws, acts, and regulations declared unconstitutional by the Supreme Court, which replaced the old federal Supreme Court and whose membership was reduced from fifteen to eleven.

The socializing tendency of the Constitution of 1934 was explicit in the obligation imposed on the government to formulate large administrative plans and create consultative technical councils. Special chapters were devoted to the economic and social order, the family, education, and culture. The Federal District was granted autonomy, and its prefect was to be chosen by popular vote. The first one to be elected, Pedro Ernesto, would end up being arrested by the federal government. The system of justice set up by the 1891 charter was preserved. The allocation of public revenues among the Union, states, and municípios was modified slightly in favor of the last two. For purposes of industrial exploitation [e.g., mining], the subsoil was made legally separate from the surface of property, thus countermanding the traditional rule of accession provided in the 1891 charter. Minimum wages and the labor court were instituted. Religious training was made optional. Like the Constitution of 1891, the new charter devoted a whole chapter to a "declaration of individual rights" relative to the state, but restricted the political rights of foreigners. The scope of the habeas corpus was delimited, and the *mandato de segurança* [a type of injunction or restraining order] was instituted for the "defense of a positive and incontestable right threatened by a manifestly illegal act." There was almost no opposition to the election of Getúlio Vargas to the presidency [by the Congress]; the Paulista bloc cast blank ballots.

The Constitution of 1934 was, in short, a set of compromises between various ideological currents, such as the Catholics and the Socialists, the Communists and the Integralistas. Some parts were accepted by party leaders only to save the whole. In its constant concern to forestall abuses by the Executive, it ended up so restricting his freedom of action that it made him more dependent than ever on the politics of the big states as expressed through their large congressional blocs. Thus the return to a constitutional regime did not give the nation the sense of security and tranquility that at least the elites had expected.

His natural tendencies, his partisan training, and his experience with arbitrary powers gave Getúlio Vargas no desire to try to correct in practice the faults of the system's theory. On the contrary, the rapid erosion of the legislative branch may have revealed to him the possibility of radically transforming the structure of the state. Furthermore, the uncertain conditions and latent unrest facilitated the propaganda of the extremist currents that were clashing in Europe and that would soon plunge nearly all of the civilized nations into World War II.

The effects of a conflict between ideological extremes are always more intense in a politically and economically weak democracy like Brazil. On the one hand there was Communism, directed by the former revolutionary lieutenant Luís Carlos Prestes, with a general staff of intellectuals and professional agitators, which employed the usual party tactics according to the instructions of the Comintern, and tried to gain a hold among the proletarian masses. On the other hand there was Integralismo, trying to win over the middle classes, which were terrified of Bolshevism.

The bases of Integralismo were launched in October 1932 in a "Manifesto to the Brazilian Nation" by Plínio Salgado, a Paulista writer, who until then had remained aloof from political activity. Aside from some secondary differences in form and method, Integralismo was a direct descendant of Italian fascism, as were other reactionary movements in Europe, such as Integralismo's closest model, the Portuguese Estado Novo that had arisen under the dictatorship of Oliveira Salazar. Integralismo was inspired, according to its leader, by the old conservative trilogy: God, Country, and Family. It was antiagnostic, Catholic, nationalist, and traditionalist. Politically, it was antifederalist and promunicipal. Economically, it was syndicalist and corporatist. In brief, it preached "an integral state, the ultimate synthesis of national realities," implying thereby an authoritarian government with a single party and a single head. Like other varieties of fascism, Integralismo had its symbols: green shirts, a banner, a hymn, a form of greeting, as well as military drill and established study centers. It met a confused conservative aspiration for a hierarchic and disciplinary system able to block Communist infiltration, and it enjoyed the sympathies of certain Catholic elements, including dignitaries of the church. It was therefore able to extend its influence over all of Brazil.

The structure of the 1934 constitutional regime seemed to justify the government's repeated allegations that the state's means of defense were precarious, a tack also taken by the Nazis during the Weimar Republic. Vargas, a master hand at the old tactic of divide and conquer, was not interested in the possibility of simply suppressing his foes, the Communists and Fascists. To set them against each other, as was done in the diplomatic and domestic politics of the great democracies, was the smart way to guarantee one's survival. The extremists thus found the field almost free not only to proselytize as legal parties but also to openly conspire against the established order. The government maintained public or secret contacts with the extremist leaders, Luís Carlos Prestes and

Plínio Salgado, and on more than one occasion offered a cabinet post to the latter.* Toward the end of 1935, bloody Communist uprisings occurred in the capitals of Pernambuco and Rio Grande do Norte, and on November 27 came an assault on a federal barracks in Rio during which loyalist officers and men were coldly murdered by Communist officers. The government's ensuing victory naturally consolidated its prestige but public tension increased.

The term of office to which Getúlio Vargas had been elected by Congress was due to end in 1938. The politicians got busy to nominate his successor. Two candidates were finally decided upon: José Américo de Almeida [of Paraíba], who was favored officially, and Armando Sales de Oliveira, governor of São Paulo, who attracted most of the opposition to Getúlio Vargas. The Communists also nominated their leader, Luís Carlos Prestes. The coalition in São Paulo that had made possible the constitutionalist revolt of 1932 was soon broken up, with the help of the federal government. The rancor of old struggles was again placed ahead of the interests of a Paulista candidate. In 1930 the Democratic party had sided with the revolutionists opposed to Washington Luís and Júlio Prestes. Now, in 1937, the Paulista Republican party, routed and persecuted by their 1930 allies, came out in support of Vargas and José Américo.

From the very start the campaign of the two candidates was heated, which to the more timid seemed a bad omen. Perhaps going against their own intentions and those of their more prudent and experienced followers, the campaigners divided the country into two seemingly irreconcilable camps. José Américo appeared to symbolize the purest revolutionary spirit; he was a candidate from the poorest part of the country and from the masses, in short, a man from the left most capable of stemming the Communist tide. Armando Sales, from the richest state, seemed to personify traditional representative democracy and the aspirations of the capitalist upper classes, that is, the spirit of conservatism that had been, after all, the mark of the Old Republic and the inspiration for the victorious movement of 1930. However, this distorted appraisal of the two candidates did not keep regional partisan issues from dividing the Paulistas, nor did it prevent what was left of the former dominant parties in the North, even though they were persecuted by the revolutionists of 1930, from supporting the candidacy of José Américo, which they did more for local economic reasons than out of regional sentiment for a Nortista.

In the troubled atmosphere created by Communists and Integralistas,

* Plínio Salgado: *O Integralismo perante a Nação.* JMB

Vargas was able to obtain extraordinary powers from Congress, laws that placed the country on a war footing and restored to him the better part of his former dictatorial powers, in spite of tough opposition from a group of adversaries in Congress who banded together as the Combined Opposition. One of the candidates would have to withdraw in favor of the other, or both in favor of a third, some of their followers believed, to allay the crisis and prevent a possible coup, of which the more vigilant were already suspicious. But as they aways are, such warnings were useless, at least in the beginning.

A kind of palace conspiracy to institute an authoritarian state—an "estado novo" or new state—began to take shape. The principal plotters, in addition to Vargas himself, were the War Minister, General Eurico Gaspar Dutra; the army's Chief of Staff, General Góis Monteiro; and the Ministers of Justice and Labor, Francisco Campos and Agamemnon Magalhães. A forged document revealing a vast Communist revolution about to explode appeared. The general uneasiness, the headway being made by the extreme right, the sterility of Congress and its resultant loss of prestige, the ably fostered dread of disorder and anarchy in Congress and in the armed forces, were all singularly propitious for the coup planned by the Executive. Antônio Carlos, a possible contender for the presidency, was ousted as president of the Chamber. An emissary from the Minister of Justice had got the state governors, who would soon be converted into federal interventors, to asquiesce in the coup. However, the governor of Rio Grande do Sul, Flôres da Cunha, sounded out ahead of the others, had opposed the step. Using the state of war as a pretext, the federal government was able to dissolve the provisional battalions that supported him, undermine his local police, and finally force him to abandon his office and take refuge in Uruguay.

Preoccupied with holding onto his personal power, Vargas used every means to widen the split in the democratic forces. Part of his strategy was to incite extremist groups of the right and left against each other, and to hold them up as a permanent scarecrow to the center. He therefore maintained direct and indirect contacts with the Communists and especially with the Integralistas. After the Communist uprising of 1935 had been put down, its leader [Luís Carlos Prestes] jailed, and the party outlawed, Vargas drew closer to the Integralistas. He asked Plínio Salgado, according to the latter's testimony, to support the coup then being prepared; he also asked him for his opinion of the new constitution. Salgado was in accord with the corporatist bases of the Estado Novo, "although I thought that a simple revision of the 1934 charter would suffice to replace universal suffrage with corporate suffrage, enlarge the state's economic functions, and strengthen the central authority." In any case, "as long as the government had the support of the armed forces, Integralismo would give it no trouble." The shrewd and more ironic Minister of Justice, Francisco Campos, allegedly stated that "the Integralista doctrine constituted the basis of the Estado Novo, but it was necessary, nevertheless, for the party to open its doors to all Brazilians who wanted to cooperate in building a great body of support for the aims of the head of the nation." In this way [Salgado thought], Integralismo would achieve its doctrinal victory by other means. But he soon realized his mistake. The November 10th coup came as a complete surprise to him; greater still, as he confessed, was Getúlio Vargas's speech declaring the suppression of all political parties, including the Integralistas. Not even as a cultural, sports, or benevolent association would any party be permitted to survive. The One Party of official fascism would tolerate no competition.

Six months afterward, on May 11, 1938, some Integralistas, hand in hand with some liberal politicians, would attempt a night raid on Guanabara palace, the President's residence, and be quickly repulsed by loyal troops under the command of the War Minister. Once again Getúlio Vargas would triumph over his disunited and precipitate foes. On being outlawed, Integralismo would suffer the same fate as Communism: some of its principal figures arrested, and its leader politely exiled to Portugal.

On November 10, 1937, and meeting no protest, police in Rio closed the doors of the two houses of Congress, just as the Portuguese parliament had been closed six years before. If the politicians and the greater part of the nation's elites, faithful to the liberal tradition, received the coup with consternation and deep inner revolt, the masses and even the nonpolitical middle classes received it with vague sympathy or at least with indifference. The coup surprised even the ministers, who applauded it or resigned themselves gracefully to it, but held onto their portfolios; the Minister of Agriculture, Odilon Braga, was the only one who resigned.

That evening at the Guanabara palace, surrounded by partisans and friends, including members of the dissolved Congress, Getúlio Vargas read over the radio a "Proclamation to the Nation." The democratic institutions the Republic had inherited from the monarchy were foundering. Brazil was entering the ranks of the totalitarian states. Vargas's justifications were no different from those of other dictators: obsolescence of liberalism, artificiality of political and economic structure, incurable ills of the administrative machinery, excessive regionalism damaging national unity, impotence of the Executive, sterility of the Legislature,

threats of anarchy aggravated by the presidential campaign, etc. Heed-
ing, therefore, "the legitimate aspirations of the Brazilian people for
social and political peace . . . [and] the state of apprehension created by
Communist infiltration . . . the President of the Republic, with the support of the armed forces, hereby decrees the new constitution."

The Constitution of 1937, whose principal inspirer and evident fram-
er was Minister Francisco Campos, retained none of the old liberal principles. It made a complete political dictator of the President of the Republic, who became "the supreme authority of the State, who coordi-
nates the upper representative organs, conducts domestic and foreign
policy, promotes or guides national legislative policy, and superintends
the administration of the country." In addition to the traditional powers
of the President, he was granted the right to dissolve Congress, to decree
laws, and to nominate candidates to the presidency. If he nominated no
one, the selection would be made by the Presidential Electoral College,
composed of electors chosen by the chambers of the municípios, the
National Economic Council, the Chamber of Deputies, and the Federal
Council; otherwise, the election would be made by universal suffrage,
and the incumbent President's term would be extended until his successor took office. The legislative power was exercised by the Chamber
of Deputies, with the collaboration of the President and the Federal
Council. The Chamber was to be chosen by a special electorate. The
mandate was for four years, with not more than ten or fewer than three
representatives from each state. The Federal Council was to be made up
of a representative from each state and ten members appointed by the
President, with a six-year mandate; its president was to be chosen by the
head of state. The National Economic Council was composed of representatives, divided equally between employers and employees, of the nation's industry, chosen by legally recognized professional or trade unions,
and presided over by a minister of state. In principle the proposing of
legislation was the province of the government. Bills initiated by any of
the chambers could not be considered if they related to budget matters
or involved increased expenses, and those affecting the national economy were submitted to the Economic Council for an opinion. Budget
matters and administrative policies as a whole were placed in the hands
of an administrative council under the President. The result of these
provisions was to minimize the legislature's field of action.

The judicial branch was composed of its traditional organs: a federal Supreme Court, judges and courts in the states, Federal District,
and territories, and military judges and courts, all with more or less
their former duties. If a law were declared unconstitutional by the Su-

preme Court, the President could resubmit it to Congress, which could invalidate the court's decision by a two-thirds vote.

Included in the constitution of the Estado Novo was a chapter on individual rights and guarantees. Censorship of the press, cinema, and radio was instituted. The death penalty, until then unknown in Brazil except for war crimes, was made applicable to certain criminal acts against public order and the state. Marriage was made indissoluble, and illegitimate children were recognized. Elementary education was made compulsory.

The existing labor laws were consolidated and others added. Professional and labor unions were free, but since only the unions recognized by the state had the right to local representation [in the National Economic Council], their freeedom was nothing but a farce. Strikes and lockouts were declared to be antisocial measures, and corporations were placed under the care and protection of the state as organs for its exercise of public power. Thus Brazil was made a fascist corporative state, with strong nationalist coloration. During a state of emergency, the President could suspend congressional immunities. The dictatorial constitution was subject to approval by plebiscite, the President's mandate being extended meanwhile. Federal intervention was to be imposed in the states whose governors' mandates were not confirmed by the voting. (Only the governor of Minas had his mandate confirmed.) As a fitting climax, a state of emergency was declared for the whole country.

Vargas's 1937 constitution was a historical document that mirrored a certain moment in the life of Brazil. The Republic's first constitution, in 1891, was brief in text and sober in form, and interpreted the aspirations of liberal democracy dominant at the end of the century. The historical Republicans—foremost among them, Rui Barbosa—were survivors of the struggle against the centralizing and parliamentarist monarchy, and effected a fundamental change in the structure of the state. The United States, tempered by Argentina, was naturally the model followed. Although vitiated and debased in practice during its forty years, the Constitution of 1891 withstood, on the whole, the challenge of serious troubles. The Constitution of 1937 imposed upon the nation by Getúlio Vargas, with the absolutism of John VI or Pedro I, was a queer chapter in the nation's democratic evolution. After dissolving the constituent assembly in 1823, Pedro I had granted a charter more liberal in some respects than the one that assembly had elaborated. The 1937 charter was arbitrarily decreed by a few men who were the country's ruling force at the moment. Because of this, the Constitution of 1937 was never put into practice or even submitted to the plebiscite its own terms called for.

By means of the new constitution, or in spite of it, Getúlio Vargas's vast powers were restored to him. His tendency to leave everything in a fluid state was ironically defined by a popular phrase, "Leave it alone till we see how it turns out." More than once, his adversaries and other nonconformists were sentenced by oppressive tribunals to banishment or imprisonment under cruel conditions clearly typical of a police state. Others tried to adjust to the situation. Gagging of the press and of other public media by the ever-vigilant censor was followed by intense propaganda in behalf of the Estado Novo and its dictator, conducted by a specially created agency, the DIP (Departmento de Imprensa e Propaganda). The techniques used were no different from those of other totalitarian regimes, nor were the results obtained any different.

Getúlio Vargas was an approachable and amiable man, a patient listener who was extremely discreet and cautious in speech and careful never to commit himself. Though he possessed no personal magnetism, he had always inspired sincere popular sympathies. During the early downfall of some of the 1930 revolution's most significant figures, Vargas had survived unscathed. A legend, partly true, grew up of his good nature, his instinctive kindness and tolerance. His political cunning was also a source of public esteem; stories were always going around about his cleverness in avoiding a dangerous crisis, or in getting rid of a hard-to-handle adversary or presumptuous friend. Shrewdly, he took advantage of these popular tendencies. We can suppose that both his sincere revulsion against the harsh inequalities in Brazilian society and his clearly demagogic intents caused him to seek among the masses, who were kept permanently worked up by the official propaganda, the support denied or grudgingly given him by the elites.

Republican politics, with its imperial tradition, had always been conducted at the summit, by a small, tight circle that formed a sort of syndicate. In a country that was restricted to an agrarian export economy, that had no effective middle classes, that was inured to fraudulent elections that were boycotted by the educated, the masses had hardly been considered except in large urban centers and during passionate political campaigns. They were therefore a new field to be cultivated. The new labor laws, directly benefiting the growing working classes in the cities, gave them the beginnings of class consciousness. Vargas shrewdly used the workers' improved situation to improve his own. His propaganda blamed anything that went wrong on the carelessness or bad faith of his leading assistants; anything that was successful was credited to him. It was a mystique against which any reaction seemed useless.

Brazil lived in comparative quiet during the two years before the outbreak of World War II. Rural Brazil still retained her archaic aspect and old-fashioned methods, and had little if any transportation. The starvation wages and the near-total absence of state aid led to chronic underconsumption by her workers. But major changes had taken place in the urban centers, especially in Rio and São Paulo. The surge of manufacturing industries, encouraged by high tariff protection, attracted growing masses of peasants who could not be absorbed or even decently housed. Behind the opulent houses and apartment buildings of Copacabana there sprang up sordid *favelas* [shantytowns] with their marginal inhabitants. Whereas the city of São Paulo's growth was part of the growth of that state, Rio grew artificially. It was a bureaucratic and parasitic city. Its topography was picturesque because it was on the edge of a zone that lacked natural resources. The inhabitants of Rio were therefore forced to import their daily needs over great distances. The public utilities could not keep up with the city's disorderly growth; shortages of water, transportation, electric power, food, etc., became more severe and more frequent. The opening up of new boulevards and new roads to the outside by the energetic prefect Henrique Dodsworth during the dictatorship lessened the crisis in transportation only slightly.

The rapid crowding of the big cities, the move to apartment houses, the competition of women for government and business jobs formerly held exclusively by men, and the growing influence of American habits, accelerated the sharp changes in urban life. The old tradition of large, patriarchal families living secluded in outlying districts, in houses with front gardens and back yards, but usually without modern conveniences, was being lost. Later, with increasing monetary and credit inflation, the old contrasts between wealth and poverty would become even more shocking, and the temptation to get rich quick would become overpowering. Speculation in real estate—incorporating office and apartment buildings, subdividing land into building lots—would become one of the most fabulous businesses in the world. Easily obtained long-term mortgage loans enabled the middle classes to realize the formerly absurd dream of owning their own homes, just as installment buying would permit them to own even luxury domestic appliances. But on the other hand, two-thirds of the national income was going into urban investments and expenditures that did nothing to strengthen the country's economy.

Under Roosevelt's policies, the United States had gradually emerged from the 1929 depression, and with American recovery came an improvement in the world economic and financial situation, including Brazil's. Unfortunately, this did not mean a cessation of Brazil's chronic ups and downs. Nevertheless, under the conservative Finance Minister Artur de Sousa Costa, who had replaced Aranha [in 1934] and retained the post until the end of the Vargas regime, business gradually began to resume its normal pace. Exports of products other than coffee, such as Paulista cotton, began to increase, which improved the balance of trade. Brazil's efforts to equalize sales and production of coffee, principally by imposing quotas on the coffeegrowers, were not emulated by her foreign competitors. The government therefore terminated the outstanding agreements and reduced the export tax on coffee, whose exports began to increase rapidly but were again reduced by the outbreak of World War II. However, the decrease in volume was offset by an increase in prices.

After a series of schemes and agreements, such as Osvaldo Aranha's with the Rothschilds, the consolidated foreign debt had been greatly reduced. When foreign loans were cut off by World War II, the government turned to voluntary and compulsory domestic loans, such as Treasury notes and war bonds. The volume of paper money in circulation rose from 2.8 billion milreis in 1930 to 17 billion [in 1939], and the foreign exchange rate dropped to the lowest point in Brazil's history. Nevertheless, Brazil's coin retained its domestic purchasing power, because of both the natural growth in Brazil's industrial productivity and the merely moderate increases in domestic prices.

The first signs of World War II of course greatly stimulated Brazil's business activity, and the ensuing prosperity allayed criticism of the Estado Novo. Everything Brazil could supply, especially raw materials, was in demand as in 1914, but on a larger scale. The unavailability of the civilian goods she usually imported, especially from the United States, forced her to accumulate a large favorable balance of trade, and also stimulated her industrial development, even though her production was hamstrung, as in 1914, by irrational improvisation, profiteering, inadequate transportation, and bureaucratic red tape.

Brazil's new coin, the cruzeiro [Southern Cross], which replaced the outmoded milreis, was finally issued [on November 1, 1942]. At the Bretton Woods international conference in the United States [July 1944], its value in dollars was set at more than twice that of the stabilization of 1926. This is still the official rate of exchange, though it is only one-fourth the current rate on the open market.*

---

* Since this was written, continued inflation has rendered the cruzeiro practically worthless. At the end of 1965 the rate was 2,200 to the dollar, which forced some government financial figures to be expressed in trillions of cruzeiros. A new cruzeiro worth two or three thousand times the present one is expected to be issued in 1966, as soon as the government is satisfied that its measures to control inflation have succeeded in stabilizing prices. JLT

Economic progress was both uncertain and disorganized. The steel mill at Volta Redonda [state of Rio de Janeiro] was built, and the formation of the Rio Doce Valley Company began larger-scale mining and exportation of iron ore from Minas Gerais [through the port of Vitória, state of Espírito Santo]. Very little was done to meet vital transportation and fuel needs. The railroads were nearly all operated at a loss, and were, like the roads, in very bad repair. Neither system was being appreciably enlarged. In short, despite her industrial spurt, Brazil was still the typical large underdeveloped country, with a low and wildly varying per capita income, heavily reliant on foreign trade, and with more than two-thirds of her poor production consisting of primary commodities. All of these factors resulted in a low standard of living and an extreme sensitivity to economic events.*

Brazil continued to depend on foreign sources for all her oil and half her coal. The utilization of hydroelectric power was minimum. Her vastness and her deficient land and sea communications did, however, precipitate the growth of commercial aviation. A special Ministry of Civil and Military Aeronautics was created, under which air routes into the practically undiscovered backlands were pioneered. In the civil and military ministries, routine work, and a few bolder and more efficient projects, went on, but the traditional slowness, the red tape, the congestion and stalling of the bureaucratic machinery, persisted everywhere.

The social aspects of the Vargas government will always be the most interesting ones. In the new atmosphere created by growing industrialization and by the consequent supremacy of the large modern cities over the rural areas, the demands of the wage-earning masses had made themselves heard. Vargas's labor legislation and propaganda had roused deep and even fanatic popular sympathies for him. By cultivating them, and with the armed forces solidly behind him, he could afford to dispense with the cooperation of old-style democratic politicians. But the populist character of his government did not keep it from being supported by magnates of business and industry who believed it provided a diversion for the extremist tendencies of the working classes. It was pre-

---

* Since the official and unofficial statistics are unreliable, it would be foolish to quote too many figures about Brazil's economic development. In an era of chronic inflation even the estimated national income is a very relative index. Nevertheless, the percentages of increase in real production, especially since the start of the war in 1939 and in the manufacturing industry, were encouraging, being greater than the increase in population. Agricultural production between 1939 and 1953 rose 30 per cent; mineral production, 55 per cent; industrial production, 163 per cent; transportation and communications, 142 per cent; and commerce, 94 per cent. The rise in all real production was 74 per cent, as against the increase in population of 38 per cent, resulting in a 26 per cent increase in per capita production. JMB

cisely in the richest and most industrialized state, São Paulo, which in the 1930 revolution had lost its leadership in federal politics and which had been beaten in its 1932 constitutionalist rebellion, that Vargas achieved his highest personal prestige.

The nation was morally and socially, at least in the urban centers, very different from what she had been before 1930, partly because of the universal unrest and subversion of values between the first and second world wars, but also because of the changes in her own economic and social structure, which had been brought about not only by the brusque and disorderly shift of political control from the rural areas to the cities, but also by the hiatus in her political life as this concept is understood in democracies. With neither elections nor legislative assemblies, without full freedom of expression, the new generation had no way to exercise its political thinking. To some extent, this forced abstention from active participation in politics contributed to the flourishing of literature, both fictional and nonfictional. At the same time, rapid monetary and credit inflation excited the desire for quick riches, ostentatious luxury, and material pleasures. The authoritarian state—and this is one of the paradoxes of the time—was supported by an undisciplined society, just as, in another context, the yearning for spiritual rebirth existed in the midst of a neopaganism brought on by a general breakdown of customs.

There is no room in this book for an account of World War II. We limit ourself, therefore, to a summary of its influence on Brazilian life.

Brazil did not and could not have a foreign policy in the sense that the countries of Europe had one. Brazil's international rank was quite secondary; like the rest of Latin America she lived, actually, under the aegis of the Pax Britannica, which had helped her achieve her independence, but gave so many pinpricks to her pride.

Franklin Roosevelt had tried to revive Pan-Americanism by giving it a new role of positive political and economic coordination. The simple Pan-American Bureau of Commerce, born of the first conference [April 14, 1890], had become the Pan-American Union, with headquarters in Washington. Its name was later changed to the Organization of American States. Like the United Nations, it was based on equal rights and votes for all of the "good neighbor" countries. Its main purpose was to prevent conflicts between the members, and to assure their complete autonomy by guaranteeing noninterference in their domestic affairs. Various meetings and congresses, always filled with romantic speeches, followed one another closely, from the one "Consolidating the Peace" held in Buenos Aires in 1936, which President Roosevelt attended, to the Pan-American ones proper, and to meetings of foreign ministers in Havana, Lima, Montevideo, Mexico City, Rio de Janeiro, etc. Inspired by her desire for balanced solutions, harmony, and cooperation, Brazil tried to maintain her diplomatic continuity regardless of the state of her domestic affairs, and took an active part in all international movements aspiring to harmony. In the field of Pan-American affairs, she felt it incumbent upon her to be a mediator or shock-absorber between the United States and the Spanish-American republics, especially Argentina, which was nearly always a discordant element in the meetings she attended.

The war in 1939 brought to Brazil, as to all nations, the same agonizing apprehensions as the war of 1914. But there was a distinct difference in the reactions of those segments of her population who were more aware of the world's general problems. Regardless of its indirect causes, which were the old political and economic rivalries of European countries, and its direct ones, born of Germany's aggressive imperialism, the impact of the conflagration in 1914 was like that of a tidal wave, sweeping away the individualist, liberal, democratic values inherited from the nineteenth century. It was a collision, therefore, between a late conception of autocracy and the ideal of free representative government. Brazilian sympathies had been almost unanimously for the Allies, the stronghold of liberalism. The 1939 conflagration, on the other hand, divided the ruling classes in every country to some degree. The democratic majorities were opposed by the Nazis, who were convinced of Hitler's impending victory, and by the Communists, who expected their position to be the one Russia would take on the grounds that the struggle was simply a duel between the imperialisms of the right and the center for world leadership. The Integralistas, who worshiped Mussolini and Hitler as the inspirers of their doctrine and even as their supranational leaders, as Stalin was to the Bolsheviks; military apologists for strong governments, who were impressed by Germany's powerful war machine; some conservative groups in permanent dread of social upheavals; and certain advocates of the totalitarian state, including Getúlio Vargas, were the minority of Brazilians, who, whether they admitted it or not, were the champions of Nazi-fascism. The floaters and opportunists, who always side with those they consider closest to victory and who thought the liberal state to be on its deathbed, attached themselves to this minority.

The direct participation of the United States in the war ended Brazil's neutrality, as it had during World War I, as well as that of other Latin-American countries. In declaring war [August 22, 1942], Brazil was following her traditional foreign policy; the wartime Foreign Minister was Osvaldo Aranha, who was considered above suspicion by the democratic powers and was faithful to the spirit of Pan-Americanism. Brazil was living up to her intercontinental commitments, among them the 1942 Conference of Foreign Ministers held in Rio; and she was acting in keeping with the nation's sentiment. In becoming a belligerent against Germany and Italy, Brazil was also replying to their fifth-column activities, and to the brutal torpedoing of Brazilian vessels in Brazilian waters. But this time she took more than a symbolic position in the conflict. Within the limits of her modest resources, Brazil undertook to defend not only her seacoast but also the adjacent seas. A contingent of her military air force joined the American forces in Italy, and later an expeditionary force of 26,000 men took part in the fighting on the Italian peninsula, where they left about 500 dead. Brazil granted the United States air and naval bases in the North and Northeast, whose geographical position made it a strategic zone of great importance. With Rio Grande do Norte and Pernambuco as the main centers, it became a bridgehead, or as Roosevelt called it, a "corridor to victory," for the invasion of Africa. When Russia entered the war, Brazil at once established relations with her. Russian participation changed the meaning of the war for the Communists; instead of a fight between two brands of imperialism, it became an implacable war of destruction against Nazi-fascist tyranny. Thus the positions of the Integralistas and Communists were inverted: the latter triumphant, the former persecuted.

As the war drew to a close, with the defeat of the Axis certain, it became increasingly obvious that the indefinite continuation in Brazil of such an authoritarian system as she was helping to destroy on a far-off battlefield in Italy was the greatest of absurdities. The reaction against the Estado Novo grew stronger. The opposition secretly tried to consolidate itself. The armed forces, which had endorsed the bloodless coup in 1937, began to take a second look at their duty to restore democracy. A manifesto by some outstanding Mineiros in late 1943 was the first public sign of rebellion. Although the manifesto was mild, it provoked reprisals by the government, which arrested some of its signers, dismissed state commissioners, and put pressure on some private concerns. But Getúlio Vargas could not long resist a public opinion that was directly supported by the military. He was forced to declare a general amnesty. In April 1945 General Góis Monteiro, returning from a diplomatic mission in Uruguay, would openly declare in a newspaper interview: "I have come to put an end to the Estado Novo."

Late in 1944 the President called on his ministers to "suggest practical steps for consulting the nation." He was referring to a constitutional amendment that, though it revoked the plebiscitary system of the 1937 charter, could combine its general features with direct elections to office. Naturally, such a concession did not satisfy those who wanted to reinstitute democratic processes. On February 22, 1945, José Américo, with the apparent support of the War Minister, gave a trenchant interview calling for elections to a large Rio newspaper. According to him, three politicians were morally impeded from running for the Presidency: Getúlio Vargas, Armando Sales, and himself, all of whom had run in 1937. A fourth person, whom he named later to another newspaper, combined the highest qualifications and the best position for the contest: Brigadier Eduardo Gomes, then the sole survivor of the "march toward death" during the 1922 uprising of the Copacabana fort. He was a military chieftain, a revolutionist of great prestige, and one of the few who had not subscribed to the totalitarian state. On February 28 the constitutional amendment elaborated by the ministers was published, as was the law regulating the "voter registration and elections for the presidency of the Republic, state governorships, national parliament, and legislative assemblies." Other, increasingly resolute public demonstrations by individuals and organized bodies followed, upholding the position taken by José Américo. The dams of official censorship had broken.

Although the opposition at first combated the February law on the grounds that the authority that had decreed it was illegal, they finally accepted it on the condition that the parliament to be convoked would be given ample constitutional powers. National political parties were organized as prescribed in the call for elections: the UDN (National Democratic Union) took in all the opposition elements and the PSD (Social Democratic Party) those favoring the government. Getúlio Vargas launched the PTB (Brazilian Labor Party). Under the system of proportional representation, various small parties, including those of the extremists, would arise. The ideological differences between the two major conservative parties were secondary. The Labor party, inspired by unionism, addressed itself mainly to the wage earners, but was, as usual, hurriedly adhered to by numerous capitalists and businessmen, and entered a coalition for campaign purposes with other, apparently antithetical parties.

In spite of the new law and the setting of December 2 as the date for elections, political agitation did not cease. Vargas's adversaries feared that he was preparing a new coup, or that he was using the official machinery of the states, which were controlled by his interventors, to rig the election. Thus two currents were formed: one demanded elections for a constituent congress and the presidency without Vargas as a contestant, and the other, which had been joined by the Communists under Luís Carlos Prestes, would be content simply with a constituent congress; in other words, a "constituent without Getúlio" versus a "constituent with Getúlio." The attitude of the Vargas supporters was thus dubbed "queremismo" [we-want-ism], derived from the slogan "Queremos Getúlio" [we want Getúlio].

The candidacy of Brigadier Eduardo Gomes of the UDN was matched by that of another military man, the War Minister, General Eurico Gaspar Dutra, put up by the PSD. The year 1945 passed by in an atmosphere of doubt and suspicion. If Eduardo Gomes had the enthusiastic support of his followers, the solidarity of the ruling politicians backing Dutra always seemed precarious. The political campaign resounded in the press, freed from years of censorship.

It is possible that the partisans of the two military candidates had agreed on joint action at the proper time. Getúlio Vargas seemed confident that he had the sympathies not only of the populace, including the Communists, but also of part of the military. He therefore insisted on continuing to head the government. The appointment of his brother, who was known to be given to violence, to replace João Alberto, who had become suspect, as head of the Rio police was the last straw. After some hours of dramatic suspense, the motorized troops of the Rio garrison occupied the city [Oct. 29, 1945]. Without the slightest show of resistance, Vargas renounced his office. For the first time in the chronicle of revolutions and coups, in either Latin America or countries elsewhere, a deposed head of state was not exiled or even deprived of his political rights. Vargas was free to fly, with official protection, to his ranch in Rio Grande do Sul.

Thus, after fifteen years of supreme authority under various guises, the Rio-Grandense politician closed his public career. One would have thought that, with his departure, the revolutionary cycle begun in 1930 would come to an end too. That illusion was widely held.

24. Brazil, 1945–54

Return to a democratic regime — Presidential candidacies —
The Dutra administration — The Constitution of 1946 —
Political parties — The Communists — Foreign affairs — Fi-
nances — Return of Vargas to the presidency — Economic
policies — The social milieu — Political scandals — Death of
Getúlio Vargas.

The bloodless ousting of Getúlio Vargas left the military chieftains who were directly responsible for it, and especially the two who were running for election, General Dutra and Brigadier Eduardo Gomes, with the problem of replacing him. Since there was no longer any semblance of constitutional order, and since they did not want to repeat the usual pattern of setting up a temporary junta like the one in 1930, they turned the government over to the President of the Federal Supreme Court, José Linhares, a native of Ceará and a career magistrate. He at once appointed an emergency and nonpartisan cabinet. Under the circumstances, the Linhares government could not formulate a definite program of action. Preserving law and order, maintaining normal administrative services, and guaranteeing impartial elections were the extent of its duties.

The two democratic candidates stepped up the electoral campaign. Dutra, backed by the PSD, was tied more or less to the state machines that had been dominant since 1930. Gomes was put forward by the UDN, in which the various factions opposed to Vargas and his totalitarian state were merged. There was no essential difference between the platforms of the two parties, which both proclaimed themselves conservative-liberal. Insofar as it is possible to assess public opinion trends in Brazil, the UDN found its main support among the intellectual elites and partly among the liberal middle classes, and hence largely in the cities. The PSD was backed by the upper classes and the lower-middle classes, and also by the still intact official machine, hence largely by the rural electorate, which was more submissive to bosses and petty politicians than were the urban voters. The third electoral force—the PTB—was chiefly an urban party that sought to control the votes of organized workers. Undecided at first, it ended up supporting Dutra on express instructions from Vargas, the party's founder. The largest of the minor parties, the Communist party, apparently expected Vargas to cancel the presidential elections, but to permit the election of a constituent assembly. It tried, therefore, to capitalize on the popularity of Luís Carlos Prestes among the working classes in order to elect a large delegation to the legislature, where, according to widespread rumor, its members would support Vargas's efforts to remain in office. Surprised by the overthrow of the Estado Novo, the Communists presented a political nonentity and non-Communist, Iedo Fiuza, as their presidential candidate only two weeks before the election.

On the date that had been set by Getúlio Vargas, December 2, 1945, presidential and parliamentary elections were held peacefully throughout the entire country. These were the first national elections since 1934. After eleven years the electorate had increased five-fold, in part because women had been enfranchised, but primarily because so many more citizens were now able to meet the literacy requirement for voting. In the presidential race the swing to Dutra by the PTB, and the massive electoral support of the rural political bosses, gave him the victory with an absolute majority. Dutra polled over 3,250,000 votes for 55 per cent, as opposed to Gomes, who ran well ahead in the large cities but received only 35 per cent with slightly over 2,000,000 votes. Nearly 570,000 ballots, 10 per cent of the total, were cast for Iedo Fiuza, largely in protest against the two military candidates. There was no election for Vice-President, an office that had not existed in Brazil since 1930. On January 31, 1946, after his victory had been proclaimed by the Electoral Court, General Dutra was inaugurated as President of the Republic for the 1946–51 term.

Dutra was born into a modest family in Mato Grosso in 1885. He followed a military career, in which he rose steadily to the top by always staying on the side of legality in all of the revolutionary movements that agitated the nation, including that of 1930 and the Paulista one of 1932. He was Vargas's War Minister for nine years, and was among those mainly responsible for the coup in 1937 that resulted in the Estado Novo. He was also among those who destroyed it eight years later. He was simple, unpretentious, silent, polite, and brave without being boastful. Dutra lived modestly. He was so unaggressive he sometimes seemed irresolute, but was nevertheless tenacious in working for certain objectives (as he was to demonstrate later in outlawing the Communist party). He was also imperturbable, and shrewder than he appeared to be in dealing with men. He lacked political and administrative training, except in military affairs. His exercise of the presidency reflected his easily understood personal qualities, whereas his immediate predecessor (and successor) was always the subject of controversial psychological analyses. For his first cabinet he chose some men from parties that had supported him and some who were nonaligned; later, in an effort to promote a national union of politicians of the center, he included representatives of the former opposition, which, in fact, had not fought him very hard.

The congressional elections of 1945 gave the PSD a substantial majority in both houses, thus assuring cooperation between the new President and the legislature. The distribution of strength between the political parties was shown clearly in the Senate race, where candidates were elected by direct vote. Here the power and nationwide organization of the major parties were evident, as the PSD won 26 and the UDN 12 of the 42 seats at stake. Of the remaining Senators, two were elected by the PTB, one by the Communists, and one by the small Popular Syndicalist party. The PSD and UDN fared equally well in the contests for the Chamber of Deputies, placing 151 and 83 candidates, respectively, in the 286-member body, to which five minor parties managed to elect only 16 federal deputies. The rest of the seats were won by the PTB and the Communist party, which were able to exploit innovations in the electoral law to gain a disproportionately large representation in the lower house. Although candidates were allowed to hold only one public office, they were nonetheless permitted to campaign from several states simultaneously, and to transfer any surplus seats they might win to other members of their party. The number of seats awarded to a party, moreover, was determined by a complex formula based on the total votes received by its candidates in the electoral district. Thus, a candidate with great voter appeal could sweep weaker members of the ticket into office. This role was played for the PTB by Getúlio Vargas and for the Communist party by Luís Carlos Prestes. Vargas did not participate directly in the campaign, but allowed his name to be entered at the discretion of state PTB leaders. At the same time, he was a PSD candidate for the Senate from Rio Grande do Sul, a post he won handily. Vargas also won election to the Chamber of Deputies on the PTB ticket from six states and the Federal District, contributing over 300,000 votes to the party to account for 17 of the 22 federal deputies elected by the PTB. Prestes, who campaigned vigorously, was elected as a federal deputy or alternate from five states and the Federal District, and as a Senator from the

Federal District. In the contest for the lower house he polled well over 60,000 votes, enough to place at least 4 of the 14 successful Communist candidates in office, where they helped to draft the new constitution.

The fourth republican constitution was promulgated on September 18, 1946. Like the Constitution of 1934, it maintained the framework of federation and presidentialism, although at many points it veered away from the orthodoxy of 1891. In keeping with the strong trend toward centralization in the rest of the continent, as well as in the United States, the new constitution generally strengthened the Union in relation to the states, though it eliminated the Union's right to intervene in the states for noncompliance with federal laws. It also kept the provisions of the previous charter that required cabinet members to appear before Congress when called upon to give information and answer questions, that held them to account for acts they had sanctioned, and that instituted, after the example of the United States, congressional committees of investigation. Ministers drawn from Congress were permitted to retain their legislative mandates. Though less marked ideologically than the 1934 charter, the 1946 constitution reflected the same socializing motivation. It also retained the invocation to God in its preamble. Some of its authors, and some of the Presidents who ruled under it, were of the opinion that several of its provisions made efficient public administration difficult. The way it allocated public revenues, to the detriment of the states and municípios, has also been much criticized. Altogether, then, the new charter was destined to be revised. By failing to enact laws supporting it, Congress permitted part of the legislation of the Estado Novo to remain in force.

The vice-presidency was restored by the Constitution of 1946, under which Congress elected Nereu Ramos, a Senator from Santa Catarina and President of the PSD, as Vice-President for the first term; his competitor for the office was José Américo de Almeida of the UDN.

The Constitution of 1946 increased the size of the national legislature and provided for the election of governors and state assemblies throughout the nation. The addition of 18 federal deputies from five states and three territories raised the Chamber of Deputies to 304 members, and the Senate was expanded to 63 by the provision for a third Senator from each state and the Federal District. The new charter also specified that an alternate should be elected with each Senator. Elections to fill these posts, more than a thousand in all, were held on January 19, 1947.

The voting pattern in 1947 was similar to that in 1945, although the turnout was somewhat smaller and 14 parties were now competing. The four leading parties retained their respective positions. The PSD, which gained twelve seats in the Senate, six in the Chamber of Deputies, nine governorships, and forty per cent of the state offices, remained by far the strongest party. The UDN elected five Senators, six governors, and over a quarter of the other positions. The PTB, the only one of the top four to increase its vote in 1947, emerged as a truly national party, placing 94 of its candidates at the state level in all but three states, electing one federal deputy, and contributing to the election of five governors and three Senators. The Communist vote dropped below half a million, but it was adequate to elect 46 assemblymen in 15 states and a plurality of 18 members on the Municipal Council of the Federal District. In addition, two Communists running on the PSP ticket were elected to the Chamber of Deputies from São Paulo. Among the smaller parties, three drew enough votes to attract national attention. These were the Republican Party (PR), led by ex-President Artur Bernardes; the new Social Progressive Party (PSP), dominated by Adhemar de Barros, the ex-Interventor of São Paulo; and the Popular Representation Party (PRP), which was the former Integralista party of Plínio Salgado in a new guise. The PR, formed of remnants of pre-1930 state machines, polled nearly 400,000 votes to elect the third Senator from Minas Gerais and 53 state officials in 10 states and the Federal District. It also contributed to the election of five federal deputies. The PSP became a significant political force by capturing the governorship of São Paulo and electing the third Senator from that state. Elsewhere the party's organization was weak. The PSP elected only 26 Assemblymen in four states, including nine in São Paulo. The PRP received less than 3 per cent of the vote, electing 15 assemblymen in 10 states and the Federal District. The party gained national recognition, however, by winning the governorship of Paraná. The remaining parties shared less than 6 per cent of the total vote and an even smaller percentage of the elective offices.

Electoral alliances and coalitions were a new feature of the 1947 campaign. Half of the governors, two-thirds of the federal deputies, and a fourth of the Senators elected in January 1947 were endorsed by two or more parties, some by as many as five. All of the larger parties and most of the smaller ones participated in temporary alliances wherever it seemed to their advantage. There was no consistency in the coalitions, which varied from state to state according to the immediate interests and convenience of local party leaders. Thus, parties that competed bitterly in most of the states cooperated in others. And even where alliances were formed, they did not necessarily extend to all of the contests within a single state. Two or more parties might support a common candidate for governor while presenting rival slates for all other offices. This practice, which made party platforms meaningless, was to become an increasingly vital aspect of the political system under the Constitution of 1946.

The Dutra administration was marked politically by respect for democratic freedom and for normal functioning of constituted authorities. Dutra absolutely refused to decree federal intervention in São Paulo, though it was urged upon him by his political supporters. Such action would have violated the constitution. He also hewed strictly to the constitution in outlawing the Communist party, largely on his own initiative. The Dutra government was alarmed by the party's increasingly open identification with the Soviet Union. Beginning in March 1946 Senator Prestes had said publicly and repeatedly that in the event of war between Brazil and the Soviet Union, the Communists would fight against the government of Brazil. Dutra, who had been War Minister at the time of the Communist revolt in 1935, took these statements seriously, though the general public did not. His administration still might have ignored an insignificant Communist party, but it could not tolerate one with a large national following. On May 7, 1947, the party's registration was revoked by the Electoral Court, on the grounds that the published objectives of the party were diametrically opposed to the "democratic system of government based on the plurality of parties" that was guaranteed in the 1946 constitution. In January 1948 Congress canceled the mandates of all Communists elected to state or national office on the party ticket. The two Communists elected to the Chamber of Deputies on the PSP slate were allowed to serve out their terms. Some liberals held that the banning of the Communist party was unnecessary, but no large group rose to the defense of the Brazilian Communists, whose constitutional rights as citizens were respected by the Dutra government. It was in part because of the outlawing of the Communist party that Brazil and the Soviet Union broke off diplomatic relations in October 1947.

Under the direction of João Neves da Fontoura of the PSD, and afterwards of Raul Fernandes of the UDN, the foreign office resumed its traditional balance and discretion. It worked to promote closer intercontinental relations, especially with the United States, both through bilateral agreements and through the Organization of American States, whose headquarters were in Washington. Brazil's relations with the United States involved both civil and military affairs. In 1946 an Air Transport Treaty, to regulate civilian air travel between Brazil and the United States, was signed. Two years later the Joint Brazil–United States Technical Commission was formed to investigate and recommend measures for the rapid development of health, food, transportation, and power resources throughout the nation. Its report, submitted in 1949, served as the basis for future government programs in these areas. Similar agencies were established for closer collaboration between the South American republics and Brazil. After World War II numerous military agreements lapsed and new treaties were negotiated. A major issue during the first year of the Dutra administration was the restoration of the air and naval bases leased to the United States after 1942. The last of these were returned to Brazil early in 1947. Brazil continued to participate in the deliberations of the Inter-American Defense Board in Washington, to obtain military equipment from the United States, and to request and receive advisory missions from United States military services, such as the one in 1948 that helped establish the Superior War College for senior officers of the armed forces. In 1947 the Inter-American Conference for the Maintenance of Continental Peace and Security was held in Petrópolis. The closing session was attended by President Truman, whose visit was afterwards returned by President Dutra. The Conference drew up the Inter-American Treaty of Reciprocal Assistance, which provided for the mutual defense of the American states against armed attack. The Treaty, signed at Rio de Janeiro on September 2, 1947, and hence known as the Rio Treaty, had its first application the following year, when the OAS intervened directly in the conflict between Costa Rica and Nicaragua. Brazil continued to be active in international organizations, such as the UN and its related organs.

On returning to the presidency in 1951, Getúlio Vargas would publicize the sound economic and financial conditions that had prevailed when he was ousted five years earlier: six billion cruzeiros in foreign credits, seven billion in gold, seventeen billion in paper money in circulation, etc. In reality, the conditions were much less auspicious than they seemed. The foreign credits would be wiped out by foreign debts. As had happened after the first world war, exports fell off sharply and imports increased. In 1919 the deficit in the balance of payments had been reflected especially in the falling rate of exchange, which was the principal indicator at the time; in 1945 it was manifested by the rapid erosion of the credits abroad. During the war there had been continual budget deficits, inflation, and ballooning speculation in every field, especially real estate.

As his first three Finance Ministers, who served for short periods, President Dutra appointed a banker, a businessman, and an industrialist, from São Paulo or Rio. This was the general practice after 1930, contrary to that of the monarchy and of the Republic of 1889, which had been to appoint politicians to the post. But his administration lacked well-defined direction in national economic and financial matters. At first it cut back on expenses, which reduced deficits and slowed down inflation. Afterward, under the pressure of such factors as salary increases for civil servants and the military, past-due bills, large public works, and most of all, financing agriculture and industry, it returned to budget deficits, emissions of inconvertible paper, and inflation. The credit balances abroad were largely used up in reducing foreign loans (those in sterling and French francs were wiped out almost entirely) and in purchasing and nationalizing burdensome, run-down railroads. The coffee situation, however, was improved by higher prices in the foreign markets. With the depletion of the credits abroad and of the gold reserves at home, the exchange market, hitherto free, came under the strict control of the Banco do Brasil, which put a brake on imports and required the other banks to make 30 per cent of the purchases of foreign exchange. Still, the Dutra administration left its successor a balance of 200 million dollars in New York. The volume of Treasury notes in circulation rose to 31 billion cruzeiros.

Among its constructive accomplishments, the 1946–51 government deserves credit for such worthwhile programs as rebuilding and paving the Rio–São Paulo highway, starting a Rio–Bahia highway, constructing oil refineries, a tanker fleet, and port installations, and beginning the Paulo Afonso hydroelectric project.* The Department of Agriculture, which after the cabinet shakeup had been entrusted to a Mineiro, Daniel de Carvalho of the PR, intensified the campaign for wheat production, and improved the food supply situation in the Federal District and elsewhere in the country.

With the desire to unite the democratic or anti-extremist parties constantly in mind, President Dutra tried to bring them together to support a candidate to succeed himself. But divided as they were, not by ideological differences, but by the usual personal, group, and regional rivalries and ambitions, the politicians could not agree among themselves. The names of various potential candidates came to the fore, some of whom had genuine political competence, others of whom were suggested simply as feelers. The UDN held out for its prestigious leader, Brigadier Eduardo Gomes. The PSD, the majority party, nominated, without enthusiasm and perhaps feeling certain of his defeat, a Mineiro politician, Cristiano Machado. The small Socialist party nominated João Mangabeira, a distinguished public man of the Old Republic. The fragmentation of the parties of the center and the indecision of the PSD

---

* Located on the São Francisco River at a point central to the four states it now serves: Bahia, Pernambuco, Alagôas, and Sergipe. J L T

made it possible for the PTB, in alliance with the PSP, to nominate Getúlio Vargas, and for him to win the election.

Except for two-thirds of the Senate, all elective offices in the nation were at stake in the general elections of 1950. Thirteen parties were competing for the votes of more than 8,250,000 electors, who went to the polls on October 3. In the absence of the Communist party, the PSP occupied the fourth rank after the PSD, UDN, and PTB. The top four parties received a much smaller share of the ballots than in 1945 and 1947, but still accounted for 80 per cent or more of the governors, Senators, federal deputies, and assemblymen elected to office. Among the leading parties the PTB registered strong gains, chiefly in the cities and at the expense of the UDN. The PR led the minor parties with about 3 per cent of the vote, electing two Senators, and eleven federal deputies to the national legislature.

In the 1950 presidential race Getúlio Vargas polled nearly 3,850,000 votes for a plurality of 49 per cent. Gomes received 30 per cent with over 2,300,000 votes. All but a handful of the remainder went to Machado, who ran third with 21 per cent. Vargas's running mate, João Café Filho of the PSP, led a field of five candidates in the separate vice-presidential contest to win with less than a third of the votes cast. Vargas and Café took office without incident on January 31, 1951.

Thus, once again, the civilian leader of the revolution of 1930 and the beneficiary of the 1937 coup d'etat attained the highest post in the Republic, more because his adversaries lacked political vision and cohesion than because of his own efforts. His unresisting departure from the political scene in 1945 had not hurt his popular prestige. Though he did not win an absolute majority of the votes, his election was something in the nature of a plebiscite. And once again, as during his previous administrations, he was supported by representatives of the upper classes and of industry, commerce, banks, and business, as well as by the proletarian masses.

It is hard to analyze the Dutra administration because it was so recent. It is, naturally, twice as hard to analyze Getúlio Vargas's second experience as a President with limited powers. We can merely outline in a general way the facts and conditions that can lead one to understand its dramatic epilogue.

As we have seen, when Vargas resumed the presidency he publicized the situation that had existed when he was deposed, in order to contrast it with the one he now inherited: budget deficits, one billion cruzeiros; bills payable, two billion; owing to the Treasury by the Banco do Brasil, one billion; paper in circulation, 31 billion; reduction in credits abroad, one billion, and in the gold reserve, 700 million. All this, according to

Vargas, was without an increase in production and with continual deficits in the balance of payments. A policy of rigid financial housecleaning was therefore imperative as the basis for economic recovery. But
that is not what took place. New measures were useless or self-defeating,
especially in the area of foreign exchange, when drafts on foreign banks,
used to pay for imports, were being sold at auction by the Banco do
Brasil. Unrestricted importation of luxury items, and stockpiling on
the gratuitous assumption that the Korean War would spread, used up
the remainder of the foreign credits. The volume of paper currency rose
from 31 billion in 1951 to 50 billion in 1954, equivalent to 1,000 cruzeiros
per capita, as compared with 600 in 1950 and 80 in 1930. With spiraling
inflation came an uncontrollable increase in prices and in speculation,
including foreign exchange. Exchange parity, as determined in international agreements, was maintained, thus increasing the depreciation
of the currency on the domestic market, which in turn, among other
effects, made it impossible to sell Brazil's traditional export items
abroad; they were referred to as *produtos gravosos* [products that are
overpriced in foreign money]. The monetary inflation was accompanied
by credit inflation, which was brought on mainly by financing schemes,
many of them scandalous, underwritten by the Banco do Brasil and
the semiautonomous government agencies, such as the Social Security
Institute.

Among the official achievements were the expansion of the steel mill
at Volta Redonda and of the hydroelectric plant at the Paulo Afonso
falls. The restriction on imports, the high premium on foreign exchange,
and inflation all combined to stimulate the rapid development of urban
industries, which were concentrated around the country's two largest
cities [São Paulo and Rio], and were owned or controlled by a few groups
and families. The increase in agricultural production was more the result of cultivation of new areas, such as northern Paraná, than of greater
yields from those already in use. Domestic transportation, except the
airlines, progressed little; the shortage of fuel became chronic. Attraction of foreign capital was made difficult by a rigidly nationalistic mentality, which was typically expressed in the exclusion of foreigners, except as engineers and technicians, from participation in the oil industry
or in Petrobrás, the State oil monopoly. Even native-born Brazilians, if
married to foreigners, could not own shares in Petrobrás, though they
might be fully qualified for the highest public posts, including the presidency itself. The sudden upheavals in the economic structure were reflected ever more sharply in the general tone of Brazilian society, which
revealed all the well-known symptoms of social maladjustment that are

precipitated by inflation: a prosperity often more apparent than real; a growing disparity between the living standards of the small, wealthy groups and those of the masses and the lower-middle class; the contagious decline in morals; and the universal temptation to indulge in luxury and display. This phenomenon was also manifested in the glaring contrast between the poor regions and the South, especially São Paulo, which contained 80 per cent of the nation's economic and financial resources and produced the same percentage of the national income, now increased by inflation to nearly 400 billion cruzeiros. The old political elite, pushed aside in 1930, had seemed to want to return to public life under the new constitutional regime, but had refrained from doing so because of self-interest, skepticism, an inability to understand or adjust to the changes in the Brazilian social landscape, or an aversion to rampant demagoguery and electoral corruption.

Brazil continued to echo, with the usual lag, the philosophical, literary, and artistic trends of Europe: Bergsonism, Neo-Thomism, Neo-Kantianism, that is, all the different forms of the spiritual reaction that had begun early in the century. The postwar reaction in European thought was not to reach Brazil until later. In the plastic arts early French impressionism had been left behind. Brazilian music, inspired by native folklore, had developed along more original lines, although the nation's most outstanding composer, Heitor Villa-Lobos, was appreciated more abroad than at home. Brazilian architecture, especially in public buildings and skyscrapers, was renowned throughout the world for its imagination and style. Fiction, after living through the experimentation of the "modernists" of the 1920s and 1930s, had achieved better balance. Free verse was in the ascendant. There was a marked trend toward political, sociological, and historical essays. There was an improvement in the makeup of newspapers, and an expansion of publishing houses and bookstores. Brazilian motion pictures devoted to native themes began to attract favorable attention at European film festivals. The first television stations made their appearance. Revisions and reforms of education legislation followed one after another. With Minister Gustavo Capanema's reform of education, new public and private universities sprang into being, some of them on solid ground, but most of them not. Because of her immense territory, potential wealth, and economic evolution, and the continuity of her diplomatic policy, Brazil aroused greater interest in the world. She stopped being a rather unknown and picturesque country, easily confused with the others in Latin America, and began to acquire her own distinctive personality.

After spending five years on his frontier ranch in Rio Grande do Sul, with no interest in travel and, it appears, almost no social contacts, Getúlio Vargas seemed more withdrawn, more silent, and more weary. He returned to the Catete, therefore, a different man from the one who had entered it in 1930, or even from the one who had left it in 1945. His ouster from power that year had perhaps heightened his prejudice against politicians and his distrust of the military. The nation, however, seemed to take him back tranquilly. Even those who had fought him the hardest seemed to have some confidence in him. By appointing four members of the PSD and one representative of the UDN to his cabinet, Vargas revealed his peacemaking intentions. Afterwards, as General Dutra had done, he reshuffled the cabinet, but merely replaced the PSD ministers with other members of the same party, and retained João Cleofas of the UDN as Minister of Agriculture. The political truce did not last long. As in 1937 and 1945, the suspicion spread that Vargas, relying on the support of the masses, was plotting to perpetuate himself in power. The tone of the opposition in Congress and in the press became more vehement day by day. More and more frequently his administration was accused of corruption, public graft, embezzlement, illicit gains, and indefensible financing by the Banco do Brasil, which was a powerful hybrid machine, sovereign manipulator of the national credit, and virtually under the exclusive control of the Executive. The scandalous mismanagement of the Treasury, which had been all but plundered with complete impunity, could no longer be hidden from the public, especially when the inquiry ordered by Vargas into the conduct of the Banco do Brasil during Dutra's administration proved fruitless. Inconclusive investigations into charges of graft and corruption became the order of the day.

The government's authority was severely impaired by the scandal-filled atmosphere. Much of the opposition campaign was directed against João Goulart, Vargas's protégé and the Vice-President of the PTB, who became Labor Minister in 1953. According to the opposition, Goulart was employing the power and financial resources of his office illegally to convert the labor unions and federations into a vast political machine, in order to establish a syndicalist republic in the image of Peron's justicialismo. Some of his bitterest critics were army officers, who demanded his dismissal in the so-called "Colonels' Manifesto" of February 1954. The officers were provoked by Goulart's proposal to double the minimum wage, which would set off another round of inflation, and, incidentally, raise the income of unskilled workers above that of army sergeants. Under pressure from the army, Goulart was removed from office, but he remained a member of Vargas's political household and his wage bill was enacted into law. There was no letup in the violence of the opposition campaign or in the general unrest.

The final crisis of the Vargas regime began on August 5, 1954, with an attempt to assassinate Carlos Lacerda, a newspaper editor and virulent critic of the government. On that night Lacerda, returning from a political meeting and accompanied by an air force officer, Major Rubem Florentino Vaz, was fired upon as he got out of his car in front of his apartment house in Copacabana. The officer was killed and Lacerda wounded. The crime became known as the "crime da Rua Toneleros." The first clues uncovered pointed suspiciously to President Vargas's own large personal guard. The President permitted the officer corps of the air force to take over the criminal investigation from the police, who were suspect. The clues proved correct, and the chief of the palace guard [one Gregório Fortunato] confessed to being the direct instigator of the crime. The chief was a coarse and arrogant half-breed, and the guards were largely characters with bad police records who peddled their palace influence and exploited the "sea of mud," to use Vargas's own desperate expression.

The public outcry could no longer be quelled. In Congress, in the press, in the military clubs, everywhere, the President's resignation was demanded. Vice-President João Café Filho himself suggested they should both resign. Depending possibly on his War Minister's control of part of the army, Vargas considered resisting at all costs; only when he was convinced that he had no means of resistance was he willing to resign temporarily. A final, dramatic cabinet meeting was held on the night of August 23, 1954. Getúlio Vargas announced, not that he would resign, but that he would temporarily step aside as chief of state. This did not satisfy the military. On the morning of the 24th, in his private quarters, after being informed of the unalterable demand for his unconditional resignation, he killed himself with a bullet in the heart.

There followed a whole day of indefinable anguish in the appalled city and across the nation, like the suffocating atmosphere of an impending storm; but prompt military measures, plus perhaps the stupefaction caused by the unprecedented tragedy, kept the storm from bursting. In political circumstances not unlike those of 1945, the military chiefs called on Vice-President João Café Filho to assume the government, perhaps in the belief, soon to prove wrong, that he could carry out within the constitutional framework the reforms necessary to rectify the former state of affairs.

Getúlio Vargas left two brief suicide messages that quickly became known as his "political testament." Here he attributed to unspecified foreign and domestic "interests" the pressures that had forced him to take his own life, and described his suicide as a sacrifice to free the Brazilian people from bondage. His name was to be their battle flag and his blood the price of their ransom. Only in time can the full psychological content and meaning of his testament be calmly interpreted and its long-range effects assessed. But if, as seems likely, it was intended to provoke an immediate popular reaction against his enemies, it failed miserably in its purpose. The common people, to whom he addressed his message, did not respond. There were even some who doubted its authenticity. Thus, it was on a note of apparent futility that Vargas, to use his final words, should "depart from life to enter history."

25. Brazil Since 1954
by Rollie E. Poppino

Background — Political environment of the post-Vargas decade — The Café administration — The "countercoup" of 1955 — The Kubitschek administration — Brasília — Jânio Quadros — Crisis of 1961 — The parliamentary experiment — Plebiscite — The Goulart administration — The revolution of 1964 — Castello Branco — The crisis of democracy in Brazil.

The dramatic suicide of Getúlio Vargas marked the end of an era in Brazil. The man who had dominated the Republic for a generation was dead, and for at least a decade no figure of comparable stature would emerge to replace him. It is too early to assess the full impact of Vargas and his times on Brazil, but there is no doubt that profound economic, social, and psychological changes occurred during the Vargas years to alter the complexion of national politics. During those years the central government asserted its political power over the states and municipalities, and made deep inroads into areas of the economy formerly reserved for private capital, foreign and domestic. At the same time and as part of the same process, painful strides were taken to build an industrial economy. The factory and the steel mill became the symbols of the new Brazil. The cities of the central and southern regions grew in size, wealth, and political influence at the expense of the traditional rural zones. Millions of persons migrated from the backlands to São Paulo, Rio de Janeiro, and other metropolitan areas, moving simultaneously into an urban milieu and the money economy. With the restoration of democratic government at the end of World War II, the urban working force and the industrial middle class entered the political arena as well, offering a mass vote in exchange for satisfaction of their recently acquired needs and aspirations. These new groups were particularly susceptible to the growing sense of nationalism, which by 1954 had become the common property of every political party on the national scene. Nationalism, with its varying degrees of optimism and xenophobia, was and remains unquestionably the most pervasive and volatile element of the Vargas heritage.

In the decade after 1954 a broad complex of trends and attitudes fixed during the Vargas era continued to exert decisive influence on the course of national politics. The urgency for economic development was intensified under the spur of nationalism and the explosive expansion of population, which threatened to outstrip increases in the resources available to meet the material needs of the people. Concurrently, the deep-seated and poorly comprehended unrest of a society in transition from an agrarian to an industrial way of life was channeled into demands for economic reforms and social justice. The repeated frustration of such demands, as the decade wore on, made demagoguery and "revolutionary" appeals standard forms of political expression. Political leaders of the most varied persuasions agreed, with enthusiasm or resignation, that Brazil was caught in a "revolutionary" current that seemed irreversible. They disagreed, at times violently, over the nature of the drastic measures required to avert national disaster.

Efforts to work out a viable political solution to national problems after 1954 were impeded by the persistent legend that had grown up around Getúlio Vargas, which conditioned public and official reaction to the basic issues confronting the Republic. It is now apparent that the changes in the economic and social structure since 1930 were too great to have been caused by only one man, but while Vargas lived it was difficult to distinguish the man from the processes his policies had set in motion. As an astute politician, moreover, Vargas had claimed credit for creating a new Brazil. This claim was vociferously endorsed by his admirers, and unwittingly supported by his enemies, who denounced him for jeopardizing traditional institutions and values. The bitter controversy surrounding him, which obscured the real issues underlying the crises of his last administration, continued after his suicide to divide those who had supported or opposed him in life. To his adversaries Vargas remained the nemesis whose miscalculations and greed for power had brought Brazil to a perilous impasse. To his vast popular following, on the other hand, he was now a martyr to Brazilian nationalism, a victim of those who would retard Brazil's inevitable ascent to great-power status. Gradually, as memory of him receded, attention was shifted from Vargas's personality to the issues associated with his regimes, but the broad division of political forces into pro-Vargas and anti-Vargas camps continued. In a real sense, national politics after 1954 may be viewed as a continuing contest for power between the heirs and foes of the former dictator.

Perhaps the most striking and far-reaching political development of the post-Vargas decade was the decision by the armed forces to resume a key role in the direction of national affairs. Since the founding of the Republic the military services had regarded themselves—and were identified in successive constitutions—as permanent national institutions responsible for preserving constitutional powers. It was further generally accepted that the military enjoyed the right, above the law, to intervene in the political process during moments of national crisis, when the basic institutions of the Republic appeared to be in jeopardy. This extralegal power had been used sparingly, however, and then only to transfer political control from one civilian regime to another. Between the inauguration of President Prudente de Morais in 1894 and that of President Getúlio Vargas in 1951, there had been three successful military interventions against the established government. This record was to be equaled between 1954 and 1964, when force or the threat of force was employed to topple three administrations. The rising frequency of armed intervention revealed the progress of the military's disillusionment with civilian political leadership and of their loss of confidence in the effectiveness of the democratic process as it had evolved in Brazil. Finally, the unwillingness of the armed forces to restore full political authority to civilians after the 1964 revolution added an ingredient to Brazilian politics that had not been present since the early years of the Republic.

With the overthrow and suicide of Vargas, political power passed into the hands of his opponents. For the first time since the restoration of representative democracy in Brazil, men who had resisted the Estado Novo before 1945 were in a position to determine the policies of the federal government. The former Vice-President, João Café Filho, who assumed the presidency on August 24, 1954, immediately began to reorganize the cabinet to reflect the new political situation. His appointees were drawn from the four leading parties, but key positions were reserved largely for members of the UDN. This party controlled the Ministry of Finance through the appointments of Eugenio Gudin, a highly orthodox economist of international reputation, and his successor, the São Paulo banker José Maria Whitaker; the Foreign Ministry, headed by Raul Fernandes, an elder statesman whose political concepts had been formed under the Old Republic; and, after April 1955, the vital Ministry of Justice, under the direction of UDN president José Eduardo de Prado Kelly. The Minister of Justice was made responsible for the orderly conduct of national elections. The cabinet also included two ex-*tenentes* ["lieutenants"] who had played prominent roles in the political ferment of the 1920s and in the revolution of 1930, only to break with Vargas when the dictatorship was imposed in 1937. These were the new Air Minister, Brigadier Eduardo Gomes, the twice-defeated presidential candidate of the UDN, and General Juarez Távora, a man of Christian Democratic leanings but without firm party ties, who became chief of Café's military household. The most important position in the cabinet, that of War Minister, was assigned to General Henrique Teixeira Lott, a little-known non-political officer who had signed the "generals' manifesto" of August 22 that brought about Vargas's resignation. It was widely assumed that this government would be receptive to the recommendations of the so-called "producing classes," and that the major objectives of the anti-Vargas groups would now be realized. The new administration was expected to enact strong measures to curb inflation, to encourage economic development by assisting private enterprise, to circumscribe the political activities of organized labor, and to use its authority to prevent the election of another Vargas-style regime in 1955. Given the political climate of the moment, this was a reasonable assumption, but it proved to be invalid, for it overlooked the attitudes and determination of President Café.

Under normal circumstances João Café Filho could never have become President of Brazil. His credentials for the nation's highest office were deficient on at least three practical political counts. He was from the wrong part of the country, he was a member of the wrong party, and he had compiled no record of accomplishments as a civil or military administrator. Since the founding of the Republic, victorious candidates for the presidency had ordinarily been drawn from the wealthy, populous states of São Paulo, Minas Gerais, and Rio Grande do Sul. Café was a native of Rio Grande do Norte, an economically depressed state that in 1950 accounted for only two per cent of the national electorate. The President usually represented a nation-wide party. Café had been a regional leader of the Social Progressive Party (PSP), which was primarily the personal vehicle of Adhemar de Barros, whose electoral following was concentrated overwhelmingly in São Paulo. In addition, Café had spent his political career almost entirely as a member of the opposition. In 1928, as a young journalist in Pernambuco, he had been jailed for criticizing the state administration. An ardent supporter of the Liberal Alliance in 1930, he was elected to Congress in 1934, but was exiled in 1937 for his bitter public attacks on the dictatorship. In the Constituent Assembly and Congress from 1946 to 1950, Café gained recognition as a formidable critic of the regime, quick to denounce arbitrary uses of power or actions that appeared to infringe on the constitutional rights of the individual.

He was respected as a sincere democrat and crusader against corruption in public office, but was not looked upon as a constructive political leader of presidential stature. It was only as a result of the chance coalition of the PTB and PSP in the 1950 campaign that Café was selected to balance the ticket as Vargas's running mate. In the separate balloting for President and Vice-President, Café ran more than a million votes behind the former dictator from Rio Grande do Sul, polling barely 30 per cent of the total as opposed to 47 per cent for Vargas. After the elections he avoided publicity, attracting little attention until the final days of the Vargas administration, when he proposed the joint resignation of President and Vice-President as a solution to the crisis of August 1954. Vargas refused to entertain this suggestion. His resignation and suicide, and the military's willingness to honor the constitutional rule of succession, completed the series of coincidences by which João Café Filho became the seventeenth President of Brazil.

Café's background as a champion of the rule of law, and his appraisal of the circumstances under which he had come to power, combined to give him a narrow, legalistic view of his responsibilities as President. He was fully aware that confidence in the political institutions of the Republic had been badly shaken by the overthrow of Vargas, and was convinced that the survival of representative, democratic government depended upon his staying in office for the remainder of Vargas's term. Café was primarily concerned with the preservation of constitutional government and with the right of the people to select their political representatives freely. Thus, he consistently resisted demands by a vociferous minority for the installation of a temporary dictatorship that would suspend all normal political activity until the passions aroused by the demise of Vargas had been allowed to cool. Café appealed, on grounds of the national interest, for cooperation among the major political parties, but left no doubt that he would permit unbridled partisan politics, if necessary, rather than violate the constitutional provisions respecting freedom of political expression. This sincere, but essentially negative, defense of the political provisions of the Constitution was the extent of Café's program. He seemed awed by the office he had so unexpectedly inherited, and appeared to doubt his competence or right to exercise all the authority at his command. In his opinion, since he had not been elected to the presidency, he held no mandate from the Brazilian people to depart sharply from the policies set down by his predecessor. Thus, although he tended privately to agree with many of the objectives of moderate conservative leaders, Café refused to employ the full powers of the presidency to implement a thorough anti-Vargas program. During the entire fifteen months of his administration, Café regarded himself as the head of a caretaker regime whose chief duties were to maintain law and order, to preside over open national elections, and to transfer power on schedule to a successor chosen by the people. It is a credit to his tenacity that he was able to accomplish two of these goals within the letter and spirit of the law, and that he was prevented from fulfilling the third only by the armed forces' violation of the Constitution he had sought to preserve.

The great majority of elected officials in Brazil were subject to reelection or replacement during the Café administration. Throughout the Republic national and state officials with four- and eight-year terms were up for election in October 1954, and those with five-year terms were up for election twelve months later. In addition, most municipal elections were scheduled to coincide with one or another of the major contests. Preparations for these elections kept the country in a state of continuous political agitation. The 1954 campaign was already well under way when Vargas was removed from power, and no one could predict how the August crisis would affect the balloting on October 3. At stake were eleven governorships, the legislatures of the twenty states and the Federal District, two-thirds of the Senate, and all seats in the Chamber of Deputies, which had been increased from 304 to 326 to reflect the population growth recorded in the 1950 census. Anti-Vargas extremists, fearing a resurgence of popular sympathy for the "martyred" President, clamored for postponement of the elections, but the heirs of Vargas and their moderate opponents insisted upon the right to seek vindication at the polls.

Neither the fears nor the expectations of the politicians were fully realized. The elections of October 3, 1954, failed to resolve the political dilemma or to provide a clear indication of public attitudes toward the Café regime and the events that had brought it to power. The inconclusiveness of the returns was due, in large part, to the persistence of campaign practices that compounded the confusion already prevalent among the electorate. No party ran on a consistently pro- or anti-Vargas platform. Although some candidates campaigned on a record of opposition to the Vargas administration, the majority in every party was competing for the now leaderless following of the former President. At the same time, nominally pro- and anti-Vargas factions were frequently allied at the state level, and in numerous congressional contests as well. In each state temporary electoral coalitions continued to be determined more by local issues and convenience than by the broad policy pronouncements of national party leaders. In these circumstances, the Vargas crisis proved to have little impact on normal voting patterns.

On the whole, the results of the 1954 elections were disappointing to the parties supporting the administration. The UDN remained the nation's second party, but declined somewhat in overall strength. It won two governorships and contributed to the defeat of João Goulart, the candidate of the PTB in Vargas's home state, but dropped to third place in the Senate and was unable to maintain its previous representation in the Chamber of Deputies. The PSP strengthened its fourth-ranking position in the Chamber, but fell to fifth place in the Senate, behind the small Republican party, and failed to elect a single governor. Party organization and prestige were damaged by Adhemar de Barros's loss to Jânio Quadros, a political independent, in a close race for the governorship of São Paulo. On the other hand, the PSD remained clearly the leading party, even though it was wracked with factionalism in several states and polled a slightly lower percentage of the total vote than formerly. It continued to provide far more governors, state legislators, Senators, and federal deputies than any other party. The PTB, despite its setback in Rio Grande do Sul, added to its following throughout the country and placed members in every state legislature. It also elected one governor, surpassed the UDN in the Senate, and gained substantially on the UDN in the Chamber of Deputies. Thus, the two parties most closely identified with the Vargas legend accounted for well over half of the Senate and Chamber of Deputies, whereas the UDN and PSP supplied fewer than one-third of the members of either house. The remaining legislators, drawn from the eight minor parties, were divided about evenly between the administration and the opposition. Although party labels gave only a rough indication of the political leanings of individual members of Congress, it was evident that the legislature could not be expected to offer sustained leadership or majority support for the changes advocated by the anti-Vargas factions.

Even before the congressional ballots were tallied, attention shifted to the presidential campaign, which presented serious difficulties for all parties. Since Café continued to resist pressure for an extraconstitutional solution, and no party commanded enough votes to win the presidency alone, negotiations were immediately begun for a reshaping of electoral alliances. It was assumed the successful candidate would need the backing of two large parties and at least tacit approval of the armed forces. These conditions appeared to restrict the range of possible candidates, for an anti-Vargas extremist would be unlikely to attract broad popular support, whereas the election of a candidate appealing to the Vargas legend would invite further military intervention. Debate over these questions was still raging in the press and in party circles when Juscelino Kubitschek, the PSD governor of Minas Gerais, declared his candidacy and launched a whirlwind campaign to gain his party's nomination.

Kubitschek's actions provoked the military members of the government to recommend a compromise. Their proposal, announced to the nation by President Café in a radio and television address on January 27, 1955, called for a "national unity" candidate to be endorsed by all parties. The drafters of the appeal counseled against a military candidate, and each pledged himself not to accept nomination as head of a national unity ticket. The UDN hailed the proposal as an altruistic gesture designed to promote national tranquility at a time of grave social and economic crisis. The PTB was not seriously expected to accept the national unity idea, but its proponents hoped a UDN-PSD-PSP coalition would agree to a quiet campaign behind a common candidate, who would be assured well over half the national vote. The proposal, thus, was directed chiefly against Kubitschek, and incidentally against the presidential aspirations of Adhemar de Barros. Neither man was acceptable to the UDN. Kubitschek, however, refused to withdraw from the contest. His formal nomination by the PSD in February virtually doomed the national unity concept to failure. Its last chance for success disappeared when Adhemar de Barros emerged as the candidate of the PSP. The extreme right was represented by Plínio Salgado, the nominee of his own Popular Representation party, which derived from the pre-war Integralista movement. After much hesitation the UDN threw its support to General Juarez Távora, who had secured the backing of the small Christian Democratic party and the Brazilian Socialist party. Milton Campos, of the UDN, was Távora's running mate in the vice-presidential race. Meanwhile, the PTB indicated strong preference for its chairman, João Goulart, but authorized him to negotiate with other parties. In June the PTB leader accepted the vice-presidential nomination of the PSD, reaffirming the bonds that linked the two parties created by Getúlio Vargas. Five minor parties, including the illegal Communist party, publicly endorsed the Kubitschek-Goulart ticket, to the consternation of the anti-Vargas camp. The field was completed with the entry of Danton Coelho, a PTB dissident vying with Goulart for control of organized labor, as a candidate for the vice-presidency on the de Barros ticket.

The campaign was waged in an atmosphere of extreme political tension. Rumors and charges of an impending coup d'etat circulated on all sides. The controversy centered chiefly on Goulart, the former protégé of Vargas, who was regarded by many conservatives as too blatantly pro-labor and pro-Communist to hold high public office. Some outspoken anti-Vargas elements called openly for military intervention to forestall the possibility of a Kubitschek-Goulart victory. Goulart's backers asserted with equal vehemence that legalists within the army would stage a "countercoup" if necessary to prevent interference with the campaign and the balloting. The armed forces, who were responsible for guaranteeing orderly elections, were torn between their respect for the Constitution and their concern over the prospect of another Vargas-style regime. A faction known as the Constitutional Military Movement, identified with ex-War Minister Zenobio da Costa, now Inspector General of the Army, insisted that the will of the electorate must prevail, no matter how repugnant the winning candidates might be to the military. This view was unacceptable to a majority of navy and air force officers and to the army element called the Democratic Crusade. This group was led by ailing General Canrobert Pereira da Costa, president of the Military Club, who had played an active role in the overthrow of Vargas in 1945 and again in 1954. The Democratic Crusade held that the election of Kubitschek and Goulart would restore the kind of corrupt, irresponsible rule the armed forces had been compelled to destroy the preceding year. Both groups, however, preferred to avoid intervention in the hope that the electorate would choose candidates acceptable to all military factions.

Through it all President Café preserved an attitude of calm, reiterating his conviction that the elections would take place on schedule and without incident. His predictions proved sound. On October 3, 1955, in the most honest and orderly elections the Republic had yet known, Juscelino Kubitschek and João Goulart were elected President and Vice-President of Brazil. Neither received an absolute majority of the more than nine million votes. Kubitschek polled 34 per cent of the total, and Goulart received nearly 40 per cent in the three-way vice-presidential race. Távora and Campos ran second, with 29 per cent and 37 per cent, respectively. Almost one-fourth of the presidential vote went to Adhemar de Barros. Coelho, his companion on the ticket, received over one million votes, largely at the expense of Goulart. Távora's backers maintained that the more than 700,000 ballots cast for Plínio Salgado would otherwise have gone to their candidate, giving him the victory. Each of the candidates, however, accepted the results without serious protest.

Kubitschek and Goulart had been elected by the people, but their right to take office was to be decided by the army. After a brief period of quiet while the ballots were counted, the rumors of a coup d'etat became even more intense than before. In this atmosphere, a politically inflammatory peroration at the funeral of General Canrobert Pereira da Costa, on November 1, set in motion a series of events that culminated in the paradoxical "countercoup" of November 11, 1955. The speaker, Colonel Jurandir Mamede of the Superior War College, in his fiery denunciation of the "suicidal insanity" of politicians who placed personal and partisan interests before "the higher interests of the Fatherland," appeared to be reiterating the intransigent opposition of the Democratic Crusade to Kubitschek and Goulart. War Minister Lott demanded that Mamede be disciplined for violating military regulations barring officers from publicly expressing controversial political views. He had previously dismissed pro-Vargas officers from their posts for similar violations. But Lott lacked jurisdiction over staff members of the War College, and Mamede's superiors held that no infringement of regulations had occurred. The press immediately inflated the Mamede affair all out of proportion to its true significance, presenting it as a test of strength between the War Minister and proponents of a coup d'etat. In the glare of publicity neither side could compromise gracefully. Both appealed to the President, who alone could resolve the question. Meanwhile, however, President Café had suffered a mild heart attack on November 3. Five days later he entered the hospital, after transferring power temporarily to his constitutional successor, Carlos Luz, Speaker of the Chamber of Deputies. Thus, Acting President Luz, a PSD dissident who had opposed the Kubitschek candidacy, faced the alternative of ruling in Lott's favor or accepting the War Minister's resignation. Luz chose the latter course. On November 10, he arranged with Lott for the formal installation of a new War Minister the following afternoon. This decision was acceptable to Lott, but not to the leaders of the Constitutional Military Movement, who persuaded him that the Mamede speech, Café's illness, and Luz's actions were all deliberate steps in a plot to nullify the verdict of the polls. At the behest of General Odílio Denys, commander of the army garrison in Rio de Janeiro, Lott decided to remain in office and to assume leadership of a "countercoup" to assure the inauguration of Kubitschek and Goulart.

In the early morning hours of November 11, 1955, the deposed War Minister led troops and tanks in a bloodless revolt against the regime. Luz, accompanied by Colonel Mamede, Congressman Carlos Lacerda, and some members of the cabinet, took refuge aboard the naval cruiser *Tamandaré*, and steamed under fire for Santos, where he hoped to organize resistance against the rebels. The effort failed, however, since the army remained loyal to Lott, and Governor Jânio Quadros refused to aid the Acting President. Two days later Luz returned to Rio de Janeiro aboard the *Tamandaré*. In the meantime Congress had acted promptly to replace him with the Vice-President of the Senate, Nereu Ramos, next in the constitutional order of succession to the presidency. No serious penalties were levied against the defenders of the brief Luz administration, although Colonel Mamede was transferred to a remote army recruiting station in the interior, and Carlos Lacerda chose voluntary exile in Portugal. Luz resigned as Speaker of the Chamber of Deputies, but resumed his seat as a representative from Minas Gerais. General Lott remained as head of the War Ministry and as unofficial strong man of Brazil. On November 22, 1955, when Café sought to resume the presidency, Congress voted to impede him, authorizing an *ex post facto* state of siege from November 11 in order to deny him access to the courts. The state of siege was subsequently renewed to run until January 31, 1956, when Nereu Ramos formally transferred the presidency to Juscelino Kubitschek. In the same ceremony João Goulart took the oath of office as Vice-President. As a result of the "countercoup," which violated the Constitution on the pretext of preventing a more drastic departure from constitutional norms, Kubitschek in fact owed his office to War Minister Lott and the army rather than to the electorate.

Juscelino Kubitschek de Oliveira, the new President of Brazil, was a product of the Vargas era and a self-made man. He was born at Diamantina, Minas Gerais, in 1902. Left fatherless when still an infant, he was raised by his mother, a grammar school teacher of Czech descent, who inspired in her son a deep respect and desire for learning, and a burning ambition to rise above the genteel poverty that marked his early years. Kubitschek was largely self-supporting from the age of twelve, working as a delivery boy in Diamantina, and later as a telegraph operator while attending medical school in Belo Horizonte. After a period of travel and postgraduate study in Europe, he returned home in 1930 to establish a private practice and accept a position as surgeon in the state police force. During the revolution of 1932 he was officer in charge of medical services on the São Paulo front, where he attracted the attention of Benedito Valadares, a rising figure in the Vargas political machine in Minas Gerais. As a protégé of Valadares, his political career was assured. In the next two years he occupied several positions in the state administration, then served as a federal deputy from 1934 to 1937, and was appointed mayor of Belo Horizonte in 1940, a post he retained until the end of the Estado Novo. In 1945, with Valadares, he became a charter member of the PSD in Minas Gerais. Kubitschek campaigned successfully for the Constituent Assembly, helped to draft the Constitution of 1946, and served in the Chamber of Deputies until 1951. In that year he was elected governor of his home state and began to acquire national stature as a dynamic administrator. Kubitschek achieved remarkable material progress in his program to improve his state's economic structure—chiefly in power and transportation—in order to attract industry there. His greatest innovation was the creation of joint capital corporations, through which the state government and private enterprise cooperated in constructing thermo- and hydroelectric generating facilities. During his four-year term as governor, highway mileage in the state increased five-fold and electric power output tripled. It was largely on the strength of these accomplishments that Kubitschek received the presidential nomination of his party in 1954.

As a candidate for the presidency, Kubitschek appealed to the Vargas legend, to the widespread spirit of nationalism, and above all to the nearly universal desire of Brazilians for rapid economic development. Presenting industrialization as the panacea that would permit Brazil to provide a higher standard of living for its burgeoning population, he offered the nation a modified version of the program and techniques that had proved successful in Minas Gerais. Like his rivals in the presidential race, Kubitschek also promised improvements in public health, social welfare, and education. Unlike them, he vowed to transfer the federal capital to the interior of the country. This pledge later became a vital element in his administrative program, but during the campaign itself his platform and public pronouncements focused predominantly on a list of thirty specific objectives—chiefly production goals—to be attained by 1960 in the fields of transportation, power, food, and basic industries. Kubitschek insisted the Republic must have daring, imaginative leadership with confidence in the future, willing to spend heavily to develop domestic sources of energy, determined to create a vast network of roads and highways to unite the distant regions of the country, and prepared to supply the credits, tariff protection, and other incentives necessary to speed the growth of private industry. He promised that his program would give Brazil "fifty years of progress in five." Only in this way, he maintained, building on the foundations laid by Getúlio Vargas, would Brazil become a modern, industrial nation able to achieve its great destiny as a world power.

Kubitschek's five years in office were a period of political peace and tremendous economic activity in Brazil. An atmosphere of optimism and expectation prevailed, in sharp contrast to the political climate of the preceding presidential term. Partisan politics continued to be waged as intensely as before, but virtually all factions now seemed content to follow democratic, constitutional procedures. The possibility of military intervention was not seriously considered by the armed forces or the political parties, either in the congressional elections of 1958 or in the hotly contested presidential campaign of 1960. Kubitschek was able to complete his full term with only two insignificant, if dramatic, protests by a handful of air force officers. During his administration Brazil seemed finally to have achieved the balance of political order and economic progress that had been a goal of the Republic since its inception.

The record of the Kubitschek administration in the economic sphere was truly impressive. The great majority of the President's highly publicized production goals in both the public and private sectors were achieved or surpassed. Electric-power-generating capacity was raised from three million kilowatts to five million, and construction was begun on additional projects to add another three million kilowatts by 1965. Comparable gains were registered in the petroleum field. Proven reserves were expanded by 1,400 per cent, daily production was raised to 100,000 barrels, the tanker fleet was doubled, and refinery capacity was tripled, enabling it to meet current domestic needs. The opening of new roads and highways—more than 11,000 miles, of which nearly one-third were paved—represented an increase of 80 per cent over the mileage existing in 1955. The government subsidized the acquisition of new aircraft by private airlines, and revived Brazil's moribund merchant fleet with the purchase of eighty modern vessels, making it the largest in Latin America. Agriculture, which continued to account for more than half of the labor force, received comparatively little attention from the Kubitschek administration, but even here some notable gains were made. Storage facilities for grains and perishables were expanded by more than 500 per cent, the production of fertilizers exceeded the original goal by more than one-third, over twenty-five thousand tractors were imported for farm use, and by the end of 1960 tractors of Brazilian manufacture were beginning to appear on the market. It was the industrial sector, however, that benefited most directly from the policies of the regime. The output of steel was nearly doubled to about two million tons per year, and two additional mixed-capital plants with a potential capacity of two million tons were under construction at the end of Kubitschek's term. Increases of up to 800 per cent were recorded in the production of aluminum and other nonferrous metals, and Brazil became self-sufficient in the production of cement. The availability of these materials, and of power and transportation, permitted the introduction or expansion of a broad range of manufacturing industries. The most striking innovation was the creation—behind prohibitive tariff barriers—of an automobile industry that produced 130,000 trucks and cars in 1960. The announced goals in the output of wheat, coal, rubber, and iron ore were not met, although there was a substantial increase in the production of each of these commodities during the Kubitschek administration.

Overall, Kubitschek may have given Brazil something less than the promised fifty years of progress, as measured in strictly material terms, but it is evident that his administration sparked an unprecedented burst of economic expansion. There is no question, moreover, of the impact of the Kubitschek years on Brazilian attitudes toward economic development. During those years, as the Brazilian people surpassed the "impossible" goals Kubitschek had established, doubts about the feasibility of rapid economic growth, and their own ability to sustain such growth, were swept away. The President's infectious confidence in Brazil's continued progress was accepted, consciously or otherwise, as a veritable article of faith by nationalists of all political persuasions.

The construction of Brasília, which became the capital of Brazil in 1960, seems likely to stand as the most far-reaching accomplishment of the Kubitschek administration and as a lasting monument to Brazilian nationalism. A long-cherished dream of Brazilian visionaries was realized with the establishment of this futuristic city in the wilderness. The transfer of the capital to the interior had been proposed in the eighteenth century by Tiradentes, the precursor of independence, and in 1823 by José Bonifácio de Andrada e Silva. The dream had been transformed into a national aspiration and a continuing commitment of the Republic when it was incorporated into the Constitution of 1891 and reiterated in the charters promulgated in 1934 and 1946. A tentative site on the remote and empty plateau of eastern Goiás was selected in 1892, a symbolic cornerstone was placed by President Epitácio Pessoa on the first centenary of independence in 1922, and until at least 1950 official maps of Brazil regularly showed the location of the future Federal District. For practical purposes, however, the constitutional provision remained a dead letter until Kubitschek seized upon it, almost by chance, in his campaign for the presidency. Encountering unexpected public enthusiasm for the proposal, he vowed to complete his term in the new capital.

Brasília proved to be the capstone and principal symbol of Kubitschek's developmental program. The shift of the capital was justified by the administration on political, economic, social, and psychological grounds. The existence of Brasília would hasten effective settlement and economic development of the interior. The location of the capital near the geographic center of the nation would facilitate the integration of the hinterland with the populous coastal areas, bringing an end to the isolation and backwardness of the rural population. And, at least incidentally, government leaders, legislators, and bureaucrats might be expected to view national problems more objectively, once they were removed from the pressures and distractions of Rio de Janeiro. The basic purpose of Brasília, however, was to break the "colonial" mentality of the Brazilian people and to reduce their traditional dependence upon the world overseas. Brasília would force them to look inward upon the country and its untapped potential, to rely more heavily upon their own resources, rather than to seek inspiration, assistance, and prosperity abroad, as they had always done. Advocates of the new capital insisted that these changes would never come as long as the seat of the government remained on the Atlantic seaboard.

Once in office, Kubitschek gave the Brasília project top priority. Enabling legislation for the transfer of the capital was approved by Congress, with considerable skepticism, in September 1956. An international competition—won by Lúcio Costa—was held to select a plan for the city, and world-famed architect Oscar Niemeyer was placed in charge of architectural design. For three-and-one-half years construction was pushed at a frantic pace, with men and equipment being flown to the site until access roads were opened. While it was still under construction, Brasília became the hub of a network of trunk highways connecting the northern and western regions of the country with Rio de Janeiro, São Paulo, and the south of Brazil. A steady stream of workmen and their families poured into Brasília over these new routes, giving the future Federal District a population of more than 140,000 by 1960. Although construction was by no means completed, the formal inauguration took place on schedule. On Tiradentes Day, April 21, 1960, the seat of government was officially transferred to Brasília. By the same act Rio de Janeiro became the State of Guanabara. The transfer, however, was largely symbolic. In effect, Brazil now had two capitals. The Congress met in Brasília, but the cabinet ministries remained in Rio de Janeiro, where much of the business of government continued to be conducted as it had for the preceding 197 years. Nevertheless, the attainment of Kubitschek's most difficult goal was hailed by most of the population outside Rio de Janeiro as an irreversible step toward national greatness. In the euphoria of the moment few persons were concerned about, or even acutely conscious of, the unnecessarily high cost of the new capital.

The remarkable material progress in Brazil under Kubitschek was balanced by a spectacular expansion of the public debt and depreciation of the currency. The five-year program of development was financed in large part by heavy foreign borrowing, deficit spending, and inflation. At the same time, the boom psychology and the progressive reduction of the real income of salaried persons combined to encourage a general lowering of standards against graft and corruption by government officials and tax evasion by the public. These problems were not new to Brazil, but during the Kubitschek administration they assumed new and staggering proportions, drawing increasingly bitter criticism from opponents of the regime. Government expenditures consistently outran revenues by a wide margin, contributing to a three-fold rise in the money supply and in the cost of living, as well as to a comparable decline in the value of the cruzeiro. The external public debt, which had stood at 600 million dollars in 1955, soared to more than 2,000 million. The Kubitschek administration contracted over 500 million dollars in short- and medium-term loans from the United States alone. To a large extent the financial policies of the administration were adopted as a calculated risk. Kubitschek and his advisers regarded inflation as a necessary concomitant of economic growth, and large foreign loans as indispensable for the desired rapid rate of expansion in the basic services that were required to attract ever-larger investments of private capital in the industrial sector. They expected that increases in production, which they saw as the real wealth of the nation, would provide the means to repay the huge investment in the economy, that local manufactures would supply most of the demand for consumer goods, and that a substantial increase in exports would earn the foreign exchange necessary to amortize loans from abroad. These calculations—highly optimistic, if not visionary—were undermined by an unexpected rise in domestic consumption that reduced the quantity of products available for sale abroad, and by a simultaneous sharp drop in the world market price for Brazil's major exports. Thus, before Kubitschek left office he was forced to resort to further borrowing in order to service the public debt. He bequeathed his successor a heavy schedule of payments that seemed likely to require either difficult renegotiations with foreign creditors or a drastic and politically unpalatable reduction in the level of public expenditures.

The Kubitschek administration maintained Brazil's well-established foreign policies of close and friendly cooperation with the United States, and active participation in international bodies. At the United Nations and in the Organization of American States, Brazil was a consistent advocate of disarmament, peaceful settlement of disputes, and greater assistance by the industrial powers in the economic development of Latin America. Following the Suez crisis in 1956 and the Congo crisis in 1960, Brazil contributed military detachments to the United Nations Emergency Forces in those areas. In 1957, after a year of acrimonious debate in the press and Congress, the Kubitschek administration granted the United States authorization to construct and operate for five years a missile-tracking station on the island of Fernando de Noronha. The decision was made over the strenuous protests of leftist nationalists, who denounced it as a limitation on Brazilian sovereignty. Kubitschek's most important foreign policy innovation was Operation Pan-America (OPA), later hailed as the forerunner of the Alliance For Progress. OPA was a proposal for a massive and coordinated program of economic development throughout Latin America, involving reciprocal assistance by the Latin-American governments with unprecedented financial support from the United States and international lending agencies. The cool reception of this proposal abroad apparently contributed to the sharp deterioration of Brazil's relations with the International Monetary Fund in the last year of Kubitschek's term. During that year Brazil's relations with Cuba also became controversial. Ultranationalists praised the Castro revolution as a precedent to be followed in Brazil, while moderates and conservatives publicly deplored the violence of the Castro regime and its disregard for legal norms. The Kubitschek government pursued a policy between these extremes, reiterating Brazil's traditional defense of the principle of self-determination, but granting asylum to Cuban refugees and voting in the Organization of American States to condemn international Communist intervention in the island republic. Controversy over the Cuban question added to the atmosphere of exaggerated nationalism in which the electoral campaign of 1960 was conducted.

Significantly, appeals to the Vargas legend were muted in the presidential campaign. The established political leadership continued to be divided roughly into pro-Vargas and anti-Vargas camps, for the underlying social and political questions of the Vargas era were still unresolved. But these questions were increasingly identified with new personalities, who expressed them in different terms to a young and rapidly expanding electorate. At least half of the voters—those who had come of age since the fall of the Estado Novo—seemed indifferent to the name of the ex-dictator. They had been stimulated, however, by Kubitschek's approach to national development, and entered vociferously into the debate over the errors and omissions of his program.

The successes and shortcomings of Kubitschek's policies thus largely determined the issues in the 1960 campaign. For the great majority of the people, the most serious and immediate issue was inflation, which kept living costs spiraling constantly upward ahead of increases in wages and salaries. Indignant protests were also lodged against inefficiency and corruption in government, and against the neglect of agriculture, education, health, and social welfare. Spokesmen for outlying regions complained that the new industries had been concentrated overwhelmingly in São Paulo, that the economic needs of other areas were being ignored. Conservatives objected that labor exerted an undue influence on the regime, and that Kubitschek was overly tolerant of agitation and propaganda by students and left-wing groups seeking to undermine traditional Brazilian institutions. The political left, and ultranationalists generally, countered with charges that the Kubitschek program favored the wealthy and had opened Brazil to selfish exploitation by foreign capital. The regime was denounced for failure to revise the tax structure, to nationalize basic industries, to tighten controls on the entry of foreign investments, and to restrict the remission of profits abroad. Those seeking to lead the rural populace into the political arena also denounced Kubitschek's failure to effect a sweeping agrarian reform. In the conduct of foreign affairs the administration was attacked for alleged servility to the United States, and for refusal to take full advantage of opportunities to open new markets in the Communist bloc. For months before the elections the public was subjected to an incessant barrage of such charges and denunciations declaimed in highly nationalistic terms. Under the circumstances, all presidential aspirants presented themselves as ardent nationalists, determined to solve the problem of inflation without slowing the pace of economic growth.

The presidential campaign developed into a three-way race between Marshal Henrique Teixeira Lott, Adhemar de Barros, now mayor of São Paulo, and Jânio Quadros, a congressman from Paraná and former governor of São Paulo. Lott, who resigned from the War Ministry to become the administration candidate, was backed by the PSD, the PTB, and a coalition of minor leftist parties. He waged a lackluster campaign on the basis of the Kubitschek record and on his own reputation for impeccable honesty and a deep sense of responsibility to the nation. De Barros, again the nominee of his own PSP, did not present a coherent program, but in his flamboyant oratory seemed to promise a larger role for private capital and a substantial increase in social welfare. Both Lott and de Barros promised to preserve Brazil's customary foreign policies, including firm alignment with the West in the Cold War. The unpredictable and charismatic Quadros, who had risen from political obscurity to national prominence in less than a decade, headed the UDN ticket. Quadros carried the burden of the opposition. With a new broom as his symbol, he promised to sweep out corruption, to administer the nation's finances with efficiency and scrupulous honesty, as he had done in São Paulo, to bring social justice to the underprivileged, and to give Brazil a truly "independent" foreign policy. These appeals reached every major sector of society. The vice-presidential candidates were João "Jango" Goulart, who was seeking to succeed himself in office; Fernando Ferrari, a reform-minded dissident from the PTB who sought to convert that organization into a genuine labor party; and Milton Campos, again the candidate of the UDN.

The inconsistencies and paradoxes of the 1960 campaign were underscored by the actions of the illegal Communist party and Vice-President Goulart. Logically, the Communists should have thrown their support to Quadros, who was promising to carry out the major reforms they had long demanded. The party, however, opposed him with all the means at its disposal, giving its full backing to the Lott-Goulart ticket, despite Lott's well-known anti-Communist views. Communist leaders reasoned, privately, that after ten years of the Kubitschek-Lott program Brazil would be ripe for revolution from the left. At the same time, Goulart allowed his supporters to link his name with the Quadros campaign. Throughout the country Jânio-Jango committees were more active than the administration-sponsored committees promoting the Lott-Goulart slate. In this welter of confusion, over twelve million voters went to the polls on October 3, 1960, to give Quadros the largest vote ever received by a candidate for public office in Brazil. He polled 5,636,623 ballots, nearly 45 per cent of the total, as opposed to about 31 per cent for Lott and just over 17 per cent for Adhemar de Barros. The effectiveness of the Jânio-Jango campaign was seen in the vice-presidential vote, for Goulart won reelection with a plurality of 36 per cent, over Campos with about 34 per cent. Ferrari polled 17 per cent of the total. Goulart's narrow victory over Quadros's running mate was to have far-reaching implications for Brazil within a year after the elections.

Jânio da Silva Quadros was a new phenomenon on the political scene. His meteoric career was unparalleled in Brazil. As the champion of the common man he had gone from victory to victory, defying the normal standards and taboos of the successful politician. Where others were polished and urbane, Quadros was disheveled and brusque. He converted his gaunt, wall-eyed features into political assets by a flair for stagecraft that both intrigued his audiences and led his early adversaries to dismiss him as a harmless clown. Quadros won a huge popular following with his consistent and convincing public display of respect for the dignity of the individual, no matter how humble. Yet in his personal contacts he was often oblivious to the sensibilities of colleagues and subordinates who displeased him. In an environment in which party loyalties were easily transferred, Quadros was notorious for his cavalier attitude toward political parties. His path was strewn with the wreckage of small parties he had used and discarded at his convenience. His insatiable ego gave him confidence that such organizations would always be at his disposal.

Quadros was born in Mato Grosso and lived as a boy in Paraná, but was identified in politics with São Paulo. It was there that he completed his education and entered public service as a secondary-school teacher. In 1948, at the age of thirty, he ran successfully on the Brazilian Socialist party ticket for the São Paulo city council, a post he resigned in 1951 to enter the state legislature as a representative of the Christian Democratic party. Two years later, as the candidate of a Christian Democratic–National Labor party coalition, Quadros attracted national attention with his surprise election as prefect of the city of São Paulo. His growing reputation as a giant-killer was confirmed in 1954, when he defeated Adhemar de Barros for the governorship of the state. To this point each of his posts had been used as a springboard to higher office. Now, for the first time in his career, Quadros served out the full term for which he had been elected. As governor he made no secret of his presidential aspirations, but devoted his energies primarily to the problems of the state government and to consolidation of his political strength in São Paulo. By employing drastic methods to eliminate waste and inefficiency, Quadros gave the state the most effective and personal administration it had known for many years. At the end of his term, in 1958, he had little difficulty in getting his Finance Secretary, Professor Carlos Carvalho Pinto, elected as his successor, and won election for himself as a federal deputy from Paraná on the PTB ticket. Of the 326 candidates elected to the Chamber of Deputies, only four veteran campaigners seeking reelection polled larger votes than Quadros in his first bid for national office. This resounding victory added further to his prestige and political appeal throughout Brazil, enabling him to secure the backing of the UDN in the campaign for the presidency of the nation.

The election of Quadros as President of Brazil was acclaimed as a revolution at the polls. By a decisive margin the people had rejected the political crowd that had controlled the executive branch almost without interruption since 1945. The anti-Vargas forces, who had missed their opportunity to rule six years earlier, had been given a second chance. It seemed that Brazil was now to have a genuine alternation of power between the opposition and administration parties. This government was expected to continue all that was positive in Kubitschek's developmental program, but to eliminate the inequities and injustices that had been tolerated by the outgoing regime. São Paulo could not fail to benefit. For the first time in thirty years a Paulista occupied the presidency. But at the same time the economically depressed regions of the country, the Northeast in particular, were also to know the blessings of industrialization, and to receive a more generous subsidy from the national treasury. The legitimate grievances of the underprivileged, whose quest for dignity and a better life had been subordinated to the urgency of material progress, were now to be acknowledged. And in its relations with foreign powers the Quadros administration was expected to demonstrate that Brazil was capable of making its own decisions in the light of its own interests. In short, virtually every vocal group that had felt thwarted or disappointed by the Kubitschek administration looked to Quadros to resolve its difficulties and satisfy its aspirations. Never had so many Brazilians pinned their hopes on a single national leader.

Few of these hopes and expectations were to be realized under the new President. On August 25, 1961, less than seven months after taking office, Quadros resigned. This unheralded action came as a complete surprise and shock to both the public and his most intimate colleagues. His motives can only be surmised, for aside from a vague and unconvincing statement about "terrible forces" that made it impossible for him to govern the country, Quadros has not sought to explain them. Clearly, during his brief tenure he had not been able to work miracles, but he faced no hazards that had not been encountered by earlier Presidents. The problems of inflation and the public debt had not succumbed to palliatives or rhetoric. The bureaucracy, the political parties, and the state administrations had resisted his efforts to impose fiscal responsibility and a higher standard for conduct in public office. He had irritated members of the administration by his close personal supervision of cabinet ministers, whom he deluged in a flow of hastily scribbled directives. Even his most successful venture, the redirection of Brazil's foreign policies away from the United States and the West toward the neutralist and Communist blocs, which had been enthusiastically received by his popular following, had caused serious misgivings in other quarters. Moderate supporters of the regime doubted that Quadros's aggressively "independent" policies in fact served the nation's best interests. In his few months in power, Quadros had arranged to establish or resume diplomatic relations with the Communist countries of Europe, had resisted all pressures from the inter-American community for joint action on Cuba, had pointedly and publicly affronted the personal representative of President Kennedy, had bestowed Brazil's highest medal for foreigners on the Cuban Minister of Industries, Ernesto "Che" Guevara, and had sent Vice-President Goulart as head of a state mission to visit the Soviet Union and Communist China. Quadros's pursuit of controversial foreign policy goals and his conduct of domestic affairs disillusioned some UDN leaders, and led to an open break with Carlos Lacerda, now governor of Guanabara. Formerly one of Quadros's staunchest supporters in the UDN, Lacerda denounced him bitterly, accusing him of seeking to become a dictator. There may have been some validity in Lacerda's charges, for Quadros had certainly been frustrated in his dealings with Congress. This body, elected in 1958, did not reflect the realignment of political forces or the zeal for reform evident in the election of Quadros. Obliged to meet in Brasília, against the wishes of the majority of its members, Congress frequently lacked a quorum to pass on Quadros's peremptory demands for legislation. None of the key bills in the administration's domestic program were enacted into law during the seven months Jânio Quadros served as President of Brazil. The legislators would neither cooperate on his terms, nor permit him to rule by decree.

Under the circumstances, it seems clear that Quadros's offer of resignation was intended to be a power play to strengthen his position at the expense of the legislature. He must have felt confident either that Congress would refuse to accept the resignation or that the people would insist he remain in office. He could reasonably assume that the alternative—the elevation of Vice-President João Goulart to the presidency—would be unacceptable to the administration parties and, more importantly, to the armed forces. It is significant that Quadros made his dramatic gesture while Goulart was absent from the country, thus allowing time for public reaction to the resignation before the Vice-President might be formally installed as chief of state. Quadros must have been stunned by the alacrity with which the leaders of Congress accepted the resignation, declared the presidency vacant, and, as provided in the Constitution, installed the Speaker of the Chamber of Deputies, Pascoal Ranieri Mazzilli, as interim President. For reasons known only to himself, he issued no call to his popular following, which remained inert in the absence of leadership. Returning to São Paulo, Quadros boarded a ship for Europe and for temporary, self-imposed exile, leaving the country embroiled in the crisis he had caused.

Brazil's democratic institutions were strained almost to the breaking point by Quadros's resignation, for it posed a dilemma that appeared insoluble by legal means. The immediate question was whether the armed forces, which had intervened ostensibly to preserve the Constitution in 1955, would now violate the Constitution to prevent Vice-President Goulart from assuming the presidency. There was no legal cloud on Goulart's claim to the highest office upon his return to Brazil. Nonetheless, the military cabinet officers, led by War Minister Odílio Denys, insisted that Goulart could not become President, and called upon the Congress to find a constitutional solution to the impasse. Had the Congress been meeting in Rio de Janeiro, where most military commanders and the Lacerda administration applauded the War Minister's demand, it would almost certainly have acquiesced to military pressure. But in the comparative isolation of Brasília, the majority of the legislators refused to submit to dictation by the armed forces. Even bitter political foes of the Vice-President upheld his constitutional right to take office. For a week, while Goulart slowly made his way home from the Orient, the nation hovered on the brink of civil war. In Rio Grande do Sul, Governor Leonel Brizola, Goulart's brother-in-law, began arming a popular militia and threatened to install his kinsman by force if necessary. In Rio de Janeiro, Marshal Lott, now in retirement, issued a public statement supporting Goulart and appealing to the army to defend the letter of the law. Lott was arrested, but his appeal on behalf of legality was cheered by most of the press and public elsewhere in Brazil. Following this appeal, General José Machado Lopes, commander of the army garrison in Pôrto Alegre, cast his lot with Governor Brizola, defying further orders from Denys. The crisis heightened when Goulart arrived in Pôrto Alegre, at which point army troops from São Paulo were marching south to suppress the resistance to the War Minister.

At this juncture, to avert open warfare between elements of the army, a dramatic compromise was reached in Brasília. By constitutional amendment Congress changed the form of government. For the first time since 1889 Brazil was to have parliamentary rule. The President was reduced to little more than a figurehead, for executive powers would be exercised by a council of ministers drawn from and responsible to the legislature. Under this arrangement the military ministers resigned, and Goulart was permitted to take office formally on September 7, 1961. The compromise was jubilantly, if prematurely, interpreted by the press and Congress as a victory for civilian democracy and as proof that it was no longer necessary or proper for the military to determine the national interest in moments of crisis.

The experiment with parliamentary government was a complete failure. Goulart had accepted the compromise as the price he must pay to attain the presidency, and used all of his influence as President and as head of the PTB to discredit the parliamentary system. Congress, except for a tiny band of enthusiasts, had accepted it as a convenient expedient to resolve the political crisis. And public opinion appeared to range from total indifference to opposition. In short, no important group was vitally concerned to make the system work effectively. Yet, the legislators were unwilling to surrender their new-found political power to the President. The result was a stalemate. Prime Ministers and cabinets changed with increasing frequency as Goulart and Congress exchanged recriminations. Each sought to blame the other for governmental inaction, while mounting social and economic grievances went unattended. After sixteen months Congress was obliged to authorize a plebiscite by which the electorate might vote to retain the parliamentary system or restore the traditional form of government. In the balloting on January 6, 1963, over nine million of twelve million voters rejected the compromise, and Goulart was granted full presidential powers. The armed forces, discredited by the failure of their intervention in 1961, made no effort to protest the verdict of the polls.

João Goulart was not yet forty-five years of age when he became President in his own right, although he had been active in national politics for a decade and a half. He had served as vice-president and subsequently as president of the PTB, as Minister of Labor, twice as Vice-President of the Republic, and most recently as titular chief of state. He had never held public office at the local or state level. Goulart was born March 1, 1918, near São Borja, Rio Grande do Sul, where his father was a prominent rancher. He was trained in the law, but never practiced the profession, preferring to manage the family cattle business until he met Getúlio Vargas in 1945. Goulart became a close friend and protégé of the ex-dictator, who made him responsible for organizing trade-union support for the PTB. In this capacity Goulart entered the political arena, working closely and effectively with a broad spectrum of labor politicians, including Communists. Until he was driven from power in 1964, the urban labor movement was to be his principal source of strength, although he always tried to develop an electoral following in the rural areas, within the military, and among the middle and upper classes as well. Goulart held no strong ideological convictions. His basic tenets in politics, which he had learned from Vargas, were to make no permanent enemies and to avoid total commitment to any one group. He was widely respected as an adroit manipulator, admired by friends for his political flexibility, and denounced by his enemies as an unprincipled opportunist. This was the man who was expected to bring order, fiscal sanity, and social justice out of the wreckage of the parliamentary experiment.

The air of optimism and confidence that had prevailed at the beginning of the Kubitschek and Quadros administrations was noticeably absent in January 1963. The climate of opinion was conducive neither to optimism nor to effective political compromise. The economic situation, while not yet desperate, had deteriorated markedly since Quadros's resignation. The cost of living had risen by 60 per cent, and there had been a 200 per cent drop in the exchange value of the cruzeiro. The gross national product, after rising steadily through 1960, had entered a period of decline that was not to be reversed for nearly four years. Inflation, previously regarded as a sign of healthy economic growth, now became the major obstacle to further growth, and the primary political problem facing the country. The economic trend was reflected in mounting social unrest and increasing polarization in politics. Xenophobic nationalism and demagoguery were on the rise. "Revolution" was a prominent expression in the vocabulary of every politician seeking public office. This was particularly evident in the Northeast, where the rural lower class had been made aware of its plight and of the possibility of agrarian reform. The need for basic reforms in landholding, education, the electoral system, the tax structure, and the nation's finances was generally recognized, but there was no consensus among or within the political parties on what the priority or exact nature of such reforms should be. No politically articulate group in the population was prepared to sacrifice its immediate interests for the national welfare.

Despite the serious difficulties confronting the regime, Goulart still might have provided the dynamic leadership the nation had demanded on January 6. He enjoyed several strong political assets and appeared to be using them to full advantage during the early weeks of his administration. The plebiscite had been an overwhelming vote of confidence in civilian, presidential rule. Goulart was virtually free from interference by the armed forces, and could look forward to three years in office. In anticipation of the plebiscite, he had called upon one of Brazil's foremost economists, Celso Furtado, to draft a three-year economic recovery plan to reduce inflation to manageable proportions, to appease foreign creditors, and to accelerate the pace of industrial and social development. As Finance Minister, responsible for carrying out the economic program, Goulart appointed Congressman Francisco Santiago Dantas, a moderate nationalist respected by the major political parties. Prospects for congressional support had brightened, for the administration was now backed by the PSD as well as by Goulart's PTB. The two parties commanded a large majority in both houses of the new Congress, which had been elected on October 7, 1962, for the term beginning in March 1963. In these promising circumstances, the Goulart

administration received a commitment for substantial financial assistance from the United States. After a year and a half of continuous crisis,
it seemed that the nation had found the route to political stability and
orderly socio-economic progress.

The success of Goulart's program depended upon his ability to impose unpopular austerity measures that in the short run would be felt
most severely by the working class and by salaried employees of the government and the business community. Had he been willing to resist the
demands of labor and the bureaucracy, and to ignore virulent criticism
by the ultranationalist minority within the administration parties, he
could have secured the indispensable cooperation of congressional moderates. As a labor politician, however, he was unwilling to risk losing
his following to radical extremists who were competing for control of
the mass urban vote and the newly aroused peasantry. Consequently, he
vacillated. In attempting to please both moderates and leftists, he satisfied neither and widened the gap between them. By authorizing un-
scheduled wage and salary increases, and tolerating widespread corruption in public office, he negated measures taken to contain the inflationary spiral. By allowing Communists and other leftists to strengthen their
position in the labor movement, to infiltrate the bureaucracy, and to
appear conspicuously among his advisers, Goulart gave the impression
that he was seeking to destroy the bases of constitutional government
and to perpetuate himself in power. These actions not only drove the
moderates into the arms of the old anti-Vargas civilian elements, but
brought the military back into the political arena in its traditional role
as guarantor of national institutions.

Congress and the political parties shared responsibility with Goulart
for prolonging the deadlock between the executive and the legislature.
And the congressional opposition was at least partially responsible for
forcing Goulart to adopt a more extreme position than he would
otherwise have chosen. To an increasingly disgruntled public, Congress seemed to have degenerated into a sterile debating society, advo-
cating incompatible extremist solutions to national problems while enjoying the lavish perquisites of office. A majority of the legislators in
all the parties appeared to be more interested in blocking the administration program than in working out feasible alternatives. The negative
attitude of Congress was illustrated in its treatment of Goulart's agrarian
reform bill, which was submitted in March 1963. The bill violated constitutional provisions that expropriated properties be paid for in full
at the time of expropriation. Clearly, here was a controversial question
within the jurisdiction of the legislature. It might reject the bill, modify

it, or approve it and amend the Constitution. Congress, however, took a fourth course. With its members deadlocked, it shelved the agrarian reform measure for an entire year. When Goulart later denounced congressional inaction as deliberate and called for a constituent assembly to revise the Constitution, ostensibly to permit enactment of his basic reform program, opponents in Congress attacked the proposal as a smokescreen. They claimed, not without apparent justification, that he intended to alter the Constitution to allow his own reelection. When neither the President nor the legislature had faith in the integrity of the other, all possibility of meaningful cooperation between them vanished.

By early 1964 the situation was calamitous, and there seemed no constitutional way to avert disaster. Under Goulart inflation was completely uncontrolled. The cost of living had risen by 70 per cent during 1963 and was rising twice as fast in the first three months of the new year. Despite higher wages, the living standards of the urban working force had fallen. Sporadic violence had already broken out in some rural areas, as peasant leagues attempted to seize the lands to which they felt entitled, and property owners resisted force with force. The middle class was almost entirely alienated from the regime, for it was convinced that Goulart was leading the nation to chaos, perhaps even to a Communist seizure of power. And it feared that the common people would support him if his bid for a constituent assembly were put to a vote.

In these circumstances the anti-Vargas forces, who had been excluded from power since the resignation of Quadros, gained renewed strength and determination. During 1963, sensing that they must either reverse the trend of events or risk becoming a permanent opposition that would have no real chance to gain power by legal means, they had intensified the attack on Goulart as the chief heir and beneficiary of the Vargas tradition. Governor Carlos Lacerda of Guanabara was again the most virulent spokesman of the opposition, publicly denouncing the regime as a mortal threat to national institutions and to Brazil's Christian heritage. At the same time, the UDN governor of Minas Gerais, José de Magalhães Pinto, was working quietly with Lacerda and the PSP governor of São Paulo, Adhemar de Barros, to enlist civilian and military support for a revolution.

Goulart's effectiveness as President was lost when the public abandoned its intransigent defense of civilian constitutional rule, which had been a major bulwark of his administration. Nonetheless, he might have survived in office for the remainder of his term had he not also united the armed services against him. Although he did not initially fear serious opposition by the armed forces, Goulart was fully aware of the suspicions of many officers and of their grave concern over the leftward drift of national politics since 1961. Accordingly, he took special pains to praise the military's tradition of legality, and to reward those officers who placed this tradition above their extraconstitutional role as arbiters of the political process. In this respect Goulart's military policy did not differ noticeably from that of his predecessors in the presidency. He departed radically from precedent, however, in seeking to develop a personal following among enlisted and noncommissioned ranks. Goulart permitted Communists and other leftist agitators to infiltrate the military establishments, and he actively encouraged the political aspirations of sergeants and corporals, who were barred from public office under existing laws. His objective was to create a labor-military apparatus that would both reinforce popular pressures in support of his reform program and be a counterweight to the officer corps. In pursuing this goal, Goulart assured the hostility of the military commanders. During 1963 uncoordinated plotting by disgruntled officers spread rapidly and almost spontaneously throughout the services, as it became evident that Goulart's courting of subalterns was greatly reducing the military and political effectiveness of the navy and air force. By the end of the year the overwhelming majority of officers in each service were convinced that Goulart must be checked or removed from office, for he was undermining the very foundations of the military structure, discipline and hierarchy. Early in 1964 the currents of civilian and military protest were joined. Only a spark was needed to ignite the revolution.

Goulart's actions during March 1964 provoked the military uprising that toppled his regime. Aware that his position was becoming untenable, he tried in one bold stroke to intimidate the conservative opposition and to reassert his leadership of labor and ultranationalist forces throughout the country. Flanked by recognized Communists and extreme nationalists, on Friday, March 13, he addressed a televised open-air rally in Rio de Janeiro attended by 150,000 enthusiastic admirers. Here Goulart reiterated his demand for a new constitution, insisted that a sweeping program of social and economic reforms be enacted, and defied the Congress by announcing presidential decrees nationalizing foreign-owned oil refineries and instituting a partial agrarian reform. His performance seemed to solidify labor-nationalist support for the government, but its impact on the rest of the population was not what he had anticipated. The civilian and military opposition was now certain that he sought to establish a left-wing dictatorship. Middle-class reaction was spontaneous and massive. A hastily organized March of the Family with God for Liberty attracted nearly 500,000 participants in São Paulo on March 19. Five days later in Santos a similar procession drew 150,000 marchers. Before additional demonstrations could be prepared, a new incident convinced nearly all military commanders that the revolution could no longer be postponed. The crisis stemmed from a strike—soon to be regarded as mutiny—by pro-Goulart sailors and marines in Rio de Janeiro, who rejected orders by their superiors to cease political activity and return to duty. Goulart refused to punish this breach of discipline. Rather, when the Navy Minister resigned in protest, Goulart replaced him with a figurehead, and pointedly confirmed the commands of those few officers who had expressed sympathy with the strikers. The revolutionary commanders then set March 31 as the date for the armed assault on the Goulart administration.

The revolution broke out in Minas Gerais, midway between Brasília, Rio de Janeiro, and São Paulo. The military phase lasted only three days, although the revolutionaries had been prepared to wage war on the central government for as long as three months. State and army troops were dispatched from Minas Gerais to occupy Brasília and to engage forces loyal to Goulart in Rio de Janeiro. Most of the interior towns were brought under rebel control within a few hours, as army garrisons followed prearranged plans to adhere to the revolution. In São Paulo, after vainly attempting to persuade Goulart to break with his Communist supporters, General Amaury Kruel declared the key Second Army in revolt on April 1. Goulart, shocked by the magnitude of the uprising against him, flew to Brasília to rally support, but abandoned hope when his defenders in Rio de Janeiro joined the rebel cause. There was no presidential call for armed action by the people, and no volunteers arose to defend the government. With all major cities except Pôrto Alegre in rebel hands, Goulart departed for exile in Uruguay on April 2, 1964. On that same date, Ranieri Mazzilli was again installed by the Congress as interim President of the Republic.

The Goulart regime collapsed before the civilian and military leaders of the revolution could define a common set of objectives. There was broad agreement among them on the need to preserve the Constitution and traditional national values against the dangers of presidential irresponsibility and subversion. No clear vision of the future government and its policies, however, emerged from the rash of proclamations and manifestos issued during the brief period of violence. Under the circumstances, the army chiefs who had planned and executed the overthrow of the government imposed a program of action that was much more severe than their civilian allies would have preferred. Most of these officers had taken part in the ouster of Getúlio Vargas a decade earlier, and had been disillusioned by the failure of successive civilian administrations to effect the moral regeneration of national politics that had been demanded at that time. In their view the Republic could no longer afford the luxury of tolerating leftist subversion, wholesale corruption in public office, and continual partisan bickering by self-serving politicians. The political institutions of the nation must be cleansed of obstructionists so that the revolutionary government might carry out the "economic, financial, political, and moral reconstruction of Brazil," in the name of the people and within the bounds of Western, Christian traditions. To this end, on April 9 the new military ministers issued the so-called Institutional Act, greatly enlarging the powers of the Executive at the expense of the legislature and the judiciary. This document was promptly approved by a compliant Congress as an amendment to the Constitution, to remain in force for the remainder of the presidential term.

The Institutional Act provided the legal basis for subsequent actions of the revolutionary regime. Among the first of these was the most sweeping purge of officeholders since 1930. For six months normal judicial processes and civil rights were suspended to permit the arrest and trial by police-military courts of all persons suspected of corruption or subversion as defined by the regime. Even before publication of the Institutional Act many thousands of persons had been jailed. The great majority of these were later released without charge, but more than one thousand were convicted by special tribunals and dismissed without appeal from elective and appointive office at all levels throughout the nation. Nearly four hundred persons, including ex-Presidents Goulart, Quadros, and Kubitschek, were deprived of all political rights for ten years. Congress survived, but was divested of its undesirable members, who were replaced by legal alternates acceptable to the new administration. Although the legislators could still debate and amend proposed legislation, they could no longer delay or prevent passage of measures submitted by the Executive.

Not until the military phase of the revolution was concluded did the public learn the identity of the man most responsible for the success of the uprising against the Goulart administration. He was General Humberto de Alencar Castello Branco, a professional soldier highly regarded by his colleagues but little-known outside the armed forces. He was born into a military family in 1900 near Fortaleza, Ceará, and entered the army as a cadet in 1918. He saw combat against revolutionaries in the

São Francisco Valley during the 1920s and in Italy with the Brazilian Expeditionary Force during World War II. Nonetheless, Castello Branco was primarily a school officer, recognized as one of the leading intellectuals of the army. He attended the Superior War College in France, the Army Command and General Staff School in the United States, and the Army General Staff School in Rio de Janeiro, where he also served at various times as instructor of tactics and military history, and eventually as commander. In 1960 he became director-general of army instruction. After serving briefly as commander of the Fourth Army in Recife in 1962, he was transferred to Rio de Janeiro as Chief of the Army General Staff. Here he was strategically situated to coordinate the various and contradictory plans for the revolution and to provide, within the army, articulate expression of the fears and grievances of the armed forces against the Goulart administration. His only prior venture into politics had occurred in 1954, when he signed the generals' manifesto calling for the resignation of Vargas. As the senior officer uniformly acceptable to all the military currents of the revolution, Castello Branco was elected by Congress on April 11. Retiring from the army with the rank of Marshal, he was formally inaugurated as President of the Republic on April 15, 1964, for the term ending January 13, 1966. It was the first nonmilitary post he had ever held. In July 1964, at the insistence of the armed forces and the civilian leaders of Congress, he accepted a constitutional amendment extending his term until March 1967.

The revolution of 1964 appears as the most serious of the crises in Brazilian democracy that have recurred periodically since the establishment of the Republic. It may also be interpreted as an indictment of civilian political leadership. In effect, when the elected heads of the political parties encouraged, or failed to discourage, the overthrow of President Goulart by the armed forces, they were acknowledging the failure of representative democracy, as known in Brazil, to cope with the urgent problems of the day within the letter and spirit of the Constitution. The alternative appeared to be either military rule or anarchy. Neither the President, the political parties, nor the elected representatives of the people were able to plot a viable course between these extremes. Thus, by their actions or inaction, they were surrendering to the armed forces authority and responsibility for national leadership, apparently hoping the military would make and enforce the painful decisions they had been unable or unwilling to reach. Under the circumstances, the military commanders acted with remarkable self-denial, refusing to establish an outright dictatorship, retaining the forms and much of the spirit of representative government, and vowing to return the nation to civilian rule when overdue institutional changes had been effected. The spokesmen for the badly fragmented political parties could only hope that the armed forces and the people would, in fact, be willing to elect a civilian to the presidency at the expiration of Castello Branco's term.

Index